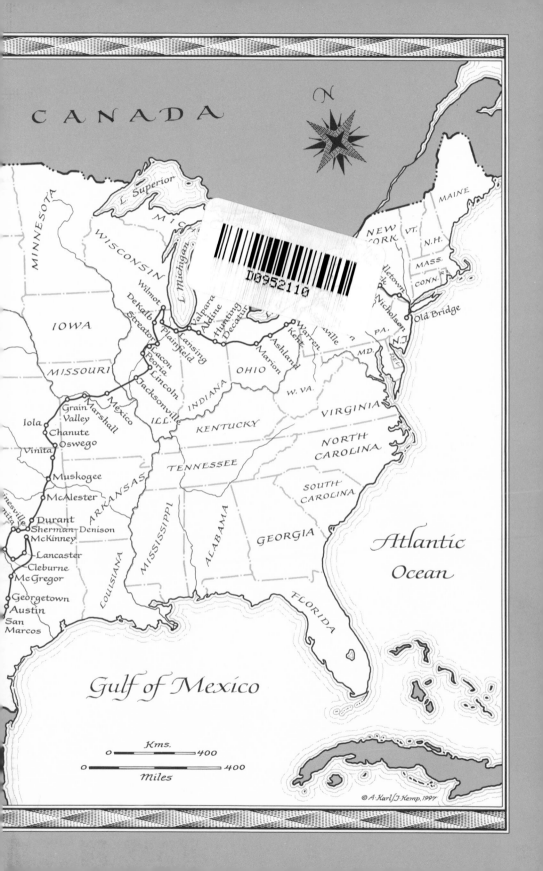

# FLIGHT OF THE GIN FIZZ

## Also by Henry Kisor

---

*Zephyr: Tracking a Dream Across America*

*What's that Pig Outdoors?:*
*A Memoir of Deafness*

# Flight of the Gin Fizz

## Midlife at 4,500 Feet

---

# HENRY KISOR

BasicBooks
*A Division of* HarperCollins*Publishers*

Published by BasicBooks,
A Division of HarperCollins Publishers Inc.

*Designed by Elliott Beard*

Library of Congress Cataloging-in-Publication Data

Kisor, Henry
  Flight of the Gin Fizz : midlife at 4,500 feet / Henry
Kisor.
    p.  cm.
  Includes index.
  ISBN 0-465-02425-4
  1. Kisor, Henry—Journeys.  2. Deaf air pilots—United
States.   3. Cross-country flying—United States.
I. Title.
TL540.K53K58   1997
629.13'092—dc21                                        97-5911
                                                       CIP

97 98 99 00 01 ❖/RRD 10 9 8 7 6 5 4 3 2 1

For Tom Horton and Bob Locher
*and pilots everywhere*

I fly because it releases my mind from the tyranny of petty things.

ANTOINE DE SAINT-EXUPÉRY

# Contents

# PART I

# PREFLIGHT

Lake Superior

Ontonagon

Ontonagon
County
Airport

MICHIGAN

N

WISCONSIN

Taxiway        × "The Hole"

14                    21

3-21
Asphalt Runway

14-32
Grass
Runway

1480'

Taxiways

2850'

32

3

Hangars

Pilot Lounge

Hangars

WESTOSHA
AIRPORT

Wilmot, Wisconsin

Oshkosh

Wittman
Field

Lake

Michigan

MICHIGAN

Baraboo        Portage Airport
Airport
          Portage
Baraboo

Tri-Cities
Airport
                Madison
Lone
Rock

Watertown
      Watertown
      Airport

Milwaukee

Ft. Atkinson
Ft. Atkinson
Airport                East Troy
Platteville                        East Troy Airport
    Grant        Janesville        Burlington
County Airport              Lake        Burlington Airport
          Rock County        Geneva
          Airport              Wilmot
                    Westosha
                    Airport
          Palwaukee Airport        Wheeling
                         Evanston
          Chicago

ILLINOIS

Mississippi R.

Galesburg Airport        Lacon
      Galesburg        Marshall
                County
                Airport

Kms.
0 ————————— 100

0 ————————— 100
Miles

© A. Karl/J. Kemp, 1997

# 1

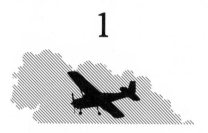

It was from a train that I was launched into flight.

On a transcontinental railroad trip a couple of years ago, an offhand remark from a fellow traveler inadvertently changed the course of my life. Like me, Bob Locher is on the shady side of fifty yet an overgrown boy at heart, one who never quite lost the sense of adventure that fueled his youthful fantasies. We both are mystery-novel addicts, and one lovely afternoon as the *California Zephyr* threaded its way through the Rocky Mountains, he and I dreamily concocted the plot for a modern-day James Gang train robbery. At one point I wondered aloud how the crooks could make a getaway from deep inside the Colorado canyon the train was then traversing, and Bob replied that he had seen a wind sock high atop a cliff just east of the gorge. He was a relatively new private pilot, having earned his ticket in his late forties, and was the owner of a four-seater Cessna 172. Immediately he saw the possibilities. A helicopter could pluck the felons from the canyon and carry them to the airport, where they could make good their escape to Mexico in a fast twin-engine plane.

For the rest of the trip, I thought no more of the idea, not even at our journey's end in San Francisco when Bob turned to me, shook my hand, and said, "When we get home, come flying with me." Bob was living in Deerfield, Illinois, not far from my home in the Chicago suburb of Evanston, and a few months later I took him up on his offer. We drove to his home field, Westosha Airport, just west of the little town of Wilmot, Wisconsin, near the Illinois state line. There we climbed into his white, maroon, and brown high-winged Cessna Skyhawk, registration number N3979Q emblazoned on its swept-back fin. As I buckled myself into the right front seat, the array of dials and gauges on the instrument panel bewildered me. All I could identify were the airspeed indicator and altimeter; the rest seemed arcane mysteries whose secrets could be vouchsafed only to members of holy orders.

As I watched silently, Bob recited his checklist as if it were a litany, fingering switches like beads on a rosary and muttering incantations—"Breakers in!" "Carb heat off!" "Mixture rich!"—like a vicar at matins, his radio headset and mike the alb and stole of his calling. Briefly he peered in all directions, then opened his side window, shouted "Clear!" in a loud benediction, and turned the key. Almost instantly the 150-horsepower engine two feet in front of our knees coughed alive, shaking awake the Skyhawk. As the slipstream from the propeller stroked the plane's tail surfaces, the aircraft rose on its landing gear like a churchyard cat stretching from sleep.

A spell of wonder slowly began to envelop me as the engine settled down to a creamy purr. Bob cracked open the throttle, and the airplane rolled off its hardstand onto the turf toward the narrow runway, scarcely thirty-eight feet wide. As we reached the asphalt, Bob keyed his mike and intoned, "Cessna three-niner-seven-niner-Quebec back-taxiing on Runway Three!" He then pulled off the runway onto a taxiway, locked the brakes, and raced the engine as he watched the gauges and indicators on the instrument panel. Satisfied with whatever he saw, Bob turned back onto the runway and swung the tail so the plane's nose pointed into the wind. Calling "Cessna seven-niner-Quebec departing Runway Three," he thrust the throttle forward to the stop. As the engine bellowed into full revolutions, the plane sprang forward, gathering speed with every stride. Before we had eaten up a third of the runway, the Cessna leaped into the air like a winged lioness, my heart rising with it.

I thought back to one of my earliest memories, wiggling the joystick in the cockpit of an Avenger torpedo bomber in a hangar at the Fort Lauderdale Naval Air Station, where my father was a supply officer. The year was 1944, and I was four. A few months later Dad's aircraft carrier, *Randolph,* its decks awash with Avengers,

Hellcat fighters, and Helldiver dive bombers, stood out to sea from Hampton Roads, Virginia, bound for the Pacific. Like just about every other American boy whose earliest memories were formed during that war, I thought of aviators as the noblest warriors of all, knights with aluminum steeds performing chivalrous deeds high in the clouds far above the grimy fray. Even at age five I could distinguish a Zero from a Hellcat and a Messerschmitt from a Spitfire, thanks to the aircraft silhouette–recognition charts tacked to my bedroom wall.

After the war Dad introduced me to gasoline-powered model aircraft that flew round and round the "pilot" at the end of twin nylon tethers. Pulling on one made the plane climb; pulling on the other made it dive. Patiently Dad rebuilt all the airplanes I flew into the ground, although I had to use my own money to replace the propellers I splintered on every landing.

At age eleven I took my first ride in a lightplane, a shiny aluminum postwar two-seater called a Globe Swift 125. The pilot, who owned the grass airstrip in Hallstead, Pennsylvania—which he grandiosely named Hallstead International Airport because a Canadian pilot had once landed there—took me up to 2,000 feet (I remember reading the numbers on the altimeter) and briefly let me steer the airplane. I gave him a start when I pushed the yoke forward sharply, causing the Swift to enter a dive. Before he could grab the controls, I pulled back the yoke, leveling off the plane.

"Take it easy," he said. More gently I guided the plane into a climb, then a descent.

"Want to try a roll?" he asked.

"Yeah!" I shouted. The pilot tightened my seat belt, then smartly turned the yoke to the left so the Swift entered a barrel roll. I looked up and there was the ground. I looked down and there it was again. I was annoyed when the pilot said our fifteen-minutes-for-five-dollars were up and we had to land.

As I grew into a teenager, however, model trains and then girls shouldered aside airplanes as objects of adoration. Though I had indulged small-boy fantasies of being a pint-sized combat pilot ("He's only nine," said the grizzled colonel, "but the little lieutenant can outfly everybody else in the squadron!"), I had never truly dreamed of becoming an aviator. At age three and a half I had contracted meningitis, becoming totally deaf. Like my hearing friends, I grew up with the widespread and ignorant belief that, of course, deaf people can't fly—since they're not able to use the radio and all—so I was not particularly upset, having absorbed the common sense that some human pursuits, such as conducting a symphony orchestra, require fully functioning ears. All through my teenage years I didn't give flying a thought.

Now, sitting next to Bob during that first takeoff in a small plane since my childhood, I began to understand aviators' mysticism, the techno-transcendental notion that flying unites one with a higher power or transports one into a different dimension. Indeed, flight seemed to lift me away from my land-bound cares in a fashion I had never imagined, the next best thing to an out-of-body experience. It brought alive that graceful phrase from John Gillespie Magee Jr.'s poem "High Flight" about "slipping the surly bonds of Earth," a line that may seem sentimental and hackneyed to the nonpilot but always carries exultant truth for the flier.

For the next hour Bob frolicked in the air, tiptoeing through canyons of cumulus and swooping lazily, like a mellow falcon, through holes in the clouds to shoot landings and takeoffs at nearby airports. We flew low over the resorts of Lake Geneva a few miles west of Westosha, then turned east, climbed, and headed for the deep blue-green of Lake Michigan. Banking gently over the beach near Kenosha, Bob turned to me, smiled, and said, "It's all yours!"

I was sitting too far back for my feet to reach the rudder pedals, but grasped the control yoke and rolled it ever so slightly to the left. The plane responded immediately, first curtsying to the right, then segueing into a smooth bank and turn to the left. My heart leaped—a machine was doing my bidding 2,000 feet above the surface of the earth. Rarely had I experienced such exhilaration. The ineffable, almost undefinable impulse to fly, so long buried, had at last overtaken and captured me.

"Male menopause!" my wife, Debby, said in mixed horror and exasperation upon hearing that I wanted to learn to fly. She had a point. My yearning for a pilot's license was partly a middle-ager's struggle to preserve the remnants of his fading youth. When I looked in the mirror, I saw a man who had worked the same job for almost a quarter of a century and was short, fat, bald, bespectacled, and deaf. At age fifty-three, I realized that I had neither hope nor desire for advancement or adultery.

Over the course of my half century on the planet, I had built a modestly successful newspaper career, working my way up to the book-review editorship at the *Chicago Daily News* and, when that illustrious afternoon paper folded, taking over the same job at the morning *Chicago Sun-Times.* I reviewed books, interviewed authors and wrote profiles of them, and in general covered the literary world as competently as any of my hearing colleagues at other newspapers. My employers valued my work enough to make sure I had expert assistance with the things my deafness prevented me from doing—speaking with people on the telephone and transcribing long taped interviews of authors. I even had a generous travel budget. I was a Somebody—a minor-league Somebody, to be sure, but with respect and standing in my profession.

Things change, however. By the early 1990s American newspapers, including my own, had suffered an unhappy transformation. Circulation was hemorrhaging, and profits were dwindling. Second newspapers in two-paper markets were either folding or barely hanging on. In Chicago, the *Tribune* had grown fat, the *Sun-Times* lean. Trying to keep the paper decently profitable, a succession of owners had tried new formulas, all of which promoted entertainment and sports rather than news; selling snappy graphics rather than thoughtful text; and serving the amorphous mass market rather than distinct interlocking audiences, including educated lovers of books. "Make the book section 'poppier,' " I was ordered. "Focus on the best-sellers." I became another link in the Great Chain of Hype.

Over the past few years, the "leaning" of America has choked operating budgets everywhere, those of newspapers in particular. For me that meant less money for big-name reviewers and none for travel and interview transcripts and a greater reliance on material from the wire services of the big national newspapers. I saw the squeeze happening in other departments, too. Soon the staff was decimated in a series of buyouts and layoffs, and management even reassigned the sweet-tempered editorial assistant who had been making my telephone calls and opening the scores of packages containing new books that arrived each day.

Suddenly what is indelicately called "shitwork" became a great part of my job. For hours a day I had to open boxes of books like a Barnes & Noble clerk and deal with publishers' secretaries on the telephone with the help of the cumbersome voice-relay system for deaf customers. In this scheme, an operator voices to a hearing party on the other end of the line the words I type on a TTY (short for text telephone), an apparatus resembling a laptop computer. (It was earlier called a TDD, or telephone device for the deaf.) The operator then types to me what the other party says. This is a slow and inefficient way to communicate, although it beats not communicating at all. (To lessen the pain, the paper did obtain an Internet address for me, and the departmental fax machine helped plug the holes as well.)

Like most of the older writers and editors at the *Sun-Times,* long accustomed to producing painstaking work of high quality for sophisticated readers, I was demoralized. Many of my contemporaries (some of whom were close friends) either took buyouts or opted for early retirement or quit in disgust to work elsewhere at newspapers that better appreciated their talents. My circle of trusted colleagues had shrunk drastically.

Why didn't I join them in the exodus? Book editorships on American newspapers are rare, and when one falls open, it is usually filled by a younger, lower-paid member of the staff. I was over fifty and on the upper rungs of the salary scale, not the kind of person tightfisted newspapers were looking for. Moreover, I was a deaf man, one who sometimes had difficulty communicating with the hearing. My speech, though serviceable, is not always easily understood in noisy environments, and my lipreading skills are not always reliable. I was also an *aging* deaf man, no longer a promising and unusual prospect for a generous and good-hearted mentor to mold. Looking at myself through the eyes of a prospective employer, I saw that I was not a particularly attractive candidate. The most I could do was hang on to my job, performing as best as I could until I was old enough to go out to pasture with an adequate financial cushion. This was hardly a sentiment of pride. It was little better than a depressed feeling of superannuated uselessness. Was I destined to a long, unhappy slide into retirement, brooding as I held on desperately to my paycheck?

All that said, however, this was not entirely a gloomy time. I wrote and published two books, one a memoir of growing up deaf and the other an account of that transcontinental railroad trip on which I encountered Bob Locher. Although neither had set sales records, both had pleased the critics—in fact, each was what the French call, with sweet irony, a *succès d'estime.* The books had done well enough so that a sideline career as an author seemed a good way to keep my professional self-respect while I plodded along as a veteran editor in an industry for which I had lost my youthful passion.

Meanwhile, my elder son had graduated from college and my younger one was about to. Debby had embarked on a career of her own and was now an experienced librarian in a prestigious suburban school district, as well as a respected reviewer of children's books. In the normal—and, in this case, happy—course of generational change, my family had outgrown its singular reliance on me.

But a vacuum yawned. I needed not only to come to terms with events but also to do something new and exciting, something that would keep me from falling into the passive routine and crabbed expectation so common in people over fifty. I needed to reshape my life, to reinvent myself. At the time, however, I understood these things only dimly. They simply percolated in my unconscious while I felt vaguely fretful about events I could not control.

The hour-long flight with Bob Locher had done more than awaken an old dream. It had also freed some long-dormant thoughts about the sorts of things I can and cannot do. Throughout my youth and early years as a journalist, I never accepted the idea that my deafness was an insurmountable hurdle to doing the things I wanted to do, and through a combination of luck and stubbornness, I was able to make my way in the hearing world.

As a fresh young college graduate, for instance, I had been told that I could never become a newspaperman—that not only was my written English likely to fall short of the mark but also that I could not cope with the vagaries of the telephone, of interviewing a source, and of communicating in person with my co-workers. I had also been informed—by a freshly minted and still ignorant pilot—that deaf people could not fly for "all the obvious reasons, the radio being only one."

Barely before the propeller of Bob's plane had stopped whirling, I recalled a conversation from twenty years earlier at a convention of the Alexander Graham Bell Association for the Deaf, where I had met James Marsters, a deaf orthodontist from California. Jim told me that he owned an airplane, a four-seater Piper Tri-Pacer, which he flew regularly. I was impressed and a little mystified.

"How do you do it?" I asked simply.

"Nothing to it," Jim replied. The secret, he explained, was that except for the large airfields that serve commercial aviation, most American airports do not use control towers, and most of the country's low-altitude airspace, in which lightplanes fly for the most part, does not require radio communications during good weather. In fact, except for certain circumstances, pilots who are flying under Visual Flight Rules (VFR for short) generally do not talk to air traffic controllers or to pilots of other aircraft while en route. From time to time they may call a weather station for updated information, but for the most part, their radio communications are limited to announcing their presence and intentions at uncontrolled airports. Those communications are not required. In fact, many small airplanes still do not carry radios; and even when they do, there is no guarantee that the radios will be on or that the pilots will be paying attention to them. In these circumstances, all pilots rely on their eyes and established landing-pattern procedures to avoid running into each other.

Hence there was no reason why deaf and hard-of-hearing people could not fly. Indeed, the Federal Aviation Administration had long ago set up rules and procedures to qualify them as pilots, and today eighty or ninety active pilots have licenses bearing the restriction "Not Valid for Flights Requiring the Use of Radio." I learned that deaf pilots have been around since the 1920s and that a deaf South Dakotan named Nellie Zabel Willhite made her first solo flight on January 13, 1928. Three years later, a Canadian linotype operator, Edward Thomas Payne, became the world's first licensed male deaf aviator. In 1947 an American printer, Rhulin Thomas, flew a Piper Cub from coast to coast and was considered the first deaf pilot to accomplish the feat.

It was in this frame of mind that I ran my idea by Debby. On principle she took a dim view of lightplane flying. She had suffered a frightening experience years before while flying to Marathon in the Florida Keys with our older son Colin, who was about three years old at the time. Her Chicago-to-Miami flight had been delayed, causing her to miss the commuter flight connection from Miami to Marathon. The commuter line put her in an air taxi, a four-seat Beechcraft Bonanza, for the rest of the trip. Unhappily, the extraordinarily turbulent weather tumbled and tossed the Bonanza as if it were a sparrow in a cyclone. When she and Colin finally landed, she felt as if she had narrowly survived a trip through a Mixmaster.

She vowed never again to set foot in an airplane too small to have its own washroom or, preferably, two.

And it was difficult for her to come to grips with the idea that her deaf husband longed to be up in the air risking his neck in crowded airspace without using a radio. This, I thought, was truly ironic—during the more than a quarter of a century we have been married, Debby has supported my right and ability as a deaf person to do the things hearing people can do. She also has been deeply involved in my journalism, traveling with me on many trips to serve as my ears and voice when they were needed. She knew that one way or another, learning to fly would lead to another book for me to write, and she felt that her antipathy to small planes meant that she could not be a part of it. Besides, she knew it was going to cost a fortune. All the same, she came to terms with my dream—slowly and grudgingly—after a few small skirmishes.

As often happens when I hit upon a new enthusiasm, I began reading voraciously on the subject, starting with the great aviator-writers—Antoine de Saint-Exupéry, Charles A. Lindbergh, and Ernest K. Gann—gradually moving on to more general aviation histories. And it was in one of these books that I discovered the story of Cal Rodgers. Though today he is just a footnote in aviation history, in 1911 Rodgers was the first aviator to fly across America, from New York to Pasadena by way of Chicago, Kansas City, Dallas, El Paso, and Phoenix, in a flimsy biplane built by the Wright brothers. He was one of several pilots hoping to collect a $50,000 prize offered by a newspaper mogul of the time. It took Rodgers forty-nine days to make it from coast to coast, and the germ of an idea—reenacting his journey—began to form in my head.

I investigated further on the public library shelves. On one lay a recent biography of Rodgers, a Smithsonian Institution Press publication titled *Cal Rodgers and the Vin Fiz,* written by Eileen Lebow and published in 1989. I checked it out. The first pages were encouraging. Rodgers had landed seventy-three times in his six-week odyssey across the United States. I could do that, too, I thought, and wouldn't need a very big and expensive airplane, either. All those stops meant opportunities to meet people, to learn about aviation in America, to see new parts of the country.

And then with a "Eureka!" I discovered that Cal Rodgers suffered from a severe hearing loss. He was not completely deaf, as I am, but enough so that his impairment profoundly affected his life and the views his contemporaries had of him. As I read on, I realized that although Lebow had expertly summarized the external events of Rodgers's life, she had encountered difficulty entering his mind and uncovering his inner self, for he had left behind nothing revealing about that. Like so many early aviation heroes, Rodgers had died young, before contemporary biographers had been able to plumb his thoughts.

Perhaps as I retraced his flight, I thought, I could bring my own meaning to his journey and a new perspective to the vague frustrations of my life. But first I needed to know more about Rodgers himself, to get a feeling for what I would be up against.

Calbraith Perry Rodgers was a member of a breed common in his time but almost extinct today: the well-born amateur sportsman with an independent income and no occupation. He never worked a day for pay as long as he lived. In one important way, however, he was different from those of his wealthy peers: He was no hail-fellow-well-met, no witty social lion comfortable in the presence of the mighty. Though with friends and family he could be laughing and impish, with strangers he was often ill at ease, even darkly taciturn and withdrawn. For a deaf person, communicating with a hearing world is full of pitfalls. Lipreading is an imperfect art, and dealing with the often low expectations the hearing world has for the deaf can be frustrating and wearying.

Rodgers's lineage was distinguished not merely for its affluence but also for its deeds. If fearlessness, steadfastness, and love of adventure are personal qualities that can be handed down through the generations, Cal inherited them from a surprising number of illustrious forebears. One of his great-grandfathers, Matthew Calbraith Perry, commanded the naval squadron that sailed into Tokyo Bay in 1853 and opened Japan to American trade. Matthew's older brother Oliver Hazard Perry defeated a British fleet at the Battle of Lake Erie in 1813, after which he dispatched the famous message, "We have met the enemy, and they are ours." Another great-grandfather, John Rodgers, was also a distinguished naval officer, having commanded the frigate *Constellation* of the fledgling U.S. Navy. Cal's father, Calbraith Perry Rodgers, had served ably as a U.S. Cavalry captain during the Indian Wars, earning mentions in dispatches while fighting the Sioux in the Big Horn Mountains and the Nez Percé in the Wind River country. On August 23, 1878, he was killed by lightning while returning to his station near Fort McKinney in the Wyoming Territory.

(In Rodgers's family history I found modest correspondences to my own lineage. A great-grandfather of mine had been U.S. minister to Colombia during the events leading to the building of the Panama Canal and had presciently warned Teddy Roosevelt against offending Latin Americans with a high-handed land grab. My maternal grandfather had risen high in the Central Intelligence Agency after a distinguished career in Naval Intelligence before World War II and the wartime Office of Strategic Services. My father was a Naval Academy graduate, and various uncles and cousins had done their bit, too. As Rodgers must have been, I was conscious of the example my forebears had set, and I wanted to live up to it as best I could.)

Five months after Captain Calbraith Perry Rodgers's death, his son and namesake was born in Pittsburgh on January 12, 1879. The infant's mother, the former Maria Chambers, was the daughter of a prominent Pittsburgher, Alexander Chambers, a glass manufacturer and bank director. Young Cal was, his family said, "lovable and affectionate." He also was a big child who always looked older than his age and early on displayed an interest in mechanical things, at one point declaring that he was going to grow up to be a locomotive engineer.

In 1885 six-year-old Cal contracted scarlet fever. For a week his temperature soared, an angry red flush covering his body, and for two months thereafter he was quarantined. He was a "different child," Lebow wrote, when he recovered. Most of his hearing was gone, and his speech was "less clear." His sense of balance had been impaired as well, and "the happy engineer-to-be had lost some of his bounce," Lebow wrote. "Just as his formal education was to begin, Cal was missing half of what was said to him. Without concentration, most of a conversation was lost to him, adding greatly to the woes of a boy about to begin school. As if to compensate for this loss, the boy grew taller and stronger than other children of his age."

Just how deaf Cal was is open to conjecture. No records exist of any assessment of his hearing loss, except a newspaper story that declared him totally deaf in one ear and 50 percent deaf in the other—a crude and primitive measurement, probably a reporter's wild guess. His mother, like so many at the time whose children's hearing was less than perfect, evidently chose to ignore it; in her letters she wrote nothing of her son's affliction. In fact, when he turned out to be not much of a student in school, his mother said he was "just like his father," choosing to explain her son's antipathy for books as hereditary, rather than as a result of his unrecognized problems with communication. Cal also showed little interest in religion, although his family was stoutly Presbyterian. It's more than conceivable that his lack of spirituality came from an inability to listen to sermons and to join easily in the Sunday fellowship of the church.

Later, when Cal became famous, reporters along his transcontinental route often wrote revealing details—details that when lumped together offer considerable evidence that the consequences of his hearing loss were profound enough to isolate him from much of the hearing world. Some reporters assumed that Cal was only temporarily deaf from the roar of the motor next to him and that his hearing would recover quickly. Others wrote, however, that not only did he seem to hear little that was said to him but that he spoke "with an effort, and very slowly" and was hard to understand. One newspaper story declared that Cal had a "defect in speech which makes him timid about associating with other aviators."

Other accounts described him as "tall, taciturn and with a distant look in his eye" and noted that "he wasn't the most talkative chap in the world." Still another said, "The famous birdman is rather a hard person to approach in a conversational way." It is striking how often reporters described Rodgers as being aloof and unresponsive, without connecting that idiosyncrasy—common among the deaf, especially those who lose their hearing after having learned language—with his hearing impairment. Such was the popular knowledge about deafness during the early years of the twentieth century.

As I continued my research, I found it striking that many people who knew Rodgers—sometimes quite well—never seemed to mention his deafness, either to others or in their own memoirs. Clearly he compensated well enough, at least with them, so they could put it out of their minds. This paralleled my own experience. As a child and an adult, I never lacked for friends, and those who spent any amount of time with me grew used to both my breathy articulation and the "quirks" of my deafness. I'm sure that those who knew Cal grew used to his flawed speech, too. Like me, Cal probably could communicate relatively easily with people he knew well by combining the remnants of his hearing with a talent for reading both lips and body language, although no contemporary account mentions that he did.

Isolated he may have been as an adult, but as a youngster Cal did not lack friends. Athletic competence often wins respect among adolescents who otherwise may be inclined to tease or shun a child for a physical disability. Cal may have compensated in part with sheer energy bordering on hyperactivity, especially in sports. At Mercersburg Academy he was the biggest player on the football team, at six feet three and 175 pounds. He also was a vigorous member of many school organizations, and this youthful club-bability probably helped make up for his lack of scholastic prowess. "The experience of being with young men of his age and standing on his own two feet to be judged for his deeds alone was as beneficial as learning," Lebow noted. Perhaps this foot in the door of the hearing world was all that Cal needed to be able to function, however clumsily, in it.

Cal had hoped to enter the Naval Academy, but his deafness kept him out, and for a decade—1901 to 1911—he lived the unproductive life of a wellborn gentleman, enjoying his membership in the New York Yacht Club and serving as a crewman on rich men's boats. He also raced automobiles and motorcycles and married a well-to-do young Vermonter, Mabel Graves, not long after he rescued her mother when she fell into the water while climbing aboard a yacht.

In early 1911 a favorite cousin, John Rodgers, who had graduated from Annapolis, was selected by the U.S. Navy to become one of its first aviators and was sent to Dayton, Ohio, to learn to fly with the Wright brothers. According to Lebow, John told his cousin, "There's nothing like it. You're up there, watching the land glide by, bobbing, dipping as if in a boat, but you can see nothing, only feel it. For speed, you can't beat flying." Cal visited Dayton to see what John was doing, and though he had not yet taken his first ride in an airplane, he was immediately hooked—just as I was when Bob Locher's Cessna 172 freed me from the grip of the earth.

# 2

If I was going to take to the air in Cal Rodgers's wake, I first had to learn to fly. To do so, I needed to find an instructor and a flying school. The closest school, a branch of a nationwide chain, lay at Palwaukee Airport in Wheeling, Illinois, twenty minutes from my home in Evanston. One February day I called the school, using the TTY relay system, and asked if they would take on a deaf student. "Umm . . . Let me talk to our chief instructor," said the voice at the other end. Almost immediately she added, "I'm sorry, we're all full up."

"What about the summer?" I said.

"We're full then, too," she replied.

"You mean you just don't want a deaf student," I responded, but by then she had hung up.

I wasn't terribly surprised by her reaction—not after experiencing the inevitable discrimination of half a century of deafness—but I wasn't all that dismayed. Palwaukee is a tower-controlled airport; I would not be able to talk on the radio to the tower. Other deaf student pilots have learned at controlled airports, but with cumbersome arrangements to do their solo flying out of uncontrolled fields, usually with the instructor going along for the ride out of the controlled airport. I called the schools at a few outlying uncontrolled airports, but the answer was always a nervous variation on "Sorry, we're not set up to train handicapped pilots." I thought about siccing the courts on the schools courtesy of the Americans

with Disabilities Act, which prohibits such discrimination, but decided that such an action would raise ill feelings—hardly a good
beginning to an endeavor that requires mutual and delicate trust.
From the first, an instructor and a student ought to get along.

In the end I decided to take up Bob Locher's suggestion that I
approach Tom Horton, his old instructor at Westosha Airport near
Wilmot in southern Wisconsin. Bob told me that Tom was a corporate jet pilot with more than 17,000 hours in the air who still taught
flying on weekends for the love of the experience. I was further encouraged when I learned that years before, Tom had taught a deaf
pilot; he and I would not be reinventing the wheel, feeling our way
through the complications of deaf-and-hearing in-flight communications. Nor would I have to persuade a skeptic of the capabilities
of deaf student pilots. I called, and Tom was willing to take me on.
And so the Westosha Flying Club (one hour and five minutes by car
from Evanston, if I stretched the tollway speed limit a little) became my weekend home-away-from-home for the twelve months of
instruction it took me to earn the certificate and rating of "Private
Pilot, Airplane Single Engine Land."

Worried that the FAA might be slow to issue me an official student
pilot's certificate, I had a bright idea: I'd call an old colleague from
the late *Chicago Daily News* who was now the local press relations
chief at the FAA. What good is clout if you don't use it? Enthusiastically he said he'd obtain all available FAA documentation on deaf
pilots and would call the chief flight physical examiner on my be-
half. I never heard from him again.

So I forged ahead and made an appointment with Dr. Hermann
Spee, a suburban physician and FAA medical examiner. He said to
bring documentary evidence that I am deaf—the FAA wouldn't accept my word for it. I called my family physician's office to ask for a
Note from the Doctor attesting to my deafness.

Dr. Spee turned out to be a pleasant old bird, with a photo of
himself in front of a Skyhawk in his examining room. The exam for
the FAA third-class medical certificate seemed astonishingly perfunctory. First, I filled out a brief form swearing that I did not suffer
from half a hundred medical conditions. Then I peed in a cup and
looked through a scope at several cards so that Dr. Spee could be
sure my vision was corrected to 20/30 with eyeglasses and that I
wasn't color-blind. He listened to my chest just a few seconds, took

the blood pressure rapidly, and had me cough while he held a finger delicately to each side of my groin. He said the FAA would need at least two weeks to pass on the student pilot certificate and to call him if there was a problem. (The certificate arrived within ten days; I must have caught the bureaucracy during a particularly efficient period.) At one point, Spee said his late father had been deaf, but I was not so sure he had much experience with deaf people because he talked to the wall and the floor and not to my face unless I reminded him to look at me. I was in and out in fifteen minutes. The cost was thirty-five dollars.

A week later, I took my first flight at Westosha. Tom Horton turned out to be a pleasant man on the cusp of forty with dark salt-and-pepper hair; easygoing; relaxed; and, best of all, very easy to lip-read. My biggest worry, failure to communicate, was not going to happen. We spent half an hour in a small office off the scruffy pilot's lounge looking over the preflight instructions in the 1984 Cessna 152 manual. All the gauges and instruments seemed intimidating, but Tom said I'd soon get used to them. In slow, carefully enunciated speech, so I could read his lips easily, he told me precisely what we would do during our first flight, and I responded that anticipating our tasks in each lesson would make my understanding them much easier.

We went up in one of the Westosha Flying Club's planes, a cute little high-winged, 108-horsepower Cessna 152 two-seater trainer with seemingly not too many hours on it. Shoehorning myself through the door into the left seat wasn't easy, for those airplanes are cramped. And it was freezing cold—about ten degrees Fahrenheit, with a light wind from the north. Tom led me through the preflight checklist and had me start the engine—not difficult at all—and then showed me how to taxi using the rudder and brakes. Taxiing is not easy unless you are used to it, for the rudder pedals, not the control yoke, steer the plane on the ground. I wandered all over the runway like a mouse in a maze. Tom guided the plane through the takeoff, and once we had climbed to 2,000 feet above the ground, he demonstrated how to do gentle turns, climbs, and glides. I did a lot of the flying myself and soon picked up the rhythm, to my immense pleasure and Tom's approval. He landed the plane, and I tried to stifle a wide grin as we walked into the lounge. "Do you think I have the right stuff?" I asked. He smiled and nodded.

I had read that from beginning to end Cal Rodgers needed just *ninety minutes* of instruction at the Wright school in Dayton (plus probably quite a few more minutes of solo practice) before he was ready to take the flight test for his pilot's license. Today this amount of time seems akin to showing a baby how to windmill his arms and then throwing him into the pool and seeing whether he can swim. I knew that I would be no ninety-minute wonder, not just because of my deafness but because my comparative advanced age—and the fears I had accumulated like barnacles over the decades—would be a drag in overcoming the inevitable problems and plateaus every fledgling pilot faces.

And there was a great deal more to learn than in 1911. I had to absorb not only copious quantities of information on the physics of flight and the arts of navigation but also reams of Federal Aviation Regulations and the mysteries of weather. The workload and the mental power needed to earn a private pilot's certificate was that of an undergraduate course in basic science. This was not heavy intellectual lifting, but it did require a punctilious attention to detail. I was a much more conscientious student than I had been as an undergraduate because what I was learning could save my life if I got into trouble—and what I failed to learn could kill me.

On that first day with Tom, I learned immediately that the project was not going to be cheap. The airplane manual was $16; the plane rental, $28 for an hour; the instructor's fee, $25; the initiation fee into the Westosha Flying Club, $150; and the first month's dues $16. That was $235, just for openers. Later that week I ordered a pair of trifocal prescription sunglasses, expensive at $179. But when I complained about the cost, Debby surprised me by saying I must have them if I was going to be a safe pilot. For both of us, this acknowledgment was some kind of watershed.

Rain and low clouds greeted the day of the second lesson. I called Tom. "Go or no-go?" I asked. "No-go," he said. Damn. I felt like a kid who missed Christmas. But then the weather cleared the next day, and Tom allowed me to execute the takeoff. I felt good about that, even though the airplane wallowed all over the runway under my clumsy hands. Whirling propellers cause torque, which makes the airplane veer to the left, like a spaniel with short legs on the port side. To counter the torque, I had to press down on the right rudder pedal with a nervous foot—now too much pressure, now too little, and the plane's nose followed willy-nilly.

We climbed to 2,500 feet to try gentle banks and turns, and I did coordinated exercises in which the pilot rolls the wings from right to left and repeats the maneuver, trying to keep the nose fixed on a point on the horizon with the help of the rudder. I overcontrolled wildly, the plane hunting hither and yon, like a bloodhound frantically trying to pick up an elusive scent. I tended to stand rigidly on the rudder pedals, too. Tom quietly told me to fly with one hand, rather than clutch the yoke in a two-fisted death grip. "You need to develop a lighter touch," he said.

I was also brought up short when Tom asked, "Where are we at now?" I had absolutely no idea. Tom gently informed me that we were about five miles south of the airport, and, thoroughly embarrassed, I flew north, then made the standard landing approach. First, I flew one leg "downwind" along the runway and past the threshold, reducing power and dropping ten degrees of flaps. The plane sank gently. About a quarter mile past the threshold, I turned left on "base leg" perpendicular to the runway, adding another ten degrees of flaps. At last I turned on "final" approach, lining up the plane with the runway as it descended, adding still another ten degrees of flaps so that the plane glided slowly downward at a sharp angle. I left my hands and feet on the controls while Tom made the actual landing.

For the next several months, I would repeat these circuits of the airfield several times during each lesson. And it was here that my deafness intruded most insistently. During touch-and-go practice—in which the airplane does not come to a stop on the runway after landing but accelerates immediately into a takeoff—an instructor can discuss the student's errors while he is maneuvering back into the landing pattern. But as a lip-reader, I could not divide my attention between the airplane and Tom. After each touchdown, we had to pull off on the taxiway to discuss the landing and then get into line for takeoff. This process was time consuming, but there was no other way to do it.

On just one occasion was there an outright misunderstanding. To speed communications in the air, we had worked out a series of simple gestures. One gesture, a finger thrust suddenly forward over the instrument panel, meant "Climb away at full throttle." One morning I had the plane lined up perfectly with the runway, at just the right height, and was crossing the threshold when Tom's arm snaked out over the instrument panel, pointing ahead. Thinking he was ordering me to do a go-around, I rammed home the throttle and pulled back the yoke. Quickly Tom took the yoke, closed the throttle, and landed the plane. "I was just trying to tell you to keep your eye on the other end of the runway," he said. We laughed, and that was the last miscommunication we had.

Fog skunked the next two dates. And on the third I was almost skunked by the recurrence of an old terror. Tom demonstrated a steep turn to the left—in which the wings lie at a forty-five-degree angle to the ground—and as I looked down, I suddenly became aware that only a seat belt and a flimsy aluminum door kept me from falling 3,000 feet to splatter on the ground like an overripe eggplant. My mouth turned dry, and I burst into a trembling sweat. Having lost my balance organs to meningitis, I have no inner sense of equilibrium. I cannot function without a visual horizon. Looking down from the tops of tall buildings causes my heart to race. The sight of Harold Lloyd dangling from a clock face makes me swoon. Instead of remaining straight in my seat and following the plane through the turn, I leaned away from it, unconsciously trying to align my body with the horizon. The result was that I pressed up against Tom in the tight confines of the little Cessna.

He nudged me sharply. "You've got it," he said, pointing at the yoke. "Do a 360-degree steep turn to the left, then one to the right." Gingerly, glancing fearfully at the ground through the pilot window, I put the Cessna into a left turn so shallow that Tom reached up and firmly swiveled the yoke farther to the left to steepen the bank. "You can do it," he said. I made a right turn, looking straight ahead rather than down, and was surprised that we did not plunge screaming to our deaths. "Do it again," Tom said. I did, stifling my terror. And again. And again.

Letting one's body ride into that first steep turn, some aviators will say, is a sure sign that the student is a natural, that to him the movement of stick and rudder will come instinctively. The result will be a "hot pilot who can fly anything and the box it came in." But I would have to deliberate over everything I did in the air. Later Tom would declare, in his hardheaded and unsentimental way, "There's no such thing as a natural pilot. It's not natural for man to fly."

Adding to the discomfort of those early lessons was turbulence, those jounces and jolts in the atmosphere that the uninitiated call "air pockets." They are caused by thermals—long, ragged, rapidly rising columns of air kicked up by the sun's uneven heating of the earth's varicolored surface. Though on a sunny day the gently rolling farmlands of southern Wisconsin may look fluffy as a feather-bed, flying over them can be like driving over a potholed corduroy road, steady bump-bumps strewn with sickening dips. Stiff, gusty breezes coursing in off Lake Michigan can add their bounces and rolls to the invisible devil's brew. To a passenger in a Boeing 767 descending for a landing, flying through "light turbulence" is a mild annoyance, but in a Cessna 152 it can be hair-raising, the airplane seeming to be on the edge of falling out of control as unseen forces try to knock it helter-skelter. For many months I hated and feared turbulence, often deliberately scheduling my lessons with Tom for 7 A.M., well before the morning sun could awaken the thermals.

I did not know it then, but the slow process of accustoming myself to turbulence, making repeated steep turns—and learning to fly under a hood to block out the view outside, using instruments alone to keep the airplane flying straight and level—would allow me to overcome my deep-seated horror of losing my visual horizon and falling. In time, I even turned that fear upon itself, bringing home the comforting awareness that aloft I was master of my fate. This is a common phenomenon. Even Lindbergh experienced it; in his autobiography, he vividly recounted how on his first flight he suddenly realized he had a terrible fear of heights. He dealt with it by first becoming a barnstorming "wing walker," but sweating through terrible dreams nearly every night, and finally conquering the demon by jumping into the void under a parachute.

Today, many people who are deathly afraid of air travel conquer their dread by learning to fly. Some, however, are brave only when they're "Pilot in Command." On a train I once met a man who said he was a private pilot. "I own a small plane," he declared. "As long as I'm in the left seat flying the plane, I'm fine. But I can't stand to fly with a pilot I don't know. He might kill us all. That's why I take long trips by train." At that time the notion sounded eccentric, but today it seems logical. Many private pilots are nervous about flying the airlines because, as one said, "I'm noticing what the planes are doing, especially on landing, and sometimes I'm not convinced that what the pilot is doing is correct."

And as time passed and I learned to fly higher and higher, I came to realize that altitude is the pilot's best friend. I would even develop a healthy apprehension at being too low because an engine failure at minimum altitude usually means a forced landing on inhospitable terrain. The higher the airplane, the better the pilot's chances of finding a good spot for an emergency set-down.

As our early lessons continued I learned not to overcontrol so much and to relax. Slowly, experience was teaching me, but with frequent setbacks. Landings still scared me pale—trying to put the plane down on a thirty-eight-foot-wide runway at sixty miles per hour* was like trying to thread a needle aboard a galloping horse. Westosha has two runways, one a grass lane called 14-32 and the other an asphalt strip known as 3-21. Runway 3-21 is famous for being one of the trickiest in southern Wisconsin. Not only is it narrow, but one end—the threshold of Runway 3—lies close to a long hangar, which roils a crosswind from the east into a maelstrom that causes planes landing on it to do merry dipsy-doodles a few feet above the asphalt. A few feet from the other end—the threshold of Runway 21—lies a sharp drop-off that Westosha pilots call "the Hole." A strong southwest wind down the runway dips sharply as it blows over the threshold, and a pilot landing close to the edge of 21 must take care lest the breeze drops his plane below the edge of the asphalt. (Runways are numbered according to their magnetic headings to the nearest ten degrees, with the trailing zero omitted. The magnetic heading of Westosha's Runway 3—often pronounced "Tree" on the radio, because a "th" can sound like a "f"—is 30 degrees. If the plane is taking off in the opposite direction, the heading is 210 degrees, and the runway is called Runway 21, or "Two-One.")

Months later Tom told me that the Hole had given him his most frightening moment as an instructor. Once he and a student were coming in on "short final"—only a few hundred yards shy of the runway—when their airplane's engine failed. At an ordinary field, the pilot could have stretched the glide enough to touch down on level ground close to the threshold, perhaps taking out a runway light or two in the process, but the Hole intervened. The trainer

---

*Pilots today measure distance and speed in nautical miles and knots. One nautical mile equals 1.15 statute miles. To simplify matters in this book I use statute miles and statute miles per hour.

plunged into it, and despite Tom's best efforts to save the landing, struck the Hole just five feet from and a couple of feet below the runway pavement. The impact bent back the plane's landing gear, but both the instructor and the student walked away from the wreck.

After one of my lessons, I went up with Bob Locher in his Sky-hawk and noticed how his landings weren't all that perfect—on one he came in a little too fast and too low, floating down the run-way, and on another, he touched down off the centerline. But each time he got us down without much of a jar. "Each landing is going to be different," Tom kept telling me as I struggled to make them all smooth and jar-free. "Perfect landings are rare."

I also began to learn more about the culture of flying. One day Bob and I flew to Janesville, about forty miles away, for lunch at the airport restaurant. Just about every pilot from northern Illinois and southern Wisconsin seemed to be there, too; the restaurant was packed. "That's what airplane owners do on Sunday," Bob said. "Their planes have to be flown regularly so the engines will re-main lubricated and unrusted, so without anywhere in particular to go, they will take a short and expensive hop for a very cheap lunch. They call it 'going for a hundred-dollar hamburger.' "

As my first month drew to a close, Tom seemed pleased with my progress and did not display irritation when, firmly strapped into the pilot's seat, I told him I had completed the preflight checklist—but had not looked to see that the left wing's rope tiedown had been undone. Tom had untied the tail and the right wing tiedowns, but sneakily ignored the left wing rope to see if I would catch it—and I didn't. "Are we going to fly in circles on the ground?" Tom asked with a small smile. As the architect Ludwig Mies van der Rohe observed, "God is in the details." Mies would have made a splendid pilot.

For my part, I was taking two steps forward and one step back. I had begun to do landings all by myself, without Tom's hand on the yoke, and my slips were improving. A slip is a maneuver in which the pilot banks in one direction but holds the rudder in the oppo-site direction, so the airplane seems to fly sideways. Slips are used to line up the airplane with the runway in a crosswind and to lose altitude in a hurry. My approaches and landings weren't too bad, either. It all seemed to be coming together. Tom did observe that in my landing patterns, I was turning much too tightly and banking very steeply, and that it would "scare the shit out of a passenger." At least it's not scaring the shit out of *me*—not any more. I had no time to be frightened. My mind was racing ahead, thinking about setting up the next turn.

The next day, however, I couldn't do anything right, but at least I knew what I was doing wrong, and why. But that didn't stop me from receiving the Lecture from Tom, when, on final approach with power off and full flaps down, I pulled up the nose of the airplane because I perceived myself as being too low. "That's the best way to kill yourself," he said. "When you do that, the plane loses forward speed and stalls—it just stops flying and falls into a spin. You're not high enough to recover." There was one and only one solution, he said, and that was to apply power, to give the engine gas. He was right, of course. I should have known that, and I was terribly embarrassed.

On the way back from the next flight, Tom had me fly at 3,000 feet directly over Westosha; then he pulled back the throttle to a slow idle and said, "Engine failure. Now what?" I knew enough to put the plane into a sixty-five-miles-per-hour spiral glide down to the runway, but made a messy landing of it—helped to be less so by Tom's quick hand. Afterward, Tom told me to aim for the center of the runway, not the threshold, when my engine was out. "I'd rather you went off the end of the runway at slow speed rather than crashing short of the threshold," he said. "Don't worry about the plane," he said. "We want to save your life. Screw the plane. Smash it up. You want to walk away from it."

As May began, I learned another important lesson: I had to *do* something when I got into trouble; I couldn't hesitate and wait for my instructor to save my sorry hide. The flight instructor and his student have a relationship like no other mentor-pupil association in the world: The student's life literally depends on the skill and conscientiousness of the instructor. But sometimes I allowed myself to get too dependent. On one approach to Runway 21, I was too low and did not apply full power as I should have. I froze, waiting for Tom to make a move. At the last second, just before the plane splattered against the Hole, he drove home the throttle, shaking his head in disgust. I took his reaction to mean that I must learn to make my own decisions; I would never become a pilot until I cut the umbilical cord to my instructor. I couldn't understand myself. I was a grown man, a husband, a father, a published writer and critic, an authority in my field, a world traveler, a person of parts. Yet here I was meekly wanting my hand held, like a small boy on his first foray on a two-wheel bicycle. I had to lose the emotional training wheels. Moreover, I needed to *think* about the mistakes I made each time and correct for them so I wouldn't commit them again. "I don't know where the term *winging it* came from," Tom said, "but it sure wasn't from flying. You've got to think about everything you do."

Debby was still upset about my learning to fly. One evening, my childhood friend Sam Williamson told me that Debby had called and had gone on and on with his wife, Cass, about my flying. Sam spoke to me with grave concern, like a marriage counselor. He said I ought to listen to Debby, that she felt I was making a terrible and even fatal mistake thinking I could learn to fly. Hear her out, he said. (Sam, who is a professor of economics at Miami of Ohio, hardly presented a role model of the dutiful husband. Not long after our conversation, *he* became a student pilot, too.)

The following day I brought up the subject with Debby. She complained that I was too obsessed with flying, was gone for long hours every weekend, leaving her isolated without a car, and that she did not feel connected to this new part of my life. I replied that I thought she was still overly fearful of what she considered the dangers and was walling herself off. But I said I would help her buy a car if it would make her happier. Some weeks later, we bought a new Saturn, and that relieved some of the pressure.

The next afternoon, when I had to have a molar extracted owing to the failure of a root canal, I asked for novocaine instead of pentothal because I wanted to be clearheaded for a lesson with Tom the next morning. "Fat chance," said the oral surgeon after I confessed. He spoke the truth; even with novocaine, I was in no shape the next day to drive to Wisconsin, let alone fly an airplane. Debby was right. This was obsession, although I preferred to call it devotion. Whatever its name, like a *passion grande* with a beautiful countess, it had lifted me out of the rut my life had fallen into. With a new focus, each day gave me refreshed energy.

Some days, however, I wondered whether Debby was right, after all. In the air one Saturday, Tom asked, "Shall we do a spin?" I didn't like the sound of that, but replied, "Sure." At 3,500 feet Tom pulled up the nose and put the plane into a stall, in which, airspeed having been lost, the plane simply stops flying. Immediately we dropped into a sickening spin straight down that turned my bowels watery as the horizon corkscrewed madly. After two revolutions, Tom pulled back the power, centered the control surfaces, and sharply thrust the yoke forward. The plane recovered smoothly into level flight. "Now you try it," he said. Shakily I demurred. "Could we do it sometime else?" I asked quaveringly. Then I realized that if I didn't get back on that horse right now, I might never ride again. So I did a spin, and although it was scary enough, it wasn't as frightening as Tom's. I was still terrified, but at least I wasn't disoriented. I knew which way was up and which way was down—how to regain that vital visual horizon. I was in control. Sort of.

During the next lesson, Tom snaked back the throttle at 2,000 feet two miles north of Westosha, said "Engine failure," and folded his arms. This time I misjudged the wind badly and never got the airplane close to the runway. At about 100 feet, just as I realized the 152 would wipe out its landing gear in tall corn, I cursed and drove home the throttle, the airplane arching away into the sky. Damn! I should have nailed that one. In embarrassment I peeked at Tom out of the corner of my eye. Far from gazing stonily out the window, as I had expected, he was nodding with satisfaction. Then I understood. I had at last let go. I was relying on my own judgment and taking decisive action. Tom had reached that conclusion, too.

Three days later I passed another milestone. With Tom aboard, I shot three first-rate takeoffs and landings and one excellent simulated engine-out set-down after Tom pulled the plug on the downwind leg. My fifth landing was a perfect "greaser" in which the airplane touches down without the slightest jar, just a hum of the wheels on asphalt. My sixth was just a bit inelegant, and my seventh was a fine no-flaps landing in which I did a slip to lose speed. Tom directed me to a stop on the taxiway and said, "Do you think you can handle it alone?" After gulping a moment, I replied, "I think so." To which Tom said, "The plane will seem a little lighter and faster without me. Go around once, land, and come back to this spot." I took off, flew around the circuit, and greased her in.

To my surprise, I felt no exultation flying alone for the first time—I was concentrating too hard on performing every task correctly. It didn't matter whether anyone was sitting next to me. After my landing, Tom sauntered over to the plane and told me to do two more circuits and then return to the ramp by the pilot's lounge and shut down the engine. I did so, without incident. Then I walked into the lounge, where Tom smilingly brandished a sharp pair of scissors. "Turn around," he said. With swelling pride I stood still as Tom performed the traditional ritual marking one's first solo: He snipped off my shirttail and mounted it, suitably inscribed with my name, the date, and the aircraft number, on the wall of the lounge. I drove home, at last feeling unconditionally pleased with myself.

# 3

ow that I could land an airplane by myself, my next task was to learn how to go somewhere in it. And so Tom and I set about to study the rudiments of pilotage and dead reckoning. Pilotage is simply comparing the landmarks one sees below with the symbols on an aviator's map, called a sectional chart because it shows one section of the United States, typically portions of two or three states. Pilotage is much easier said than done. One kidney-shaped lake looks like another. Railroads and highways crisscross each other willy-nilly. And folding and unfolding a two-foot-by-five-foot accordion-pleated paper chart inside a cramped airplane while flying it at the same time is like trying to read the *Wall Street Journal* in a windstorm.

Dead reckoning is a little easier, but not very accurate. The pilot measures his magnetic course on the chart and then finds his bearing—the angle into the wind that he must fly to remain on course—while calculating his ground speed. Some pilots use an aluminum rotary slide rule to determine bearing, ground speed, and time between waypoints. Others, like me, prefer an electronic pilot's calculator.

Once the student has figured out how to combine pilotage and dead reckoning to fly from point to point on his chart, the instructor takes him out for several cross-country flights. I took to these flights like a homing pigeon, hitting my destinations right on the nose from the beginning. I may have trouble with crosswind landings, but at least I'm good at navigation. This was a confidence builder.

My first dual-instruction cross-country flight was a short hop to Fort Atkinson, forty-three miles northwest of Westosha, hitting the target bang on. I felt so pleased with myself that I forgot (dammit!) to reset the directional gyro while on the ground. In the air the vacuum-driven gyro—set by hand to point in the same direction as the magnetic compass—holds a steady indication, unlike the compass, which swings from side to side with every dip and curtsy of the airplane. The directional gyro, however, slowly precesses, or winds down like a child's top, and needs to be reset every fifteen or twenty minutes to jibe with the compass. As a result of my failure to reset the gyro, on the way back we drifted twenty degrees off course. Tom said nothing, and I realized my error only when I looked down and saw Burlington airport a couple of miles south of my intended course instead of a couple of miles north. So much for my knack for navigation.

Once, touching down in a gusty crosswind, I reverted to my early student days and tried to "drive" the plane on the runway with the yoke, like a school bus, instead of the rudder pedals—a tendency often hard to thwart in older student pilots who have spent decades guiding an automobile with the steering wheel. (This is one reason why, Tom said, he finds sixteen-year-olds easier to teach. They don't need to unlearn a lifetime of habits.) As a result, the 152 careened off the runway and nearly ground-looped. Only Tom's quick save prevented a broken airplane and damaged passengers. "You're gonna kill yourself that way!" was all he needed to say.

This two-steps-forward, one-step-backward progress sometimes disheartened me. After one difficult, discouraging lesson, I asked Tom, almost challengingly, "How do you think I'm doing?" If I should be gently told that perhaps I'd be better off not being a pilot, now was the time. To my surprise he said, "Fine. Don't be so hard on yourself."

Tom somehow found the strength to remain encouraging, no matter how often I repeated the same mistakes despite his patient corrections. As our lessons progressed, I soon realized how lucky I was to have Tom for an instructor. All too many certified flight instructors teach only to build the thousands of hours needed to reach that first rung on the ladder to an airline job and couldn't care less about the welfare of their students. Not Tom. He is well known all over southern Wisconsin as a superb instructor. Few of his students—perhaps 5 percent—fail their flight tests for the private pilot's license.

I tried to get closer to this man, to take his measure as a person as well as an instructor, but that proved difficult. Tom is a short, spare, handsome man who jogs to keep himself fit for the cockpit and is both generous and laconic. Although he charged a little more per hour than most instructors, he ran the meter only in the air, not on the ground. In the pilot's lounge he would patiently explain concepts to me for hours, waving away my offers of payment for his time. But subtly he seemed to resist my efforts to become friendlier, to find out more about him and his life. Another student always seemed to be waiting, and after the last one had tied down the plane, Tom was gone in his beat-up Subaru. Perhaps this was his way of keeping his students at arm's length, maintaining detachment like a physician with his patients, in case one killed himself in the air. I did not think any had; Tom's emphasis on safety is legendary, and I experienced it during every lesson.

It's possible that Tom may have been just too weary for idle chat. He and his wife, Lynn, have three young sons, and they were in the midst of building an addition to their house. To earn extra money, Tom was teaching as many as fifteen hours a week on his days off from his full-time job, flying a Cessna Citation for Modine Corporation.

"Isn't it difficult to find a job flying corporate jets?" I once asked him.

"It is, yeah," Tom said.

"How did you do it?"

"It's not what you know," he replied; "it's who you know." And that's all he said. I suspect that the personal connections Tom made at Westosha, where many corporate executives keep their airplanes, led to the left seat of that Citation. He has taught about 250 students by his count, half a dozen at a time, and many of the veterans have remained under his spell. Not only does he ride right seat during their biennial flight reviews—the brush-ups all private pilots must take every two years—but he has also taken many to advanced licenses and ratings. To them, he is a guru, invariably the first instructor consulted for advice in the pilot's lounge. Learning to fly is such an intense experience, by turns painful and pleasurable, that a former student tends to remember and, if he was lucky, cherish his relationship with his instructor, however long ago he cut the umbilical cord. I have seen well-to-do owners of $100,000 Bonanzas shut down their engines at the fuel pumps, spot Tom on the ramp, and make a beeline to tell him where they've been and what they've done, like graying acolytes at a twentieth-year high school reunion seeking a benediction from a beloved math teacher.

Among professional pilots, who tend to be footloose, Tom is unusual. He is a homeboy who married the girl next door, and he and Lynn still live in the town of his childhood. In that Citation he flies all over the country, but "Wilmot still seems like the best," he said sincerely. "I always come back."

I asked Tom why he kept on instructing when flying executive jets is a comfortable living. His reply was simple, direct, and modest—the essence, I suspect, of the man: "I just enjoy it. I guess I get a lot of gratification out of seeing people learn, and then when they solo, seeing how excited and happy they are. It makes me feel good." But the jets are still something special. "They're the nearest thing to a magic carpet," he said, grinning.

Sometimes I flustered myself, too. When we arrived over Watertown during the second dual cross-country flight, I started to enter the usual left-hand landing pattern—in which all turns are made to the left—for the active runway, but Tom snatched the yoke and pointed out that the arrangement of whitewashed markers around the wind sock below proclaimed that the runway required a *right-hand* pattern, to keep low-flying airplanes away from the city. Suddenly I was nonplused. I could not for the life of me figure out how to make the approach to the runway. When my carefully laid plans were jogged by something unexpected, I would get upset, and my judgment would collapse until I could scratch it together again. This was how I learned to sail as a boy; at the moment of truth my wits deserted me, and the boat either tipped over or ran aground. It took a long time for me to master sailing, learning from catastrophe after catastrophe. In the air, however, a student does not have the luxury of learning that way. I needed to stay ahead of the airplane by anticipating every maneuver, to predict rather than react.

Eventually, at Tom's suggestion, I bought a three-volume set of *Flight Guide,* a popular reference manual that contains diagrams of the runways and landing patterns at every airport in the United

States. Before every cross-country flight to a new airport, I'd study it carefully, sketching on paper a diagram of every possible approach to its runways. Soon, as I gained confidence in my ability to perform this simple geometry, I no longer needed to draw the approaches. I was learning the discipline of thinking ahead.

But I still had my lapses. On takeoff from Watertown, I set course for home—114 degrees magnetic—but read it as 141 degrees on both the gyro and compass. Had I stayed on that course, I would have flown right into the Janesville Airport airspace, which requires communication with the tower by radio. Fortunately, I caught my mistake in time. But when I arrived home that afternoon, I had all but convinced myself I was not cut out to be a pilot. Stumbling into the house, I poured out my tale of woe to Debby. Astonishingly it brought from her a halftime pep talk. Gently she took my face between her palms and said, "I have full faith in you. You are too far along to quit now. If you just stick with it, you will overcome your problems." I was stunned. If Debby had really felt that I should not be flying, she would have told me to face my limitations and just bag it. But her nurturing side emerged, as always, when I needed it. I felt whole again. Maybe she would never fly with me, as she kept saying, but her affectionate steadfastness was a comfort.

The next day's lesson turned out to be much happier. I performed beautiful crosswind takeoffs and landings and was rewarded with an introduction to radio work. My speech, Tom said, is intelligible enough to be readily understood on the radio. I could enhance my safety and that of others by broadcasting my intentions in the blind, though I, of course, could not receive transmissions. After a few quick instructions, Tom stepped out of the plane and told me to do three takeoffs and landings alone—this was only the second day I had soloed—and announce my intentions on the radio each time. Afterward he told me my radio transmissions had come through loud and clear on the speaker in the pilot's lounge. From then on, I would let the world know that I was taking off: "Westosha traffic, Cessna six-four-niner-two-zero departing Runway Two-One, Westosha," I'd say, in the best imitation of a Chuck Yeager drawl I could muster.

"I just knew you felt lower than a snake's belly yesterday," Bob Locher said that night. "You needed a day like today." And so I did. After I told him about broadcasting my intentions on the radio, he suddenly became lost in thought. "The one problem with that," he said, "is that because you can't hear another pilot talking, you might step on his transmission. Both of you will come in garbled. But I think there's a solution, and let me work on it."

I grinned. I had no doubt that he would find one. Sometimes I think Bob was born with a soldering iron in his fist. He is a basement tinkerer and a serious ham radio enthusiast, as well as a comfortable half-owner of a Chicago business that manufactures radio, photographic, and video equipment. He also runs a successful kitchen-table mail-order business from his home, making kits for ham operators. A few days later, Bob arrived at the airport with a small black box the size of a pack of cigarettes. On its front protruded a large red light–emitting diode. Out of its back looped a coiled cord with a plug. "Plug the cord into the headphone jack on your radio," Bob said. "When there's any traffic on the frequency the radio's using, the LED will light up. When it's dark you can make your broadcasts."

Ever since, I have rarely sat in the pilot's seat without the little box I immediately dubbed a Locherometer, although it is generically called a "radio level meter." The few times I forgot to take it along aboard a rental airplane, I immediately missed it, as if someone had removed the rearview mirrors from my car. Today, several other deaf pilots use Locherometers built from Bob's plans.

On August 3, after boning up on the books for two weeks, I took the written test for the private pilot's license at a computer testing center in Chicago's Loop and scored 95 out of 100. What a boost to my confidence! Because of my deafness, I didn't attend ground-school classes, typically a series of lectures to twenty or more students in a large room. Instead, I had designed my own ground-school curriculum: close reading of half a dozen textbooks on flying, plus the FAA's *Federal Aviation Regulations/Aeronautical Information Manual*. As I had learned as a schoolboy, I compensated for my deafness by doing extra reading and by using the arts of research I had picked up in high school and college.

And it seemed as if I was about to cross still another watershed; I anticipated that soon Tom would at last turn me loose by giving me a gas card, which operates both the fuel pumps and the steel safe in the pilot's lounge that guards the keys to the planes, proclaiming the student pilot's right to fly solo whenever he wishes, provided he remains within twenty-five miles of his home airport and lands nowhere else without being "signed off" by his instructor to do so. After our lesson on August 20, at the end of which I did three solo landings and takeoffs, Tom did give me the gas card. I was progressing.

August 24 was my first real solo day, in which I preflighted, took off, flew, landed, and tied down the plane, all by my lonesome, away from Tom's paternal eye. That night I had a dream in which the entire membership of the Westosha Flying Club voted me out of the organization as a danger to them and myself, not because I was a deaf pilot but because I was a lousy one. Actually, I was becoming friendly with many of the members, especially those in their forties and fifties. I suspected most of them were fairly new pilots themselves, if not students. I was beginning to feel the stirrings of a new kinship.

Three solo cross-country flights—one of them at least 336 statute miles long—are required for the private pilot's license. They are a giant step forward for every student pilot. On my first flight on September 5, I hit all my checkpoints bang on. First I flew to Baraboo, 103 miles northwest of Westosha, then fourteen miles east to Portage, and ninety-five miles back to Westosha. My time-en route calculations were off three minutes long going, four minutes short returning—a pittance. This day did wonders for my self-esteem. Like a falcon on the edge of adulthood, I was leaving the nest, stretching my wings, flying free for the horizon.

Nothing in the world matched being aloft alone in a little airplane, surveying one's domain in absolute freedom. In no other endeavor did my life depend so utterly on the skills I had learned— and was still learning. In such surroundings, I could feel my cares drop away and my mind become riveted on the task at hand. I would drive up to Westosha, my mind swirling with office politics, worried about the latest change in editorial philosophy or the newest graphic makeover, and wondering whether I was up to the chore of dealing with them. Two hours later, I would drive home refreshed, ready to rassle the bear. As had nothing else during my life, flying was taking me outside myself.

As September turned to October, several bouts of bad weather delayed the second of my three solo cross-country flights, and I itched to return to the air. I tarried around the airport one entire morning, hoping the fog would lift enough to provide the six miles' visibility Tom required for a student cross-country. "I'll give it another half hour," I said every half hour from 8 A.M. until about noon.

To which the two other student pilots in the lounge replied, "You're not planning to go out in *that,* are you?" For a while I wondered why they were hanging around in the all-but-empty lounge until I realized that they were worried about me, that they didn't trust me to do the right thing and stand down. I didn't know whether to be annoyed by their patronization or gratified by their concern. At noon I went home—and so did they.

But later that week the weather cleared, and I flew the second and third solo cross-countries. One was a 354-mile trip west to Lone Rock and Grant County Airports and back. The other was a 325-mile journey south to Lacon and Galesburg in Illinois. Flying free was still new to me, and keeping one eye on the sky and the other on the ground, watching for both traffic and landmarks, was wearying—not to mention scoping out the active runway at the destination (wind socks are hard to see from the air, and their direction is even harder to judge) and getting down in one piece.

On these cross-country flights, pilots relaxing in the lounges had pricked up their ears when I walked in and announced my deafness to the attendant behind the counter. Ordinarily I don't advertise my lack of hearing—it's irrelevant in most situations—but around airports and their whirling propellers, making sure other pilots knew that among them was a visiting student who couldn't hear seemed a prudent act of self-preservation. To my surprise, their response almost invariably was one of genial interest. Many would hand me a cup of the ghastly coffee common to grassroots airports and ask not only how a deaf pilot goes about his business but also for the highlights of my training; whether I might buy an airplane someday; if so, which one; what I thought of the Clinton administration's proposal to privatize the FAA; and so on.

This was something new for me. As a deaf person, I have grown accustomed to apprehensive diffidence from people who are fearful of encounters with those who cannot hear or who struggle to speak clearly. By contrast, pilots seemed to welcome me with open arms—so much so that I felt a member of the Brotherhood of the Right Stuff, Tom Wolfe's ironically grandiose term for fighter-pilot camaraderie. Perhaps pilots felt a subtle bond with all who had shared the experience of flight training. Maybe, I thought, there was even a genuine fraternity among them, one that transcended the differences that divided us.

In the meantime there was more work to be done. By October 15

I had amassed seventy-six hours in the air and needed just the three required hours of night flying, plus a few hours of brush-up work before I could take the "check ride," the official flight test for the private pilot's certificate. I felt increasingly confident in my skills and was well on the way to defeating an old bugaboo, crosswind landings. But I was not in a race, Tom reminded me; I'd be ready when I was ready and not a moment before.

His wisdom came home to me one sunny day in mid-November, when I experienced something new: wind shear. On the ground the wind sock barely twitched, while the sock on top of a hangar stood straight out. That should have warned me. At about 200 feet in my takeoff climb, the airplane lurched abruptly to starboard as if a giant fist had plucked it from the air, and my stomach turned to ice. I thought something was wrong with the Cessna. When I saw that my airplane was drifting rapidly to the right instead of flying straight and true over the ground, I drew the obvious conclusion that the winds above 200 feet were brisk while those on the ground were light. The wind shear was comparatively gentle. But I had had my first real taste of what the unseen caprices of weather could do with an airplane. From then on, I resolved to take nothing for granted, even on a pleasant day. Again, easier said than done.

On the last day of the month came my first night flight. Tom and I flew to Burlington thirteen miles northwest for landings on its ample runway, its edges outlined with dim lamps. On my first touchdown, I very nearly landed on a highway paralleling the runway—only an oncoming car warned me of my error. In some ways, however, flying in the dark is actually easier than driving an automobile, for there is no glare of oncoming traffic. It is also easier to see and avoid the traffic because airplanes at night burn bright navigation lights on their wings and tails, as well as flashing strobe lights atop their rudders. With no daytime thermals rising to create turbulence, the air is smooth. Flying at night in a clear sky is like wrapping oneself in a velvet blanket speckled with diamonds. It also can be deceptive and dangerous, especially for a middle-aged student pilot whose eyes aren't what they used to be. On our landing back at Westosha, I fell into the common illusion, from watching the angle of the runway lights ahead, that my approach was too high and pulled back the throttle to lose a little altitude. Immediately Tom poured on the power, and in the beam of the landing light I saw the tops of trees rushing upward. I had been too low, not too high. Then and there I resolved never to fly at night. The accident rate for lightplanes flying at night is significant, so much so that a veteran Boeing 747 pilot I once met said he would never fly past sundown in a small airplane. Other pilots disagree. To each his own.

After the Christmas holidays, and a welcome vacation from work, January 2 saw the beginning of the brush-up lessons for the check ride. Mainly it was a day for sanding off the rough spots. Slowly I was attaining the polish required for taking the flight test. A week later, however, Tom and I did another hour of brushup, during which, recovering from a power-on stall at 3,000 feet, I accidentally fell into a spin—absolute grounds for failing the test. I was not terrified, but the inadvertent spin told me that even after ninety-six hours of flight, I still was not ready for the moment of truth.

Over the next two months, typical Wisconsin winter conditions—a deep freeze, heavy snow, and ice storms—effectively grounded me. I did get in some flying time toward the end of February, and after two practice check rides on March 5 and 6, Tom called Jimmy Szajkovics, a safety inspector at the FAA's Milwaukee Flight Standards District Office, and scheduled my test for 9 A.M. on April 8 at East Troy, an uncontrolled airport less than an hour from Milwaukee. A student pilot with any kind of physical disability must take a special FAA medical flight test, which must be administered by an FAA inspector, not a civilian designated examiner. Reputedly, FAA inspectors are tougher than designated examiners—they are said to fail candidates at a much higher rate—but those who ride with the governmental employees don't have to pay a fee, while some designated examiners charge $175 for the ride. If I failed, I wouldn't be out any money, while a hearing flunkee riding with a civilian check pilot still has to pay the fee and pay it again for the next test. And the next, if it comes to that.

April 8 arrived, but bad weather canceled the check ride. And again. And again. Each time we set a date, something else would come up. Crankily I observed to a fellow student pilot, "Getting laid in high school was easier."

Finally, on May 5, Jimmy Szajkovics, a tall, pleasant fellow with the cheerful concern of a born teacher, took me through an hour and a half of oral quizzing, during which my knowledge expanded hugely; safety inspectors are born lecturers. The weather was still not ideal, and he had suggested that we wait until the next day. But conditions were good enough (ceiling 8,000 feet, visibility seven miles, wind nine miles per hour from the southwest), and I was champing at the bit. While we were in the air, however, an unfore-cast weak front rolled through, and suddenly the winds shot up to seventeen and twenty miles per hour, with gusts of twenty-eight miles per hour. At East Troy Szajkovics had to snatch the yoke to keep the plane from a hard landing when it flew from a gust into al-most dead air above the threshold of the runway—and I froze at the controls.

That alone, I thought, should have flunked me. I was also not pleased with my performance in "lost procedures," in which the ex-aminer thoroughly disorients the pilot's sense of direction while he is flying "under the hood" on instruments only, without being able to see outside the airplane, and then tells him to locate the air-plane's position on the chart once the hood is removed. I was thor-oughly bewildered, heading west when I thought I was heading north. Only after Szajkovics's broad hints did I finally determine my location and direction.

Thinking I had already failed the test and that Szajkovics was just going through the motions on the rest, I relaxed and began to look at the exercise as an interesting challenge instead of a pass-or-fail examination. I made a splendid emergency engine-out landing through the gusts and crosswinds at a private field and greased the final landing, a hot one without flaps in a stiff crosswind at East Troy.

"How do you think you did?" Szajkovics asked after I shut down the engine.

"Not very well," I said. "I got lost, and you had to take over that one time."

He smiled and extended his hand. "Congratulations," he said. "You're a private pilot. You simply nailed those last two landings in tough conditions, and I'm just gonna trust you to have the sense not to fly in winds like this until you have more experience."

I was astonished and a little dismayed. I had been *given* this li-cense, I felt. I had not earned it. Szajkovics, I thought, was giving me a leg up because he wanted to see a pilot with a disability make good. When I landed at Westosha and the pilots tumbled out of the lounge, asking eagerly, "Did you pass?" I nodded neutrally, trying to hide my consternation. I felt I did not deserve the backslaps and handshakes they showered on me. In the lounge, Tom sauntered out of the club's office with a big smile and shook my hand. I confessed my state of mind. "I shouldn't have passed," I said, and told him of the botched landing.

"Henry," Tom replied, "Jimmy wouldn't have given you that license if he didn't think you deserved it. You're a private pilot." Then he reached up on the wall, took down the shirttail he had cut off my back almost a year earlier, and presented it to me with solemn ceremony, the final ritual in the initiation. Then Tom pronounced the familiar blessing of the flight instructor, the one that proclaims to every newly minted private pilot that education in the mysteries of aviation is never ending: "Now you have a license to learn."

On the way home down the interstate, I finally began to believe. Slowly a broad grin crossed my face, the momentous smile every pilot remembers all his career. "When you get that license, sonny," a septuagenarian aviator had said, "you'll feel like a real man." Now I knew what he meant.

I embraced Debby as I walked in the door. "I'm a *pilot*," I said as she gazed at me with all the welter of love, worry, and exasperation she had displayed during the fifteen-month enterprise.

"I knew you could do it, Henry," she said simply, giving me a warm kiss. But when I opened my briefcase and took out the grimy shirttail that was cut off for my first solo and tried to tack it up on the kitchen bulletin board, Debby exclaimed, "Oh, God, no—that's horrible! We have to *eat* in here!"

# 4

*T*om was right. I still had a great deal to learn before I'd be ready to retrace Cal Rodgers's flight from New York to California. A new pilot is only a sophomore as far as knowledge is concerned. I needed the seasoning of experience, just as a rookie outfielder needs a year or two at Peoria before he steps up to the Cubs.

And the first thing to learn was how to fly with a passenger who is not a pilot. Just three days after I came home with the private pilot's certificate, I asked my older son, Colin, to be my first human cargo. With a certain trepidation—he shared much of his mother's view of small planes—he assented. Later I realized that he had suppressed his fear in his desire to respect his father's feelings. Fortunately the flight was uneventful; we took one of the Westosha Flying Club's 152s west over Lake Geneva and then flew low over Lake Michigan at Kenosha. Colin didn't want me to shoot landings, so we stayed up just an hour. I kept my turns shallow and my control inputs gentle, and the turbulence was mercifully light. Colin seemed only a bit nervous, although he did observe, "This plane's a lot smaller than I thought it'd be."

His brother, Conan, was my next passenger, this time on a long cross-country flight. We flew nearly 300 miles from Westosha north to Ontonagon, Michigan, a little town on Lake Superior where Debby's parents keep a summer home. The flight was a textbook example of planning and execution—brand-new pilots tend to be as meticulous as surgeons—except for one thing: In gathering weather information, I had failed to study the next day's forecast. I had not seen the oncoming front in central Minnesota. The result was that our two-day weekend at Ontonagon stretched into three days, as Conan and I sat fidgeting on the runway, hoping the low clouds and light rain over the Upper Peninsula of Michigan would lift enough to permit a legal VFR flight home. Conan is not the kind of young man who complains when things don't go his way, but I could sense his impatience and irritation with his father's lack of foresight.

In those early weeks my sons were my only passengers. For the most part, my friends and colleagues always were "too busy" or had "already made plans" whenever I asked them if they'd like to go for a ride. Whether they did not trust a freshly minted pilot or a deaf one I was not sure, but the result was the same. I usually flew alone. The solitude did not disturb me because there was still a great deal for me to learn about flying. In any case, the newness of a private pilot's certificate does not necessarily jeopardize the safety of the passengers. Still conscious of his shortcomings, a new pilot—at least a cautious middle-aged one—tends to be conscientious in the extreme, scanning the sky like a nervous hawk and ticking off the preflight checklist religiously. It's when he has just a couple of hundred hours of flight time under his belt that he starts to become overconfident.

"If you learn to land at Westosha," a veteran pilot had told me, "you can land *anywhere*." That was true enough. But month after month of threading the needle on a runway 38 feet wide by 2,800 feet long had an unintended consequence: I could land smoothly on a postage stamp, but I had a hard time with vast expanses—runways 75 feet wide by 5,000 feet long. My depth perception is not what it used to be, so what looked to me like a proper approach to a wide runway often wasn't. I would be way too high when I started the landing flare—in which the plane's nose is lifted slowly as it loses speed so the main wheels touch down before the nosewheel—and, as a result, would "drop her in" with a thunk at best and a bone-rattling jolt at worst. It was like trying to land on an imaginary surface ten feet higher than the real one. I needed weeks of practice at strange airports before I learned the trick of focusing on a familiar object, like an automobile, to judge my height above the ground accurately.

A happier task was to step up to a bigger airplane. With Mel Everhart, a retired navy jet pilot who was manager of the Westosha Flying Club, I took out a Cessna 172 for a spin. I was surprised at the difference between it and the 152s I had trained in. The Skyhawk (as the 172 is nicknamed) was much more of an airplane and required more muscle to control. I was stepping up to 160 horsepower from 108, from two seats to four. Because it was heavier and more powerful, the 172 was much more stable than the 152, easier to keep on course, brisker in the climb, and smoother in turbulence, and its cruising speed was twenty-five miles per hour faster. Its panel boasted more navigation instruments; indeed, the club's 172s were fully equipped for Instrument Flight Rules—flying in bad weather and poor visibility by watching the instruments and following radioed instructions from Air Traffic Control. This was a *serious* airplane, one made for long cross-country flights, and so were the club's Piper Archer and Piper Arrow, low-wing airplanes with even more complexity—the Arrow in particular, with retractable landing gear and a geared propeller that could be adjusted in flight for either speed or climbing power.

All these airplanes were considerably more expensive to rent than a 152, and only when I was able to talk more than one friend into flying with me did I take a Skyhawk. Otherwise I stuck with the more economical 152s for solo flying and for puttering around the neighborhood with a single passenger. With Bob Locher in the right seat, however, I had to rent a 172; he is such a big man—a long-legged six feet, three inches, and 250 pounds—that the two of us would have burdened the 152 well past its legal useful load.

Though I stifled my desire for a larger airplane to fly, I did begin to yearn for another navigation instrument. Besides its compass, the typical Cessna 152 has in its instrument panel a VOR (for VHF Omni Range) radio. This is a receiver with a swinging needle that tells whether the plane is flying directly to a navigational broadcasting station and on what magnetic course. It is 1940s technology, but so widespread and well established that the FAA plans to use it into the first decade of the twenty-first century, despite newer, cheaper, and far more reliable methods of navigation. This is all very well, but if a VOR ground transmitter or the plane's receiver goes dead and I lose my bearings, I cannot radio Air Traffic Control for a radar steer to get out of trouble. I needed a backup system.

For $700 I bought a battery-powered handheld GPS (Global Positioning System) receiver. The GPS is a tiny computer, no bigger than a camera, that can calculate the airplane's position on earth—its latitude, longitude, and altitude—*within 30 feet* by triangulating radio waves emitted from a constellation of 24 satellites high above the earth. At this writing, however, the U.S. Department of Defense, which operates the system, deliberately degrades the accuracy of the signals to about 300 feet, presumably to keep unseen enemies from lobbing a missile into the president's ear.

With the GPS strapped to the yoke, I can, at a glance, read not only my position but also my course and ground speed. This wonderful instrument tells me not only the direction to and distance from my destination, but also how long it will take to get there. Moreover, if I run into trouble and must land in a hurry, the press of a single button will display the ten nearest airports and the course to and distance from each.

Aviation isn't the only use for GPS. Trucking companies use it to find stolen eighteen-wheel rigs. Auto manufacturers are now putting GPS into luxury cars, and within a few years high-quality digital road maps will be visible on every new automobile's dashboard. Biologists strap paperback-sized receivers onto tortoises and sheep to track their migration ranges and grazing habits. Hikers use simple $200 receivers that display a little map pinpointing their exact location on earth.

Modern electronics—the TTY and the computer in particular—have made a deaf person's life easier, and the GPS was a godsend. I took it along on every cross-country flight, making myself use the VOR as my chief navigation instrument as much to keep up my proficiency with it as anything else. I relied on the GPS not only as a backup, but also to keep from intruding into the O'Hare and Milwaukee controlled airspace, which could bring the wrath of the FAA down on my head. Pilots are always nicking the edge, and Air Traffic Control usually will look the other way, but if the incursion is blatant—say three miles or more—the tower will track the offender on radar to his landing spot and send a cop to intercept the airplane on the runway and take names. Later the FAA will kick ass, usually ordering the pilot to undergo remedial training but sometimes suspending his license. The GPS told me how close I was to the center of that airspace, enabling me to keep a comfortable two miles or more away from its edge. In time the GPS proved so easy to use, so accurate, and so reliable that it became my primary navigation instrument, and I used the VOR mainly as a backup—when I used it at all.

One Sunday morning I flew to East Troy to shoot crosswind landings, and as I began my approach I saw that the grassy expanses of the little field were crowded with airplanes, a steady stream of them entering the landing pattern above. I slotted myself into the flow and landed, and during my rollout, I saw not only gaily striped tents but also a big four-engine C-130 Hercules transport parked on the ramp.

Summer had begun, and so had the fly-ins and breakfasts ubiquitous to grassroots airfields everywhere. One might be a gathering pegged to a particular kind of airplane, such as the classic Stinsons of the 1930s and 1940s, in which owners of the antiques fly them to the airport for a big grown-up show-and-tell. Or the event might be a fund-raising pancake breakfast hosted by the community that owns the airport, as this one was. Part church supper, part flea market, part air show, part Fourth of July parade, the breakfast fly-in attracts pilots from scores, even hundreds, of miles around who are looking for a reason other than a $100 hamburger to exercise their engines. *Everybody* comes. Old-timers, students, spouses, youngsters, hucksters, hangers-on, mendicants from the local chapter of the Experimental Aircraft Association who are seeking handouts to restore old warbirds, and Air National Guardsmen who are glad to have someplace to fly their birds to do a little public relations. Hence the Hercules.

As I collected a stack of sausages and pancakes—they're always soggy, but nobody complains—and found a place at a long picnic table in the hangar, I looked about me, eavesdropping with my eyes. Pilots boasted about their airplanes and cursed with envy over other people's airplanes. Others mingled with townspeople, touting the joys of flight. A few arranged to sell rides, and everyone signed up for a "bomb drop" contest later in the day, during which low-flying planes would dump water-filled balloons or refrigerator bags packed with flour on a tractor sitting in a field off the runway. Young children cooed as jumpsuit-clad guardsmen showed them the cavernous interior of the Hercules. Everyone stopped and watched as a rich fellow zoomed his World War II P-51 Mustang in a flyby along the runway, thrilling the crowd with the throaty roar of its high-horsepower engine. There is nothing else like it in the world.

And yet these communal fly-ins are a threatened species. "I haven't seen anything like this before," I said to my neighbor at the picnic table. "How come this doesn't go on every day?" In answer, he surprised me with a tirade against the federal government, with frequent hostile asides about the legal profession. As the year wore on, I would hear and read more and more about the economic crisis that has enveloped general aviation, the smallest of the three categories of American aviation. General aviation embraces sport airplanes, as well as small-business, corporate, and agricultural aircraft. The military and the airlines make up the other two categories.

For more than a decade, the business of small airplanes has been about as healthy as the Egyptian air force after the Six-Day War. In 1982 the bottom dropped out of the new airplane market. Cessna stopped building piston-engined airplanes in 1986. Piper went bankrupt. Mooney almost went under. Beechcraft still built Bonanzas and Barons, but only millionaires could afford them. By 1994 the number of active general-aviation airplanes had slumped to 170,600—a drop of almost 14 percent in four years—and the FAA was forecasting that the number of planes would bottom out at 165,400 in 1997 before resuming a modest growth.

What went wrong? As my tablemate said, just about any pilot will tell you it was "the damn government" or "those damn lawyers"—or both. There have been infamous cases in which multimillion-dollar product-liability judgments have gone against deep-pocketed airplane manufacturers, despite the proved errors of pilots who crashed decades-old airplanes that were considered perfectly safe at the time they were built. While much blame can be pinned on an overzealous federal bureaucracy and an explosion of greedy personal-injury lawyers, the matter is considerably more complex.

It turns out that the boom years for lightplane makers in the 1970s had been artificially stimulated by an astonishingly generous tax code meant to invigorate the industry. The buyer of a new airplane could take a huge investment credit off the bottom line of his income tax return and, what's more, take an enormous first-year "bonus" depreciation on the plane as well as a speedy depreciation on the rest of its cost. Added up, all the tax benefits meant that a new plane cost no more than a used one.

All those breaks vanished when the tax code was overhauled in the early 1980s. Now, almost nobody could afford to buy a new airplane, and the manufacturers ceased producing all but a few single-engine models. Without an infusion of new aircraft, the single-engine fleet grew old, so old that many aging airplanes became good investments. A pilot could buy a twenty-year-old Cessna 172 in good shape, fly it for a couple of years, and sell it for more than he paid—if he could afford to keep it up. The cost of parts skyrocketed, and the FAA issued directive after directive requiring costly inspections of elderly airplanes, even if they had been lovingly maintained.

New pilots ate the increasing costs in the form of sharply higher rental rates for training airplanes. Between 1984 and 1993, the number of student pilots had declined almost 20 percent, and the number of private pilots had fallen by 11 percent. As a result, the average age of the American grassroots pilot shot from 35.7 years in 1970 to 41.3 years in the mid-1990s. Flying for sport seemed to be turning into a rich old man's pastime. (At that fact I felt a shock of recognition, although I am hardly well-to-do.)

Suburban airports—at least those that weren't plowed under for new housing developments—continued to survive and even thrive, kept afloat by business aviation and wealthy young professionals who still could afford to fly for fun. Rural airfields, however, rapidly declined, and many of them went under. As I extended my cross-country range across Wisconsin, Illinois, Iowa, and Missouri, I flew into country airport after country airport and saw no one out and about, even on weekends. Many of these airports were no longer attended and sold fuel only in emergencies.

There was some hope for the future, however. In 1994 Congress passed the General Aviation Revitalization Act, which limited a manufacturer's legal liability to the first eighteen years of an airplane's life. No longer having to worry about being sued in crashes involving airplanes as old as half a century, Cessna geared up to produce new 172s and their bigger brothers, 182s, for the first time in a decade. Piper reorganized and emerged from bankruptcy. Old power-plant manufacturers, such as Teledyne Continental, invested in modernization. And the used-airplane fleet was shrinking from attrition enough so that new airplanes, however more expensive they were, began to look attractive. The old Cessna two-seaters used as trainers were wearing out after many thousands of hours of abuse, and smaller aircraft manufacturers began to put new two-seaters through the long, arduous, and expensive process of winning FAA certification as safe to fly commercially.

Nobody in aviation expected a return of the high-flying go-go years of the 1970s, when it looked as if the airplane-in-every-garage hope of post–World War II American aviation would at last come true. And if grassroots flying was indeed revived, the new lease on life, it seemed, would come slowly. For now it seemed that the precipitous decline had finally been slowed, if not halted.

There was one technique I had not yet learned: the light-signal landing, which would allow me to fly into and out of some tower-controlled airports. During the 1920s and 1930s, most light airplanes did not carry radios, and a system was developed that allowed controllers to keep them from colliding overhead at airports: the portable light-signal gun. With the gun, a controller in the tower would issue orders by pointing a powerful beam of light at an airplane. Two green flashes signified "Approach for landing." A steady green light meant "Cleared to land." A steady red light told the pilot to "Give way to other aircraft and continue circling." A flashing red light meant "Airport unsafe; do not land." An alternating red-and-green signal meant "Exercise extreme caution." This system is still used, to land mostly airplanes with ailing radios, but also antique aircraft without transceivers and, once in a blue moon, deaf pilots like me.

Ordinarily I would much rather land at an uncontrolled airport close by, just because traffic is lighter, but if I have a good reason to land at a controlled airport—it may be the only airport within many miles or the only nearby airport with an aviation electronics repair shop—I will do so if I can get clearance. Most control towers at smaller airports will quickly grant it, although when traffic is heavy, they'll ask me to stay away until a better time.

One morning I took my portable TTY to Westosha. After preflighting a 152 and parking it outside the pilot's lounge, I phoned the tower at Rock County Airport in Janesville, half an hour west. "I'm a deaf pilot," I said through the relay operator, "and I've never done a light-gun landing. I need some practice. Can you give it to me?"

Evidently, whatever small fame I had as Westosha's deaf pilot had begun to spread across southern Wisconsin. "Sure, we've been waiting for you to call," the controller said immediately. "What's your ETA and where are you coming from?"

"Fourteen hundred hours Zulu," I said. Aviation time runs according to a twenty-four-hour clock at the meridian of longitude that runs through Greenwich Observatory in England, once known as GMT, or Greenwich mean time, but now called UTC, for universal coordinated time. (The official term was originally French, hence the odd arrangement of the initials.) *Zulu* is the long-standing international aviation shorthand for both GMT and UTC. I was telling the tower I would arrive at 1400Z aviation time, or 9 A.M. central daylight time. "I'm November niner-five-five-five-eight, a Cessna One Five Two, white and brown, and I'm coming from Whiskey India One Zero," the FAA airport code for Westosha. I chuckled silently. I had walked the walk; now I was talking the talk.

"Here's what to do," replied the tower. "Since you're approaching from the east, you should enter the Class Delta* airspace on base for Runway One-Three at 1,500 feet. While you're on base leg, we'll give you the signal. If there's a problem, continue circling, and watch for the signal."

"I can speak," I said, "and I could tell you on the radio when I enter the airspace."

"Great," said the tower. "Announce your presence as you cross the interstate about four miles northeast of the airport. We'll be watching for you. And, by the way, would you like to pay a visit to the tower when you arrive? We'd like to meet you."

"Sure," I said.

"We'll have someone pick you up when you shut down. OK, see you later."

Immediately, I climbed into N95558 and took off, arriving fifteen minutes early at Janesville, thanks to a swift tailwind. Wanting to announce my presence at the precise moment, I climbed and circled over the airport above the ceiling of its controlled airspace, checking runway numbers and the location of the tower. At 8:55 A.M. I headed back northeast, losing altitude, to get onto base leg for Runway 13. At precisely 9 A.M., the airplane crossed the interstate, and I

---

*Class D airspace surrounds smaller airports that require tower-to-air radio communications. Class C (Charlie, in the international phonetic alphabet) surrounds bigger and busier fields, and Class B (Bravo) the major metropolitan airports, such as O'Hare and Kennedy. Class A (Alpha) airspace is that above 18,000 feet, where jetliners fly. Class E (Echo) and Class G (Golf) do not require radio communications. (There is no Class F airspace.)

keyed the mike. "Janesville Tower, Cessna niner-five-five-five-eight entering base for Runway One-Three," I said. "Request light signal."

About a mile east, I saw the first signal—but it appeared white, not green. A white signal does not have a meaning to a pilot in the air. On the ground it means "Return to starting point on airport." I was confused. I was still 700 feet above the runway, and so I proceeded to fly a wide circle around the airport as instructed, keying the mike and asking for a repeat of the light signal. As I passed the tower while flying parallel to Runway 13, I saw two brief green flashes that meant, in essence, "Return for landing. Get into the pattern." I waggled my wings and sang on the radio, "Janesville Tower, Cessna five-eight. Signal received and understood. Janesville." On base leg, a steady, but nearly imperceptible, green signal shone from the tower. Just before turning on final, I waggled my wings again. Smoothly the airplane touched down, and while I was still on the rollout past the tower, I received the double green blink that gave me clearance to taxi.

After shutting down on the apron by the airport restaurant, a wide grin enveloping my face, I was greeted by the young controller who had lighted my way in. "Don Medernach," he said, shaking my hand with a smile as broad as mine. As we rode in his car to the tower, he said, "I know ASL. Do you?" Nope, I said, I don't know American Sign Language. He nodded, unsurprised. He very likely knew that a deaf man in his fifties who used lipreading and speech would have grown up at a time when sign language was discouraged, even forbidden. He told me that he had a two-year-old deaf-born child who was being raised bilingually, with ASL the primary language and English the second.

But when we reached the control room at the top of the tower, my landing was the more immediate subject of conversation. I had done everything correctly. The white signal I had seen was easily explained. At my angle of approach, the prismatic effect of the reverse-slanted windows in the tower had changed the green to white.

"You were easier to land than a complete no-radio pilot," Don said, "because we knew you were gonna do what we told you to do. Some pilots prefer to do it their way, if you know what I mean. And your being able to talk on the radio let us know what you planned to do at all times and helped us keep other airplanes away. You owned the airport until you landed."

Most small Class D airports like Janesville's have no radar. All controlling is done by eyeballing aircraft in the air with the help of binoculars. "That's one reason we don't want you coming in on Saturdays and Sundays," Don said. "It's not just the heavy weekend traffic then, but it's also that pilots don't always mind us, and we can't be sure we'll always be able to divert every other airplane away from you."

I told them about Cal Rodgers and my plans to reenact his transcontinental flight. "Before you go," Don said, "let us know, and we'll call all the Class Delta towers on your route and put in a good word for you."

Afterward Don drove me back to the restaurant, where I sat down for a cup of coffee. Suddenly there was a tap on my shoulder. I looked up into the face of Jimmy Szajkovics, the FAA safety inspector who had given me my check ride a few months before. He was smiling tightly. "I was approaching Janesville when you landed, and I immediately recognized your voice. Why did you do a light-signal landing?"

I explained and added that I hoped to do four or five such landings on my reenactment of Rodgers's flight.

"What does your license say?" he asked dubiously.

"'Not valid for flights requiring the use of radio,'" I answered. "But once I have received advance permission from a tower to enter controlled airspace for a light-gun landing," I argued, "that flight officially does not require the use of radio. Does it?"

Szajkovics's expression remained doubtful, but he didn't argue the point. I hoped I wouldn't receive a finger-wagging letter from the FAA. I didn't, but later I would learn from another deaf pilot that not all FAA safety inspectors and controllers interpret the rules so flexibly. A few controllers will not allow deaf aviators to perform light-signal landings or takeoffs under any circumstances, contending that they cannot issue instructions to the pilots during the brief intervals of flight between the outer edge of the airspace and the moment the light gun is triggered. Yes, but that's also true of hearing pilots without radios. And in either case, the controllers can warn other aircraft away from the arriving or departing no-radio airplane.

Later, back on the ramp, I pointed N55558 at the tower, turned on the landing lights, and broadcast a request for a signal giving me permission to taxi. In a few seconds, two green flashes winked from the tower. I waggled my ailerons—the movable surfaces of the trailing edges of the wings that allow the airplane to be rolled or banked—turned off the landing lights, and broadcast an acknowledgment; I immediately received a series of red-green-red-green flashes, which meant, "Exercise extreme caution." Looking about, I saw four other airplanes in line on the taxiway to Runway 13. An airplane took off, another landed, the next took off, and so on until I had reached the threshold. I turned the plane toward the tower, turned on the landing light, and waited. Immediately the steady green came, and I was away for Westosha.

Afterward I realized that I had broken radio etiquette by saying "Received and understood" alone a couple of times instead of the full "Janesville Tower, Cessna five-eight, received and understood, Janesville," as specified in the rules. Since my speech is distinctive, however, I was sure the folks in the tower forgave that. All in all, it was a satisfying morning in the air, with something new learned and learned well.

As the summer drew to a close, I devoted more of my energies to studying the history of Cal Rodgers's epic flight. The story began in 1910, when William Randolph Hearst, one of the richest newspaper magnates of the time, offered a $50,000 prize to the first aviator to fly from coast to coast in either direction within thirty days. The rules were simple. Competitors could start from either coast and fly whatever route they wanted, but had to stop in Chicago. Each aviator had to use the same airplane throughout, but it could be repaired or even rebuilt as much as needed with parts from other machines. Anybody, even foreigners, could compete. And contestants must tip off Hearst's *New York American* fourteen days before they set out. That was all.

The offer was good for one year, beginning October 10, 1910. Hearst declared that he wanted American aviation to wrest the technological lead from the Europeans, who had been faster than the Americans to embrace the Wright brothers' achievements in 1903. He also wanted American aviators to shift their emphasis from barnstorming exhibition flights toward building machines for more practical use—carrying paying passengers over long distances, for instance. And, of course, he wanted to harness the new public passion for aviation to sell more newspapers.

The reaction from aviators was immediate and enthusiastic, but over the next few months, their interest cooled. Airplanes were still too flimsy, engines were too unreliable, and the terrain was vast and inhospitable. The long trip would demand time and money, single-mindedness, and courage. Even Orville Wright said he thought the arts of aviation had not yet advanced far enough for such an endeavor.

But the Hearst offer still stood, and by the time of the big Chicago International Aviation Meet in August 1911, several men and their machines were ready to make the effort. One of them was Cal Rodgers. Rodgers had won his license that same month and had immediately gone to Chicago, where he was the third highest prizewinner at the meet, thrilling crowds of 500,000 that jammed Grant Park. He took home $11,285 of the total $80,000 purse, including the richest prize, $5,000 for flying the longest during the nine-day meet—more than twenty-five hours. Cal's feat was like breaking into the big leagues directly from sandlot baseball and slashing a two-run double his first time at bat.

Flushed with success, Cal decided to go for the Hearst prize if he could persuade someone to sponsor him. The meatpacking tycoon J. Ogden Armour had watched the meet, and his company was getting ready to market a new product. An advertising campaign was being discussed, and Cal figured that a transcontinental flight just might fit into the scheme. With the help of a hired business manager, he approached an Armour executive, and on September 10 they forged an agreement. In exchange for Armour's financial support, Rodgers would emblazon the name of the company's new sparkling grape soft drink, Vin Fiz, on the underside of the lower wings and rudder of his airplane.

The Armour Company hoped that Vin Fiz would become forever linked in the public mind with aviation, America's newest rage. The drink was delicious and refreshing, the company declared, and also a mild laxative—just what the doctor ordered. As so many beverage manufacturers have claimed, Vin Fiz not only tasted good but was also good for you.

As part of the deal, Rodgers would carry small cards imprinted with the name and price of the drink and scatter them when flying over crowds. In turn, Armour would finance a special three-car chase train that included a hangar car full of tools and spare parts, its exterior walls decorated with the name *Vin Fiz* and bunches of grapes, a baggage car containing a Palmer-Singer touring automobile for emergencies, and a luxurious Pullman buffet-broiler-sleeper for Rodgers's entourage of no fewer than twenty-five people—Armour officials; mechanics; correspondents; photographers; and Cal's wife, Mabel. In addition, Armour would pay Rodgers five dollars per mile east of the Mississippi and four dollars per mile west of the river because the population there was sparser. Cal was responsible for fuel, oil, spare parts, and repairs.

Cal needed a new airplane, a single-seater with greater range than the Wright Model B he had purchased while still a student and in which he had competed at the Chicago meet. Its fuel supply would have to be sufficient for three hours and, along with the engine, be within reach of the pilot for quick in-flight adjustments. He also needed a footrest that would carry his long legs and serve as a "gas pedal" of sorts—an apparatus to advance the spark of the primitive gasoline engine. For Cal, the Wright brothers constructed the Model EX, slightly smaller than the Model B.

*Vin Fiz*—as she was named—was a biplane whose spruce frame was covered with muslin and strengthened with many exposed steel wires. She was pushed forward by a thirty-five-horsepower engine that, with a bicycle chain, drove two propellers mounted on the rear of the wings. The pilot perched outside next to the engine on the bottom wing, exposed to wind, dust, and rain. There was just one primitive instrument: a strip of yarn tied to a bracing wire in front of the pilot. The direction the yarn blew indicated whether the airplane was flying straight and true or yawing from side to side or up and down.

This was the typical configuration of an American airplane of its day, although in sophistication, the Wright designs had already fallen behind those of the Europeans. In 1909 the Frenchman Louis Blériot had flown across the English Channel in an aircraft of his own design, the first recognizable ancestor of today's familiar single-engine airplane. It was a monoplane with a single rudder and stabilizer in the rear and the engine in the nose; its propeller pulled the craft through the air. Cal Rodgers would not be flying west in a state-of-the-art airplane.

Like Rodgers, I, too, began to realize that I would need a plane of my own to make the trip from New York to Pasadena. Mastering the idiosyncrasies of a single airplane seemed like a better idea than learning those of a different rented aircraft each time I flew—and for the next two years I would be flying a great deal. At about 120 hours' flying per year, owning becomes cheaper than renting. Besides, I *wanted* my own airplane, just as a young man I *had* to have a car; acquiring a license had also brought the yen for pride of ownership. And so I went tire-kicking, visiting airport after airport to examine used airplanes like a determined car buyer with his nose in *Consumer Reports.*

I first considered four-seaters, such as the Cessna 172 and the Piper Tri-Pacer. But a few honest calculations revealed that I did not have enough money for a four-seater in decent condition, plus the cost of the trip. However, I could comfortably finance a capable two-seater—roughly the price of a well-equipped family car—and have enough left over for gas, oil, insurance, tiedown fees, motels, meals, and the like.

So I began examining two-seaters. Fabric-covered Piper Cubs and Aeroncas would not do, for I planned to keep my airplane outdoors on an inexpensive tiedown during the harsh Wisconsin winter, and "stick-and-rag" airplanes do not thrive under snow and ice. An all-metal airplane was a necessity, and the Cessna 150 seemed the most affordable of that type—as well as the easiest to find.

To learn as much about the airplane as I could, I bought a clutch of books about used aircraft in general and the 150 in particular. In the fall of 1958, when the Cessna Aircraft Company rolled out the first 150—a high-winged two-seater with tricycle landing gear (two main wheels and a nosewheel)—Dwight D. Eisenhower was president and I was an eighteen-year-old college freshman. Much has changed since then, but still the 150 has kept flying.

Designed as a low-powered, easy-to-fly trainer, the Cessna 150 was an immediate hit in the marketplace, and over the past four decades, the type has schooled more civilian pilots than any other airplane. Some 22,000 Model 150s—plus 6,600 examples of the later Model 152, the same airframe with a slightly more powerful engine in which I had learned to fly—were built in the United States until 1986, after which the market for new small planes all but collapsed. There isn't an American grassroots airport that isn't home to at least two or three well-worn 150s or 152s.

Although it's considered a "simple" airplane, the Cessna 150 boasts an array of modern instruments. An airspeed indicator and an altimeter reveal speed and altitude. A compass shows magnetic direction. Other indicators show whether the plane is climbing or diving or tilting right or left, which could save a pilot's life if the airplane accidentally wanders into a cloud and he can't see a horizon outside. Various gauges indicate the level of fuel and the condition of the engine. A transponder answers transmissions from ground radar, telling controllers where the airplane is and how high. An emergency locator transmitter (ELT) automatically sends out a distress signal if the airplane crashes. And that is just the most basic equipment for visual flight.

As I traveled around, none of the 150s that were up for sale seemed satisfactory. Like a hopeful auto buyer disappointed by a steady stream of old beaters advertised as creampuffs, I would drop by an airport time and again to look at a tired, weathered airplane whose seller had declared her an "eight in, eight out" on a scale of one to ten, and I would mutter to myself, "That isn't even a five." Though the sellers certainly weren't as disingenuous as used-car salesmen, they certainly wanted to present their wares in the best possible light. Unlike a used car, however, a used airplane must, according to FAA regulations, come with carefully kept logbooks, each bit of maintenance or repair meticulously entered each time it was done and signed by the certified mechanic who performed it. A couple of 150s looked promising, and I flew them to Westosha for a prepurchase once-over by the mechanics, only to learn that they needed expensive work that would quickly break my budget. The cost of the mechanics' examination was high enough so that I could see that I would quickly deplete my money just getting a few more candidates checked out.

But I had also noticed a silvery high-winged Cessna on the field at Westosha. On her wings and vertical stabilizer was emblazoned the number N5859E. I learned that she belonged to the Westosha mechanics, who had painstakingly rebuilt her during their spare time over five winters. Her previous owner had landed her in a cornfield after her engine failed. She was for sale.

One afternoon I looked her over. She was one of the first of her kind, a 1959 model. She was gorgeous. Her polished aluminum flanks, trimmed with dark blue in the original 1959 paint scheme, gleamed under the sun so brightly that my eyes hurt. From a few yards away, she looked pristine, restored to factory-fresh condition. Her interior was brand-new, her seats recently reupholstered. Her engine had undergone a major overhaul and was nearly as good as new, having been run only a few hours.

A closer examination, however, revealed that this was not a new airplane. Some of the sheet metal, especially on the ailerons, was wrinkled with "hangar rash"—the dings airplanes collect when they are knocked against each other in tight confines—which is no danger to flight. The top of the cowling bore a few small wrinkles. And when the afternoon sun lowered into the western sky, one could spot in its slanting rays a few shallow pocks in the aluminum on top of the wings, evidence that N5859E had been through a hailstorm or two. Where the wings joined the fuselage, I could see traces of paint that had escaped stripping.

But the things that mattered were either new or completely refurbished; her imperfections were mostly cosmetic. I took her up for a couple of test flights and was delighted. These early Model 150s weigh 170 pounds less than the 152s I was accustomed to; as a result, they are noticeably lighter on the controls. Flying N5859E was a joy. It seemed almost as if all I had to do was think about a turn, and she would instantly lean into it like an eager and loving Labrador under its master's hand.

While a Cessna 150 does not make the world's most comfortable long-distance cross-country airplane—so light is it on the controls that its pilot can never relax and woolgather—it was nevertheless perfect for sport flying around the Midwest, and it was more than capable of the 100-mile hops I needed to make during the *Vin Fiz* reenactment. N5859E was in more than decent shape, and if I bought her and kept her at Westosha, her maintenance would be supervised by those who knew her best—her rebuilders, mechanics who had first-rate reputations. The brothers Mike and Pat Waynen and their colleague Brian Petri had labored on N5859E during odd hours at Westosha Aviation, Mike's moonlighting enterprise. Mike was an American Airlines maintenance manager at O'Hare, and Brian was chief of maintenance for American Eagle there. Both men, who are deskbound supervisors, work on small planes in their spare time for the love of grassroots aviation and the feel of smooth, oiled steel in their hands, as well as for a few extra dollars. They were so confident about the job they had done on N5859E, they said, that they would give her an unconditional guarantee for a year after they did an annual inspection upon purchase. A year's warranty on any used small airplane is rare and almost unheard of for a thirty-five-year-old veteran. But their asking price was too high for my taste.

\*    \*    \*

Still, N5859E looked as if she might be a good buy if I could talk the mechanics down a little. She had a number of strong selling points. For example, in her instrument panel was a loran (short for "Long-Range Navigation") receiver—a small on-board radio and computer similar to my portable GPS. It listens to an array of special ground transmitters across the country and uses their broadcasts to calculate the plane's course and location with an accuracy of 300 feet. During the 1970s and 1980s, loran—born during World War II for sea navigation—was the state of the art, but it is rapidly being supplanted by GPS, and by the year 2000 both the FAA and the Coast Guard plan to drop loran from their navigation systems. For the time being, I surmised, I could enjoy two levels of redundancy with a loran, GPS, and VOR before having to rely on pilotage and dead reckoning. This was important to a deaf pilot who could not talk to Air Traffic Control.

I also noticed that N5859E was different from most of her sisters. This early-model 150 boasts the classic lines of a lightplane of the Eisenhower Age. Her fin and rudder stick straight up, unlike those of the post-1966 models, whose fin and rudder were slanted backward solely to imitate the lines of the sleek jets. Moreover, N5859E has no bulbous rear window. The top of her fuselage sweeps back in a smooth, unbroken line from the high wing in fastback fashion like an early World War II fighter or a 1970s sports car.

This characteristic was both bad and good. The lack of a rear window hurts visibility; the pilot of N5859E can't look back to see if something is gaining on him. But her relatively rare straight-tail fastback lines mean that it would be unlikely that she—and her occupant—would be mistaken by the denizens of a strange airport for a commonplace trainer carrying a student pilot on a cross-country exercise. After more than thirty-five years in the air, she was just too old to be knocked about by student pilots anymore. In fact, 150s of this vintage are considered near-classic airplanes, and when one in well-kept condition visits an airport, idle pilots often wander out to the flight line to view her up close and ask questions. This phenomenon, I speculated, could turn out to be a great advantage for me: It might be a splendid conversational icebreaker that would help overcome any shyness or the disbelief others might feel about encountering a deaf pilot.

N5859E's advantages were strong enough to impel me to borrow her logbooks and study them carefully to learn her history. She was the 359th Model 150 off the production line at the Cessna factory in Wichita, Kansas, and spent much of the first decade of her life at a flight school in Teterboro, New Jersey, before being sold to a pilot who lived in Hartford, Connecticut. In the early 1970s she arrived at a flight school at Clow Airport in Plainfield, Illinois. Later in the decade she became the personal aircraft of a number of private pilots in northeastern Illinois and southeastern Wisconsin. By the middle 1980s she was getting on in years. Her engine was elderly, her cream-and-green livery scratched and faded, her window plastic fogged and crazed, and her interior threadbare. But she was still airworthy, enough so that her last owner, Riley O'Brien, equipped her with that loran receiver and flew her for fun around the lakes and dales of northern Illinois and southern Wisconsin until the day when her engine failed and he had to put her down in a cow pasture.

I went to see O'Brien in his home in Winnetka, Illinois, to ask what had happened. Airplanes are often banged up in off-airport landings, and I wanted to know if there had been structural damage. It seemed to me that someone who had seen the incident, but no longer had a financial interest in the airplane, would be the most reliable witness.

O'Brien is a retired Inland Steel executive who, at a white-haired but merry eighty-four years of age, still looks and talks like a double-barreled Irish yarn spinner. "Did you know how she got her name?" he asked as we sat down in his living room. In 1985, he said, he owned a half interest in a Beechcraft Bonanza, an expensive airplane. When his first wife fell ill with cancer, he decided he'd better scale down, sold his half of the Bonanza, "and within a week bought N5859E from an American Airlines pilot for a song. My wife had seen it, too, and when I told her I'd bought this scruffy 150, she said, 'Riley, I will never fly with you in that shitty little fucking airplane.' When I asked her if she'd be good enough to crack a bottle of champagne over her, she said, 'I won't go near the airplane or christen it or anything else!' So I went to the hardware store and bought the stick-on letters S, L, F, A for *Shitty Little Fucking Airplane* and put them on the cowling just ahead of the doors." He chuckled at the memory.

On May 14, 1988, O'Brien was flying *SLFA* with a friend about twenty-five miles north of Westosha when suddenly "it seemed to get hazy, and I thought, gee, the weather's changed. Maybe it's the sun. I turned and looked out the side window, and it wasn't the sun. It was oil mist on the windshield. And the engine began to make clunking noises. Six miles from the nearest airport, Burlington, the engine went 'bing, bang, boom, clang, clang, clang,' and the propeller stopped."

The oil-smeared windshield blocked O'Brien's view, so he yawed the plane from side to side to see ahead. "I looked down and saw what looked like a cleared field, and I came around and slipped and slithered it in, a perfect landing, not a bit of damage. It was a cornfield that had been plowed, harrowed, and planted but hadn't yet sprouted.

"I radioed Burlington and told them I'd landed safely. Then a tractor came down the farm lane. The lady driving it said to me, 'Sir, this is not an airport.' I said, 'Lady, I know it's not an airport. My engine quit.' I got some rope out of the baggage compartment and tied it to the nosewheel and the tractor, and she towed me to her barnyard.

When O'Brien and an FAA inspector looked over the plane the next morning, they found that one of the engine's cylinders had broken off the crankcase and had bounced up against the cowling. That explained the slightly wrinkled sheet metal in the cowling—the only damage the airplane had suffered in the incident. O'Brien didn't want to deal with the chores of disassembling the plane and hauling her away and then handling the voluminous paperwork required to bring back to airworthiness an old airplane with a nearly run-out engine that had been landed off-airport. "So I sold her to the mechanics at Westosha as is, where is, for the sum of one dollar," he told me, "and they took her apart and hauled her away on a flatbed truck."

Riley O'Brien retired from flying at age seventy-nine in 1991, saying, "I'm just going to quit while I'm ahead. I have no accidents, no injuries, no damages to airplanes, no violations, so I'm going to hang it up after sixty-one years of flying." But there was still a soft spot in his heart for his *Shitty Little Fucking Airplane,* and he paid periodic visits to the mechanics' hangar to watch the progress of the rebuilding. "Mike didn't have the money for new cylinders for the engine," Riley said, "so I bought them." That was remarkably generous; a set of four new cylinders costs about $3,000.

\*     \*     \*

At last, I realized that I had fallen in hopeless love with this airplane, just as I had been smitten by the brand-new, bright-red 1963 Bug in the showroom of the Volkswagen dealer all those years ago when I was a graduate student. I had to have her. I made an offer—a few thousand dollars lower than the asking price—but it was so low that the mechanics did not bother to respond. Instead they took N5859E to the annual fly-in of the Experimental Aircraft Association in Oshkosh, hoping to sell her for a better price. A week later, though, I saw the airplane back on its tie-down at Westosha, so I knew she had not been sold. Early in the fall, I raised my offer, but with one request: that the mechanics replace the airplane's communications and navigation radio with a newer one. By January 1997, all airplane radios would have to conform to tighter Federal Communications Commission standards, and N5859E's ancient model could not meet them.

It was a deal. On a sunny October day, I officially took ownership of N5859E, a.k.a. *Shitty Little Fucking Airplane,* and renamed her *Gin Fizz* in resonant honor of *Vin Fiz.*

Over the winter months I visited *Gin Fizz* frequently, often making the long drive up from Evanston in poor flying weather simply to bask in her presence, justifying each trip by shining a few square feet of her surface with heavy paste aluminum polish, cornstarch, and roll upon roll of paper towels. No prideful young father with a garden hose and a brand-new Chevrolet in the driveway took greater pains than I did with that old Cessna. Each Sunday evening I would come home, my hands dingy with the residue of aluminum polish, my fingernails cracked and blackened.

I flew her every bit I could, too, learning her idiosyncrasies and capabilities and wringing her out to make sure all her parts were in good shape. With approval, I noticed that on a perfectly smooth day, without gusts or turbulence, she held a steady course with my hands off the yoke, flying straight and true without falling off to one side. She was perfectly rigged, her flight controls consummately balanced. She had just one quirk: Like all her sisters from the first two model years of the Cessna 150, she was slightly tail-heavy on the ground. If I ran her tanks nearly dry and climbed out of her at the tiedown or fuel pumps, the sudden shift in the center of gravity caused her to tilt backward slowly and majestically, her nose rising in the air like an astonished dowager, until her tail ring kissed the ground. In 1961 Cessna solved the problem by moving the landing gear two inches aft. I learned to deal with this eccentricity by never letting her tanks get below five gallons—which was sensible, anyway, because that gave me an hour's fuel reserve. All pilots must carry at least a thirty-minute fuel reserve on daytime cross-country flights and forty-five minutes' worth at night. Because I am deaf and can't get a radar steer, an extra half-hour's reserve made sense.

A month after I bought the airplane, a strong smell of exhaust suddenly filled the cockpit while I was aloft. I opened the windows wide, landed immediately, and taxied over to the mechanics' hangar. Instantly, the mechanics removed the cowling and probed the innards. One of the two engine mufflers had cracked, leaking toxic exhaust gases into the cabin. True to their word, the mechanics sent the muffler out at their expense for rebuilding, which cost several hundred dollars. Otherwise *Gin Fizz* stayed in fine prideful shape, although rain, snow, and air pollution kept me busy with paper towels and aluminum polish out on her tiedown.

Later that autumn I turned my thoughts back to research and made a pilgrimage to Washington. Eagerly, Debby came along to help—of course, we flew on a commercial airliner—and to enjoy a long weekend in the nation's capital. We began with a visit to the National Air and Space Museum to view the restored *Vin Fiz* at her place of honor in an alcove off the second-floor mezzanine and to see if I could find anything that had gone unmentioned in Eileen Lebow's biography. Alas, *Vin Fiz* was not there—she had been shipped off a few months before to Japan as part of a traveling Smithsonian exhibit—but close by, a small model of the Wright airplane allowed me a good view of her proportions.

I had no better luck turning up anything fresh in the museum's archives, a huge reading room in which a dozen writers and scholars labored on literary projects. The Rodgers files and microfilms yielded little that Lebow hadn't already digested. Conspicuously missing, however, was any scrap of paper written in Cal Rodgers's hand. Could this omission be important? I did find one telling item Lebow hadn't mentioned: a contemporary news report from the *Los Angeles Times* written the day after Rodgers's death. Stewart De Krafft, the manager of Rodgers's transcontinental enterprise, told the newspapers that "Rodgers was purely a man's man, despite his many queer characteristics. His infirmities won him more enemies than friends. He would often turn away when spoken to; not because he intentionally desired to be rude, but because his defective hearing did not make him realize that he had been spoken to. Because of the lack of imagination his temper was short. Many things greatly vexed him that other men would have overlooked."

*Lack of imagination?* What did that mean? An inability to empathize with others? A shortchanging of intelligence? What, exactly, was Cal's mental capacity? At the museum I could not find answers to those questions, but it seemed from the sources Lebow cited that many who had known Cal, either contemporaneously—like De Krafft—or later, through studying the aviator's life, thought he was dull-witted. No written composition in Cal's hand seemed to exist to prove that Cal was at all literate, judging from the notes to Lebow's book, as well as the void at the Smithsonian.

Direct quotations from the popular press of the time are highly suspect because journalists then not only believed in quoting a person in the best English of which the newspapers were capable, but also were not above "cooking" quotes for the sake of color. "Two hundred and four miles nearer Chicago tonight," Cal was supposed to have told the journalist who wrote the daily Hearst dispatch under Rodgers's byline during the flight across the country, "and it might have been another fifty if the last gasp of the hoodoo had not blighted me today." That is clearly the hand of the newspaper hack.

Two other items jumped out at me. In 1961 a pilot from Seattle had tried to promote a full-dress fiftieth-anniversary reenactment, but was unable to raise the necessary funds and was never heard from again. In 1986, on the seventy-fifth anniversary, an IBM engineer from Fishkill, New York, had officially reenacted the flight in a replica of *Vin Fiz*. His name was James R. Lloyd. I made a mental note to search him out before embarking on my own trip.

The next morning we made a brief stop in northwest Washington to visit Eileen Lebow and her husband, Mort. Fine-boned and birdlike, warm and friendly, Eileen is a retired junior high school Spanish and English teacher. She is nearly a dead ringer for the late actress Jessica Tandy, with the same impeccable but unobtrusive manners. "How'd you become interested in Cal Rodgers?" I asked as the four of us settled in her living room.

In the late 1960s, she said, when the Smithsonian's aeronautical collection was still housed in a Quonset hut on the Mall, Mort saw *Vin Fiz* sitting forlorn in a corner.

"You should see this plane," he told Eileen. "This man flew from coast to coast sitting on the lower wing. Why don't we write a book about it?" Years later, she continued, "I went up to Air and Space and started researching, and it was fascinating. It was difficult to find out any hard facts about Rodgers. The accounts were generally wrong. They gave the wrong dates, especially of his birth, and they offered very few facts about his life. I started digging hard."

By car the Lebows followed Rodgers's route. "We drove to Salamanca, New York, where Rodgers had one of those crashes that held him up for a week or so. The evening we got there we went into the public library, and the first person we spoke to knew the Rodgers story." The woman's father had helped drag the pieces of the airplane to the hangar car for repair, and "the family had had a piece of it sitting around the house for many, many years. 'You must talk to so-and-so in town,' she said. I called them, and they told me stories. One man who was almost ninety remembered seeing Rodgers as a youngster. That was very exciting."

Eileen had hoped to publish the book in 1986 for the seventy-fifth anniversary of the flight, but she was still teaching. At first, she thought she could teach in the morning and come home to write in the afternoon. "It didn't work out that way. Too much paperwork from school. A long time went by. I finally finished the manuscript and looked for a publisher. Commercially, no one was interested. The subject was too specialized. Then I thought maybe the Smithsonian would be interested—and they were, because the Press has a historical aviation series. That was just luck."

That morning, I said, I had rummaged in the Rodgers files at the National Air and Space Museum and could find nothing in Rodgers's hand that would have proved he was literate.

Eileen nodded. "I found just two examples. One was the marriage license he signed 'C. P. Rodgers'—he never wrote out the whole name. It's a very long name, Calbraith Perry Rodgers. The other was a letter all the people on the chase train gave to the man who had been in charge of it and had gotten them from New York to Chicago. Again he signed his name 'C. P. Rodgers.' That's all I've ever seen. Oh, yes, on his application for the Chicago air meet, he wrote 'C. P. Rodgers' again."

Eileen had been unable to locate any surviving letters, which might have challenged the idea that Cal was a simpleton by showing the level of his competence with language, as well as his feelings about deafness and its consequences. It certainly may be true that Cal was not terribly bright, but the isolating nature of deafness often leads to the mistaken conclusion that people who cannot communicate easily are also lacking in intellectual prowess. Time and again, reticence and a lack of sophistication are mistaken for limited intelligence. It has happened to me, too, though thankfully not often. Once, when asked what I did for a living, I replied simply, "I work for a newspaper." The response: "Oh? On the trucks?"

As we stood up to leave, Eileen brought out a huge file of photographs taken during Rodgers's flight. "These you can keep," she said. "I don't need any of this. I need to clean out my files. Here's the takeoff from the little racetrack on Long Island. That's Mabel in the light dress, Mama in the veil, Cal in his leather jacket, the man from Armour." For ten minutes we stood in the foyer, leafing through the photos and the copies of documents she had found during her research.

A generous and helpful human being, Eileen is. But she is not a professional writer, one who makes her living at the literary trade. I was glad of that. Professional authors are so jealous of their bailiwicks, so hostile to competitors, that they just don't share.

Later that same afternoon, we drove to Silver Spring, Maryland, to meet Ted Robinson, an African American pilot who volunteers at the Air and Space Museum. The folks at the museum had put me in touch with Ted, who is a genuine aviation pioneer. He learned to fly in the 1940s in the cradle of black aviation, Harlem Airport on Chicago's South Side, home to the pioneer black pilots Cornelius Coffey and Willa Brown. Ted was a Tuskegee Airman, a member of that historic group of black pilots who were trained during World War II at the segregated army air base at Tuskegee, Alabama. Many had covered themselves with glory over North Africa and Europe as members of the storied all-black 332nd Fighter Group. The 332nd, whose P-40s and P-51s often led escort missions for white-flown B-17s and B-24s, was so good at its job that it never lost a single bomber to enemy fighters. Ted, however, saw no combat. He did not graduate as a B-25 pilot until November 1945, after the war ended.

That's where Ted's story took a turn. In 1946, shortly after he left active duty, he said, he looked for a job at the airlines. Although he had the qualifications and the experience, he encountered the Catch-22 of racism. "They were expanding, they were hiring, and I went to TWA in Chicago," Ted said. "They told me I had to be a member of the Air Line Pilots Association before I could get a job as an airline pilot. I went over to the ALPA and was told I had to become an airline pilot before I could join the union."

Two years later, he was a student at the University of Illinois when the operator of a Springfield flight school approached him. The school had recruited a group of black veterans to learn to fly on the GI Bill, but the all-white staff of flight instructors refused to teach them. The operator had learned that Ted and another Tuskegee Airman were not only attending the university but also held instructors' tickets, so he hired them to teach black students on the weekends.

"It was clear these white instructors and particularly the chief instructor, Frank, didn't want any part of us," said Ted, "and one manifestation of this rejection was the aircraft they assigned to us. One was an Aeronca Scout with one set of brakes (two are needed for instruction) and a Piper J-3 Cub. The white instructors were flying brand-new Cessna 120s with full dual controls.

"The Aeronca didn't perform right. It had a very sluggish climb rate far below what it was supposed to have. We complained to Frank, and he said, 'Naw, there's nothing wrong with this airplane,' leaving the clear implication that the problem was my piloting skill or lack thereof."

One day, after a flight in which Ted and his student had a fight with the brakes and throttle on the Aeronca, a mechanic walked over to the airplane and removed the cowling. "He said to another mechanic, 'Hey, isn't that the airplane that nosed over recently?' He pointed out a bent engine mount that changed the engine's thrust alignment. This clearly was the reason for the poor climb performance."

They asked for a meeting with "the big boss, Frank's boss," and were told he would meet with them early Sunday, so Ted and the other instructor could depart for Champaign-Urbana in time to make an important date—a church confirmation ceremony. The big boss, of course, never showed up. "We left and never went back," Ted said.

Unable to find full-time work as a flight instructor because of discrimination, Ted went to work as a streetcar motorman for the Chicago Transit Authority. He also worked part time as a flight instructor, teaching blacks at Harlem Airport, and kept up his flying proficiency in the U.S. Air Force Reserve. He flew early jets—the F-80 and T-33—with a reserve fighter-bomber group at Milwaukee.

In 1954 United Air Lines was hiring, but "they gave me a personality test and decided that I didn't have the right one to be a pilot," he said. United was just being disingenuous; not until 1963 did the scheduled airlines finally open the door to black pilots, when a black former air force pilot won a series of lawsuits that ultimately ended with the U.S. Supreme Court ordering Continental Airlines to hire him.

In 1957 things began to look up for Ted. He landed a job in Dayton, Ohio, as a professional mechanical engineer in the crew-station design section at Wright-Patterson Air Force Base. "Because of my flying ability and interest in human factors," he said, his career finally took off, and people began to notice him. In the meantime he rose to captain in the reserves.

In 1962 Ted joined the FAA as a research engineer in Atlantic City, and in 1966 became the FAA's first black general aviation inspector. He also had become a member of the Negro Airmen International Organization, which held a ceremony in 1979 to honor the black aviation pioneers who were flying before World War II. A couple of officials from the Air and Space Museum attended the ceremony, and not long afterward, the museum asked Ted to help a new curator mount an exhibit on the history of blacks in aviation. The exhibit opened in 1982 and is still one of the museum's drawing cards. In retirement, Ted does a great deal of volunteer work for the museum, especially for the Smithsonian Institution Press, where he helps edit the press's series of books on pioneer black pilots. Until recently, he was also active in Opportunities Skyway, a national program that helps young people from disadvantaged backgrounds learn to fly. "One of our first participants is now at the Air Force Academy," Ted said proudly.

On this hopeful note, I told Ted how accepting other pilots had been of my lack of hearing and how perhaps there was a brotherhood among aviators that transcended prejudice.

"No, that's not been my experience," he said in a masterpiece of quiet understatement, slowly shaking his head. "I've encountered resentment and rejection on account of my color throughout my aviation career despite the fact that when I'm with compatible groups of whites, we like to talk about the brotherhood of aviation. It's not true. I ran into open hostility in the FAA, though I had very good friends there, too."

Ted sat forward in his chair for emphasis. Recently, he said, he'd talked with several pioneer black airline pilots from the mid-1960s about the issue. "Blacks didn't become airline pilots until almost twenty years after the war! And now, another thirty years after that, the guys who started then are reaching the mandatory retirement age of sixty, and still the percentage of black airline pilots is less than one-half of one percent. They were resented, but they became captains, and they still run into open hostility. I think that attitude runs throughout the industry. You don't see any blacks in substantial jobs in the airline industry. All the significant management jobs are held by whites. There's a lot of talk about diversity, but no action."

I was embarrassed. The ignorant and often well-meaning prejudice that deaf people—deaf *white* people—encounter is great and similar in some ways, but it cannot compare with the length, depth, and breadth of historical American racism, and I had made the common mistake of assuming that Ted and I had suffered the same slings and arrows. "But, Ted, I've got to say this," I persisted. "As a deaf person I've found a lot of acceptance from hearing pilots. Isn't there something special about flying that maybe helps aviators overcome ignorance and prejudice?"

Ted shook his head. "Pilots are just like other people. They're individuals. There is, however, a culture of conservatism throughout the industry, and conservatism is not generally open to diversity. But I've been surprised. In late 1960, Jolee [his second wife, who is white] and I flew to Columbia, Missouri, in a Bonanza belonging to the aero club when I was at Wright-Patterson, to visit some old friends. We arrived at night, landed, and checked in. No problem. The operator tied the airplane down. Next day we flew up and down the Missouri River gorge with our friends and returned and landed. The man who ran the flight service, a white man, made a point of coming up and shaking my hand, as if thanking me for coming." Today, Ted said, airports everywhere give him excellent service as a matter of course, "and that has included Atlanta, Albuquerque, and San Antonio. Everywhere we've gone in recent years we've had a decent reception. That's about all I can say on that."

Ted stood up. "Want to go flying?" he asked. That is never a question I need to be asked more than once. And we were off to College Park Airport, where Ted keeps his Mooney four-seater. I watched as Ted preflighted his airplane far more painstakingly than most pilots I have seen—that, I thought, is one reason why he has lasted half a century as a pilot. It was nearly dusk, so our circuit above the winking lights of metropolitan Washington was short, and we landed after a while and put the airplane to bed.

"Now," I said as we walked off the ramp, "I can say I flew with Ted Robinson."

Without missing a beat, Ted replied with a broad smile, "And I can say I flew with Henry Kisor." Then we went out with our spouses to dine on Maryland crab cakes and bask some more in—I'll say it—the brotherhood of aviation.

# PART II

# TAKEOFF

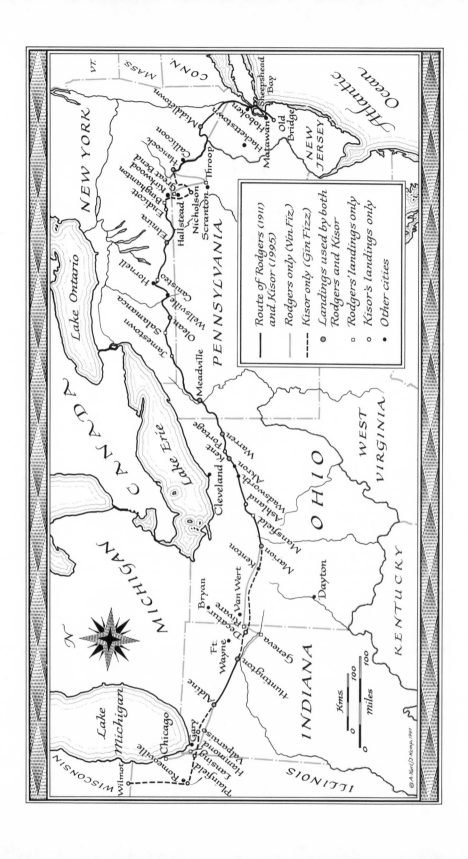

# 5

hen Cal Rodgers and his crew set to planning their route across the United States, they faced a welter of problems. The first, of course, was that no airports existed in 1911, much less aerial navigation aids. *Vin Fiz* had to follow the railroads all the way, as much for Cal to see where he was going as to provide a route for the chase train that was his lifeline. The best routes followed the lowest altitudes, and for this reason Rodgers picked the Erie Railroad between New York and Illinois and the Southern Pacific from Texas to California. The latter would provide the most comfortable course around the forbidding Rocky Mountains. As his starting point, Rodgers chose the smooth, flat expanse of the infield of the Sheepshead Bay race track in Brooklyn, on the southwestern edge of Long Island. As his goal he picked Pasadena, California.

More than eighty years later, I faced an easier task as I laid preliminary plans to pursue Rodgers's route, landing at the airports nearest the spots where he had set down *Vin Fiz*. Briefly I thought about employing a friend or two to drive a chase van behind me, but quickly dropped the idea as unnecessary. Airports, mechanics, and motels abound along the route today, and I could take everything I needed aboard the plane. Soon I had roughed out a scheme of daytime landings and overnight stops along the route. From New York, Cal had flown to Chicago and then turned south to Springfield, Illinois; flying west to Kansas City and south to Dallas and San

Antonio, he next turned west once more for El Paso and Phoenix before his official landing at Pasadena. None of his flights had been more than 130 miles long. In a modern airplane the journey would hardly be strenuous, and I could make it in six days if I pushed. But I would take four or five leisurely weeks, six at the most, leaving plenty of time to tarry at airports to talk to people as well as to stand down during bad weather.

The first problem to solve was Debby's adamancy. Though she had accepted my pilothood, in no way would she allow me to be away from her for six whole weeks, flying through who knows what perils over godforsaken mountains and deserts. Six unbroken weeks of worry, she said, would simply consume her alive. And so we struck a bargain: I would make the trip in three legs—Chicago to New York and back, then Chicago to Austin, and finally Austin to Los Angeles and back to Chicago—with lengthy furloughs between segments at home, where she could keep an eye on me and enjoy my company for a short while before I went out again to put my life on the line.

I sighed. I could not persuade her that she had exaggerated the perils in her mind—that with the caution of middle age, the act of flying a little airplane across the country in short hops could be as safe as an errand to the corner store in a station wagon. I was not headstrong and impulsive; if anything, I was a bit of a coward compared to Rodgers. Unlike him, I would fly a strongly built airplane that was certified for commercial use in a variety of weather conditions.

Tom Horton, I heard, had once ferried a Cessna 120—a predecessor of the 150, slightly smaller, less powerful, and with a tailwheel rather than a more modern nosewheel—from Chicago to Los Angeles. I found him one afternoon in the pilot's lounge and asked his advice.

"Watch out for the winds," he said. "They'll be right in your face, and they're fierce during the summer and early fall, especially west of Albuquerque." Tom had flown a more direct route than Rodgers, from Chicago on a beeline to the 7,600-foot mountain pass at Albuquerque, then almost directly west through the Rockies. "Fly in the morning and the late evening, when the winds are quieter and the turbulence isn't so bad. It took me five days to get to L.A. that way."

When he passed Albuquerque, he said, the winds at altitude

were so strong that the Cessna made little headway, and he decided to set down for the day at Gallup. The surface wind at that
high airport—it sits almost 6,500 feet above sea level—blew so
hard that as soon as he landed, two burly line attendants had to
come out and grab each wingtip to keep the airplane from blowing
upside down. "The plane didn't have a radio," Tom said, "so I didn't
know the wind was blowing at forty knots"—almost fifty miles per
hour. "If I knew that, I'd have been scared."

He was scaring *me*. "Do you think I'm capable of making this
trip?" I asked. I had little more than 200 hours under my belt.

"Oh, of course. Just be sensible and you'll do fine."

Unfortunately, my timorous middle-aged sensibility kept telling
me, though I kept stifling it, "Don't be stupid. Don't do it. Wait a few
years until you're an experienced pilot." I didn't dare tell Debby—
or anyone else—about my fears.

I kept the beast at bay by spreading sectional charts—seventeen of
them—on the living-room floor and scoping out the airports closest to Rodgers's landing sites. According to Eileen Lebow, he had
landed at or near seventy-three towns. There was no airport rea-
sonably close to eleven of those towns, which left sixty-two airports for me to visit. Carefully I drew up a sixteen-page list, heading
each entry with the name of the town, followed by the name of the
airport, its FAA code, its location in relation to its municipality, its
phone number, the times its fixed-base operation was open (FBO
is aviationese for the local airplane garage/filling station/flight
school/pilot's lounge/rental emporium found at most general-
aviation airports), the grade of fuel it sold, its runway alignment
and length, the field elevation and landing pattern altitude, and its
radio frequency. I added the phone number and address of the
nearest motel and inserted the flying distance between each airport, noting that the typical flight would be some 50 miles and the
longest flight about 140.

I would start not at Sheepshead Bay but at "MATAWAN, N.J.:
Marlboro Airport (2N8). 3 mi S of city. Phone 908-591-1591. 100LL.
Runway 9-27 2,156' x 40'. Elevation 122', pattern alt. 1300'. CTAF
122.7." That was the uncontrolled airport closest to the spot where
Cal Rodgers had begun his flight.

Excruciating detail? Yes, but it was all necessary—even basic—
to the planning. Gathering this information lifted my spirits; it was

like arranging a long and exotic vacation on the road. Even the names of the towns where I would land set me to chanting. "Elmira, Canisteo, Salamanca. Nebo, Mexico, Marshall. Vinita, Muskogee, McAlester. San Marcos, San Antonio, Del Rio. Deming, Lordsburg, Wilcox. Tucson, Maricopa, Phoenix." So exciting was the song in my head that I all but forgot the depressing daily events at the paper, where morale—and circulation—had continued to plunge as our editorial executives' latest schemes to save the ever more pinched *Sun-Times*'s fading reputation (graphic makeovers and a more intense focus on celebrities among them) floundered with readers and advertisers. Having an adventure to look forward to enabled me to endure this latest time of troubles and keep on working diligently at my job. I was consumed by the joy of a new passion. No wonder men have affairs. But my mistress was a shapely thirty-six-year-old with silver wings.

There was one more brain to pick before I started the trip, and that belonged to James R. Lloyd, the pilot who had flown the 1986 reenactment and whose name I had discovered at the Air and Space Museum. When my family and friends heard that somebody had already flown the route, they said, "But doesn't that ruin your project?" Nope, I replied. Our intentions were wholly different. Lloyd, who had flown in a distant replica of *Vin Fiz,* no doubt sought to reenact the flight as closely as possible to the original; my purpose was to enjoy a different kind of adventure, an emotional and intellectual one that would restart my engines at midlife. But I did want to find out how Lloyd had done things, what problems he had encountered, how he had dealt with them, and ask his advice on a number of issues. I didn't want to reinvent the wheel if somebody would lend me the blueprints. Besides, the more I knew what to expect, the better off I would be. Forewarned is forearmed, or so I hoped.

Locating Lloyd, however, was difficult. In the intervening decade he had moved several times, and his mail forwarding had expired. Letters to his old addresses came back unopened. Phone books and public libraries, the journalist's standard sources, were no help. Fortunately, I remembered that the clipping I had seen at the Air and Space Museum had said that Lloyd was a graduate of the Stevens Institute of Technology. Finally, I sent a letter to Lloyd via the Stevens alumni association, the covering note telling them of my plan and my hope to reach their alumnus. Pay dirt! Within three weeks, I had a response and an invitation to visit.

When I paid the visit to Lloyd, I found remarkable correspondences between Cal Rodgers and him. The Armour Company bankrolled Lloyd's enterprise, as it had Rodgers's, and helped drum up publicity that, if not equal to the national hoopla surrounding Rodgers, sometimes came close. What's more, both pilots were born in Pittsburgh, both were tall (Lloyd was six-feet-three and Rodgers was six-feet-four), and both were in their thirties at the time of their flights (Rodgers was thirty-two and Lloyd was thirty-eight). Neither pilot had had much experience in the air before setting out.

And both flew biplanes with remarkable similarities. Lloyd's aircraft, a modified modern ultralight airplane, was powered by a thirty-five horsepower engine, just as Rodgers's was. Both airplanes had the same maximum speed, 55 miles per hour, and the same range, 130 to 135 miles. *Vin Fiz* could carry a payload of 203 pounds and *Vin Fiz II,* 260 pounds. At 250 pounds empty, *Vin Fiz II* was considerably smaller and lighter than the 700-pound original. "It wasn't really the *Vin Fiz,*" Lloyd said of his airplane. "It wasn't a replica. But if you stood back 200 yards and took off your glasses, it looked like the *Vin Fiz.*"

A professional electronics engineer with three degrees, including a doctorate from the Stevens Institute of Technology, Lloyd is an independent consultant, a reliability engineer for integrated circuits. In 1986 he was an engineer for IBM, and at the time of our talk he and a friend were starting a consulting company to test chips for reliability. "I'm tired of working for other people who are too annoying to talk about," he said with an airy wave. Indeed, a towering fellow—he fills the room he is in, almost dangerously so when he demonstrates flight in pilot fashion with his long arms and huge hands—he is a man of rich, loquacious, and sometimes acerbic humor, often directed at himself (he has a heroic nose, and frequently jokes about it) as well as others. What follows is only a small part of our two-hour conversation.

His plan, he said, was born, much as mine was, as the seemingly absurd dream of a brand-new and overimaginative pilot to fly coast to coast, a dream that eventually was refined by circumstance and fortune. "Originally I was going to do it the way you are, in a Cessna," he said. "But when I saw *Vin Fiz* hanging in the National

Air and Space Museum, I said to myself, 'No, not a Cessna. I need something more like the original.'" At that, I smiled to myself, musing that Debby ought to be grateful our visit to the Smithsonian didn't inspire similar thoughts.

While visiting Plum Island Airport at Newburyport, Massachusetts, Lloyd saw an ultralight biplane he thought might do the job. An ultralight aircraft is defined by the FAA as one that weighs 254 pounds or less, carries no more than five gallons of gas, and cannot exceed fifty-five knots, or sixty-one miles per hour. This one looked more like the Wright brothers' original 1903 Flyer, with the horizontal stabilizer, called a canard, in front of the wings, than like the Wright EX that Rodgers had flown. Lloyd found the owner of the plane, who told him it was a one-of-a-kind that had been made by an outfit called Pterodactyl. Its designer, Jack McCornack, had also once dreamed of reenacting the *Vin Fiz* flight.

"Right away Jack said, 'Could I come along as your mechanic?'" Lloyd recounted. "Stevie Noyes, a local Newburyport celebrity who was quite a character in his own right, built *Vin Fiz II*. He was just about nineteen or twenty years old when he started his ultralight company. Jack made some changes to the original design. He put the canard in back. We put in a ten-gallon gas tank, which, according to the FAA rules, made *Vin Fiz II* an experimental aircraft rather than an ultralight. So we had to get an official registration number and an airworthiness certificate. Jack had reserved the number N75TH ten years before, because he'd always wanted to do this flight, and we used it."

Meanwhile, Lloyd had written to the Armour Company, asking for its financial support. "I said to them, 'Seventy-five years ago you supported Cal Rodgers, now why don't you support me? We can show that Armour is still in business.' I was lucky. Armour had just been purchased by another company, ConAgra in Omaha, and it wanted to maintain its identity as Armour. This was a way to do it, I told them. I flew out to visit them in Omaha, and at a corporate meeting with all the brass sitting around, I showed them my brochure. I told them I was an experienced pilot, which was a lie. I had less than 200 hours at the time. But none of them were pilots, so they didn't know the difference. Three weeks later they wrote and said the plan was on."

Indeed, Armour's support was a stroke of luck for Lloyd. Twice I had written to Armour—it had continued to merge into other companies, and it is now a division of Armour-Swift-Ekrich—before it responded. I had not asked for financial aid, only the chance to examine its files on both Lloyd's and Rodgers's flights. Finally, a factotum in the legal department sent a brief three-paragraph response. He said the only surviving item in the company's files was a four-page memo from a public relations man about promoting Lloyd's flight, and he enclosed it with his letter. Nothing remained from the 1911 era.

Lloyd began his flight in Hoboken, New Jersey. "We had two options," he explained. "The old Sheepshead Bay racetrack is now an apartment complex. Right next to it is a golf course with plenty of room for *Vin Fiz II* to take off. That was Option One. Option Two was the old Floyd Bennett Field naval air station, part of which is now the Coast Guard Air Station Brooklyn, a helicopters-only field."

Option One fell through immediately. The City of New York owns the golf course. A local bureaucrat refused permission for the takeoff, and in the same breath, Lloyd said, made a "poorly disguised" request for a bribe. "The way the guy said it was, 'I really cannot allow you to do this, but I could be persuaded.' We said to hell with that."

The authorities at Floyd Bennett also refused a takeoff, saying the former naval air station could handle only helicopters. "I said, 'My plane can take off in fifty feet, about the same distance as a helicopter.' Well, fifty feet with the right wind, 200 feet maximum anyway.

"We got in touch with the National Park Service, which had responsibility for Floyd Bennett, because the naval air station component is now part of the Gateway National Recreation Area. They said they would allow it to be used only for recreational or historic purposes that were consistent with aviation. I said, 'Well, what do you think I'm doing?' But they wouldn't let us do it. I called my congressman, and they said no to him, too. We went to Washington and had a lobbyist talk to them, and they still said no. I thought this was crazy."

The city of Hoboken, seat of Lloyd's alma mater, Stevens Institute of Technology, came through when Lloyd asked if the city would provide a takeoff site. The runway was a narrow street on the Hudson River named for Frank Sinatra, a son of Hoboken. "Armour was there, and we had high school bands, one from my old high school, one from Hoboken High. The people from Armour were a little crazy. They wanted to have the bands line up along the curb of this narrow street. My wingtips would have missed them by about three feet. I said no because if I made a mistake, I'd have taken out the bands. We convinced Armour to place the bands behind me when I took off."

On September 17, 1986, seventy-five years to the day after *Vin Fiz* departed Sheepshead Bay, Lloyd took off in *Vin Fiz II*. He dressed in period costume much like Rodgers's, with a tweed jacket, a flat cap, and goggles. Joan Lunden did a lengthy live interview with Lloyd for *Good Morning America,* and NBC-TV and other stations broadcast the takeoff live. "I went out over the Hudson, did a circle, and came back around, and they let off a thousand balloons," Lloyd said. "That was cool. Then I started up the Hudson, followed by three helicopters. That frightened me because one of the helicopters passed in front, and the wake turbulence from its rotors knocked me all over the place. That was scary, since I wasn't used to the airplane yet." Lloyd couldn't tell the choppers to stay clear because he didn't have a radio.

The television publicity had an impact. At Middletown, New York, the first stop on Rodgers's route, about fifty people greeted Lloyd, but most were friends and co-workers; IBM's headquarters was just half an hour away. The greeting at the next stop, Hancock, was a surprise. "I'm flying up the Delaware River, and I look down, and there's the field. I saw all these cars, and I knew there was a soccer field nearby. I said to myself, 'Oh, they must be having a big game today.' But there was nobody on the soccer field. As soon as I landed, about a thousand people poured out of the woods, and they just filled up the whole runway. They had been waiting for me."

But not Lloyd's crowd-control crew. "Armour told us we had to have a uniformed guard at both landing and takeoff to satisfy the insurance requirements. Our guard was Pat Kessler in a police jacket, and she was armed with a handheld radio." Pat was part of Lloyd's mobile ground crew, which included his wife, Susan Ogurian, and Jack McCornack. They had not yet arrived in Jack's van, painted with the legend "Vin Fiz Flyer" to look like the hangar car that had been part of Cal Rodgers's chase train. They were still haring over the countryside trying to find the airport; those grass fields are no easier to find from the ground than they are from the air, for they rarely are marked on road maps.

"So I was sitting here at the airport with all these people—they seemed to be more than the population of the town!—who were looking at and touching and picking at *Vin Fiz II*, and I had to keep them away, but I'm also trying to be nice because, look, they all came out to see me! It was quite an experience to have a thousand people ask you for your autograph. I kept thinking of Andy Warhol's saying that in the future, everyone will be famous for fifteen minutes, and I figured on this trip I'd get fifteen minutes in every town all across the United States!" He laughed heartily.

The next day, Lloyd encountered his first bad weather, "some turbulence that scared me half to death. The wind was blowing at thirty miles per hour, and I'd never been in an ultralight in that kind of wind. I was getting blown all over the place, and I purposely landed on the grass into the wind, rather than on the airport runway, which would have meant an impossible crosswind."

So frightening was the experience that later that day Lloyd and his crew decided to attach a parachute, not to Lloyd but to the plane itself. The parachute's brand name, a familiar one among pilots of ultralights and homebuilts, was apt: "Second Chantz." Lloyd pulled out a photograph to show the parachute, attached to the top wing of the airplane. "I'd pull a cord, and a small rocket would pull the 'chute up out of the container and the whole airplane would float down safely. If my wings broke off in turbulence, it'd save my life. I didn't have to use it, but it felt good to have it."

The bad weather grounded Lloyd for several days, "and from then on I was behind schedule. In that first month, we actually had four good flying days. All the rest were marginal. That wasn't so bad because I flew at low altitudes and at only forty-five or fifty miles per hour. I could fly legally, although there were a couple of times when it wasn't so legal."

Lloyd settled into a leisurely routine, as Tom Horton had done on his trip to Los Angeles. He flew only in the morning and in the evening, standing down at midday "because that's when the wind and the thermals pick up, and for that airplane they're pretty bad. If the wind was greater than about five to ten miles per hour, I wouldn't take off. This slowed things down a lot."

Generally, he avoided taking off in rainstorms because of the lowered visibility, "but I got caught in plenty of 'em. It's not fun. When you don't have a cockpit around you, the rain hurts. It's hitting you at forty-five miles per hour, and that hurts a lot. I was miserable."

But there were compensations. One airfield in Ohio was a historic grass strip, "one of the old original airmail airports with an old navigation beacon. I'm flying along, seeing this beacon, but it's not a normal airport beacon, which flashes green-white, green-white, green-white. This one was flashing white-white, white-white, white-white. 'What the hell is that?' I asked myself. It was the old airmail beacon. They said they hadn't turned it on in twenty years, but they had heard I was coming."

At one stop, another crowd of a thousand people greeted Lloyd. Many of them were dressed in period costume, riding "in a big parade of antique cars. They gave me a quart of milk because Rodgers had to have a quart of cream every time he stopped. They took us in the cars to a big reception, and then they said I had to get a haircut because when Rodgers landed there, he got a haircut. They had the chief barber of Ohio there—it just amazed me that any state had a chief barber—and in a big ceremony he trimmed my mustache because I'd gotten a haircut the day before starting the flight. That night I had dinner with the test pilot who flew the first Taylor Cub, the predecessor of the Piper Cub, back in 1932." Lloyd stretched and grinned at the memory.

The next day, however, *Vin Fiz II* suffered its first damaging crash. Fifteen minutes after he took off from a golf course, Lloyd struck another bad patch of turbulence. "You could see a weather front coming, and it was getting worse and worse. At one point I was in full climb, the engine wide open, and I was losing 500 feet per minute. I couldn't maintain altitude. I was all over the place, bouncing along something awful." To demonstrate the severity of the turbulence, Lloyd briskly jounced an enormous imaginary martini shaker with his long arms.

"I found another golf course with a fairway that ran into the wind, but as I got closer I realized that to make the course attractive, the builders had run the power lines on the trees, rather than on poles out in the open where I could see them. As I'm coming down, I see wires running right across the fairway where I'm landing, and so I put the plane into a shallow dive to go under them. That made me a little too fast, and when I landed, I sheared my landing gear off."

He had several adventures with squalls. In Indiana "I saw a thunderstorm over here and a thunderstorm over there, and I thought I could go between them, so I started to head there. Then the two thunderstorms came together. I said, 'Whoops, that's not going to work,' so I turned around and started to fly around one of the storms. I'm flying along, not looking at my instruments, just looking around. It was fairly calm, not too bumpy. But then I noticed everything on the ground was getting smaller and smaller. I was getting higher and higher. 'How high am I?' I asked myself, and then I realized that I had gained 1,500 feet without knowing it." Lloyd had been sucked into an updraft, one of the most dangerous places to be other than in the middle of a thunderstorm itself.

The nearest airport was about five miles away, and Lloyd closed the throttle, intending to glide down to it. "I was still gaining altitude. I'm diving with no power, and I'm still going up, and then I finally realized that I was too close to this storm. After I gained another thousand feet—I was at about 4,500 feet at this time—the storm finally let me go, and I was able to glide down and land."

One day in Illinois, the engine of *Vin Fiz II* stopped in midair. One of the spark plugs of its two-cylinder engine had backed out. "There are some good things about having an engine failure in Illinois," Jim said. "The whole state is an airport. It's absolutely flat. I found a field that was already harvested and that had been plowed in the direction of the wind, and it was real near a farmhouse. I thought I would have no problems. So I glided down. But after all this lousy weather we'd been having, the field was terribly muddy, and my landing roll was about ten feet. The mud ripped the gear right off the airplane, and it nosed over. *Vin Fiz II* was fairly heavily damaged. Not for three days were we able to get off." Good people came to the rescue, however. The owners of the farmhouse had to leave for a few days, but gave Lloyd and his crew their keys and told them to use the house, the kitchen and everything in it. "I couldn't believe it," Jim said. "That doesn't happen anywhere else."

But it did. Over Missouri, Lloyd's engine again failed. "I picked out a field and was coming into it when I realized that it was full of cows and I couldn't land there. I stretched my glide and landed in the next field, but I didn't do a good job. This was my fault. I have no excuse for this one. I didn't come down right, and I wiped out my gear again. Now, the reason *this* field had no cows was that it had a bull in it. I'm sitting in the plane saying, 'Aw, man, this is unbelievable.' "

Fortunately, three locals had looked up when Lloyd's engine quit, and they came running to rescue him before the bull could do any damage to either Jim or his airplane. "The four of us picked up the airplane and carried it out of the field away from the bull and put it down next to a house across the street. The same thing happened. This guy said we could use his yard. He let us use his house. He gave us electricity. It was just *unbelievable.*"

So moving were these incidents, Lloyd said, that Jack McCornack, who was something of a phrasemaker, "said we had met a lot of good people and a lot of bad weather. That's how it was all the way across the country. If I were to write a book about the trip, I'd call it *Good People and Bad Weather.*"

Soon it was time to draw up a bill of lading for my own mission to discover good people and avoid bad weather. A pilot who flies a Cessna 150 worries more about weight than does a lifetime member of Jenny Craig. A 150 of *Gin Fizz*'s vintage and equipage has a legal "useful load" of just 490 pounds. Part of that useful load includes fuel and part of it includes me. Aviation gas weighs six pounds a gallon, and *Gin Fizz* carries twenty-two and a half gallons of usable fuel. That's 135 pounds. Added to my stripped weight of 205 pounds, fuel and pilot take up 340 pounds, leaving 150 pounds available for a passenger plus baggage. Theoretically, that 150 pounds gives plenty of breathing room. But at full legal load on a good day—that is, a cool one at low altitude—a Cessna 150 is somewhat underpowered.

And I would be flying in the middle of the summer, when heat thins the air and sets barely adequate engines on the edge of anemia. Between New York and the Rockies, I'd have little trouble because I'd be flying at no more than 4,500 feet above sea level. West of the Pecos River in Texas, however, I'd have to take *Gin Fizz* up high, to at least 6,500 feet and sometimes more than 10,000 feet. On hot, humid days at those altitudes, her doughty little Continental would labor harder than the Little Engine That Could. *Gin Fizz* would need at least twice the runway for takeoffs and twice the time to climb. The less weight she carried, the better off she would be—and the easier it would be for me to elude thunderstorms.

So I planned carefully. At the top of my list was a lightweight canvas grip with a week's worth of clothes—underwear, socks, T-shirts, three pairs of shorts, one pair of jeans, a bathing suit, a sweatshirt, a light jacket (it can get cold in the mountains at night), a shaving and toothbrushing kit, aspirin, pills, and three paperback cop novels for wind-bound days. Then there was a "communications bag" with a laptop computer, a TTY, a modem, cables, notebooks, and pens. A camera bag held an old Pentax with short zoom and super-wide-angle lenses, plus film. (I decided to leave behind the video camera; turbulence would make it all but impossible to get good tape from the air anyway.) I carried another camera, a tiny Nikon point-and-shoot, in my pilot's rucksack, which held my electronic flight computer (which I seldom used, but decided to take just in case), sectional and terminal charts, and extra batteries for the GPS. I took along a fanny pack just big enough for my bathing suit, change of underwear and T-shirt, razor and toothbrush, and an Ed McBain novel for rainy days, so I wouldn't have to hump everything to a motel overnight. For an emergency kit, I added a two-man tent, ground cloth, foam pad and sleeping bag, a half gallon of water (I planned to take twice that in the desert Southwest), a small first-aid kit, Sterno stove, dried soup, coffee, and a large box of granola bars. All this added up to ninety carefully selected pounds.

I wasn't enthusiastic about pitching a tent under *Gin Fizz*'s wing. Two decades ago I enjoyed camping with the family, but at my age I don't sleep outdoors comfortably anymore, and pilots should be well rested. Who needs mosquitoes, chiggers, and wood smoke in the eyes? I was more than willing to pay each night for a nice motel with a soft bed, clean sheets, a pillow, soap, shampoo and towels, walls that keep away critters, doors that lock against thieves, toilets that don't stink, a telephone, an air conditioner, a Coke machine outside, and a television with cable so I could keep a constant eye on the Weather Channel. And a free breakfast. For fifty bucks a night, that's a great American bargain. With middle age, I had not merely grown soft and indolent, I had also become shrewd.

The appointed day to head east to New Jersey—a Wednesday in late June—arrived, bringing with it bad news. An occluded low had been spinning around the Midwest for two days and would likely hang around for another day. This meant hazy visibility, rain, low ceilings, and scattered thunderstorms—pure instrument-flying weather. I stayed home and went to work instead. I should have stayed home the next day, too, but Jim Lloyd's warnings about the dangers of bad weather hadn't sunk in. Learning to fly had revived not only forgotten dreams but suppressed desires. One of those last was for instant gratification. I wanted to *get going*—the hell with being mature and sensible and staying home until the weather blew over.

But that Thursday morning things did look a bit better. The front was moving east slowly, though the cloud ceiling was still too low for VFR flight. The forecast said that later in the day the weather would clear enough for me to take off and get a couple of hundred miles east, perhaps to the Indiana-Ohio border, before I had to land for the night, leaving an easy flight on Friday. This was a masterpiece of wishful thinking.

Arriving at Westosha at 7 A.M., I undid *Gin Fizz*'s tiedowns, started her engine, and taxied her to the fuel pumps, where I topped off her tanks. Then I set to loading my equipage, which proved to be a little more difficult than I anticipated. There's less room in the cabin of an early-model Cessna 150 than at first appears. Sleeping bags and foam pads are remarkably bulky. I made a command decision: I would leave behind the sleeping bag, pad, tent, and ground cloth, saving almost fifteen pounds. In an emergency I'd beg the FBO manager to let me sleep in the pilot's lounge and would sweep up afterward. *Gin Fizz* would thank me by coming unstuck from the runway a little sooner and climbing a little faster.

After I stewed for three hours, the clouds finally lifted to 2,500 feet and the visibly improved to six miles. Not great, but good enough. At 11:01 A.M. by the flight log, *Gin Fizz* was away, headed for the Jersey shore. In a few minutes she was cruising smoothly at 3,000 feet, heading south and then east around the radio-controlled airspace surrounding O'Hare. All thoughts of work and home faded from my mind. The grand adventure had begun.

And it paused not an hour later, at Lewis University Airport in Romeoville, near the southwestern edge of Chicago. The clouds had turned threatening, dark on the underside. I had had little experience distinguishing ordinary cumulus clouds from cumulonimbus, the birthing ground of thunderstorms, and couldn't radio Flight Service to ask what the weather briefers saw on their radar. So I landed to catch my breath, study the airport's computer weather report, and make a resolute Go/No-Go decision. "There's a U.S. weather station here," said the FBO attendant, pointing across the runway at a large radar dome above a low building. "Go over there and talk to the briefers."

Shyly I introduced myself, explained my mission, and asked to look at the radar readouts. A friendly technician took me to his screen. On it, a thick, ragged green, red, and purple line of violent thunderstorms had developed from southeast to northeast near Fort Wayne, effectively cutting off my forward progress. I could go on part way across Indiana, but what risk was there of running into unforeseen meteorological surprises? The technician shrugged. "You're Pilot in Command," he said.

Having vowed not to dither, I dithered. I paced the runway for an hour. I was going to be stuck; the question was where. Finally the decision was made for me when the clouds darkened and dumped half an inch of rain on the airport. I hailed a cab and holed up for the rest of the day and night at a local motel just one hour out of my starting point, thoroughly disgusted with myself.

In bed I worried that I was worrying too much about the weather, that I was too timorous in the face of billowing cumulus. Could I have gone on an hour further? If I am to complete this enterprise, I thought, I must forge ahead courageously, like Cal Rodgers in his infinitely flimsier *Vin Fiz*. Then I was struck by another worry: Would worrying too little about the weather prove disastrous? I fretted myself to sleep.

Friday turned out to be another frustrating day. I was still following a slow-moving front of five-mile-visibility haze, low scudding clouds, towering cumulus, and boomers, and the best I could do was get to Van Wert in western Ohio, two more hours eastward, after half a dozen landings to let the weather get ahead. It was like old-time college football, lurching across the field in rushes of three yards and a cloud of dust. Before I headed for a motel, however, I enjoyed a pleasant interlude.

Almost before *Gin Fizz*'s propeller stopped turning, the young manager of the Van Wert FBO dashed outside. After looking over my airplane carefully and firing a salvo of questions about it, he beckoned me to follow him. Inside a hangar sat a straight-tail Cessna 150 just a year younger than mine, and, of course, he had to indulge in a little proud show-and-tell. He and a friend were rebuilding the 150, which had just been repainted by an auto detailer and looked gorgeous. Its interior yawned empty, awaiting further refurbishment. "We're not restoring it to the original appearance as yours is," he said, "but we're gonna put in a modern panel, modern yokes, and reupholstered seats out of a 152." I smiled. There seems to be an instant bonding between owners of similar rare airplanes, even if they do not exchange names. We didn't, but we are now compatriots of a kind for the rest of our lives.

At the motel that night, the Weather Channel forecaster said the front would pick up speed during the night and reach eastern New York State by late the next afternoon, so it looked as if I would be able to reach my goal for the day: Tri-Cities Airport at Endicott, New York, just west of Binghamton.

I did, again like a checkers player jumping from one corner of the board to the other. From Van Wert to Wadsworth in eastern Ohio, I sailed at 5,500 feet in smooth air before landing to rest and refuel and let the front blow a little farther east. At noon I landed at Jamestown, New York, and telephoned my parents, who live on a farm in northeastern Pennsylvania just south of the state line from Binghamton, to say that I'd arrive at Endicott about 2 P.M. Mother said she'd meet me.

At that hour, however, I was still stuck at Wellsville, where I had landed after the clouds had lowered alarmingly over the mountains in central New York State. Right away I called Mother to tell her not to go to the airport, but she had already left, so I called Endicott and asked the attendant, if he saw a gray-haired woman in her eighties, to tell her to go home and wait, that I'd call when I arrived. Rapidly I was becoming dispirited. I'd planned to make New Jersey in two days, maybe one, and here it was the third day already. Was there some special corollary of Murphy's Law I hadn't anticipated in all my planning?

Then there was a nice surprise: "You're the guy in *AOPA Pilot!*" the attendant suddenly exclaimed. Months before, I had been interviewed by Bill Kight, a former newspaper photographer who now flies Boeing 757s for United Parcel Service, about my plan to retrace the flight of Cal Rodgers. The result, with a photo, had just appeared in *AOPA Pilot,* the official magazine of the Aircraft Owners and Pilots Association, general aviation's biggest and most powerful lobby. Quickly the attendant ran off the page on his boss's copier and handed it to me. I was elated. Just about every aviator in the world reads *AOPA Pilot,* and Kight had written a crisp, appealing piece that boosted my shaky ego. Maybe my luck was turning.

Three hours later, I put *Gin Fizz* down at Endicott, still riding that lovely fluffy cloud and looking forward to a home-cooked dinner with Mother and Dad and a bed in their house.

# 6

Cal Rodgers also had to wrestle gremlins—some of them of his own making—before getting his enterprise off the ground. Late the night before his departure from Sheepshead Bay, the disassembled *Vin Fiz* rolled into Jersey City by train from Chicago. Cal met the party at the station and helped to ferry and truck the airplane across to Brooklyn, where they arrived at a field after midnight. The crew dismounted and laboriously began putting together the airplane.

A stranger came along carrying a lantern. He watched for a time, then asked, "Isn't that Rodgers who is going to fly for the Hearst prize?" Told that it was, he observed, "Well, I'm surprised you are starting from here. I thought it was to be from Sheepshead. This is Brighton Park." Embarrassed, the crew reloaded *Vin Fiz* onto the truck and proceeded farther east, and day had nearly broken when Rodgers and his aides finished their work at the Sheepshead Bay racetrack and fell into bed in their hotel.

Cal was awakened at 2 P.M., in plenty of time for a takeoff at 4 P.M., but the milling crowds at the racetrack were so thick that he had to wait until a phalanx of policemen and volunteers had cleared enough space for his takeoff. A crewman lashed to a strut a single bottle of the soft drink for which the airplane was named. Famously a cigar devotee, Cal managed to burn his way through two stogies during that time, and when he finally mounted the pilot's seat of the Model EX, he lit a fresh one.

At 4:25 P.M. on Sunday, September 17, 1911, *Vin Fiz* finally lifted into the air to a huge roar from the crowd. Cal Rodgers was at last off, competing with two other aviators for Hearst's $50,000 prize. On September 11, a West Coast aviator, Robert G. Fowler, had departed Golden Gate Park in San Francisco, flying another Wright-built airplane, aiming to cross the Sierra Nevada and head for Denver. That day Fowler leaped 129 miles east to Auburn, California, on the western slope of the Sierra, but the next day wrecked his airplane near Colfax. The repairs would take twelve days, giving Rodgers time to catch up.

A third pilot, James Ward, a nineteen-year-old former jockey, was also trying his luck in a Curtiss biplane, having taken off from Governors Island in New York Harbor on September 13. Ward discovered, as Rodgers quickly would, that navigating by railroad was easier said than done. That day the maze of tracks around Jersey City confused him, and not until he had flown 200 miles willy-nilly did he reach Paterson, New Jersey, scarcely twenty-two miles from Governors Island. Ward made it to Middletown, New York, the next day and to Callicoon that night. In Owego on September 17, Ward tried to take off in a maelstrom of stampeding cows and frightened spectators and then flew into a fence and crumpled his lower wing. He was not hurt, but he had to delay the trip for repairs.

Meanwhile, climbing to 500 feet, Rodgers circled Coney Island, dropping a cloud of printed cards that advertised the new soft drink, then headed up over Flatbush to the Brooklyn Bridge at 800 feet. As *Vin Fiz* soared north, eyewitnesses said, the afternoon wind currents tossed her up and down like a lifeboat in heavy surf. Despite his late start, Rodgers had said he hoped to fly the rest of the trip during the mornings so the sun would be at his back, instead of in his eyes, but surely he also was considering the smoother air of the cool early hours.

Like Ward, Rodgers planned to reach Chicago by flying along the Erie Railroad's main line, and his first waypoint across the Hudson was Jersey City. He flew across lower Manhattan as crowds hung from windows and waved from housetops, and shortly after 4:30, *Vin Fiz* flew over the Erie's Jersey City terminal and Rodgers's waiting chase train.

The train was late in getting away—it had to wait for Rodgers's mechanics, who had missed the Jersey City ferry—and Rodgers continued onward. Following a warren of railroad lines is not simple, and like Ward, Rodgers took a wrong turn, finding himself mistakenly over Newburgh, New York. He turned west on the New York, Ontario & Western's main line and followed it to his intended stop at Middletown, where he landed at 6:18 P.M. after circling the field so that the throng of 10,000 could get a good look at *Vin Fiz*. As the airplane landed the crowd erupted, and Rodgers suddenly was deeply concerned for the safety of his machine. But he had made the eighty-four miles from Sheepshead Bay in 105 minutes, for an average speed of forty-eight miles per hour—not bad, considering *Vin Fiz*'s top speed of fifty-five miles per hour.

Eighty-four years later, a beautiful Sunday in July dawned with just a slight mist veiling the low mountains surrounding Hallstead, Pennsylvania, forty minutes by car from Tri-Cities Airport at Endicott, where I had put *Gin Fiz* to bed the night before. The front had blown out to sea and dissipated. So glorious was the sky—at that time of year morning fog usually chokes the valleys of the Pennsylvania Alleghenies—that, full of eagerness after having flung myself against the slow-moving front like a puppy leaping against a fence, I said good-bye to Dad and browbeat my sleepy mother into driving me early to Endicott. Having refueled the night before, I quickly performed the preflight tasks, kissed Mother good-bye, and saddled up. *Gin Fizz* took off at 7:15 A.M., and I put her into a gentle climb to 3,500 feet, her nose pointed southeast to Matawan.

That early in the day the sun hadn't yet warmed the ground, and the clear air above remained still and calm. In such smoothness, flying was downright sensuous, like sliding between silk sheets, as *Gin Fizz* sailed at 100 miles per hour over the old coal fields northeast of Scranton, then over Lake Wallenpaupack and the Pocono Mountains. Not far from the Delaware Water Gap, she crossed into New Jersey and over the long Kittatinny Mountains, the upthrust that forms the southeast border of the Appalachian Ridge and Valley region, full of shale outcrops and limestone depressions visible from the air. The low, lake-speckled New England Upland region followed, the flat-topped ridges of hard gneiss looking from the air like wrinkles that worried the green earth. Just ahead I could see shadowy shapes that marked the cities of the river-rich New Jersey Piedmont: Jersey City, Paterson, Newark, and Elizabeth.

Just before Hackettstown, I eased back the throttle to put the airplane into a gentle descent under the top layer of Newark Airport's Class B airspace. Around major airports, radio-controlled airspace is arranged like an imaginary upside-down three-layer cake, the layers growing smaller the closer to the ground. Under and over those layers, radio communications between tower and airplane are not required. A pilot who cannot hear can fly there, provided he is careful to steer clear of the unseen layers.

Over Plainfield, near the edge of the New Jersey megalopolis twenty miles northwest of Matawan, *Gin Fizz* descended below 2,000 feet and then ran into stiff turbulence that startled me when one wing suddenly lurched upward, as if kicked by an unseen foot. I gripped the yoke firmly. The ground was warming up, and thermals had started to punch through the lower altitudes. A stiff, gusty breeze coursed in off the Atlantic, too, mixing its weaving jabs with the thermals' brisk uppercuts.

The sea of buildings and streets below looked confusingly unfamiliar. I circled for a few minutes and then found Marlboro Airport right where the chart in my lap said it was. Banking sharply in the turbulence and dropping a notch of flaps, I guided *Gin Fizz* into the landing pattern—and saw that I had my work cut out for me. At 2,156 feet long and 40 feet wide, Marlboro's runway is not only short and narrow but also surrounded by tall trees and a nasty-looking high-tension power line. Worst of all, a brisk crosswind blew directly across the runway. I discovered the wind too late to correct *Gin Fizz*'s course, resulting in a high and fast final approach. Immediately, I saw that I'd land too far down the runway to stop before rolling off the far edge, so I pushed the throttle to its stop, cleaned up the flaps, and climbed away, intending to go around and try again.

As the plane curved away from the airport, I looked down and saw that the wind sock below was not only blowing almost perpendicular to the runway but also streaming straight out—meaning a wind velocity of seventeen miles per hour or more. That's too much for me, I thought. An airplane as small and light as a Cessna 150 isn't supposed to be landed in a ninety-degree crosswind greater than about thirteen miles per hour, although a truly expert pilot can stretch that envelope. Not I—not then and maybe never.

"Damn," I said. This was not the way I wanted to start my flight from New York to Los Angeles. Despite my inexperience, however, I had learned that God is not necessarily my copilot—Murphy more often rides in the right seat. Nothing involving flying is ever going to proceed exactly according to plan. Preparing for the unexpected includes choosing an alternate airport in case the first one doesn't work out, and I had done that back in Endicott while laying out my course on the chart that morning. It was Old Bridge, five miles southwest of Marlboro.

Old Bridge is a curious airport because its runway closely parallels a waterskiing course carved out of the New Jersey soil. Not long ago that course was intended for floatplanes; Old Bridge was once a seaplane base. Today an automobile drag strip also parallels the water. The entire complex is surrounded by tall light standards, but the runway is a nice long one—3,600 feet—and tall trees along one side blanket the sea breeze. The runway also stood closer to the wind than Marlboro's, the sock told me, enabling *Gin Fizz* to handle the crosswind. As an outboard boat pulled a slalom skier down the course alongside, *Gin Fizz* landed handily. On the ramp I shut down to refuel, check the weather, and call a reporter and photographer who had expressed interest in my flight. They were doubtless waiting at Marlboro, and I needed to redirect them to Old Bridge.

A month or two earlier, I had prepared a news release announcing the flight and sent it off to two dozen newspapers and television stations along the route, so I could learn a little bit more about where I was stopping, and they could know a little bit more about what a deaf pilot could achieve. I was not, however, starry-eyed about the plan. As a veteran newspaperman, I knew that the trip wouldn't interest major metropolitan media—but it might bring out reporters and television crews in smaller cities along the way, where people were much more likely to be aware that in 1911 a tall, ungainly fellow in a Wright flying machine had dropped in during a historic journey.

"I'm deaf," I told the cadaverous attendant at the Old Bridge FBO when he came in from topping the tanks of my airplane. *Gin Fizz* drank just six gallons of $1.95-per-gallon aviation gasoline—I had not been in the air much more than an hour—and he did not seem pleased by the effort it had taken to earn such a small profit. "I need to make a phone call with my TTY," I said, showing it to him.

"The public phone's right outside," he replied, jerking his head toward the door.

"This won't work with a pay phone," I said. "I need to use a regular desk phone. I'm just calling an 800 number—the New Jersey deaf relay service."

He looked at me for a skeptical moment. "Oh, all right," he said crossly, and pushed his telephone toward me.

Welcome to Greater New York, I thought to myself in equal ill humor. Fortunately, the relay operator was polite. And the reporter was still at his newspaper. His response: "Where's Old Bridge?"

Some journalist you are, I thought, if you don't know an airport ten miles from your office. "I don't know," I said, "but I'm sure you can find it on a road map."

"Uh . . ." he replied. "Look, we're kind of busy here today. Could you write something up and send it to me with a picture?"

"Sure I will," I said, swiftly intending not to. Who am I to do another reporter's job for him? His indifference, however, would be par for the *Gin Fizz*'s publicity course.

Remounting *Gin Fizz*, I lifted into the New Jersey sky in a cloud of mixed irritation and apprehension. This was not an auspicious beginning for a 4,231-mile trip, I thought, departing from the wrong airport and without the benefit of a press send-off, even from a tiny suburban weekly. I hoped nothing else would go amiss that day, not after such a beautiful beginning at Hallstead.

I felt no better as *Gin Fizz* crossed the coast of New Jersey, outbound for the Verrazano Narrows. An icy fist gripped my spine as I pointed the airplane's nose north toward the tall uprights of the bridge fourteen miles away in the bright haze, barely noticing the dozen pleasure boats tracing feathery wakes on the blue velvet of Raritan Bay. Union Beach on the Jersey shore disappeared to the southwest, and I flew steadily on over the lonely water, holding my altitude at precisely 1,000 feet above the waves. Staten Island lay just three miles west, Sandy Hook five miles east—but land seemed leagues away. If one's engine should fail over open water, there is no place to land an airplane—and I had never flown over anything larger than a small lake.

As *Gin Fizz* droned into Lower New York Bay, the broad, sandy shores of Midland Beach and the Gateway National Recreation Area on Staten Island crept closer and closer on the left, but I did not feel much better. Doubtless at 11 A.M. on a Sunday the beaches were full of bathers I could not see from three miles out, and landing there in case of trouble was not a good possibility. But *Gin Fizz*'s stout old Continental engine thrummed on contentedly, rrrrr *rum rum rrrrr*, and on the right, Coney Island approached, the entrance to Sheepshead Bay visible just to the east. It was then I realized that my little two-seater had emerged from the brisk mainland turbulence and was flying through smoother air, tempered by cool sea waters. My mood began to lighten.

My first stop in *Gin Fizz* also was to be at Middletown, but unlike Cal Rodgers I could not fly over Jersey City and follow the old Erie, now one of Conrail's many major lines. Had I done so, I would have flown illegally through the tower-controlled airspace of Newark and Teterboro Airports. Rather, I would fly up the Hudson River until I reached the Tappan Zee Bridge, well clear of the forbidden airspace, then turn west and head directly for Middletown, where I would pick up the Erie.

"How the hell can you fly up the Hudson?" I am often asked. "You've got Newark Airport on one side and Kennedy and La Guardia on the other!"

True. The tower-controlled airspace over the greater New York area is composed of three huge upside-down wedding cakes squished together in a baker's box eighty-five miles wide by seventy-five miles deep. But it is constructed so that an airplane can fly without having to contact Air Traffic Control through the "Hudson River exclusion," a gently curving corridor 1,100 feet high and forty miles long, bounded by the edge of New Jersey on one side and the New York shore on the other.

As *Gin Fizz* approached the Verrazano Narrows Bridge, I switched the radio frequency to the Hudson River "guard channel," on which aircraft announce their presence and location while flying through the corridor—which is often uncomfortably full of traffic. Picking up the microphone, I said in proper fashion, "Hudson River Traffic, Cessna five-eight-five-niner-Echo northbound over the Narrows, deaf pilot, cannot receive, Hudson River." Announcing my deafness, I reasoned, couldn't hurt and might even help; knowing that a pilot in their vicinity couldn't receive their transmissions might encourage others to keep a sharper eye out for traffic.

As *Gin Fizz* squeezed through the Narrows and New York Harbor opened up in front of me, I nearly cried for joy at the sight. On the broad blue proscenium below, ferries chugged purposefully across the wakes of pleasure boats cavorting among freighters and huge tankers riding at anchor. At stage left the Statue of Liberty lifted her mighty torch, and at stage right upriver the twin towers of the World Trade Center stolidly anchored the foot of Manhattan. I felt as if New York was putting on a Broadway show just for me.

I had wanted to circle the Statue of Liberty, the traditional beginning of a pleasure pilot's coast-to-coast flight. But there was a hitch. The regulations say that an airplane must stay 500 feet away from any people on the ground or in boats on the water. The eastern edge of the second layer of the Newark Airport wedding cake, however, lies just 500 feet west of the Statue of Liberty, its floor 500 feet above the water. Naturally, pilots who want to fly through that airspace must get permission from Air Traffic Control, but I couldn't. If I dipped down to under 500 feet, I could fly around Miss Liberty. But that Sunday morning, an entire flotilla of ferries and pleasure boats bounced on the water all about the statue—too close.

If I had any impulse to break the rules, it was stifled by a jet-propelled sightseeing helicopter that flashed south below me scarcely 300 feet away. Startled and alarmed, I looked up from the statue and scanned the sky for traffic. I could see none, except for a blimp in the distance, and I blew Miss Liberty a quick kiss as *Gin Fizz* continued northward up the Hudson, making sure to stay to the right of the river's imaginary center line and to keep my altitude at 1,000 feet, just 100 feet under the 1,100-foot floor of the La Guardia/Kennedy controlled airspace.

Past Ellis Island and Battery Park *Gin Fizz* flew. On the left I saw the docks of Hoboken, then on the right spied the greenery of Central Park through the tall buildings. A United Boeing 727 from La Guardia captured the glint of the sun as it curved west over the Hudson about a thousand feet above *Gin Fizz,* and I spotted the Triborough Bridge over the East River. The George Washington Bridge passed below, then the Cloisters on the east, Tenafly on the west, and Yonkers again on the east. I gazed in wonder alternately from left to right as the sights of New York and New Jersey pulled me north, hand over hand.

I had announced *Gin Fizz*'s presence again at the Statue of Liberty, then while passing the World Trade Center, but until the Palisades, where the floor of the La Guardia airspace rises to 1,500 feet, I saw no other aircraft. At that point, I looked down and on the water spotted the smaller shadow of another airplane overtaking me. As the shadows merged into one, I glanced upward. Four hundred feet above, a bigger and faster Cessna was drawing ahead of my airplane. Suddenly my first checkpoint, the Tappan Zee Bridge, loomed ahead. After passing over the bridge, I banked *Gin Fizz* to the west and set course inland for Middletown, twenty miles to the northwest over the rolling hills. My spirits, once again soaring, lifted with *Gin Fizz* as she climbed to 3,000 feet. My heart nearly exploded with love—for life, for flying, for my little airplane. I had experienced that intensity of emotion only three times before: on my wedding day and when my two sons were born.

Within fifteen minutes, I spotted Randall Airport through the haze just east of Middletown. The fluttering wind sock showed a brisk, gusty crosswind, but a thick protective grove of trees lay on the windward side of the long, skinny, undulating runway. I shouldn't have any difficulty landing. Little traffic was about, too; a Cessna 172 was departing, a bright yellow ultralight aircraft that looked like a flying flea was cavorting well off one end of the runway, and a small helicopter was doing chopper calisthenics nearby.

So beamish was my mood that when I touched down to the thunderous cheers of absolutely nobody at all, I didn't mind. When I shut down the engine at the terminal building—little more than a shack attached to a hangar—I was all alone as far as I could see. Randall appeared to be a typical rural field, the piebald paint of its buildings faded like weary tie-dyed Levis, with perhaps two dozen airplanes, many in need of paint themselves, squatting inside open hangars. Some of the planes seemed almost derelict, but most clearly were in flying condition. The FBO manager—a friendly, open-faced man named Charles Brodie—emerged from the office. I issued the routine announcement that I was deaf but read lips and added that I needed fuel. He pointed amiably to the pumps at the far end of the taxiway, and we exchanged pleasantries about my cross-country trip.

I dined on a Baby Ruth bar and Diet Pepsi from the FBO's vending machines—itinerant flyers never seem to be able to eat properly—and half an hour later, at 1 P.M., I left, hoping to land at three more airports before tying up for the night. I taxied onto the ramp, heading for the runway threshold. Suddenly, Brodie dashed out, pointing to a camera in one hand and waving his arms wildly. I laughed, hit the brakes, and grinned out the window while he snapped picture after picture. *Somebody* cared! Months later a couple of color prints, accompanied by a friendly note, would arrive at my house—a truly comradely gesture. Maybe my leave-taking, although pleasant enough, was not as exciting as I might have wished, but it was a great deal less hair-raising than Cal Rodgers's departure had been eighty-four years earlier.

"It's Chicago in four days, if everything goes right," Rodgers had declared grandly before spending the night in a Middletown hotel. Of course, nothing did go right, partly because of the primitiveness of the technology and partly because Cal was not yet really a *pilot*, as we know the term today. A pilot does not simply manipulate the controls of an airplane, but draws on deep reserves of experience, knowledge, and prudence. Cal's logbook showed few hours and even fewer in genuine cross-country flying.

Shortly after dawn, he took a perfunctory tour of the field, noting a willow tree along the takeoff route but nothing else. At 6:21 A.M. Cal took off—and within thirty seconds, the landing gear of *Vin Fiz* had caught in the branches of that willow, slowing its forward momentum and causing it to hit a power line he had failed to spot. In another second, the airplane struck a chicken coop, killing several birds and smashing into flinders. Cal was stunned, his forehead cut, and one ankle badly sprained. Otherwise he was unhurt. Though the newspapers of the day didn't say so, the crash clearly was his fault. He should have been more thorough in his examination of the takeoff surroundings. That is called "common sense," and Cal seems never to have had much of it. His actions tended to stem from impulsiveness, rather than considered judgment.

His mechanics worked around the clock. The Wrights shipped new parts for *Vin Fiz* by fast train from Dayton, but there was a further delay when some of the new parts turned out to be the wrong ones, and a new propeller had to be sent for as well. "The spirit is willing," the Hearst hack had Cal saying in his daily column, "but the machine is weak." In the early afternoon of September 21, *Vin Fiz* was finally ready, and at 2:18 P.M. Cal lifted into the air, headed for Hancock, New York, sixty miles due west of Middletown, but many more miles along the winding Erie.

He had planned a short landing at Callicoon, fifteen air miles downriver from Hancock, but his schedule was upset by the unreliability of the gasoline engines of the day. *Vin Fiz*'s motor was losing cooling water fast, so Cal decided to keep on to Hancock. Near that town a defective spark plug popped out as well. He chose the first good spot he saw, a potato field, and though his touchdown was decent, a landing-gear skid snapped. According to Eileen Lebow, two men digging potatoes barely looked up as Cal asked where he was and kept at their work, rushing to get the crop out before rain came. Even when a crowd "assembled as if by magic 'out of the mountains,' the two men kept at it, oblivious to the birdman."

*Gin Fizz* flew over what must have been the descendants of those potato diggers in just about every town all the way to California. Meanwhile, following Rodgers's route, I flew from Middletown directly west to the Shawangunk Mountain range and the Delaware River, picking up the old Erie main line (now Conrail's Southern Tier branch). Rodgers had found smooth air at a little more than 2,500 feet above the ground, but at that altitude, *Gin Fizz* rocked and swayed in the increasingly gusty breeze as I passed the little towns anchoring the railroad tracks to the rolling hills of southern New York State: Otisville, Port Jervis, Callicoon, and Long Eddy. I could not relax, but had to fly the plane constantly, now correcting a wing drop, then a jump in altitude. Going low and slow offers pleasant intimacies—a pilot can see close-up details of the countryside rolling past, such as houses, barns, and people and even the odd deer or two—but at the height of day, he's busy coping with turbulence. This kind of flying is not dangerous as long as the aviator is aware of radio towers and other low-lying hazards to aerial navigation, but controlling the plane through agitated air requires all his attention and is tiring in the extreme. I began to wish I had made the trip as a younger man, as Rodgers had, instead of in late middle age.

Just past Hancock, the bright blue waters of Cannonsville Reservoir on the west branch of the Delaware hove into view, and I departed the railroad tracks, looking for White Birch Airport, the spot closest to the potato field where Rodgers had landed in 1911 and the airport that had given Jim Lloyd such a rousing welcome in 1986. White Birch is a grass strip, and during much of the year turf airports blend into the green countryside, almost impossible to discern from the air. The best way for visiting pilots to find grass fields is to use loran or GPS to pinpoint them, but that would be cheating, I thought. Rodgers had to find suitable landing places in cow pastures only with his eyes. I would try do the same with airports. I looked carefully for wind socks and airplanes, and sure enough, in a few minutes two high-wing Cessnas peeked from the lee of a copse. Almost immediately, I found tire marks that bespoke a runway threshold. At 1,900 feet long and scarcely 70 feet wide, White Birch is a small landing field, even for a turf airport. Its single runway is cut into the woods atop a long mountain ridge.

After landing as gingerly as I could—holding *Gin Fizz's* nose-wheel off the ground as long as possible on the rollout, so it would not dig into the soft grass and perhaps bend its supporting leg—I taxied up to the only building on the field, a small whitewashed steel structure. As I shut down, a tall, burly man in his late sixties waved from the doorway. He was the airport manager and chief flight instructor. "Francisco?" I called. "Kisor?" he replied. He had answered a flyer I had mailed out months before to the airport managers along my route, and we had made arrangements to meet that day. Max Francisco is a former World War II–era marine who learned to fly in 1951 and drove an eighteen-wheeler truck for forty-five years. He is probably the only one-eyed certified flight instructor in the entire Northeast, and upon that hangs quite a story.

On April 28, 1991, Max told me, he was giving a routine biennial flight review to an eighty-six-year-old pilot named Lee Wulff. An internationally known authority on fly fishing, Wulff had played host to a vacationing former president, Jimmy Carter, in the Catskills during the 1980s. He was a veteran pilot with 3,700 hours in his logbook over forty-four years in the air, and Max had almost that number in his as well.

They were flying a Piper Super Cub, Max in the rear seat and Wulff in the front. "We were on our landing approach," Max said, "and when we were about forty feet from the runway, I noticed that he had failed to line up properly. It was obvious that making the runway was out of the question, so I added a little power and lightly moved my stick to guide us down the valley. At that time, I think, Wulff pulled the mixture all the way lean." That act cut off fuel to the engine, and "as the engine lost power, the airplane stalled and dropped off to the right. At this point, I wrested the controls from him but pulled out of the stall about 100 feet below a wooded hill ahead."

The Super Cub smashed into trees sixty feet high and plummeted through the branches, fetching up on the ground. "The top of the cabin was completely torn away," Max said. "I unhooked my seat belt and fell out on the ground. I tried to stand up, but had broken bones in both my feet, as well as severe facial injuries. Five compound fractures and six lacerations between my upper lip and eyebrows. After one glance at Wulff I knew that he was beyond help."

The plane had crashed only about half a mile from the airport, but no one had seen or heard it go down. "I was unable to walk," Max said. "There were houses about a third of a mile away through the woods. I headed there on my back, traveling on my heels and elbows. The going was slow, and blood kept pumping out of a wound on my face with every heartbeat. I crushed some leaves in my hands, then packed them on the cut until it stopped bleeding. As I traveled, it started up again, so I stopped and packed it with more crushed leaves."

Meanwhile, at the airfield other pilots, wondering where Max and Wulff had gone, had switched their handheld radios to 121.5, the distress frequency to which every airplane's emergency locator transmitter is tuned. A signal was emanating from nearby, but precisely where, they didn't know. They checked the ELTs on all the airplanes on the field to make sure none had been jarred into action by a hard landing.

"They didn't think anything could happen to us," Max said. "We had a combined age of 150 years and almost eighty-five years of flying as well. We had good weather and a sound airplane."

After a while it seemed that the ELT signal was strongest from the north, so two pilots took off in a search. Almost immediately after takeoff, they spotted the wreckage of the red-trimmed white Super Cub through the trees. On the ground and in the woods Max had crawled about a third of the way to the houses he was looking for when he heard the planes.

"I was unable to see them," Max said, "because my left eye was totally destroyed and my right eye was swollen shut. I could hear them, though, and knew they were looking for me." Three hours after the crash, a search party found the wreckage of the Cub, Wulff's body aboard. By following the scuff marks made by Max's odd locomotion through the woods, they soon found him, blind, disoriented, and horribly injured.

"I was conscious all the time and could recognize my old friends by their voices though I couldn't see them," Max said. "They carried me to a pickup truck in a litter and drove me to the runway. In a short time, a medevac helicopter arrived and took me to the hospital forty miles away." From a folder Max pulled a color photograph. It had been taken at the hospital just as he arrived on the helicopter. His face was utterly devastated, almost beyond recognition as belonging to a human being. It was hard to believe its owner could have survived.

Over the next six hours and thirty-five minutes, seven doctors put Max back together. They put a shunt in his throat, scooped out what remained of his left eye and drove screws into his upper jaw to make a mold for dentures. They threaded wires through his lower jaw and through his nose and from his brow to pull together the shattered cheekbones. They also reset the bones in his feet. After a few days in intensive care and a total of three weeks in bed, Max was released from the hospital, hobbling on a walker. Six weeks later, he returned to the hospital for removal of the fixtures, "and I was able to eat soft foods."

After the mandatory six-month waiting period, a letter from his ophthalmologist, and an examination by the FAA, Max was issued a third-class medical certificate with student pilot privileges—the lowest rung an aviator can occupy. After waiting for the FAA to arrange a special medical flight test at Albany, which he passed with ease, Max received a second-class medical certificate (it reads "Enucleated left eye, must wear corrective lenses") and the return of his commercial pilot's license, which allows him to instruct students. "I've been Pilot in Command for more than 300 hours since then," he said with satisfaction, "and made over 1,000 takeoffs and landings." And he's back working as a flight instructor.

The idea of a one-eyed flight instructor is no more outlandish than that of a deaf pilot. Binocular vision is effective only at distances closer than twenty feet. In flight, eyes are most often focused on infinity. Distances are judged by the relative sizes of objects, not how they appear in a three-dimensional field. Yes, a one-eyed pilot has to swivel his head constantly to take in a two-eyed field of view, but that is no more remarkable than a deaf pilot's reliance on his sense of vibration to diagnose the condition of his engine. Both kinds of pilots learn to compensate for their lacks.

Meanwhile, in its ruling, the National Transportation Safety Board blamed the crash on the incapacitation of eighty-six-year-old Lee Wulff as the result of a heart attack while flying. That explained his inadvertent shutting down of the engine in flight. Max agrees. "I will always believe that his death was the cause of the accident," he said, "rather than the result of it."

Today, thanks to the miracle of plastic surgery, the only signs of Max's injury are a slightly sunken left eye made of glass and a flattened nose bridge. They are barely visible; one must be looking for them to notice them.

I gazed out the window at *Gin Fizz* and shuddered. "I'm amazed that you returned to flying," I said. "After an experience like that, I'd never have gone back."

Max's reply was simple and direct. "It wasn't the pilot's fault, it wasn't my fault, and it wasn't the plane's fault. It was an act of God."

As I stood up to leave, I felt a lump of ice growing in my stomach. The airstrip seemed menacingly short to me—it was only two-thirds the length of Westosha Airport's asphalt runway, and the added friction of a grass surface always means a longer takeoff roll. I couldn't tell for sure, but the runway looked as if it ascended uphill a bit. Worst of all, the windward end of the runway, an open cut through the woods, ended at a row of tall trees that looked suspiciously like the grove into which Max and Lee Wulff had crashed just four years before. All this looked daunting to a low-time pilot who had landed and taken off almost entirely in midwestern flatlands with open space all around.

"I don't know about this," I said querulously. The machine was willing, but the spirit was weak. I wished I could be as stoic and accepting as Max, but that required inner resources I didn't have.

"Nothing to it," Max replied comfortably, adding that Piper Cherokees and Beechcraft Bonanzas, much bigger than *Gin Fizz* and requiring longer takeoff runs, had flown out of White Birch. He's bigger and heavier than my 200-plus pounds, and he and his students fly out of that airport in a Cessna 150. "Just use the standard soft-field takeoff technique," he said. "Drop ten degrees of flaps, wheel your plane around at the traffic cone at the threshold, gun 'er, and lift the nose at forty-five miles an hour—you'll make it easily." At that speed the wheels of a Cessna 150 will lift off the runway, the wings just barely flying, but the lessened drag allows the plane to accelerate to climbing speed more rapidly.

If anybody but Max Francisco had been watching me, I would have waited until late afternoon or early evening until the wind had died down, allowing me to take off in the other direction over an open valley. But I could not let this dauntless man think I was too timid to do what he and his student pilots do every day. I gulped and did as he said, although on the takeoff roll I raised the nose at forty miles per hour, a bit too soon, and doubtless lost thirty or forty feet of precious runway because of that. The wall of trees ahead of me grew larger and larger as *Gin Fizz* accelerated toward it.

As *Gin Fizz*'s wheels cleared the trees below, I experienced an applied demonstration of the term *high pucker factor.* There probably was plenty of room—tens of feet—but such is my mistrust in my middle-aged depth perception that to me, the clearance looked like inches. With the unpleasant feeling that a bare snag just a few yards ahead was reaching for my nether regions, I pulled the yoke back a little too much, and the indicated airspeed fell almost to 50 miles per hour. *Gin Fizz* was getting dangerously close to a departure stall—in which the airplane's wings lose lift and stop flying, causing it to plummet out of control—and I forced myself to push the yoke forward to pick up speed. I was sweating and trembling as air opened up between my wheels and the treetops, and I put the airplane into a gentle climbing left turn to avoid colliding with a mountaintop across a ravine.

*Chickenshit,* I said to myself. *What a chickenshit!* And I was taken back in time a few months to my spin training, when I had to force myself to remount my horse. Is courage—in this case no more than a willingness to face an exceedingly modest physical risk—innate or learned? It certainly isn't innate with me and even less so for a sensible man in his sixth decade, but slowly I was learning to extend my calcified middle-aged envelope, although a little voice inside me kept shouting, *"Don't do it, stupid!"*

Pilots, I would come to learn as my odyssey unfolded, constantly face this tension, trying to decide between apprehension that is grounded in good judgment and dread that's nothing more than fear of the unknown. All pilots hear two inner voices: one that counsels caution and another that declares confidence. The second gains strength only with experience. If, however, a pilot ever stops being afraid of what could happen, he could die, and that was much on my mind that afternoon. I think Debby would have felt better about my enterprise if she had known about this duality. It demonstrated, at least, that her husband was considering the risks he was taking, not just forging ahead cockily like a teenager who thinks himself invincible.

*     *     *

In 1911 American railroads boasted far more trackage than they do today, and trying to stay on the same line sometimes was like trying to follow the course of a single strand through a plate of linguini. The undeniable fact that from the air, one railroad track looks much like another caught up again with Cal Rodgers on September 22.

After staying overnight at Hancock, he scrambled aboard *Vin Fiz,* its skid repaired, fired up a cigar, and took off for Binghamton, thirty air miles west. Near Susquehanna, Pennsylvania, sixteen miles from Hancock, the Erie tracks cross the old Delaware & Hudson main line at the famous stone Starrucca Viaduct, a grail for rail buffs the world over. While the Erie follows the north bank of the Susquehanna west to Binghamton, the old D&H line dips south to Scranton, Pennsylvania. Rodgers cut over a hill, took the wrong track, and followed the D&H south. When several coal mines hove into view, Cal realized that he wasn't where he was supposed to be—he knew there were no mines near Binghamton. He landed in a rolling field, and when a crowd materialized, he learned that he was in Throop, just outside Scranton, forty-five miles south of Binghamton.

This time the unruly multitude gave him real concern. It descended on *Vin Fiz* intent upon collecting souvenirs, one woman armed with a screwdriver. Clearing the field was a problem, too— the spectators simply did not understand that an airplane needed several hundred feet of level ground over which to gather speed and leap into the sky. This turned out to be a severe predicament at many of the stops during Rodgers's trip. He may have been inexperienced and ignorant about the subtler requirements of aviation, but the crowds that watched him had no idea of the basics. At last, early in the afternoon, a weary Rodgers managed to shoo the horde back far enough so he could take off. Finally in the air, he followed the Delaware, Lackawanna & Western main line northward through the broad Salt Lick Creek valley past New Milford and Hallstead and then landed at Great Bend on the Susquehanna River, hard by the Erie tracks where his chase train waited impatiently.

After sweatily departing White Birch, I followed the Susquehanna, which meets the Delaware River at Hancock, to the spot where Rodgers took the wrong turn. The D&H line Cal followed to Throop was abandoned long ago, but much of the roadbed is still visible from the air. I traced it south of Susquehanna as far as I dared toward Cal's landing spot before turning away to avoid fouling the tower-controlled Scranton/Wilkes-Barre airspace. I had chosen Seamans Airport near Nicholson, just north of Scranton, as my touchdown spot, representing Cal's field in Throop, and found it handily with the aid of the chart. Seamans was a yuppie airport, groomed and kempt, fairly busy with large single-engine Bonanzas and small twin-engine Barons, flown by well-dressed professionals from the northern Scranton suburbs. Everybody was busy tending to his own business on this Sunday afternoon, and no one seemed much interested in conversation. I shrugged.

After downing a Diet Pepsi, I headed back aloft and followed the old Lackawanna main line, paralleling Interstate 81 directly north to the Susquehanna River. Several sailplanes were out and about, soaring on the afternoon thermals that made bumpy conditions for me. Even low mountain flying, I was learning as I traversed this outpost of the Appalachians, is different from flatland aviation. The bumps are harder, especially when a small airplane goes over a ridge; hitting an updraft feels like bottoming out in a deep pothole on a city street.

At Hallstead I dipped my wing over Spring Farm, where my parents live in a 190-year-old house atop a grassy knoll easily visible from the air, and did the same over Carl's Flats of Great Bend on the Susquehanna flood plain across the river, where Cal had landed to meet the chase train. I had hoped to land at a grass airstrip three miles farther west on the Susquehanna at Kirkwood, New York, and then make my way back on the ground to Carl's Flats. Those flats used to shelter a dairy farm in whose barn I had played as a boy and are now overgrown with shopping centers and gas stations on both sides of Interstate 81. There's no room today to land an airplane, even one as primitive as *Vin Fiz*.

An interesting historical coincidence, however, lies there. On almost the very spot where *Vin Fiz* rolled to a stop at Great Bend, my great-great-great-great-grandfather Dominicus ("Minna") Du Bois had owned a tavern and a ferry that carried travelers across the river during the first decade of the nineteenth century, when Susquehanna County was frontier country. According to family lore, he was a Revolutionary War sergeant who had been captured and imprisoned in the mountains of Wales until the war was over. He founded the Du Bois homestead on the south bank of the river in what is now Hallstead, where Mother and Dad still live in the ancient, drafty farmhouse he, or perhaps a son, is said to have built. Ever since I was a boy, I have taken pride in the Du Bois family and its homestead, and my long family history has given me a kind of emotional rootedness in a deracinated age. Visiting my parents a couple of times a year always gives me a sense of going home.

Oddly enough, the Du Bois family someday may be best remembered for a slave Minna had owned and to whom he had given his name. A couple of years ago, our family learned of a new edition of a century-old book we had never heard about: *Silvia Dubois, A Biografy of the Slav Who Whipt Her Mistres and Gand Her Fredom,* by C. W. Larison, M.D. The book was a facsimile of an 1883 volume of the transcribed reminiscences of a black New Jersey tavernkeeper. It was written in an almost unreadable phonetic alphabet invented by Dr. Larison, who was both a crank and a polymath, hence the odd spelling of the title. Thoughtfully, the modern edition—part of Oxford University Press's *Schomburg Library of Nineteenth-Century Black Women Writers*—has been "translated" into standard orthography.

Sylvia, Dr. Larison said, was 115 years old when he interviewed her. (She was actually about 94.) "I've lived a good while," she told him, "and have seen a good deal, and if I should tell you all I've seen, it would make the hair stand up all over your head." It did mine, for it is a remarkable book about a forthright, high-spirited, and courageous woman.

She was big—in her prime, Dr. Larison said, she stood five feet ten inches tall and weighed more than 200 pounds—and "was known to be the strongest person in the settlement, and the one who had the greatest endurance." By the time Sylvia was fourteen, she had learned to manage Minna's ferry for traveling hunters and traders "as well as any one could, and I often used to ferry teams across alone."

Sylvia remembered Minna with a fondness not only surprising but also horrifying in our age. "I got along with him first rate," she said. "He used to let me go to frolics and balls and to have good times away from home, with other black folks, whenever I wanted to. . . . I tried to please him and he tried to please me and we got along together pretty well—except sometimes I would be a little refractory, and then he would give me a severe flogging. . . . He never whipped me unless he was sure that I deserved it." Minna's wife,

Elizabeth, however, beat Sylvia capriciously and regularly. "Why, she'd level me with anything she could get hold of—club, stick of wood, tongs, fire-shovel, knife, axe, hatchet, anything that was handiest—and then she was so damned quick about it too."

One night, in Minna's tavern before an audience of drovers, boatmen, and hunters, Sylvia's mistress struck her once too often. "Thinks I," Sylvia said, "it's a good time to dress you out, and damned if I won't do it. I set down my tools and squared for a fight. The first whack, I struck her a hell of a blow with my fist. I didn't knock her entirely through the panels of the door, but her landing against the door made a terrible smash, and I hurt her so badly that all were frightened out of their wits, and I don't know myself that I'd killed the old devil."

Minna had his fill of the battling between his spouse and his slave. Rather than punish Sylvia, he manumitted her, and she and her young child set off for New Jersey, where the rest of her life was long, eventful, and free.

As I soared over Carl's Flats, I mused on the irony of posterity: The Du Bois family was at best a historical footnote, but their slave had achieved a kind of literary immortality. And how many of us would have the courage, as Sylvia did, to seize the moment and free ourselves?

Unfortunately for these historical resonances, the grass strip at Kirkwood had closed just a few months before. I pressed on another twenty river miles, following the undulating twin ribbons of the old Erie and the Susquehanna at 1,500 feet past Binghamton and its principal airport, tower-controlled Link Field. I set down at Tri-Cities Airport at Endicott, where I had started that morning. Not a solitary well-wisher showed up for my arrival—except Mother, who was waiting to take me back to the family homestead for the night.

That was good enough for me; one mother is worth a thousand gawkers. Especially this one, who not only taught me to speak and lip-read after I lost my hearing, but also encouraged me to test the world about me. When she learned that I was a student pilot, she was delighted. Her brother is a retired Panagra and Braniff pilot, and a son-in-law—my sister's husband—holds an air-transport rating and once was a salesman for Cessna and Mitsubishi. Judith Du Bois Kisor once was afraid to fly—it took copious infusions of dry sherry to get her aboard a DC-7—but flying in small planes with her relatives enabled her to overcome the phobia. In her early eighties she is unafraid of risk; she still rides her horse nearly every day, even after a bad fall a couple of years ago, spinal surgery, and the onset of vertigo associated with advancing age. She has flown with me. Our first flight was short; looking down from *Gin Fizz*'s windows stirred up her vertigo, and she asked quietly to return to the airport. In subsequent flights, however, she felt more comfortable. Ironically, Cal Rodgers's mother hated his flying and often grumbled and carried on from the chase train, while his wife, Mabel, loved it and encouraged her husband all along the route of his epic flight. More than once I have twitted Debby about this fact.

After relating the adventures of the day to Mother and Dad at supper on the farm, I slept the night through under the sky Cal Rodgers and I had shared eighty-four years apart, dreaming about the ghosts of forebears and of Sylvia, who may have been the doughtiest of them all.

# 7

ate in the afternoon of September 22, 1911, the city fathers of Elmira rang the fire bells when they heard that the birdman was on his way. At Binghamton forty air miles east, Rodgers had landed for a short interlude to let the crowds see *Vin Fiz* close up while he dutifully pitched Armour's grape drink to them. Crowds spilled into Elmira's streets to look for *Vin Fiz* as she approached from the south. Cal touched down on the fairgrounds without notable incident, except for an exchange with a young girl who was the first to greet the aviator. According to the Elmira *Star,* Rodgers asked her, "This Elmira?"

"Yes," she said, but it was only the nod of her head he understood, the paper said, for Rodgers was "quite deaf."

"How do you get across that river?" he then asked, and it was only after a bit of backing and filling that he was made to understand that what he saw was a pond, not a river.

That night Cal went to bed in a posh Elmira hotel weary and somewhat upset after a day battling throngs as well as winds. "It wasn't exactly dangerous," his byline account in the Hearst papers declared, "but when you lose your way, wander about 105 miles out of your way, have to fight off a bunch of hysterical people who want to tear up your machine as souvenirs, have to get up with willing but unskilled assistance, and then have to go looking for your own special train toward dusk—well, I've had enough to keep my mind occupied for one day." He didn't know the half of it.

\*     \*     \*

My adventure at Elmira was far cheerier. Early in the planning I decided to land at Elmira/Corning Regional Airport, a tower-controlled airport that is busy enough to be the center of what pilots know as a terminal radar service area, or TRSA in aviation lingo. Typically, a TRSA is a circle of airspace twenty-five miles in diameter through which airplanes that are flying by instrument flight rules are vectored by controllers who watch their progress on radar screens, and pilots who are flying by visual flight rules can request radar service if the controllers' workload permits. I can fly through a TRSA without establishing radio contact, but I cannot land at the airport in the center of the TRSA without contacting the tower. But I knew that a light-signal landing would offer an end-run around the problem. So, on Monday I pulled out my TTY and made a relay call to Elmira Tower.

"Hello, I'm a deaf pilot," I typed. "I'm calling to ask clearance for a light-gun landing at Elmira this morning."

"OK," came the answer from the tower, so quickly that I surmised light-gun landings are commonplace there. "What's your ETA, your N-number, aircraft type and color, and from what direction will you be coming?"

"Fourteen hundred hours Zulu," I said. "I'm November five-eight-five-niner-Echo, a Cessna 150, silver and blue, and I'm coming from November One Seven," the airport code for Tri-Cities Airport at Endicott, almost directly east of Elmira.

"We'll give you clearance at the proper time," said the controller. "Active runway is Two-Four, and the winds are six knots from two-two-zero. Watch for the light signal, and we'll be looking for you."

"What about a transponder squawk code?" If I was flying into a TRSA, I might as well be identifiable on radar.

There was a brief pause. "Squawk zero zero two six," the controller said.

"OK," I replied. "I can speak, and I'll use the tower frequency to tell you when I enter the airspace. See you in about an hour."

After kissing Mother good-bye, I climbed into *Gin Fizz* and immediately dialed 0026 on the transponder. That number would appear underneath the blip on the radar screens at Elmira, and the controllers would track me all the way in as soon as I was within range. That reassured me; a TRSA is, by definition, a busy place, and I'd feel more secure if the controllers not only were able to divert other blips away from mine but also knew that 0026 was the deaf pilot coming in for a light-signal landing. Sometimes it's hard for them to distinguish one airplane from another just by eyeballing.

At 9:30 A.M. I took off into the haze. The visibility was lousy, just five miles, but good enough for a short cross-country flight into airspace where ground radar controllers could vector other airplanes away from *Gin Fizz*. I felt comfortable during the twenty-minute flight along the old Erie from Endicott to Elmira, even when I spotted a tall radio tower on the mountain ridge just south of the airport, right in my path and scarcely half a mile away. I wasn't startled; the obstruction was marked on the chart, and I had been looking for it. I banked around the tower, and almost as soon as I cleared the ridge, announced my presence to the control tower, and descended to landing pattern altitude, I saw in the tower windows two dim green flashes that meant "Approach for landing." As I flew past the tower on the downwind leg, a controller flashed me the steady green signal—also dim, but a little brighter than the first. I touched down in the best landing I had made so far during the trip, and as I taxied toward the nearest off-ramp, I looked about for the attraction that had prompted me to land at Elmira: the world-renowned Schweizer Soaring School.

I couldn't find the turnoff to the school—Elmira/Corning is a *big* airport; its main runway is 7,000 feet long—so I taxied over to the terminal, where I shut down as a burly attendant carrying a hand-held radio walked out to the plane.

"Where's the glider school?" I asked as I opened *Gin Fizz*'s door.

"Away on the other side of the field," he said, pointing to a few low buildings and a copse of trees, by which a couple of sailplanes rested on the grass.

"Look," I said. "I'm deaf, and I've just come in with a light-gun landing."

"I know," he said with a smile. "We all heard the tower warning the other planes about you."

"Well," I said, "I've got to go over to the school. Would you mind calling the tower for me and asking them for clearance to taxi over?"

"Oh, sure," he said, speaking into his radio. "Tower says start your engine, point your plane at it, and wait for the green light." I did so, and a moment later, when the green signal flashed, I scuttled across the main runway, being sure to stop to look in both directions even though I had clearance—a little extra caution never hurts—and rolled onto the taxiway toward the sailplane school, where I had made arrangements to take my first glider flight.

"Sorry I'm late," I said when I arrived. "I never get lost in the air, but I get lost on the ground all the time." The sailplane instructor, Shane Lese, was a personable twenty-three-year-old elementary school physical education teacher and the son of Sally Lese, the school's director. The Leses belong to the Schweizer family, famous in soaring circles the world over. Shane had been soaring since age thirteen.

"Shane, I'm a propeller-head," I began. "I fly airplanes with engines. You fly airplanes with no engines. Tell me, what's so great about flying an airplane that has no engine?"

He grinned. This clearly was a question he'd heard thousands of times, but he answered it patiently. "Oh, it's just so totally different. You don't have to listen to engine noise. You don't have to deal with gas. You don't have to deal with electronics. It's a much freer type of flying. You're more like a bird."

Not only is sailplaning a purer form of flying than being pulled (or pushed) around the air by an engine, Shane said, but also controlling a glider is considerably different from controlling an airplane in one important way. When either a glider or a powered airplane banks into a turn, a phenomenon called "adverse yaw" causes the nose to turn momentarily in the direction *opposite* that of the bank—but if the bank is held, the nose will follow the wings into the turn. Using the rudder to help the nose turn with the wings will prevent adverse yaw before it gets started. Yaw is much less pronounced in a powered airplane because the engine provides thrust against the yaw. In a sailplane, however, "you have to use more rudder," Shane said. "With power, you can almost fly with your feet off the pedals and not really worry about the rudder. Not with sailplanes."

"The thing that makes me nervous about flying a glider," I said, "is that if you botch the landing, there's no way to do a go-around and try again. You have no engine. You have to do it right the first time. Is glider flying therefore more dangerous than power flying?"

"I don't believe so," Shane said. "You wouldn't send anybody up solo in a powered airplane unless they could land consistently on the same spot. Sailplanes are the same way. You have to land consistently before we let you solo."

I had thought that landing a glider might be inherently safer than landing an airplane because, I assumed, a glider landed more slowly than an airplane of the same size. I was wrong. A glider touches down at about forty-five to fifty miles an hour, the same as a Cessna 150.

"It may feel like it," Shane said, "but in gliders, landing speeds are not that much slower. You actually have an advantage with the 150 in that you have flaps, so you can land at a slower speed. We don't have flaps. We have dive brakes. So our stalling speed still increases instead of going down. We have to keep our speed up."

"What do dive brakes do that flaps don't?"

"Flaps increase lift. Dive brakes don't increase lift. They just disrupt the flow of the air over the wings, creating turbulence, which creates drag, which brings us down."

Thinking of how many hours it took before Tom Horton allowed me to fly alone, I asked Shane how many hours it takes the average sailplane student to solo.

"We don't figure by hours, as you do in power planes," he replied. "We go by number of flights—and the average student needs maybe twenty-five to thirty flights to solo." A typical lesson lasts only fifteen to twenty minutes. Power-plane lessons typically last an hour, with the first solo coming at the fifteenth or twentieth flight. Doing the arithmetic in my head, expecting that some sailplane flights would last an hour or more, I deduced that the actual time spent before soloing in both sailplanes and powered aircraft is much the same.

"How much flight experience do you have, Henry?" Shane asked.

"About three hundred hours," I said. He looked a little surprised, as if he didn't expect such a low-time pilot to be flying across the nation alone.

"Three hundred hours? You'll be able to handle a sailplane. You'll do most of the flying. I'll just make minor adjustments and corrections to what you're doing to help you fly a little bit more smoothly."

A thought intruded: I had learned to fly in a side-by-side two-seater, but we were going up in a tandem-seated sailplane, in which the instructor sits behind the pilot. We would be strapped in; I would be unable to turn around to read instructions on Shane's lips. I wished I had brought along a small mirror and a little Velcro or a suction cup, as a veteran deaf sailplane pilot I know had done when he learned to fly. With the mirror he was able to read the lips of his instructor in the rear seat.

"If you want to take over from me," I asked Shane, "what will you do? Tap the rudders?"

"Ah," said Shane, who obviously had already given the matter some thought. "I'll just tap you in the middle of the back if I want you to take the stick. If you're flying and I want the stick back, I'll tap you in the same place. If I want you to turn right, I'll tap you on the right shoulder. For a left turn, the left shoulder. OK?"

So simple and sensible did the plan seem that I asked, "Have you taught a deaf person before?"

"No," he said.

"So this may be an experience as interesting to you as it will for me," I said.

He chuckled. "Yes, it will."

"One more thing," I said. "I know there's a towrope release in the front of the glider. I presume you will be in control until we reach soaring altitude. Since I'm up front, you want me to pull it, is that right? Or do you reach over my shoulder and pull it yourself?"

"Nope, there's a second release in back with me," he said.

Still one more detail had to be addressed. "OK," I said. "Maybe when it's time to come down, you should take over because you have to deal with the radio." Shane nodded. Even the gliders at Elmira/Corning must carry radios to tell the tower of their intentions.

We walked over to the glider—a Schweizer 2-33 trainer—and Shane explained the controls and the instruments to me. The instruments were few, simple, and familiar to a power pilot: an airspeed indicator, an altimeter, and two rate-of-climb indicators (one more sensitive than the other). The most important instrument, Shane said, was the piece of colored yarn fluttering from a short standard on the nose. It served the same purpose as the yarn on the forward strut of *Vin Fiz*. The yarn was a yaw indicator that tells the pilot whether the sailplane is going through a turn smoothly or slightly sideways, slowing down the craft.

We watched as a Piper Pawnee crop duster towed other sailplanes off the short turf strip paralleling Elmira/Corning's main runway. In the beginning of the takeoff, a ground crewman ran alongside a glider, holding one wing level—the sailplane carried just one wheel under the fuselage—until the glider picked up enough speed for the ailerons to bite the air and keep the craft level.

Shane and I climbed into our sailplane and strapped ourselves in. He closed and latched the bubble canopy, and I immediately began to sweat as the sun baked the cockpit into an instant oven. The ground crewman hooked the towline onto the nose, and in a moment the towplane taxied slowly away until the slack was taken up, at which point the pilot gunned the engine. The plane and glider started the takeoff roll together. It was extraordinarily bumpy but mercifully short—and within seconds we were climbing in a wide circle above the airport. At 2,000 feet, Shane yanked the cable release with a soft jolt, freeing the 2-33 to soar on its own.

He headed for a mountain ridge, hoping for a thermal of warm rising air, but it was hard to find on an overcast day. Suddenly, I felt a gentle tap in the middle of my back, then one on the right shoulder. I grasped the stick, turned it to the right, and added what I thought was plenty of right rudder. Nope. The yarn yaw indicator blew sharply to the left; the sailplane was slipping into the turn, its nose coming around too slowly. I pressed harder on the rudder pedal. Now the yarn blew to the right, indicating that the nose was skidding into the turn. As I put the 2-33 through its paces, keeping the yarn straight was difficult, and the rudder pedals needed far brisker footwork than with *Gin Fizz,* which needs just a touch of pedal in a gentle turn.

For the first time, I began truly to appreciate the aerodynamics of a coordinated turn, the heart of flight. I had never given it much thought—I had just done what the instructor had ordered, letting the physics take care of itself. But as I had gained experience in flying, I had begun to understand the science of aviation—the immutable physical laws that enable a heavier-than-air machine to free itself from the ground. Now this was something new for a journalist whose education and work experience had been almost entirely in literature and the arts. In those things, one intuits from knowledge and experience, an informal process that can be messy and even chaotic. In aviation, one deduces from observation and data, a formal undertaking that is precise and methodical. The immutable physical laws of aviation had forced me to exercise the other side of my brain, sharpening all my thought processes and even making me more aware of my surroundings.

For instance, reaching the simple decision whether to take off on any given day involves much more than just looking up at the sky, seeing the sun, and saying, "Let's go flying." First, the pilot obtains a weather report. He wants to know both the present conditions and those in the near future. How high will the clouds be? How thick? Is the visibility expected to change, and when? What will the wind direction and velocity be, not only on the ground but also at 3,000 feet, 6,000 feet, and 9,000 feet? How will all those things affect his time aloft? Do the airplane's tanks contain enough fuel to reach his destination in those conditions? There are many, many more items of data that the pilot must absorb and integrate into his calculations. Aviation is a technical discipline, and as I digested its lessons over the months, I became curious about natural phenomena in the atmosphere that surrounds me and how things exist and function inside it. I have said that flying took me outside myself, that it allowed me to live for a short while without the worries of work and home. Flying also filled that vacuum with an engrossing new way to look at the world.

The orderly nature of flying even had made me a sharper, more attentive driver. All those months of taxiing along a ramp, keeping the Cessna on the yellow line—a drift off the centerline would bring a sharp elbow in the ribs from Tom—helped remind me to keep my Toyota centered in the lanes of the interstate. Those months of learning to anticipate turns in the air had sharpened my turns on the road; I no longer tended to drift into the outside lane, as so many drivers do, when making a right or left turn at an intersection. Glancing at an airspeed indicator every few seconds had made me more conscientious about keeping the Toyota speedometer nailed on the limit. I had even become a better defensive driver, watching for traffic and anticipating what it might do. Learning to handle an airplane's yoke with a light touch, executing maneuvers gracefully, had made me a smoother driver as well, gentler with the clutch and shift lever. (You can tell if a driver is also a pilot by two clues: if he grasps the steering wheel with his left hand only at eight o'clock and if he has a large "whiskey"—spirit-filled—compass on the dashboard.) In many ways, embracing aviation in my middle age had burnished youthful skills that had grown rusty.

Two years of flying had also made me mellower behind the wheel. Like so many competitive, short-fused Type-A American men, I have (to Debby's utter dismay) tended to react hotly when the idiot in a Buick in the next lane cuts me off just to show who's boss or a young cokehead in a Corvette slaloms through dense traffic at ninety miles an hour, nearly nailing my right-front fender. I'd curse, lean on the horn, flip the bird, and cut down the offender with an imaginary Uzi. But now I just shake my head in resigned dismay and drop back a little, giving the misguided soul plenty of room to display his infantility. Most of the time, anyway.

Perhaps absorbing the meticulousness of aviation simply had rounded off the rough edges of my driving, but I also had become more relaxed, less anxious, and less consumed with the cares of work and home in the two years I had been a pilot. A happier man is a happier driver.

We found a small thermal, and the sensitive climb indicator—called a variometer—showed a sudden jump, the other climb indicator following it more slowly, the needles pointing upward until we ran out of thermal at 2,800 feet. Shane constantly stayed in touch on the radio with the tower, for the airport was very close by. He was right: Sailplaning is a purer form of flight, vibration-free and quiet except for the whoosh of air from the nose ventilator, wide open against the heat of day. It did not seem as if we were at peace with the elements, however; at that low altitude close to the airport, we had to scan the sky for traffic as well as glide along ridges looking for thermals. We were just as busy as a pilot and instructor in a Cessna 150. This was, I thought, hardly flight at its most elemental. Perhaps a veteran sailplane pilot could achieve oneness with the atmosphere, but this was not a day for it.

Soon we began to descend, and a series of taps on the shoulders guided me back toward the airport. We had been up scarcely fifteen minutes when I felt the "I've got it" tap in the middle of the shoulder blades, and I raised my hands, signifying my surrender of the stick. Shane banked the sailplane into a descending spiral, and in a few minutes we lined up with the grass runway—a bit high, I thought. Then the dive brakes opened, and I surged forward slightly against my harness. The glider dropped rapidly, and near the threshold Shane closed the brakes and guided the craft smoothly to a landing. The touchdown was startlingly bumpy over the rough ground, but Shane kept the glider upright until its ground run had almost stopped. Then one wing settled to the ground grandly, the sailplane reclining like a noble Roman on one elbow at a banquet.

As Shane signed a brand-new logbook for me, recording my first twenty-minute soaring flight, I felt myself ennobled as well. Not a bad day, I thought, for an overweight middle-aged flatlander. I wasn't going to become a sailplane pilot—I already had my hands full learning to be a good propeller-head—but it was not just one more memory in the kitbag to pull out for my future grandchildren's amusement. Incrementally, the experience had made me a better pilot.

It was time to go, and after checking the weather on my laptop, I asked Shane to call the tower on his handheld radio to request clearance for takeoff. "Tower asks if you'll take off from the taxiway intersection instead of going all the way to the threshold of Two-Four," he said. "You've got almost 3,500 feet of runway there." That was more than four times the length *Gin Fizz* needed for takeoff, and I nodded. Some pilots would have declined the offer, insisting on using the full 7,000 feet of runway against the remote chance of an engine failure on takeoff, but I was growing ever more confident in my airplane—and, besides, the Big Flats of the Chemung River Valley are so broad that even in the event of a stopped engine, I could have found a smooth spot to alight upon. As soon as I approached the runway, I saw the steady green light from the tower. Turning onto the runway, I "firewalled" the throttle—thrust it forward to the stop—and was away into the haze, bound for Hornell, forty-two miles northwest.

By contrast, Cal Rodgers's departure from Elmira showed that he had learned little from his debacle at Middletown. Again he nearly met disaster for having failed to scout the terrain thoroughly. The field was small and the ground soft, flanked by a pond on one side and a tree-lined bluff on the windward end. The soft earth slowed *Vin Fiz*'s takeoff roll, and Cal had barely cleared the trees on the bluff when a gust momentarily caused his airplane to lose a bit of altitude, just as he saw telegraph wires dead ahead. He chose to go down, rather than into the wires, and *Vin Fiz* skidded to a stop just nine inches from a tree and three feet from the ledge of the bluff. The airplane, however, was only slightly damaged—some bracing wires had been sprung—and within a few hours the wires had been repaired and Cal was away.

Bad luck then piled atop bad judgment. On the way to Hornell, two of his four spark plugs popped out, and Cal had to push them back in with his right hand, holding them there while he flew with his left. That was a distinctly uncomfortable way to fly, so he decided to put down at Canisteo, four miles southeast of Hornell, for repairs. As he made his landing approach, he had to take his right hand off the engine to work the steering levers, and the engine stopped, causing *Vin Fiz* to make a hard landing and slide down a hill. The impact crumpled the lower wing and catapulted Cal out of his seat into a wing brace, causing a small cut. As his mechanics worked through the night to repair *Vin Fiz,* Cal slept in a Hornell hotel, and the next morning he took off for Olean, forty-two miles southwest.

My flight to Hornell, however, stirred no juices, except for the terrain below. These were the higher rolling mountains of the western Allegheny Plateau, and towns stood fewer and farther apart. As I flew on, I checked to the right and left constantly, sizing up fields below as possible emergency landing sites, as the careful pilot always should—and as I hadn't always done; southeastern Wisconsin is so full of airports that it's a poor pilot indeed who can't find an airfield within gliding distance if his engine cuts out at 4,000 feet. Finally, a few miles in the distance, I saw Hornell Airport and curved away from the roadway.

As *Gin Fizz* approached the airport, I saw no planes on the ground, and the runway seemed almost impossible to distinguish from the raw earth around it. Then the huge earthmover parked spang in the middle of the place leaped into view. There were no large painted *X*s on the thresholds proclaiming the airport unusable, because there were no thresholds—in fact, there was no runway, just a long gouge in the earth. Hornell was closed, obviously for the rebuilding of its runway. I was startled and puzzled. Although I had downloaded the weather on my computer that morning, I didn't recall seeing a "notam"—a Notice to Airmen from the FAA—declaring Hornell out of service.

But it was. Since I had plenty of fuel, I simply banked southwest and followed the railroad through the mountains to Wellsville and then turned west to Olean, where I put down at Cattaraugus

County Airport, seventy-five miles west of my takeoff point at Elmira. The place was almost deserted, with just three parked planes visible, and nobody out and about except the FBO manager. "There was more activity this morning," he said with a shrug, as he refueled *Gin Fizz*.

Hornell indeed was shut down for rebuilding, he confirmed, as I took the laptop inside for a weather update. I keyed in Hornell as a waypoint, and sure enough, the notam was listed: Airport 4G6—the code for Hornell—was closed. I kicked myself mentally for not studying the notams more carefully at Endicott and Elmira; what if I had flown a long distance and had been low on fuel before I arrived at Hornell? True, an alternate airport, Dansville, was close by, just twelve miles to the north. But I couldn't make this mistake in the Southwest later in the trip, where airports sometimes are hundreds of miles apart. I felt embarrassed for having judged Cal Rodgers to be a careless pilot because he didn't check his surroundings. In a more modern fashion, I'd made the same mistake.

Just before I left, the FBO manager said, "By the way, I couldn't understand you on the radio. Too much static. You sure that radio is OK?"

"I think so," I said. But I wasn't sure *I* was OK. Like many deaf people, I occasionally raise my voice unintentionally, especially under stress or in a noisy environment—at least, an environment in which the presence of powerful vibration suggests noise. The 100-horsepower engine three feet in front of me provided plenty of throbbing. When I jack up the volume on my larynx, the plosive consonants—*P*s, *T*s, and *K*s—tend to crackle noisily, and the pitch of my voice becomes unnaturally high and nasal. Over the radio the result can be—and often is—loud static.

If I remember to hold the mike an inch or two away from my face, the static diminishes markedly, but the mike then picks up outside noise from the cabin, especially the roar of the engine. There's a happy medium that's difficult to find when you can't hear yourself speak. Perhaps I'd been speaking much too loudly, unconsciously trying to overcome the noise of the engine. Now it was my turn to shrug, as *Gin Fizz* and I left for Jamestown.

Shortly after takeoff at Canisteo, Rodgers ran into a stiff and gusty headwind, the turbulent breeze causing *Vin Fiz* to rock sharply from side to side, and he had to struggle to keep the bucking plane on course and at altitude. He passed Wellsville and headed on to Olean, where he completed the twisting sixty-five-mile trip along the Erie from Hornell in a strenuous two hours and thirteen minutes. After landing he fired up another cigar and downed a quart of fresh cream—his refreshment of choice all across the country—while his mechanics refueled the tanks. Early in the afternoon, he was off again, bound for Jamestown, thirty-seven air miles west.

Just past Salamanca, almost halfway to Jamestown, *Vin Fiz*'s magneto—the small generator that shoots jolts of electricity to the engine's spark plugs—acted up. Cal decided to put down immediately and landed on a farm that was part of the Seneca Indian reservation at Red House. The mechanics tumbled off the chase train and made the necessary repairs, and in midafternoon Cal was ready to take off. One account reported that two Indians offered to take down a pair of barbed-wire fences along a farm road at the end of the takeoff run to afford *Vin Fiz* a bit of breathing room, but Cal impetuously declined the offer, declaring his airplane up to the task without help. On the first two takeoff tries, the long grass of the field grasped *Vin Fiz* by its skids, refusing to let her into the air. On the third try, the engine faltered, and when Cal tried to jump the plane into the air by suddenly yanking back the stick, it refused to cooperate, instead throwing itself into the barbed-wire fences. The impact shredded *Vin Fiz*'s wings, struts, and skids and splintered its propellers.

Cal was not hurt, but *Vin Fiz* was well and truly shattered. The extensive repair job took two days while the Dayton factory sent new parts. On the third day the task at last was done, but rain and wind kept Cal on the ground. In the interim he drove to Jamestown and spent a night there to meet his growing public. Not until September 28—a beautiful sunny day—did he take off from a different field at Salamanca, and he overflew Jamestown on his way to Meadville, Pennsylvania.

Today a small grass airport lies four miles northeast of Salamanca, but it is unattended and has no fuel for itinerant airplanes. I chose to skip it and land on the substantial Chautauqua County Airport at Jamestown, where I could not only refuel but also find a taxi to a nearby motel for the night. Jamestown is a good-size small city, and its airport is correspondingly large, with two jet-capable 100-foot-wide runways—one 5,300 feet long and the other 4,500 feet long. Several commuter flights take off and land there every day, and so do cargo haulers. It is, however, an uncontrolled airport, and I could land there without requesting clearance.

I taxied up to the United Jet Center, the only FBO at Jamestown, and shut down amid a clutch of big twin-engine airplanes, some of which were corporate jets. Two large Cessna Caravan turboprop aircraft with Federal Express markings sat in front of the FBO, awaiting loading. *Gin Fizz* was by far the smallest airplane on the ramp; I felt intimidated, like a water boy at a linebackers' convention. I was not treated like one, however.

The pilot of a twin-engine Baron noticed me fussing around *Gin Fizz,* hopped off the wing, and walked over. I had been distractedly rearranging baggage inside the cockpit, looking for a fourth battery for my handheld GPS. I had kept the GPS switched on since Endicott, just in case I lost the railroad line in the haze.

"Need anything?" he asked.

"Not really," I said, "but thanks for asking. I do need a double-A battery for my GPS. Do you know if they sell batteries at the FBO?"

"I got one," he said, climbing back into his plane and rummaging in the rear, coming up with a single battery. He handed it to me casually and brushed away my thanks, as if slightly offended that a fellow pilot would think gratitude was due for such a simple act. He walked to the FBO and disappeared.

"Going on or staying?" asked the young attendant at the FBO, where I had dragged my meager luggage. I looked up from filling out my logbook. The place clearly catered to corporate and short-haul cargo pilots, with clean carpeting and several new overstuffed couches. This was no scruffy grassroots pilot's lounge.

"Staying," I said. "Can you recommend a nearby motel?"

"The Comfort Inn four miles down the road," he said.

"Jamestown have a taxi company?"

"Yeah, but you can take our station wagon and keep it for the night," he replied. I started in surprise. He had the map to the motel all drawn and the keys in his hand. Mine was a sorry little old airplane and only a twenty-dollar tank fill for the United Jet Center, barely worth the effort. Yet he treated me with the same generous civility as he would the pilot of a $500 jet-fuel fill, even to entrusting the center's courtesy car to me for the night. Many FBOs, big and small, look upon pilots of especially small airplanes as an unprofitable pain in the neck, but the United Jet Center clearly had a soft spot in its heart for the itinerant grassroots aviator. The attendant had no idea who I was or what I was doing, just that I was a transient pilot standing down for the night. Today, I thought, the Brotherhood of the Right Stuff, or something like it, had asserted itself.

General aviation is full of down-home American neighborliness like that, and I have experienced it countless times. Once I noticed that *Gin Fizz*'s nosewheel tire was a little low. Since the FBO was closed for that day, I couldn't borrow its bottle of compressed air, so I set to with the automobile tire pump I keep in the trunk of my car. Somehow, rather than pumping it up, I managed to deflate the nosewheel completely. Damn!

While I was gazing forlornly at the tire, a fellow from the hangar next door walked by. He was a gypsy aviation mechanic, one who hired himself out for a few months, then moved on to a new town. "Trouble?" he asked. "Um," I said, pointing at the nosewheel. "No flying for me today." "Be right back," he said. In a few minutes, he returned with a rolling air compressor, inflated the tire, meticulously checking the pressure—critical if the nosewheel is not to shimmy on takeoff—and dusted off his hands.

"I am much obliged to you," I said. "What do I owe you?"

"Nothing," he said with a small wave. "Have fun."

"Hey . . ." I said. "Thank you very much. I do appreciate this."

He smiled. "No problem," he said. And then he turned and rolled the compressor back to his hangar. He had given me ten minutes of his thirty-five-dollar-an-hour time, gratis.

And so I wound up at the Comfort Inn in Jamestown, the first of a score of wayside hostelries I would frequent during my trip. It was fated that I would become a reluctant expert on motel-and-fast-food strips all across the United States. Tonight I would share with scores of yammering families not only the Comfort Inn but also a Bob Evans restaurant next door, where I smiled amiably at the manager, who wore a string tie with a blue button-down shirt, as if to announce that his neck enjoyed the best of two cultures. The roast turkey was rubbery and the mashed potatoes tasted like newsprint, but I was too gratified by the day's events to care.

One more task remained before I went to bed: to close out my flight plan. Most pilots who are flying short cross-country hops by visual flight rules do not file official flight plans with a FAA Flight Service station. A flight plan outlines the route; the takeoff time and estimated time of arrival, or ETA; the type, identification, and color of the aircraft; and other such information. Flight plans are not required, although the FAA encourages them. The point of a flight plan is to let somebody know who you are, where you're going, and when you expect to get there, so if you don't show up, rescuers will go looking.

Official flight plans are a chore, however, and must be "opened"—activated—before departure and closed out upon arrival. Most pilots radio Flight Service to do so just before takeoff and landing, and a few call on the phone afterward. If a flight plan is not closed within half an hour of ETA, Flight Service will begin calling airports along the route of the plan to see if the plane has put down unexpectedly and after a while, will mount a search by air. A pilot who forgets to close out his flight plan can cause expensive inconvenience to a lot of people, and in blatant or repeated cases the FAA will take the pilot to the woodshed. ("There are two kinds of pilots," I have been told, in one of aviation's many "two kinds" aphorisms: "those who have forgotten to close flight plans, and those who will.") In my case, I cannot radio to cancel a flight plan, and if I arrive at an unattended airport, neither my laptop computer nor my TTY will work with the usual pay phone. If I can't find anybody to phone for me to cancel the plan, I'm in trouble.

Hence I'm like most VFR pilots: my "flight plan" is a simple call to my spouse to let her know where I'm going and another to let her know that I've gotten there. And so I called Debby with TTY and relay and told her I'd arrived in Jamestown, as planned, and would go on to western Ohio the next day, probably Marion. We exchanged our news of the day—I did most of the talking, of course—and then hung up. While Debby, I suspect, called all her friends and relatives to assure them I had not yet killed myself, I went to bed, for the second consecutive night much pleased with myself and with humanity in general.

# 8

et fog grayed the dawn as I swept back the curtain. After bacon and eggs at Bob Evans—I will treat myself to an artery-stopping breakfast just a couple of times on a trip; high-cholesterol guilt keeps me from overindulging—the first task of my day was to decide whether to take off and if so, when. I turned the television to the Weather Channel, gazing with concern at the animated national map as a line of yellow, red, and purple blotches signifying regiments of thunderstorms marched east from Indiana. After downloading the computer weather to my laptop, I saw that the forecast for the next eighteen hours promised better than VFR minimums most of the day: broken clouds 1,500 to 2,000 feet above ground and visibility of five miles. The VFR pilot must stay at least 1,000 feet above clouds, 500 feet below them, and 2,000 feet from them horizontally. Visibility must be three miles or better. The forecast wasn't great, but it was good enough for the short low-altitude hops I was making, and likely I could reach western Ohio by early afternoon before having to take shelter against the boomers. It was a go, as soon as the fog lifted.

By 10 A.M. the mist had dissipated, and *Gin Fizz* and I took off, bound for Meadville, Pennsylvania, sixty air miles southwest. I climbed to 1,200 feet above the old Erie line and, just to be safe in case pockets of ground fog obscured the terrain (tendrils of it still smothered low valleys), I turned on both the GPS and loran, dialing in Port Meadville Airport as my destination. As *Gin Fizz* crossed the northwestern corner of Pennsylvania in the calm, cool morning air, the rolling foothills of the western Alleghenies began to smooth out below, like a rumpled bedsheet tugged at one end.

I recalled that Cal Rodgers had also enjoyed smooth air on his hop from Salamanca to Meadville in 1911, a modest tailwind pushing him over 104 snaking miles in 106 minutes. His landing at Meadville was routine, and he absorbed a quart of cream and smoked a fresh cigar while his mechanics dismounted from the chase train and refueled *Vin Fiz*. But back in the air, it dawned on him that he and the mechanics had forgotten to refill the engine's oil sump at Meadville. Cal and his crew had not yet mastered the art of sweating the details. He decided to land at Warren, Ohio, thirty-eight miles southwest of Meadville, to replenish the oil.

As I shut down *Gin Fizz* at Port Meadville Airport, I watched as two Cessna trainers danced a touch-and-go ballet, as common to airports as a plié is at a barre. The field was otherwise placid. I did, however, spot a young man by the self-service fuel pumps preparing his Bonanza for departure, his two young children sitting obediently on the grass close by, demurely playing with a toy truck and car. On the face of one child were the unmistakable features of Down syndrome, and the other lovingly shepherded her in their play. Maybe, I thought, there was a story here. I approached the father and went through my brief rigmarole about deafness and lipreading. Then I asked if he had a few minutes to chat. He replied pleasantly enough, as if I were a familiar local pilot, "Sorry, I'm behind schedule already. Next time, OK?" No one could take offense with that response, though I regretted missing a potentially interesting conversation. We exchanged waves as he bundled his children into the Bonanza—they clearly were veteran little fliers, buckling themselves expertly into the rear seat—then climbed in and was off to the east.

I topped off *Gin Fizz*'s tanks. After only forty minutes in the air, they didn't need replenishment. But taking off with full tanks never hurts, and the act of refueling an airplane often provides an opportunity to chat with the locals. Spending money at a FBO sometimes loosens tongues, too. I walked to the FBO and tried to strike up a conversation with the manager, but he merely grunted, more concerned with the accounts spread before him than with an itinerant top-off, but he did ask if I needed oil or anything else. Though Meadville is an agreeable-enough airport, it did not look as if it would yield any stories that day, so I departed for Warren in the fertile flatlands of the Great Lakes Plains, where Rodgers's otherwise decent landing was spoiled by an unseen ditch that caught and snapped a skid into flinders. *Vin Fiz* otherwise was undamaged, and this time the crowds came running with pies and cakes, rather than screwdrivers and scissors. They were bent on feeding the birdman, not picking his airplane to pieces.

I landed at Skeet's Airport, three miles west of Warren, after carefully keeping to the north of the old Erie main line, to avoid nicking the controlled airspace of Youngstown-Warren Regional Airport. The wind had picked up a bit, with moderate crosswind gusts, so I had to fly *Gin Fizz* all the way down to the surprisingly narrow twenty-five-foot-wide runway, instead of letting her glide softly to a touchdown. After the wheels kissed the pavement, I became aware that the runway was lined by tall trees, a thick copse squatting just past the windward threshold. The day had grown hot and humid, and I knew that taking off in an almost fully loaded, underpowered training airplane from this runway was going to scare me, even though I had 2,600 feet of rolling space.

The blacktop of the runway and ramp was in fine shape, as was the rest of the airport, I saw as I taxied up to the mobile home that served as the FBO. Skeet's is a classic country grassroots field, neatly kept with no litter, its five long hangars freshly painted. The only evidence of privation seemed to be the tattered wind sock, just shreds of cloth on a circular frame. This field looked almost like a throwback to the 1930s, and I half expected a Travel Air biplane to emerge from around a hangar, its pilot in a leather helmet, goggles, and long silk scarf. The place was deserted, however, except for a sixtyish man on a tractor mowing the turf along the runway.

I dismounted as he came by, and we entered the mobile home together. "What kind of aviation goes on here?" I asked, fishing the usual pilot's lunch from the vending machines—Diet Pepsi and peanut butter crackers—and wishing farm wives had come running up to me with pies and cakes.

"Not much," he sighed. "Too much regulation. Too expensive. Local people won't support the airport." Again for the next few minutes I heard the familiar litany against lawyers and the government, one that I would encounter a dozen times or more on my trip across the United States. As I climbed back into *Gin Fizz,* I hoped that pristine little airfields like Skeet's could hang on into the next century.

Meanwhile, a more pressing moment of truth lay at hand. I looked at that narrow runway with the tall trees at the end and cautiously did a little pilot's arithmetic on my flight computer. The runway at Skeet's is 2,600 feet long, and the elevation is 905 feet. Now, according to *Gin Fizz*'s manual, at sea level and a "standard" temperature of fifty-nine degrees Fahrenheit, a fully laden Cessna 150 requires 1,205 feet of runway to clear a 50-foot obstacle at the other end.

At a 2,500-foot elevation, the manual says, the plane needs 1,440 feet of runway to vault that 50-foot peril. So to get the runway required at Warren's 905-foot elevation, I split the difference between 1,205 feet and 1,440 feet, rounding it off to 120 feet. I added that 120 feet to the sea-level requirement, coming up with 1,325 feet of runway required to clear a 50-foot obstacle. So far so good.

But there was more. The temperature was about ninety degrees that day, and it was oppressively humid. Air grows thinner with heat and moisture, lessening its lifting capability. I added the manual's recommended 10 percent per thirty-five degrees Fahrenheit increase in temperature. The result was a rounded-off 1,460 feet of required runway.

But that was not all. A crosswind blew at about ten miles per hour, not bad but enough to affect the straight-ahead physics, so I added another 10 percent to that 1,460 feet, getting 1,606 feet of runway.

Was that enough? No. These are ideal figures for a new airplane with a new engine. *Gin Fizz* was thirty-six years old, and her engine had been overhauled several times. I added still another 10 percent for age and came up with 1,766 feet.

And to be absolutely sure, I added one more 10 percent chunk of distance just because I was an inexperienced and still chicken-hearted pilot. That made 1,942 feet of runway needed to clear the trees at the other end. I still had more than 600 feet of breathing space. There was absolutely no reason *Gin Fizz* couldn't take off.

Fortified by the courage of mathematics, I used the classic short-field takeoff technique Tom Horton had taught me at West-osha. First, I lowered the flaps ten degrees, so their added lift would help *Gin Fizz* come unstuck from the runway earlier and climb a little more steeply. Then I rolled out on the runway as close to the edge of the threshold as I could get, pointed the nose down the center line, locked the brakes, and ran up the engine to full revolutions. Engine roaring, brakes released, *Gin Fizz* slowly—all too slowly!—gathered speed, like the old, blown-out Indian motorcycle in which I once owned a quarter share at college, and lifted off well past the halfway mark of the runway. At the far end the tops of the trees seemed to lunge for the wheels like the claws of a forest of green monsters, but I am sure there was plenty of daylight, as there had been when I scared six months off my life expectancy two days earlier at White Birch Field. This time, however, I stayed cool. I was learning to trust the numbers, to put my faith in the technology of aviation.

In 1911 Rodgers had planned to spend the night at Akron, but the short delay at Warren to fix *Vin Fiz*'s broken skid meant that he would arrive over that large industrial city, center of the nation's rubber-tire production, in the dusk, as well as the pall of smoke from the factories, which would obscure his view of the fairgrounds where he planned to land. Wanting to get down before dark, Cal turned back seven miles east to the small town of Kent, where he had seen a likely field, and landed easily in a dairy pasture, welcomed by a solemn crowd of cows.

That evening he dined with Charles Seiberling, vice president of Goodyear Tire & Rubber Company, which had made *Vin Fiz*'s fabric and tires. Seiberling asked Rodgers the reason for so many deaths in aviation; the early pilots never seemed to live long before they perished in crashes. Cal responded, "Foolhardy feats. If aviators would confine themselves to straight flying, the death list would be cut down considerably." Later Seiberling would have reason to consider that an ironic answer.

That night a powerful storm scoured northern Ohio, forcing Rodgers's mechanics to turn out in the dark to keep the tarpaulin protecting *Vin Fiz* from flapping itself to pieces. They and a number of helpful spectators stood shivering in the wet all night on the loose ends of the tarp. The storm had not lifted by the following morning, and Cal decided to take the day off. Finally, early in the morning of September 30, *Vin Fiz* took to the air from Kent.

I had planned to land at Kent, too, and have a look at the airport belonging to the university—Kent State—that had figured so prominently in the history of my generation, where in 1970 nervous National Guardsmen shot four students to death, ratcheting up the consequences of protests against the Vietnam War. But as I climbed away from Warren, I saw towering cumulus clouds—harbingers of thunderstorms—gathering in the west. Were the boomers coming through earlier than the morning weather forecast had predicted? It looked that way. A hearing pilot could have called Flight Service on his radio for a weather update, but I could not do that. Chiding myself for not having dragged out the laptop at Warren for an update, I decided to land immediately at the nearest airport, Portage Liberty, about eight miles northeast of Kent, and check the forecast. There I had an encounter that badly rattled my romantic notion of the Brotherhood of the Right Stuff.

Inside the FBO, I was trying to figure out how to operate the weather computer—it gave not aviation forecasts but agricultural weather reports, which are similar but arranged in a different and unfamiliar format—when I felt hot breath on my neck and an arm snaked over my shoulder. A hand started pressing buttons on the keyboard before me. For an instant, I thought someone was trying to help me, but when I turned around and looked up into the scowling face, I realized the truth. I was being shouldered aside by an impatient pilot who no doubt had shouted at me from behind that he was in a hurry and, receiving no response, decided to arrogate matters to himself without explanation or by-your-leave. I pushed myself from the table angrily and backed away in a cloud of consternation, past a woman who shot me an embarrassed smile. In a few seconds, the pilot was finished and, taking the woman by the hand, strode roughly past me out to his airplane—a fast and expensive Mooney—waiting on the ramp. Not a word was said.

*Bastard,* I thought fiercely. I stalked over to the counter, intending to ask who the hell that pilot thought he was, but the attendant immediately ducked into his office and closed the door. The few other pilots in the room averted their eyes and walked gingerly around me, as if I was some sort of leper best dealt with by pretending he was not there. There was no use trying to explain; I would only have been apologizing for someone else's rudeness. In my mind, I began a list of airports that I would never visit again and at the head of it wrote "Portage" in large bold letters. But I did return to the weather computer, intending to wheel about and snarl at the first person to repeat that act of rudeness. Nobody came near me, however, and in a few minutes I had determined that at least three hours remained before thunderstorms would erupt in central Ohio. I departed in a dark cloud of resentment, with a picture in my mind's eye of Ted Robinson smiling sadly and saying, "I told you so."

As *Gin Fizz* climbed away from Portage and my anger dissipated, I began to chuckle at myself. An erudite friend once called me a "counter-Jansenist," sending me to the encyclopedia to see whether that was a compliment or an insult. Cornelius Jansen was a seventeenth-century Dutch heretic who held that human nature is incapable of good. In truth I am not Pollyannish enough to believe that ours is a reasonable and just world. Still, I have encountered so many pockets of generosity and decency, especially in the vast American heartland, that I just cannot help taking an optimistic view of the essential goodness of ordinary people.

This notion helps me cope with the consequences of my deafness. Time and again, even today, I encounter the prejudice of ignorance. Hearing people who meet deaf people for the first time often treat them with a standoffish mixture of pity, embarrassment, and horror. The curious and good-hearted often want to reach out, to communicate, but haven't the slightest idea how to do so and worry that their efforts will be misunderstood. The hostile (they are thankfully few) may simply reject the humanity of the deaf, as that fellow at Portage seemed to have done.

Still, when I make the effort to meet a hearing person halfway, to demonstrate that we *can* communicate with a little effort, we can enjoy the event—and often do. The simple expectation that a hearing stranger will be friendly and accommodating often serves to bring those qualities to the surface. Presenting a cheerful, guileless, and open face to the world, I have found, more often than not brings results. Yes, these can be patronization, suspicion, indifference, and even hostility, but less so than one may expect. It is true that getting older has made this notion harder for me to hold. Sometimes the game seems just not worth the candle. In the imperfect community of aviation, however, having something in common can help anybody bridge differences—most of the time.

In any event, I forgave Portage, choosing to believe that the episode was the exception that proves the rule. Besides, the offensive pilot may have been an itinerant himself, not a regular, and perhaps the attendants and other pilots were as upset and embarrassed as I was over the incident. A year later I landed at Portage to refuel while flying east to visit my parents, and a sweet-faced young female line attendant topped off *Gin Fizz*'s tanks with an endearing smile. I stopped in again on the way back, to the same pleasant welcome.

My mood had brightened considerably on the short eight-mile hop from Portage to University Airport at Kent, but I decided not to tarry there. Not only was Tuesday never a big flying day anywhere, but also it stood to reason that a college airport would be quiet during summer vacation. I did wonder, however, whether the university's aviation program thrived in that part of the country, where few airports seemed to be active. I regretted that I was not coming through on a weekend. I did a simple touch-and-go at Kent just to leave my mark on top of Rodgers's, and pressed westward.

In a few minutes I carefully threaded the five-mile-wide throat between two big tower-controlled airport areas—the giant Cleveland Hopkins International and the smaller Akron-Canton Regional—and glided into the vast farmland of central Ohio, where the low Great Lakes Plains abut the gently rolling Till Plains that form the easternmost part of the rich Corn Belt stretching westward. After departing Kent, Rodgers had circled Akron at 1,000 feet just to thrill the crowds and show off the product for Armour, but I couldn't do that, of course, because of the controlled airspace. Like Cal, I headed west toward Mansfield, seventy-two miles away, where he had landed to refuel before pressing on thirty-two miles farther to Marion. Mansfield is a small controlled airport, and though I could have called ahead for a light-gun landing, there was no reason to stop there other than because Rodgers had done so. I planned to do a touch-and-go at Galion Municipal Airport, just nine miles southwest of Mansfield, and call that my Mansfield stop.

All afternoon, however, the wind had grown increasingly gusty and bumpy. As the sky in the west darkened and the clouds billowed higher and higher, the gusts at 2,500 feet became so powerful that my left arm ached from holding the plane straight and level. I decided to climb higher, to 4,500 feet, to see if I could find calmer air. I chose that altitude because visual flight rules specify that a plane cruising higher than 3,000 feet above the ground on a course to the west of a north-south line must maintain an altitude above sea level in even numbers plus 500 feet—4,500, 6,500, 8,500,

10,500 and so on. Airplanes cruising on a course east of the north-south line fly at odd-numbered altitudes. But the headwinds at 4,500 feet, just below the broken cloud deck, were even stronger than those at 2,500 feet; the GPS reported *Gin Fizz*'s ground speed at only sixty-five miles per hour. Westbound traffic on Interstate 71 below zipped along under my wing, pulling ahead of my slow little airplane. As I descended and ran into even harsher turbulence, I decided it was time for a precautionary landing before the wind became more than I could handle.

The nearest field was Ashland County Airport, right on the old Erie line. Rodgers had flown past Ashland without landing there, but any port in a storm—especially before the storm, if there was to be one. That was a serendipitous choice. There I ran into a pilot who evidently not only believes in the Right Stuff but also shares it with everybody who comes to his airport: Doug Schoonover, the thirty-year-old chief flight instructor and general manager of the Ashland FBO, Johnston Aviation.

Over a cup of coffee in the lounge, he listened with interest as I explained my project and patiently answered my questions about the state of general aviation in his corner of Ohio. His airport serves mostly pleasure pilots and students, he said. Three of the fifteen active student pilots are his, but managing the place naturally takes up most of his time. Schoonover is an Ashlander born and bred; he grew up on a family farm nearby, but like so many, it eventually had to be sold.

"I'm making the same amount of money I did a few years ago," he said, "but the cost of living has gone up. I went to real estate school, and now I sell real estate—houses—on the side to make ends meet." He blamed the downturn in grassroots flying on the familiar *bêtes noire:* overregulation, inflation, and a stagnant local economy. He had hopes for the future but knew the trend is against him.

By about 2 P.M. the wind had diminished slightly. Schoonover had to test-fly a fuel-pump repair on the FBO's Piper Arrow and asked if I'd like to go along. Among lightplanes, the powerful low-wing, four-seater Arrow is known as a "complex" airplane because it has retractable landing gear and an adjustable-pitch propeller; it is light-years ahead of *Gin Fizz* in sophistication. I didn't need to be asked twice. After takeoff, Doug handed me the controls and told me to take the plane to 3,000 feet. I was surprised at the heaviness of the controls and the muscle it took to hold the rudder against the powerful engine torque in the climb. I realized suddenly how small, delicate, and underpowered my little Cessna is, especially when I experienced the aplomb with which the Arrow shouldered its way through the turbulence that had caused my plane to twitch and flutter all over the sky. Hither and yon I flew in bliss, wishing I was wealthy enough to afford a "real" airplane like the Arrow.

In the lounge afterward, I told Doug my concern about being understood on the radio. "Let's try it out," he said, and we spent an hour experimenting. "Ashland traffic," I'd say, sitting in *Gin Fizz* on the ground with the engine idling. "Cessna five-eight-five-niner-Echo entering downwind for Runway One-Eight." Doug sat in the FBO listening to the office radio, giving me thumbs-up and thumbs-down signals through the window. With a bit of trial and error, we determined that though I was speaking loudly enough if the mike was held six inches away from my face, the mike was also picking up extraneous noise. If I moved the mike closer to my face, the same pitch and volume of my voice would distort the vowels and my consonants would explode and crackle. If I held the mike close, almost kissing it with my lips, and spoke *softly,* the transmission would come in more clearly. Unfortunately, this was only a temporary solution and, as I discovered later, it worked only with the engine at idle, not at noisier cruising revolutions.

Later in the afternoon, Doug asked his mechanic, "Shall we loan him the Suburban?" As the mechanic nodded, Doug turned to me and said, "Can you drive a car?"

I burst into laughter. "I've been flying an airplane across the country for a week—what do you think? *Of course* I can drive a car!" The mechanic laughed and Doug looked sheepish. I wasn't surprised, however. People with no knowledge of those who do not hear often assume wrongly that automobile drivers need to be able to respond to emergency sirens, car horns, and other aural warnings that they take for granted. It doesn't occur to them that the wail of the oncoming hook-and-ladder isn't going to make a dent on the consciousness of a hearing driver with his windows rolled up and Pearl Jam blasting from the stereo. Doug shrugged and handed me the keys.

After pitching camp at the local Travelodge and refueling my person next door at a Perkins Family restaurant—Bob Evans in a green suit—I closed out my day's flight plan on the phone with

Debby and settled down with an Ed McBain, glancing from time to time at the Weather Channel. That evening, the powerful thunderstorms that had been gathering all day finally erupted over central Ohio, dumping so much water that the National Weather Service issued flood warnings for the area. At 8:30 P.M., worried that *Gin Fizz* might have been dented by hail or bent into a pretzel by high winds, I drove the Suburban back to the airport. The airplane had leaked a little through the wing roots—there were damp spots on the interior headliner—but nothing was damaged. The mechanic emerged from his house nearby, and together we gazed at the towering cumulus of the storm cloud miles away, its anvil top spotlighted red by the setting sun, its flat bottom black as if it had been grilled over coals. It was a beautiful sight against the darkening blue of the eastern sky, but the lightning flashes in its belly reminded me of its danger. Back at the motel, I snapped out the light at 10 P.M., after the Weather Channel convinced me that I'd be grounded at Ashland all the next day, as Rodgers had been at Kent in 1911.

The following morning I slept until 6:15. That's late for me, for I invariably rise with the cows, a habit ingrained after years of early-morning moonlighting as a freelance writer before going to my day job. After a quick bite of the ubiquitous free motel breakfast—Danish, juice, and coffee—I turned on the laptop and checked the weather. More thunderstorms loomed on the forecast, but they were to be scattered and arrive mostly late in the day, and with southwest winds at twelve miles per hour forecast into noon, there was nothing that morning that I couldn't handle. Outside, the sky sulked iron-gray, but with a high ceiling and a light rain. Perfectly adequate conditions. Marion was just forty minutes west, and I ought to be able to make it handily. I lifted off at 7:30 A.M. and skirted the Mansfield controlled airspace, keeping to the south. Doing the planned touch-and-go at Galion, all but deserted at that early hour, I headed for Marion. I flew through gentle rain, a little nervously because I was worried about visibility, but as long as I could see through to the other side, I knew I'd be all right. By the time *Gin Fizz* reached Marion, the wind had kicked up to a gusty fourteen miles per hour, but I made as good a crosswind landing as I'd ever done, slipping smartly into the wind as I held the nose down the runway with the rudder.

It had been twenty-five flying hours since *Gin Fizz* had last been serviced, and I taxied to Baron Enterprises for an oil-and-filter change, a plug cleaning, and replacement of a burned-out landing light—I don't use the landing lights to find my way through the dark on runways, since I don't fly at night, but just to make my airplane more visible in the landing pattern. Baron's chief mechanic, Bob Reid, a neat, compact man in his sixties whose neatly pressed work clothes were grease-free—rare for an aviation mechanic—rolled *Gin Fizz* into the hangar while I trotted off to the airport terminal.

There I had a brief chat with Dan Stover, the airport manager, who said expansively—he clearly takes pride in his town—that business at Marion Municipal was up in the last few years. An increase in light manufacturing, plus the presence of the headquarters of General Telephone and Electronics, meant a good deal of aviation activity, half business, half pleasure. I noticed a couple of Bonanzas on the ramp and a big twin-engine Navajo taking off, and that seemed about as much action as I'd seen at any airport in the middle of the week.

A large copy of an old press photo of the *Vin Fiz* landing at Marion hung on Stover's office wall. "There's a pretty good model of the *Vin Fiz* in the Marion Historical Society," he said, so naturally I had to rent a car to go see it. At the society a tiny woman in her eighties with Coke-bottle-thick spectacles and blue-rinsed hair patted me warmly on the hand and apologized for not knowing sign language. "That's all right," I said, "I don't know it either, but I read lips. Could you tell me about that airplane hanging up there?" It was a six-foot scale model of *Vin Fiz* with a tiny figure of Cal Rodgers at the controls. The detail was splendid, but I noticed that no cigar hung from the model pilot's mouth. Of course, that would not have been a good example for the generations of schoolchildren who doubtless passed under the model, oblivious to its significance. "I'm a pilot myself, and I'm retracing Cal Rodgers's route from coast to coast. I just landed this morning."

"You did?" said the elderly woman pleasantly. "Well, that's *nice*." Suddenly she launched, as if programmed, into a long, well-practiced history of Warren Gamaliel Harding, Marion's most famous citizen. Non sequitur it may have been, but her spiel was surprisingly polished and kept me rapt, even though I was not at the museum to learn about President Harding. I would like to have learned more about Rodgers's importance to the town, but I got the distinct feeling that in the history of Marion, Ohio, he was little more than a footnote, even to pilots.

Deciding to take the day off and catch up on my notes while *Gin Fizz* was serviced, I checked into the local Travelodge and spent a couple of hours at the laptop. Later in the afternoon, I returned to the airport to check on the plane.

"Your plugs looked pretty good," said Bob. "How long had it been since they were last done?"

"About 100 hours," I said.

"Not bad," he said approvingly, gazing at the engine. "Been burning much 100 octane?"

His question was not an idle one, for the issue of aviation gasoline is crucial for owners of older airplanes. This is nothing like the issue that faces automobile owners: Will burning high-test gas—89 or 93 octane—in cars built to run regular 87-octane unleaded gas damage their engines? Of course not; burning expensive high-test gas just wastes money. The engines of older airplanes, however, were designed to run on 80-octane aviation gasoline, which contains little or no added lead. The high-compression engines of light-planes built since the 1970s, however, are made for 100-octane "low-lead" aviation gasoline—something of a misnomer, for 100LL avgas contains more than four times the amount of lead allowable in 80-octane fuel.

When older engines like the 1950s-era Continental O-200 model in *Gin Fizz* are operated on 100LL, the excess lead tends to end up as thick deposits on the spark plugs and sometimes on the exhaust valves. These lead deposits cause rough running and can even damage the engine if the plugs are not removed for the lead deposits to be cleaned off them every twenty-five hours or so of operation. The problem can be lessened by using a lead-scavenging potion called TCP, or tricresyl phosphate, a few ounces of which I mix into the 100LL at every fill-up, plus careful leaning of the fuel-and-air mixture in flight, and a brief run-up at a high idle before shutting down. But these are not complete solutions. Frequent plug cleaning and occasional but costly valve polishing are necessary to keep an 80-octane engine running healthily on 100LL. Most airports in the United States have found it uneconomical to offer both 80-octane and 100LL aviation gasoline, so they keep only the latter on hand.

A few airports offer 87-octane automobile gasoline, which an older engine can burn happily and legally, provided the airplane has been certificated for it. One has to be careful, though, that the autogas is pure; the alcohol that is often added to automobile fuel in many localities tends to dissolve important nonmetallic engine parts, such as carburetor floats. A damaged carb float can cause a sudden engine failure and make life "very interesting," as pilots like to say in their understated way. Autogas, however, is a good deal cheaper than aviation gas—often two-thirds the cost—even at the inflated prices of airport fuel pumps. Many pilots, especially in Western states where the practice is legal, weld 100-gallon tanks to the beds of their pickup trucks. They buy autogas at their corner stations at the street price and refuel their airplanes from their trucks. Those who have it the best are the flying farmers who purchase tanker truckloads of nontaxed agricultural gasoline and refill both their airplanes and tractors from large tanks in the barnyard. Illegal, yes, but who's watching?

And so I was pleased with Reid's comment about my spark plugs because I had been burning 100LL all across New Jersey, New York, and Pennsylvania; 80 octane is sometimes difficult to find in the East, though it is fairly common in the Midwest, where older airplanes congregate. Clearly, I had been doing the right things to keep my engine happy.

"What time are you gonna leave tomorrow?" Reid asked. "Early," I said, "as close to dawn as possible." He frowned. "There may be thunderstorms overnight, and we don't open till eight. If you can leave later, we can store the airplane in our hangar until then. No charge." I quickly accepted. Normally, an airplane can ride out a heavy rain on a tiedown, but with electrical storms there is always the possibility of hail, which if large enough can damage the soft aluminum of a lightplane. In such conditions, I always pay the ten dollars or so for overnight storage inside. It's cheap peace of mind.

At 8:30 the next morning, after refueling *Gin Fizz* at Marion's 80-octane pumps, I took off, bound for Indiana.

Rodgers landed at Marion the morning of September 30, 1911, to collect a prize from the city and show off the plane, and after lunch he left for Huntington, Indiana. Just after he crossed the state line, he noticed that his main fuel tank was running dry, and when he turned the cock for the reserve tank, gasoline failed to flow from it. He had to land to clear the blockage and put *Vin Fiz* down in a large field near the tiny town of Rivarre, Indiana. By the time the mechanics had fixed the cock, it was too late in the day to keep going, so Cal spent the night. It had been a good day for him—he had flown 205 miles from Kent, and his chief rival—Robert Fowler—had failed in three attempts to cross the Sierra Nevada from the west. Fowler's airplane simply did not have the power to scale the mountains. He conceded defeat and took his airplane to Los Angeles.

Her plugs fully cleaned and her oil reservoir replenished, *Gin Fizz*'s engine thrummed contentedly as we followed Rodgers's route westward. After Kenton, fifteen minutes west of Marion, the old Erie line suddenly petered out. The line at this point had been abandoned decades before, when Conrail—into which the Erie Lackawanna Railroad had been merged—cut back its routes. The roadbed remained in a few places, especially along ridged property lines, but, for the most part, it had been plowed over, leveled into the surrounding countryside. Still, the outline of the old right-of-way was visible from the air in a fuzzy but unmistakable line of a darker color cutting across the green of the crops below. It was like tracing the ghost of a railroad, and in my mind's eye I could see the apparition of a passenger train below, a turn-of-the-century Ten-Wheeler belching smoke as its goggled fireman waved up from the footplate at *Vin Fiz* following it a thousand feet above.

There is no airport at Rivarre. The closest one is Decatur Hi-Way Airport, about four miles north, and I banked toward it, using both the loran and GPS to pinpoint its location, because it is a grass field difficult to distinguish from the farmland surrounding it. Arriving directly over the spot marked *X* by the two electronic navigation systems, I circled slowly, searching for the runway. There were no airplanes on the ground, but I soon spotted the bright orange cones at the ends of the runway.

I taxied up to the FBO and shut down. As I opened the pilot's door, a tiny woman, white hair blowing wildly in the wind, arrived aboard a tractor, towing the brace of gang mowers with which she had been trimming the well-kept runway. Always moving, always talking, Josephine Ivetich Richardson, the owner and manager of Decatur Hi-Way Airport, displayed all the nervous energy of a sparrow on speed. I followed her into the office.

The office turned out to be the most singular one I have ever encountered. The typical FBO office-cum-pilot's lounge at a small air-field normally looks like a cross between an adolescent boy's bed-room and a small convenience store about to go out of business if it is not first shut down by the sanitation department. Fighter-plane posters and Piper advertisements cover the cracked walls. Dusty model airplanes dangle from the ceiling. Display cases carry radio headsets, quart bottles of engine oil, logbooks, sectional charts, fuel testers, carbon monoxide detectors, ear protectors, cleaners, polishes, waxes, operating manuals, and half a hundred more avia-tion-related items. A stained, weary overstuffed couch and arm-chair, littered with crumbs and mouse turds, usually complete the ensemble. The whole displays all the ambience of a small boy's clubhouse-in-a-tree, and a crude wooden poster emblazoned NO GIRLS ALOUD would not seem out of place.

But the "pilot's lounge" of Decatur Hi-Way looked like a country gift shop of particular eccentricity. Greeting me upon entering was an enormous chandelier made of cardboard egg crates and glass beads. "Made it myself," Josephine said. On top of a large display case lay a huge Bible, a stuffed opossum, and a cast-iron trivet pro-claiming MY GET UP AND GO GOT UP AND WENT. Inside the case were hundreds—no, thousands—of pine-cone decoupages and porcelain knickknacks, many of them religious in nature. Instead of a KEEP 'EM FLYING sign, JESUS NEVER FAILS adorned one wall.

In the equally cluttered back rooms, countless floor-to-ceiling shelves played parade ground to vast armies of bottles containing herbs, vitamins, and home remedies of the Shaklee brand, ordinar-ily sold door to door. A garage contained a large array of heavy-duty power tools, including a massive table saw. An add-on hangar held a Cessna 172 that, by the look of the dust on its cowling, hadn't been flown in many months, maybe years. It was the only airplane I saw at the airport, other than *Gin Fizz*.

Out of the hail of words from the five-foot-tall dynamo who presided over the place, I managed to put together the following: Born in Chicago in 1915 to Yugoslav immigrants, Josephine Ivetich learned to fly after her brother James was killed in a crash in the field across the road from their home. She bought her first plane, a Cub, in the 1940s, and became a well-known female pilot and Pow-der Puff Derby racer, finishing twelfth in the transcontinental women's air race in 1960. In 1977 she flew a leg from Bryan, Ohio, to Chicago during a reenactment of the first New York-to-San Francisco airmail flight by a private contractor in 1927. Josephine still hosts meetings of the local chapter of the 99ers, a women's aviation organization, at Decatur Hi-Way. She holds a commercial license—the next step up from the private pilot's certificate—with a helicopter rating, but has not flown in three years.

Josephine is a fierce environmentalist, a crusader against agrichemical pollution, which she calls "aerial landfills." She showered me with copies of clippings of her letters to the editor of the local newspaper decrying ground, water, and air pollution. "If the chemical gas cloud is too thick when you come over," she said, "just fly up and down the runway a few times to blow off the cloud."

She was also upset because the state of Indiana, she said, wanted "to take another fifteen feet off my runway." The runway is 2,562 feet long by 140 feet wide, a healthy size for a grass strip, but because of overhead wires along the roads that mark the boundaries of the airport, the thresholds at either end of the runway are deeply displaced inward, shortening the usable length by about 900 feet. Josephine feared that a loss of 15 more feet would "make pilots crash and make me liable."

She built Decatur Hi-Way with her own hands in 1955. "I bought twenty acres, and the man who sold it to me laughed when I told him what I wanted it for. 'Ho ho ho,' he said. 'That I got to see.' The farmer just east of me hated me because he wanted to buy the land for himself. I personally cleared out half a mile of trees on the east side and south end of my runway. In six months I built a home and a hangar and moved in as soon as I got the roof up. I had six jobs besides building the airport and slept not more than four hours a day." She worked in the local General Electric plant and did home-improvement projects for others, eventually building an entire house in a nearby town—she is something of a pioneer in the building trades as well as the aviation industry.

Josephine is an inventor, too, and proudly showed me an official-looking patent certificate for a large sparrow trap that catches fifteen birds at a time. Sparrows are a pest around airplane hangars, building nests in engine compartments and coating windshields with their droppings. Either gas them with auto exhaust or "let a cat in to finish them off as she does," said a news story. "It also catches mice," she said.

Josephine has other talents. She can, she declared, forecast the weather for a whole year and performs "circulatory treatments," a kind of massage intended to "restore energy" to the circulatory system. She dangled a pen from a string over my knees and knuckles, letting it trace a tight circular pattern. "When you do that over a certain part of the body," she said, "it'll show that you have energy. If it doesn't swing, you're losing energy. You feel weak and tired because of the chemicals in the air." Her massage treatments "follow the nerve endings on the limbs up from every part of the body." If one's circulation is poor, "you look around and see what's going on. See if your glasses need wiping. Around here, you have to do that if you feel weak, sleepy, or tired." If I stayed much longer, she hinted darkly, I might need treatments.

But I could not tarry, for I had to follow Cal Rodgers westward. After taking off, I noticed for the first time the dark band of pollution that covered the sky at about 5,000 feet that day. I have lived in it for many years and, of late, have flown through it, but it had seemed such a part of life that I never gave it a second thought. Now, however, my knees and knuckles were beginning to ache, it seemed to me. I checked my glasses to see if they needed wiping, and since they did not, I flew on to Huntington, twenty-seven miles west of Decatur Hi-Way.

# 9

ctober 1. The clouds were high, but the weather seemed clear enough for a take-off." And that was Rodgers's latest mistake. Anytime the weather conditions "seem" just "enough" for anything ought to raise warning flags in a pilot's mind. Judging from the description of the weather that day in eastern Indiana, Cal took off at 8:45 A.M. in marginal conditions into an approaching line of thunderstorms. Today, avoiding such squalls is easy enough; all a pilot needs to do before takeoff is check the weather at airports along his route. Cal could easily have had someone telegraph or telephone ahead from Rivarre to Decatur and Huntington to inquire about the conditions. Evidently, in his impatience to get going, he didn't. Modern pilots call this dangerous antsiness "get-there-itis" and are wary of it. It can kill you, and it almost killed Rodgers. It killed Commerce Secretary Ron Brown and thirty-four others in a crash of a military version of the Boeing 737 during bad weather at Dubrovnik, Croatia, in 1996. That same year it also killed Jessica Dubroff, a seven-year-old girl who was attempting to become the youngest person to fly an airplane across the United States, when her impatient instructor—who was the real Pilot in Command and indeed had done some of the flying—allowed a take-off in bad weather in an overloaded Cessna 177 at the high-altitude (6,156 feet) airport of Cheyenne, Wyoming.

As *Vin Fiz* neared Decatur shortly after takeoff, a forty-mile-per-hour gale slammed into the airplane. A storm lay dead ahead, and

Cal wrestled *Vin Fiz* into a tight turn to escape it, but flew into heavy rain and then a tempest of thunder, lightning, and swirling clouds. "Seated on the lower wing with no protection of any kind," Lebow wrote, "he struggled to keep the *Vin Fiz* steady and his goggles clear. When that became impossible, he took the goggles off along with his gloves which he used to cover the magneto. . . . On the ground, those who saw the little Model EX plunging, tossing, spinning, and bucking in the wind never expected to see the man reach the earth alive. At times, he disappeared from view, which increased the anxiety and suspense of his viewers."

The God that watches over fools, drunks, and low-time pilots had been with Rodgers that morning. Flying into a thunderstorm in a small airplane, even today, is nearly guaranteed death for a pilot and his passengers. Flying into a thunderstorm in a primitive string bag like *Vin Fiz* and getting away with it is unthinkable. Rodgers was extraordinarily lucky. He managed to set *Vin Fiz* down in a field near Geneva, eighteen miles off course to the south, without damage. News reports said he was calm and unruffled, unconcernedly smoking a cigar when the first bystanders reached him. "A motor can go through heavy rain, if you cover your magneto with your gloves," he was supposed to have observed, as if that was all he learned from his experience. He was probably in deep denial. I would have been pale and gibbering for hours.

After the storm passed in midafternoon, Cal took off, following an interurban track, and landed at Huntington, where the entire town turned out to cheer, as Lebow described it, "the gallant pilot who had survived a 'net of fire' and brought his machine safely through the storms that threatened 'to destroy his aeroplane in midair and dash him a thousand feet to the earth.'"

My arrival at Huntington Municipal Airport, of course, went utterly unremarked. After landing on its commodious runway, I left *Gin Fizz* in a queue of small planes before the fuel pumps and strode into the FBO for a cup of coffee. As I stood by the lounge's plate-glass window, I felt a vibration building in the air, gathering force and richness as its source approached, then shaking the whole building. It was something special, I knew, but what? It must be a powerful reciprocating engine. Then I saw it as it flashed low over the runway at nearly 200 miles per hour—a silver P-51 Mustang. My heart stopped. It does not take much to turn me into a small boy again, and immediately I was transported to 1945, when I worshipped the tall, tanned gods who flew against the evil Germans and Japanese and memorized reams of aircraft minutiae. A Mustang! Its numbers tumbled out of forgotten crannies in my memory. Built by North American Aviation and powered by a Packard-built Rolls-Royce Merlin engine of 1,650 horsepower, the same one as in the vaunted British Spitfire. Capable of 437 miles per hour at 20,000 feet, with a range long enough to escort bombers to Berlin and back. The finest all-around fighter airplane of World War II.

"Who's that?" I asked the attendant.

"Jim Shuttleworth," he said. "He rebuilt that airplane from junk. It's historic."

In a few minutes the Mustang had landed, and I walked out onto the ramp to watch as she waddled up the taxiway, her long nose hunting from side to side as the pilot, whose view ahead was blocked, swung the tail back and forth so he could see where he was going. As the Mustang pulled up by the fuel pumps and the pilot slid back the canopy, I saw that she was a two-seater, pilot in front and passenger in back. Her rudder was painted bright red, the legend "*Scat VII*" on her nose. Twenty-four tiny swastika flags adorned the fuselage below the canopy. A tractor trundled out from a large hangar next to the FBO, SHUTTLEWORTH emblazoned above the huge doors, and towed *Scat VII* inside, parking her next to another familiar airplane of the same era, a North American T-6 Texan trainer. The hangar was the neatest and cleanest I had ever encountered, the concrete floor freshly painted. This was, I realized, the lair of a special kind of pilot: a wealthy warbird devotee. On its walls hung an impromptu museum of old flight jackets, helmets, uniforms, and .50-caliber cartridge belts. In one corner sat an ugly jagged lump of iron, a piece of flak dug out from an aircraft damaged long ago. A silk escape map lay atop a glass counter.

"A word?" I said as Shuttleworth walked up. Briefly I explained who I was and my mission.

"Sure," Shuttleworth said, and we settled in chairs by a large metal desk along one wall of the hangar. Like many of the fighter pilots of World War II, he is a small, compact man. He is in his late fifties, his face ruddy from the sun. He is president of the large company that bears his name, a manufacturer of electronic and mechanical automation equipment for such companies as General Motors, IBM, and Hewlett-Packard. Shuttleworth has plants in Ireland and Japan, as well as sales offices in Belgium, France, and Germany, and, soon, in Malaysia. He is a rich man, and the size of his obsession seems proportional to his wealth. It certainly dwarfs mine.

His first airplane ride, in 1945, was in a T-6 like the one in the hangar, and he had grown up around aviation ever since 1946, when his father bought "a brand-new Ercoupe and flew it out of a little grass airport about ten miles from here." As youths, he and his younger brother puttered around with a little homebuilt airplane, but he did not start flying in earnest until an airline strike in 1966 cramped his business travel. "I bought a Beech Musketeer and then a Bonanza, which I flew in business over just about all of North America, Central America, and a bit of South America. I flew it to Gander, Newfoundland; and Point Barrow, Alaska; and to Caracas, Venezuela. Then I got an Aero Commander and then a King Air"—both twin-engine airplanes—"and then the Citation, which we still fly." I couldn't keep my eyebrows from rising. A Citation is a serious airplane, a multimillion-dollar business jet. This guy, who employs his own aviation mechanic, is no mere weekend pilot who lazily bores holes through the air of the nearby countryside. I felt very much out of my league.

Shuttleworth, however, will talk airplanes with anybody, even pilots of lowly Cessna trainers. "I bought the T-6 in 1986, and that's when I started really flying for fun," he said. "My son John, who is now twenty-three, and I taught ourselves to do aerobatics in the T-6. We learned rolls and loops. John's an excellent aerobatic pilot and flies formation with other T-6s at air shows.

"But I've always been in love with the big heavy warbirds. I almost bought a Mustang in 1968, but decided owning it wouldn't be good for the business. In 1991 my wife, who is also a pilot, remembered my dream and said we should buy one. We started looking, and we bought this one in 1992. It was a wreck. It had been converted into an air racer called *Vendetta* for the unlimited class races at Reno, with Learjet wings and a much modified engine that put out about double the normal horsepower. It was wrecked when the engine failed. When I bought it, it was in pieces."

This particular P-51 is a historic airplane. She is one of only two surviving Mustangs flown by an ace in combat during World War II—the whereabouts of the other is unknown—and was the personal airplane of the celebrated Robin Olds, who scored thirteen aerial victories and eleven and a half ground kills. Olds also flew in combat in two other conflicts—Korea and Vietnam, where he scored four more victories—and rose to the rank of brigadier general before retiring from the air force in 1973.

"See," said Shuttleworth, taking down a framed photograph from scores along the wall of the hangar. "This is *Scat VII* in 1945, General Olds taking off from Wattisham in England, not far from the Channel near Ipswich—434th Fighter Squadron, 479th Fighter Group, Eighth Air Force." Shuttleworth laughed. "After we rebuilt the airplane, General Olds had to get a private pilot's license to fly it.

"Here's another airplane Olds flew in Europe. Nine days after this picture was taken, he was hit by flak. It shot off his right flap, his right aileron, and blew off the ammunition door. That's when he got *Scat VII.* He had his last four kills in her, four out of the twenty-four the airplane eventually shot down."

Still another picture to show. "This is the crew chief, Glen Wold," Shuttleworth said. "We found him fifty years later, and he came over to see the plane when we put in the rebuilt engine. Here's Fred Hayner, the wartime painter who did the nose artwork. We found him, too, and he said he was seventy-three and might die before the airplane was finished. So he did all the artwork so that I could transfer it by computer to the airplane. But he's very much alive."

"This is my wife, Carol," said Shuttleworth, taking down another photograph. "She owns the airplane. She lets me fly it." He chuckled. Parts of the aircraft, he continued, had been rebuilt all over the country—"the wings in California, the hydraulics in Ohio, the engine was overhauled elsewhere, the painting done in Canada." The airplane had been converted into a two-seater TF model P-51, much like the ten original dual-control examples North American had built for the training of wartime pilots. That was not the only departure from her 1945 appearance.

"How come," I asked, "*Scat VII* is painted in an aluminum color, rather than left the original bare aluminum, as my airplane is?"

"Too much work to polish," Shuttleworth replied.

"Amen," I said.

"We put in a modern oxygen system, improved heating and cooling," Shuttleworth continued. "Our avionics are similar to those in the Citation. I wanted to make this the safest possible fifty-year-old airplane I could fly."

The rebuild, Shuttleworth said, required forty people and 20,000 man-hours.

"How much did it all cost?" I asked incredulously.

He pursed his lips. "I don't know," he said. "I never added it up. I made a deal with my wife. If she didn't tell me how much she spent on our daughter's wedding, I wouldn't tell her how much I spent on the airplane. One day I'm going to add it up, but my guess is $750,000 to $800,000."

"Jeez," I said. "What does your wife think of all this?"

"Mostly she likes it. Sometimes when Steve [his mechanic] and I work all night on the airplanes, she gets discouraged," he said with a laugh. "And if I go to too many air shows. . . . "

"What do you do with *Scat VII* at air shows?" I asked "Flybys?"

"Flybys, and we do strafing and bombing shows with pyrotechnics. With explosions, simulated bombs." Shuttleworth attends ten air shows each year, joining other warbird pilots in thrilling the crowds.

I asked how much fuel the P-51 burns. "About sixty-five gallons per hour on a cross-country cruise," Shuttleworth replied. I gulped. *Gin Fizz* burns less than five and a half gallons per hour. Aviation gas typically costs close to $2 a gallon. That means I'm spending a little more than $10 an hour on gas, compared to Shuttleworth's $130 an hour.

"That's the least expensive part of flying," Shuttleworth reminded me. "Insurance costs me more than twice that per hour. And the cost of maintaining the engine is extremely high."

"Do you give rides to itinerant pilots?" I asked hopefully.

"No," he said. "Too much liability risk. I give rides to foreign visitors, but only a few to Americans. But if you really want to fly in a Mustang, there's a company in Florida called Stallion that sells rides in them and teaches pilots to fly them as well. That's where I learned to fly the P-51. I spent a week there. The company also teaches navy test pilots how to fly and recover from unusual attitudes because the new navy fighters are all fly-by-wire; you can't *feel* the airplane controls."

"Why do you do it?" I asked. Shuttleworth gave the answer I expected, the one every warbird pilot offers. It is a deceptively simple sentence. In it is a regression into adolescence, as well as an expression of the desire to possess a piece of history. It is truly the heart of the whole expensive, exciting, and sometimes dangerous experience of owning and flying an old combat airplane.

"It makes a glorious noise," he said.

*       *       *

In her own modest and understated way, *Gin Fizz* also makes a glorious noise, I mused, as she climbed out, throttle wide open, from Huntington Municipal Airport and I set course for the next stop, Aldine, Indiana. This time, I used the loran for navigation, entering into the instrument the code of the airport nearest Aldine, Wheeler Field. The loran's liquid-crystal display told me that Wheeler was seventy-one miles from Huntington on a bearing of 291 degrees. Automatically, it counted down the miles, seventy, sixty-nine, sixty-eight, as *Gin Fizz* droned on. Another part of the display also warned me if I was off course, showing now 288 degrees, now 295. Staying on course by means of the loran was child's play compared to following the iron road, which no longer existed anyway.

For most of the way to Aldine the old Erie line was gone, plowed over long ago, and I amused myself trying to find the ghostly traces of the railroad. Six miles southeast of Wheeler, the tracks suddenly reappeared. The line was still abandoned, but here the rails, ties, and right-of-way had not yet been dug up and carried away. Even though it was early afternoon, the day was almost windless and the rising turbulence slight, the kind of day *Gin Fizz* seemed to love. She touched down on the grass at Wheeler in the kind of super-smooth landing all pilots try to make every time but manage only about once a year, always with nobody else around to appreciate their skill and finesse.

Cal Rodgers had no such luck the day he left Huntington—or tried to. On October 2, 1911, the weather was still unsettled, with a stiff wind flattening the grass on the Huntington fair grounds. Inexplicably, Rodgers decided to take off *downwind*—never a good idea in appreciable wind and an absurd one in a strong breeze. (Takeoffs and landings are made into the wind as much as possible, to slow down the airplane's ground speed and shorten the length of runway required. Taking off downwind increases the length and ground speed of the takeoff roll, dangerously so on a short runway or when there are obstructions to be cleared.) Worse, the crowd broke free and rushed onto the field as *Vin Fiz* approached, forcing Rodgers to bank into a grove of trees to avoid the spectators. Rodgers was thrown clear and uninjured, but once again his airplane was well and truly smashed. It was the third complete wreck of the enterprise, and by now, the mechanics were growing used to rebuilding the airplane. Not until almost noon of October 5 did *Vin*

*Fiz* finally get away, landing unplanned in a field of "wire grass" at Aldine when her reserve tank line clogged. That line repaired, the first takeoff in the clinging grass resulted in a snapped skid. Rodgers's crew then had the meadow mowed—it was about time they cottoned to that idea—and shortly before 5 P.M., too late to make Chicago before dark, Rodgers took off, headed for Hammond. Rodgers hoped to make Grant Park in Chicago by 11 A.M. the next day, but it was not to be; for the next two days, the fierce, biting wind Chicagoans call "the Hawk" swept in from the north, its talons pinning *Vin Fiz* and its entourage to the ground.

Just before noon on October 8, a fine day for flying, *Vin Fiz* soared in from Hammond over the south side of Chicago and touched down before a crowd of eight thousand people. Rodgers's stop was perfunctory, just a formality to meet one of the conditions of the Hearst prize—a landing in Chicago—and at 4 P.M. he was off again, bound for California. Only two days remained before the October 10 time limit for the prize ran out, and Rodgers knew that he had no chance of winning it. Yet he was determined to press on. A contemporary account, doubtless well spiced by the Armour publicity man, quotes him thus: "I am bound for Los Angeles and the Pacific Ocean. Prize or no prize that's where I am bound and if canvas, steel and wire together with a little brawn, tendon, and brain stick with me, I mean to get there. The $50,000 prize, however, seems to be practically out of the question. But anyway it doesn't matter much. I'm going to do this whether I get $50,000 or fifty cents or nothing. I am going to cross this continent simply to be the first to cross in an aeroplane." Whether or not those were his actual words, they certainly echoed his bulldog resolve. Rodgers may have lacked skill, judgment, and experience, but he certainly did not want for tenacity.

Because Rodgers no longer had a chance at the prize, Eileen Lebow remarked, the newspaper accounts of his arrival at Grant Park in Chicago were quiet and low-key compared with the banner headlines that had greeted his takeoff from Sheepshead Bay. A more pressing reason was that Armour might drop its funding of the enterprise. Cal and Mabel Rodgers looked for alternative sources of income and returned to an idea they had hatched back in Middletown, when it seemed that the cost of rebuilding *Vin Fiz* might be harder than anticipated on the exchequer. They had come up with the idea of a private air-mail service; they printed twenty-five-cent stamps (still in high philatelic demand eighty-five years later) and postcards and sold them to all comers. "Whether such mail was actually carried by Rodgers in the *Vin Fiz* is questionable," Lebow wrote, but Mabel and Rodgers's manager, Charles Wiggins, "both claimed the mail bearing these stamps had been airborne." Probably most of it made the trip on the chase train, although some of it certainly was sent aloft with Rodgers in a mailbag tied to the lower fuel tank and stuffed in his coat pockets.

Back at Aldine, I looked about me. Wheeler Field, commodious for a turf establishment at 2,600 feet by 200 feet, was extraordinarily attractive, with a rich mat of close-cropped grass by a pretty little lake that gave it the luxuriant look of a seventh-hole fairway. It was empty, however. At one end was a single hangar and a dilapidated office that looked as if it hadn't been used for a couple of years. An elderly man ambled slowly down the hill from a house in the trees nearby and waved me over. "Need fuel?' he asked affably. "I haven't got any, but I can run you with a couple cans in my car down the road to Arens airport. It's just five miles south."

"No, thanks," I said. "Got plenty. I just landed here to see what it was like. I'm following the route of the first transcontinental flight, which was made in 1911, and . . . "

He nodded. "Cal Rodgers, right?"

"Yes."

"You're not the first one, you know," he said. "'Bout eight or ten years ago, a guy came through here in an ultralight doing the same thing."

"Jim Lloyd?" I asked.

"Yup, that's the name," he said.

Rare memories. Today, I was discovering, few people along the route know the name of either Cal Rodgers or Jim Lloyd. Andy Warhol's "fifteen minutes of fame" seems to have been applied retroactively throughout our century. It tends to be the old-timers who remember, perhaps because their brain cells have not been "imprinted" like cheap rechargeable batteries with the short memory spans of our modern age of disposable hype.

"Gotta run," said the old-timer presently. "Nice to meet you, and good luck." Slowly he trudged back uphill to his house. Reluctantly—the place was so picturesque-pretty in an idealized fashion, like a Norman Rockwell painting, that I didn't want to leave it—I climbed back into *Gin Fizz,* started her engine, and was away, bound for Hammond.

A short time later, *Gin Fizz* was boring its way through a light rain shower when I suddenly felt a sharp breeze past my left ear. I looked up and to the side and saw, to my horror, that the upper half of the pilot's door was bowing out into the wind, a good five inches of daylight between the window frame and the fuselage. After being opened and closed countless thousands of times, the light aluminum door frame had finally failed at its thinnest point, right next to the window. The top half of the door flapped alarmingly in the powerful suction from the 100-mile-per-hour slipstream. Clearly it could not hold for long before shearing in two, perhaps wresting the entire door off its hinges. I throttled back to sixty-five miles per hour to lessen the force of the wind and punched up the nearest airport on the loran. It was Porter County Airport at Valparaiso, seven miles to the northwest, and I headed *Gin Fizz* toward it.

After landing, I shakily asked the FBO attendant, "Have you got a mechanic?" He shook his head no, but pointed at a hangar on the far end of the field. I started the engine and taxied *Gin Fizz* over to it, hoping against hope that I could find someone willing to jury-rig a repair that would hold long enough for me to get the plane back to Westosha, where the mechanics could do a permanent job.

I stopped in front of a large hangar emblazoned PROFESSIONAL AVIATION. A multimillion-dollar Jet Commander squatted outside, and a couple of big turboprop-powered executive twins reclined inside. This clearly was a serious corporate aviation-maintenance facility, not the Gasoline Alley repair shops I was used to, and it looked unlikely that its proprietors would deign to address a lowly Cessna 150. I felt as if I had taken a coaster wagon to a Mercedes garage. Inside the port-engine nacelle of a Beechcraft Super King Air, a tall, balding, weather-beaten man peered into its works. He saw me. "Help ya?" he said.

"I've got a Cessna 150 out there that needs repair," I said tentatively. "I'm on my way to California, and the top of the pilot's door has cracked open."

"Let's see what ya got," said Larry Bub in the longest sentence I heard him say all afternoon. He put his tools aside, then ducked under *Gin Fizz*'s port wing and examined the yawning door. "Maybe if you just got some duct tape and sealed it shut," I said, "maybe I could climb into the plane from the right side and go on to my own airport. . . . "

Larry chuckled and shook his head. Wordlessly he pulled the nose of *Gin Fizz* into the hangar out of the wet. "This won't take long," he said, and went for his tools. As I watched from a respectful distance, he expertly fashioned a splint from a piece of aluminum angle and painstakingly test-fitted it against the door frame where the crack had gone almost all the way through. With a pneumatic riveter, he affixed the splint and smoothed the raw edges with a file and emery cloth. Then he closed the door. The frame fit snugly against the fuselage. He opened and closed the door, shook it a few times experimentally, and said with satisfaction, "There. That'll last forever."

And so it has. It was a beautiful repair, almost invisible, and solid as houses. The job took thirty-five minutes and cost twenty dollars. Larry didn't charge for the aluminum splint or the half-dozen rivets.

As I took off, much relieved that I was not stuck overnight so close to my intended destination, I recited Jim Lloyd's mantra: "Good people and bad weather."

Half an hour later, as I approached Hammond, I peeled off to the west. There is a towered airport at Gary next door, but it seemed wiser not to attempt a light-signal landing so close to Chicago's busy O'Hare-Midway-Meigs raceway. For my Hammond stop, I chose the nearest uncontrolled airport, Lansing, just south of Chicago, hard by the Indiana state line, just twenty-four miles from Valparaiso. It's a good-sized, jet-capable workaday airport, its runway long and broad, with lots of single-engine aircraft and small twins on tiedowns on the concrete apron, as well as corporate jets and turboprops in the hangars. As I shut down next to a well-worn, fabric-covered four-seater Stinson Reliant from the 1940s, I looked about at its neighbors, counting familiar Cessnas, Mooneys, low-wing Pipers, and a single pretty Navion, a large postwar lightplane that was a little brother of the P-51. The Navion's sleek lines bespoke its kinship with the Mustang, also a North American Aviation design. The place, I thought, probably was extremely busy on weekends.

That day, however, only a few aviators were out and about. Four men with a wheeled power cart struggled to start a balky Skyhawk.

The Skyhawk's propeller spun erratically, the engine failing to catch, as I walked from my tiedown to the pilot's lounge. As I stepped up into the lounge, I looked back. Two of those trying to start the Skyhawk had given up, walked over to *Gin Fizz,* and were examining the interior of the cockpit, stooping under the wings with hands grasped behind their backs, like art historians peering at an Old Master. That is always good manners around a polished aluminum airplane, which picks up handprints the way velvet attracts lint. Presumably, they were trying to determine exactly how much the airplane had been refurbished. That stirred my pride; Cessna 150s are common as Chevrolets and about as remarkable. My vintage straight-tail turtleback can still turn a head or two.

The lounge—clean but sparsely furnished—was empty. The remains of a huge rectangular lemon birthday cake sprawled invitingly on a table. Unable to resist, I pulled off a crumb and tasted it: It was still fresh. I helped myself to a good-sized chunk and a cup of coffee from the ubiquitous percolator and walked out onto the ramp. Lansing might not have been particularly active on that day and at that hour, but it was a good airport for ground-based airplane-watching. The usual cavernous hangars held the usual assortment of singles and twins, and in one hangar, a tiny Pitts Special aerobatic biplane squatted beside a brawny, long-legged T-28 Trojan, a propeller-driven air force advanced trainer of the 1950s. The T-28's massive paddle-bladed propeller looked as if it alone weighed more than the little Pitts. I wondered what rich fellow owned the Trojan, an airplane every bit as expensive to operate as a Mustang.

A few yards away, a small two-seater helicopter was landing; as I walked by, I saw that it was a Robinson R-22, a model much in the aviation news at that time for being involved in an alarming number of crashes. I was reminded that I had no intention of ever taking instruction in a helicopter. The two men inside—presumably an instructor and student—sat talking as the rotors slowed to a stop. They did not look up as I waved companionably.

At the end of the ramp, an enormous orange Sikorsky Skycrane helicopter stooped over the concrete like a giant mantis, its rotor blades drooping. ERICKSON AIR CRANE was emblazoned on the narrow spine of its fuselage. What massive lifting jobs had it performed? Perhaps it had placed the tall television antennae on top of the John Hancock Center. No one was there to ask.

A few minutes later I was away. In the hour I spent on the ground, I had seen almost no activity, except for the recalcitrant Skyhawk and the Robinson. Not a single winged airplane had landed or taken off during that time. Was that still another symptom of the malaise gripping general aviation in America, or had I simply arrived at an exceptionally slow hour? I could not tell.

My next stop, of course, was Chicago, and choosing an airport to represent Cal Rodgers's Chicago landing site had taken a bit of thought. O'Hare was out of the question, and so was Midway— those big airports are much too busy for routine light-gun landings. Meigs Field on the lakefront was a possibility, but after studying the charts, I decided to pass it up. There was a gap in the controlled airspace between Midway and Gary airports through which I could sneak, but it was only four miles wide and full of tall radio towers. I could have skirted Gary to the east, but that would have put me farther out in Lake Michigan than I would have liked, about three miles from shore. Private pilots fly over the lake every day, but my inexperience made me conservative, and so I chose to land at the uncontrolled public-use airport closest to Rodgers's landing site at Grant Park in Chicago. And that airport was Clow International in Plainfield, twenty-six miles southeast of Grant Park.

Several times I had landed at Clow, a little single-runway field whose grandiose name must have been an aviator's joke. Judging from the impressive number and variety of lightplanes tied down on its greensward, however, it's perhaps the most popular grassroots field in the southwest suburbs of Chicago. Every time I've been there, at least half a dozen planes were landing and taking off on the narrow, cracked runway, with the same number of hangars open, revealing airplane owners busy at work on their machines. It's one of the few grassroots fields I've visited that still has an operating restaurant, right off the ramp to the FBO, and the restaurant is always full of pilots indulging in burgers and "hangar flying," the aviator's camaraderie of casual conversation, hyperbolic boasting, and outright lies. It's a downright friendly place; every time I've landed there, the same old-timer has emerged from the restaurant, stepped over to the ramp, and commented admiringly on the condition of *Gin Fizz*. Perhaps N5859E looked familiar to him; O. Boyd Clow, the octogenarian founder of the airport, once owned the airplane, in the late 1970s when it was part of his FBO's rental and training stable. All my landings at Clow seem to be good ones, as if *Gin Fizz* knew she was coming home—which I don't for a moment believe—and wanted to be on her best behavior.

Popular as it may seem on the outside, Clow is hurting, too. Though it may not be hurting as much as some other airports, the downturn in general aviation has been felt at the FBO, A&M Aviation, where I stopped to see Andy James, its affable president. Andy is sixty-five, but looks ten years younger. He is one of the most prominent names in Chicago-area aviation, having trained scores of airline pilots. Among the usual photographs of favorite airplanes on the wall, I spotted pictures of James with Illinois's two Democratic senators, Paul Simon and Carol Moseley Braun.

Andy is a former AT&T executive who plunged into flying in the early 1970s to "relieve the pressures of the job" and on the side founded and operated a flying club in Morristown, New Jersey. When AT&T brought him to Chicago in the middle of the decade, he started another club. In 1981, as AT&T was being broken up, James retired and became a flight instructor. By that time the club had seventeen airplanes. The entrepreneurial spirit remained, however, and "after six months I decided to grow the club." Soon the club was huge and many legged, with thirty-five airplanes at four airports. "I once did all the teaching and got to be hands-on with all the airplanes. I love to fly. But the club got so big that I found myself in management, moving paper to keep things going, rather than getting up in the air." Even today, after cutting back with the decline in general aviation, the club still employs fifteen instructors as private contractors, plus an office staff of three and a maintenance crew of four.

In the early 1980s, at the height of the aviation boom during the go-go Reagan years, Andy bought the bankrupt FBO from O. Boyd Clow and set up shop at Clow Airport. The club trained many fledgling pilots who went on to aviation careers. "We have a young lady that came to us weighing eighty-five pounds soaking wet," James said. "She got to be a charter pilot with us, flying a big Cessna 310 twin we thought she would never be able to handle, and she's an FAA inspector today." James is particularly proud that "10 percent" of the pilots of American Eagle, the commuter carrier, are his graduates, including the airline's chief pilot. Others have gone on to fly for the transcontinentals. "To know that these captains on DC-10s and 727s and 747s came through here and learned to fly. . . . Ah, it's kind of neat, standing in your backyard and seeing a DC-10 fly over on his way to O'Hare and blinking his lights because he knows you live down here."

But "with the aviation economy going down," Andy said, "the last two or three years we've been struggling to keep the club going. So we got into everything. We got into banner towing, chartering, everything involved in aviation. We bought a prop-jet Merlin for chartering. We flew a lot of people around. Walter Mondale. Mike Singletary of the Bears. Recently, we flew Carol Moseley Braun, the senator."

Now James is reorganizing the business. "What we have to deal with is that the prices of airplanes are so high. Aviation's always been expensive, but what we've gotta do is figure out ways for more people to fly and share the costs in some way. We need to get back into the grassroots of flying. There's a lot of things happening. Cessna's coming out with new airplanes again and other companies, too. There are a lot of new homebuilt kits." Even so, the costs are still high, even higher than they were a few years ago, "and it's very, very hard for the average person to get into flying."

A couple of years ago, as James approached the normal retirement age of sixty-five, he said, "I'm thinking, 'Maybe you oughta slow down.' So I bought a place in Florida two years ago, in an airport community where I have a hangar on the house and a Stearman in it. I live two lives. We have a house in Illinois and a house in Florida. Here I work almost seven days a week. In Florida I goof off. But down there I have a fax machine, so I'm still in touch, I'm still signing all the checks. I didn't want to let that go. But I'm trying to semi-retire a little bit."

We walked out onto the ramp, and James pointed out the sweet corn growing right up to both edges of the long taxiway from the ramp to the runway. "This once was all farm," he said. "Boyd Clow was a farmer who enjoyed aviation, and he put a landing strip in amidst the corn and beans and grew this airport with the crops to what it is today. At that time, the airport was so far out from the city pilots had a difficult time finding the place at night. Now look at it. You can see the city has grown around this place. We're surrounded. At one end we got the K-Mart, and look at all those houses along the runway. Boyd's land is becoming more and more valuable, and, of course, as a private owner, he's taxed very heavily. Maybe aviation's getting better, but nothing's helping Boyd. What's going to happen ten years from now, I don't know. It's hard to say if the airport will be here that long. I don't know. I wish I knew."

As we walked back into the airport, a slim, strikingly attractive woman in her late thirties and a man in his sixties stood in the doorway. "Ah, Henry, I want you to meet Cheryl and Gene Littlefield," Andy said. "Cheryl's the office manager here. Gene's the chief of maintenance. Cheryl's our wing walker and Gene's her pilot."

"Wing walker?" I said, my eyes widening. This was an exceedingly rare profession, the kind that won people guest spots on the old television show "What's My Line?" in which a panel attempted to guess the subjects' occupations.

"When people ask you what you do for a living," I asked Cheryl, "what do you say?"

She laughed. "If I tell them I'm a wing walker, their next question is, 'Are you crazy?' I normally will say I work at a fixed-base operation at an airport." She was being too modest. Among the thousands of air-show performers in the country, perhaps only ten are active wing walkers. So rare are they that I've never seen one, although I've been to half a dozen air shows. The Littlefields are veterans of the international air-show circuit, and Gene has been president of the Professional Airshow Performers Association, as well as a Hollywood stunt pilot—he flew the aerobatics for star Robert Conrad in *Will,* the film biography of G. Gordon Liddy, the Watergate figure.

"Could you describe the air-show routine?" I asked.

Gene answered. "We take off with Cheryl on the wing, and the narrator tells the audience on the PA system who we are and what we're flying." The Littlefields fly a much-modified Boeing Stearman, the primary-trainer biplane that had schooled Ted Robinson, his fellow Tuskegee Airmen, and thousands of other World War II pilots. "And we'll gain about a thousand feet. The first maneuver with Cheryl standing on the wing is a loop. And we'll do a hammerhead coming out of the loop. That's a maneuver in which the airplane goes up and stops, then rotates around one wing and comes back down the same axis. The third maneuver is half of a Cuban eight. It's a pull, then five-eighths of a loop, and a half-roll on a down forty-five, and then we go back to level flight."

Even with Gene drawing circles in the air with his hands to illustrate the maneuvers, I was thoroughly confused. All I could do was picture the Stearman flung about the sky in mad, frightening abandon. Aerobatics, the pinnacle of aviation for grassroots adventurers, has never interested me. My imperfect sense of balance won't allow it, and my overdeveloped sense of self-preservation discourages it anyway. Straight and level flight, that's for me.

"And then we do a four-point roll—it's a hesitation roll, stopping four times during the roll, one and two and three and four, showing all sides of the airplane," Gene said. "And we do that for a reason because in the next turnaround, when the bottom of the airplane is toward the crowd, Cheryl loosens her harness, comes down off the wing, and hides in a compartment inside the airplane. People don't see her move. Coming back into the arena, we do another four-point roll to show all sides of the airplane. She's gone, disappeared. It's like magic."

When the plane does its next turnaround to fly back to the arena, Gene "turns on the smoke" to hide Cheryl from view as she scampers back atop the upper wing. "And we roll the airplane over and fly by the audience with her hanging upside down from the lower wing." The harness holds her there, and for good measure she wears two stainless steel safety cables, each five-sixteenths of an inch thick, that are attached to the airplane's structure. "If she fell, she'd be hurt, but she'd never get away from the airplane. The cables are long enough to let her move around but still not get away from the plane." She has no parachute "because of the wind pressure," she said. "If the parachute accidentally opened, I'd probably take half the airplane with me." The show ends with two more passes, Cheryl dangling from the bottom wing on the first and waving from the upper wing on the second, a slow "photo pass" for the spectators with cameras. "When we land," Gene said, "she's inside the airplane because, you know, landings can be difficult and we don't want to take a chance with her out on the wing."

They also perform the same routine at night. "We attach ten halogen lights to the airplane and light the whole thing up. The night shows are easy to do. Usually the weather is better. The wind has died down. When we taxi in, we do so with the plane lit up. It's very pretty."

Is the routine dangerous? "The idea is to make it as exciting and entertaining as possible," said Gene. "We just imply that there's some risk. We want it to appear exciting, but still be safe. I have the easy job. I just sit there. Cheryl has the tough job."

Their most unpleasant moment occurred in 1988 when the

Stearman's engine quit while it was inverted at low altitude on a fly-by past the crowd. Fortunately, the airplane was carrying enough speed so that Littlefield could roll her right side up and land immediately in the grass between the runway and its parallel taxiway. Had the airplane been flying toward the crowd, that's where it would have landed, doubtless with considerable loss of life. That's why air-show performers always fly past, rather than toward, the spectator stands; it was written into the official air-show performers' association rules with Gene's help. "Besides being the right thing to do," he said, "what kind of businessman would ever want to jeopardize his livelihood by putting his customers at risk?"

There was once a time, even in the barnstorming days of the 1920s and 1930s, when air-show performers lived hand to mouth. But with the rise in outdoor spectator sports, "it's become very lucrative," Gene said. We receive $6,000 for a weekend, and if we do twenty shows a year, that's a gross income of $120,000 a year." Of course, owning and maintaining the Stearman is costly, but "you can make a good living at it. And then we both work here for Andy. I just started last fall, but Cheryl has worked for him for twelve years. It's kind of a supplementary thing."

While Gene maintains James's planes, Cheryl does "most of the accounting and ordering of inventory and just makes sure that things run smoothly."

"That's not as exciting as wing walking," I observed unnecessarily.

"No, it's not," Cheryl said, chuckling. "I do meet just as many nice people here, though, as I do throughout the air-show industry, and I think that's a big reason that we've stayed involved in aviation. The general aviation family is its own one big happy family."

"Yes," Gene said. "It's a relatively small community, but it has a cohesiveness to it that is amazing. You know, as soon as you meet someone who flies, you have a ready identification with them. The conversation never gets dull."

What, I mused as I walked out to *Gin Fizz,* could be better than "good people and bad weather"? How about "good people and good weather"? As *Gin Fizz* curved away from Clow between the low scattered clouds in the sunny sky, I was eager to head south for Texas and California and meet some more of those good people. But it was time to go home and rest up with Debby for a couple of weeks.

Good fortune had given me mostly decent flying; I was coming home early, without having to use all four extra days I had budgeted for standing down during bad weather. So, careful not to take a bite out of the 4,000-foot floor of the top layer of the O'Hare International wedding cake, I turned *Gin Fizz*'s nose to the north for her home base at Westosha, forty minutes away.

# PART III

# CRUISE

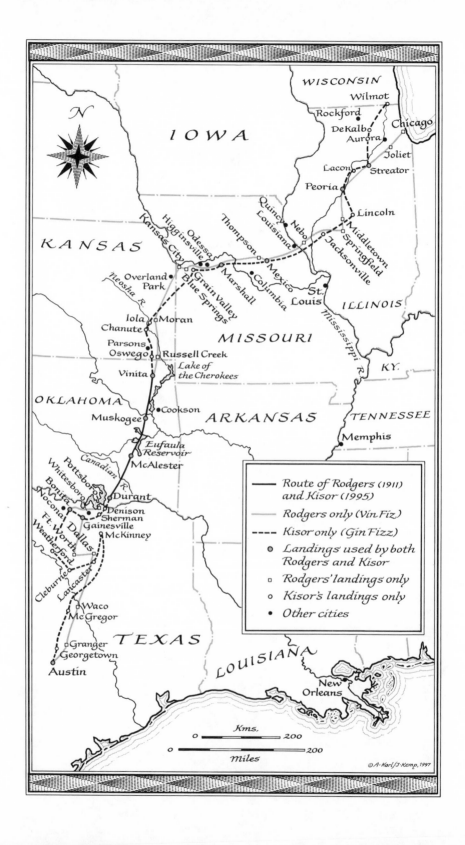

WISCONSIN

Wilmot

Rockford

DeKalb
Aurora
Chicago

Lacon
Joliet
Streator

Peoria

Lincoln

Quincy
Louisiana
Nebo
Middletown
Springfield
Jacksonville

Mexico

Columbia

St.
Louis

ILLINOIS

Mississippi R.

KY.

N

IOWA

KANSAS

Higginsville
Odessa
Thompson
Kansas City
Grain Valley
Blue Springs
Marshall

Neosha R.
Overland
Park

Iola Moran
Chanute

Parsons
Oswego Russell Creek
Vinita Lake of
the Cherokees

MISSOURI

OKLAHOMA

Muskogee
Cookson

ARKANSAS

TENNESSEE

Memphis

Eufaula
Reservoir
McAlester

Canadian

Pottsboro
Whitesboro
Bonita
Nocona
Ft. Worth
Weatherford
Cleburne

R.

Durant

Denison
Sherman
Gainesville
McKinney
Dallas

Lancaster

Waco
McGregor

Granger
Georgetown
Austin

TEXAS

LOUISIANA

New
Orleans

Route of Rodgers (1911)
and Kisor (1995)

Rodgers only (Vin Fiz)

Kisor only (Gin Fizz)

● Landings used by both
  Rodgers and Kisor

□ Rodgers' landings only

○ Kisor's landings only

● Other cities

Kms.
0 ———————— 200
0 ———————— 200
Miles

©A·Karl/J·Kemp, 1997

# 10

hen I arrived back home in Evanston after tying down *Gin Fizz* at Westosha, Debby no longer seemed quite so nervous about my coast-to-coast enterprise. Her fears seemed largely dissipated after that week's adventure. My flying to New York and back without incident finally had persuaded her that I was a safe pilot. I am certain part of the secret lay in the simple husbandly act of checking in with her every night to report the day's events; good communications ease the stresses of any marriage.

Also, she had begun to entertain dreams about an adventure of her own the following summer, a month's trip to Mexico with fellow teachers from her suburban elementary school, which had begun a dual program in Spanish and English for Latino and Anglo pupils. Such a "language-immersion" undertaking sounded good to me; the lively dinner-table details of Debby's plan brought back the bubbly, enthusiastic, idealistic young fifth-grade teacher I had married three decades before. Twenty or even ten years ago, I would have felt left out, even abandoned, had she suggested being away from me for so long—our lives were then too deeply intertwined for such a show of independence. But now I was beginning to understand how she had felt when I announced my plan to fly across the country solo. She had the courage to let go; she knew how important making the trip was to me. And her example had helped me find the maturity to let go, too. The bonds of our marriage, which had sustained both of us for so long, were loosening—and at the same time gaining strength from the trust we were showing in one another. I began to feel a genuine enthusiasm for her dreams and a pride in them as well. She was also past fifty, and she was not allowing the weeds of middle-aged disillusionment to tangle her life, either.

In fact, Debby was cheerful and relaxed at the dinner table when I spun yarns about the colorful characters I had met at all those airports between New York and Chicago. So amused did she seem that I hoped she was beginning to lose her distaste for small planes, and twice I suggested that perhaps she'd like to go for a short spin in *Gin Fizz*. Both times that brought a warning glint to her eye. "You don't make me do what I don't want to do," Debby said, "and I won't make you do what *you* don't want to do. Deal?"

"Deal," I said, backtracking hastily. No use pushing things.

Though life was happy and relaxed at home, at the *Sun-Times* some long-simmering matters were coming to a boil. The top editors had met defeat in their struggles for the purse strings with the tightfisted new publisher. The old executive editor had departed, the present editor-in-chief was on his way out the door, and the managing editor was being weighed for the drop. It seemed as if we journeymen reporters and editors were developing a permanent hunch in our shoulders from trying to keep a low profile. Morale, never high at a struggling newspaper, had plummeted to a new low. As my month's furlough drew to a close, I became increasingly anxious to get out of Chicago and head for Austin, the terminus of the second leg of the coast-to-coast trip.

But the conditions that had prevailed in northern Illinois and southern Wisconsin for an entire week that August—soaking humidity and cool air—brought thick ground fog and low ceilings in which only instrument-rated pilots could fly. I had hoped to leave Westosha on a Wednesday to start the second leg of my trip, but I had to move my departure back a day and then another day as the soup curdled over the Chicago megalopolis.

Finally, with the forecast improving on Friday, I kissed Debby good-bye before dawn and arrived at Westosha at 6 A.M., hoping for an early start for a day's flight to eastern Missouri, with stops along Rodgers's route through Illinois. But the dishrag-gray clouds still sulked close to the ground. The radar pictures on Westosha's weather computer showed clear skies just south of Chicago, but an occluded front lingered between me and those skies. If I could only get through the first sixty miles, the sailing would be clear all the way to the Mississippi River. Finally, at 11 A.M., after I had dawdled all morning polishing the airplane and praying hourly at the weather computer, the clouds lifted to 1,500 feet above the ground and the visibility improved from two miles to four. These were legal conditions in which to fly, although a little short of the personal minimums—clouds at 2,000 feet and visibility of six miles—I had imposed on myself as a low-time pilot. Since the sun was out just about forty-five minutes away, I decided to take off.

Scarcely twenty minutes later, as I flew between Rockford and the western suburbs of Chicago, the weather took a sudden shift for the worse, the clouds lowering to a shade above 1,000 feet and the visibility to about three miles—on the very edge of legality and way beyond any sensible margin of safety. "Damn," I said to myself. "Time to get down and ride this out." The nearest uncontrolled airport, De Kalb Municipal, lay ten miles away, and I found it handily with the GPS. An Aeronca preceded me into the landing pattern, and I throttled back slightly to give it plenty of room. Before turning onto final, I peered downwind into the increasing murk to make sure that no airplane was making a long straight-in final, skipping the first two legs of the recommended landing pattern. Straight-in finals are not illegal at uncontrolled airports, but they do not bespeak good airmanship. Seeing nothing, I continued the turn onto final and landed.

Scarcely a minute after I emerged from *Gin Fizz,* a big Cessna 182 rolled into the tiedown space next to mine and shut down as well. From the right seat, a middle-aged woman gazed at me with a haughty smile I couldn't decipher. A few minutes later I learned its meaning. In the pilot's lounge, tapping away at the weather computer, I looked up at a tall, looming, red-faced figure, visibly angry. "You cut me off on final!" he growled. "I was doing an instrument approach when you crossed half a mile in front of me!"

I blanched. "If it was my fault," I said, "I apologize."

"It *was* your fault," the pilot said. "Didn't you have your radio on?"

"I'm sorry, I'm deaf," I replied. "I can't receive on the radio."

"You shouldn't have been up there!" he retorted. "It's IFR!"

Now that could have been debated—I had seen the airport from a legal three miles away, and De Kalb is not an official instrument-approach airport, with higher visibility requirements—but I knew instantly that I should have seen the oncoming 182 while I was still traveling downwind in the landing pattern. It had the right of way. And I knew that good sense dictated that no low-time pilot should have been aloft in visual flight rules in those conditions, even if they were legal. Still, the arrogance of the other pilot was uncalled for.

"Well," I responded, digging in my heels a little, "I *am* sorry. But I think I had a right to be up there. When I took off in Wisconsin, the conditions were a lot better, and I was making a precautionary landing here because the visibility had gone to hell. I'm just sorry I didn't see you on that long final."

The other pilot grunted disgustedly, waved his hand in contemptuous dismissal, and stalked away, leaving me in a puddle of embarrassment and concern. Even though our encounter fell into a gray area—pilots on instrument approaches to uncontrolled airports are still bound, under FAA rules, to "see and avoid" other traffic—I shared the blame. This was the first time my inability to use the radio had caused potential danger, and I was upset about it, especially since the situation could have been avoided if I had kept a sharper lookout for traffic and if I had not chosen to take off below my self-imposed minimums. I shouldn't be criticizing Cal Rodgers for carelessness, I thought. The bug of get-there-itis had bitten me, too.

An hour later things looked better, and I simmered down. There is no weather station at De Kalb, but the one at Aurora, fifteen miles southeast, was reporting a 2,500-foot ceiling and six miles visibility, and Rockford, twenty-five miles northwest, a 1,000-foot ceiling and three miles visibility. Splitting the difference, I decided to go and lifted off into markedly better conditions. After twenty-five minutes, I finally emerged, just above the Illinois River, into scattered clouds and hazy sunlight.

Cal Rodgers had a tough time getting out of Chicago, too, thanks once again to the confounding spaghetti that was the Iron Road in the big city. On October 8, 1911, *Vin Fiz* departed Grant Park at 4 P.M., headed for Joliet, thirty-five miles southwest, but Rodgers immediately lost his way, unable to find the Chicago & Alton (now Santa Fe) tracks that he had planned to follow to St. Louis. He circled over Lake Calumet, then Jackson Park, and then found the waiting chase train at Argo. By then, dusk had fallen, so he put down at Lockport, three miles northeast of Joliet. The next morning he took off again, circling the Illinois State Penitentiary at Joliet to thrill the prisoners, and made a beeline for Streator, forty-five miles away, where he landed for refueling.

I passed up the stop at Joliet to get out of the murk. A few minutes after escaping the clouds, I saw Streator Airport below and glided down for a landing. Streator, fifty-five miles south of De Kalb, is a singular airport. For one thing, its paved runway is pencil-narrow, at eighteen feet wide, and in the gusty crosswind I had to fly *Gin Fizz* all the way down to thread that needle. On the rollout, three things caught my eye: an old buckboard buggy underneath the wind sock, a children's swing set close by, and a lovingly re-stored Santa Fe caboose parked on a pristinely ballasted forty-foot section of track by the gas pumps. Two lights burned in its vestibules.

In a nearby hangar a ruddy, linebacker-sized man in his late forties bent over the engine of a beautifully restored early Piper Cub, a J-3 model. On his head was a baseball cap emblazoned STEARMAN FLY-IN, GALESBURG. He introduced himself as Virgil Rothrock, adding, "Call me Rocky." Though still in his late forties, he had retired a year before as a farm-implements dealer and bought the airport.

"What's with the caboose?" I asked in my best David Letterman fashion. Rocky chuckled. When America's railroads got rid of their cabooses several years before, he said, the Santa Fe had put it up for sale. A local undertaker who also flew a Piper Archer bought the caboose because the railroad, which runs through Streator, was important to the town's history. "He rebuilt it to where it was almost like brand new," Rocky recalled. "He had a little airstrip about a mile from here. And one day he comes in to make a landing and he misses. He runs off the end of the runway he's landed on all his life. It was the last time he ever flew an airplane. Right away he went to the doctor. He was only forty-five or fifty years old. Within ninety days he was gone, from brain cancer. His son inherited the caboose and his daughter inherited the airplane, and I ended up buying both of them."

"Why?"

"The history," he said. "Besides, the caboose's not a bad-looking thing. You need something unique at your airport. Yesterday was a good example. Two little kids and a mother and a father landed in a 172. They had flown overhead, the kids saw the swing set and the father saw the caboose, so they landed here for a picnic. What normally would have been an hour's stop became three hours. We've also got chickens here"—he pointed through the window at a small shack by the hangars—"and next thing you know the kids are looking at the baby chickens, and the caboose fascinates them, too.

"The state of Illinois has been trying to help me get a big twin-engine helicopter," he added. "I want to get that set up out there on the field as a static display, so kids can play on it." He leaned forward for emphasis. "Aviation is slipping, and the only way to get it back is through the kids. That's what aviation has forgotten."

Still, a minor Disneyfication of his airfield to attract business did not seem to be the reason Rocky collects historical artifacts. "Yeah, I like to buy things that are old, restore them, and keep them here," he said. "I was looking at a 1904 world atlas not long ago, and it showed Streator as the fourth biggest city in central Illinois. The population was 14,000. It's still 14,000, and when the coal got all mined out, the city stayed the same size. It never grew." Because of the town's earlier prominence, Streator is the third oldest airport in Illinois, Rocky said. "It was really popular in the 1920s through '50s, when there used to be 50 to 100 airplanes on the field. Right after World War II, the place used to train 200 to 300 veterans a year through the GI Bill. Now the older guys are in their seventies and don't feel so safe flying anymore. They learned in old Cubs and later airplanes just got too complex. When coal mining died here, so did the airport. I've tried to bring it back. We spent the first year cleaning up and tearing down and redoing the buildings. We're starting to get more pilots."

But these pilots are not the youngsters, it seems. Many of the newcomers, he said, are "laid-back retired guys," older owners of expensive restored vintage "taildragger" airplanes—machines with two main landing wheels and a tailwheel. "Someone with a nice old plane isn't going to want to pound it onto asphalt," so Rothrock spends "probably four to five thousand dollars every year" on keeping the two turf runways pristine, rather than widening the narrow blacktop runway. This literally is grassroots aviation.

"Speaking of taildraggers," I said, "is that pretty Cub your only airplane?"

"No, I got thirteen of them," he said with a laugh. "Come with me." And he led me down to an outbuilding and showed me his gleaming 1942 Stearman biplane, next to which were nestled a 1927 Plymouth sedan and a 1919 Model T Ford, as well as several ancient motorcycles. "Back in 1983," he said, "I went to the Stearman fly-in at Galesburg and wanted to buy one. The one I wanted was a Pete Jones Air-Repair Special. That Stearman was on the block for $30,000. My dad pitched a fit. He said, 'You need farmland worse than you need them Stearmans. Use your money, make that down payment, do whatever you want, but don't buy that stupid Stearman.' In 1993, ten years later, I went back to Galesburg and that Pete Jones was up for sale again. I paid $142,000 for it. That farm I own is not worth anywhere near the inflation of that Stearman price."

Rocky first fell in love with aviation at the age of six, when his parents took him to a fair whose most exciting attraction was a man parachuting out of a hot-air balloon. "From that point on I always wanted to be a hot-air balloon pilot," he said, though he never could persuade his parents to buy him a balloon. "Back in the old days, one of them cost more than three cars," Rocky told me. It has been only in the last six years that he was able to return to this first love.

In fact, the prizes offered in balloon competitions make the sport profitable for serious balloonists. "You get to go to nice big cities and they'll pay your room and board and they'll wine and dine you, and you work two, three hours a day, and then you can leave with $3,000 or $4,000 for a weekend's work. That's not a bad job," he said. "Last Labor Day, down in Jackson, Mississippi, I won fifty grand over a four-day weekend. You're working weekends, yes, but it gives you all week to work on your airplanes and you don't have to be working for somebody else."

As I walked out to *Gin Fizz*, Rocky's parting words echoed behind me: "You don't have to be working for somebody else." Now that was appealing. Not long before, when professional disillusionment had begun to set in for me, Debby's career was starting to gather steam; in fact, her income had begun to approach mine. I toyed with a dream of retiring at fifty-five, and she did not discourage the idea because the boys had left the nest and she was no longer so dependent on my bringing home the bread. Perhaps, I thought, I could work part time and goof off part time, maybe even write another book or two. After I learned to fly, I added thoughts about taking a course in aviation mechanics, so I would be able to work on my own airplane. But I am not and never will be a wealthy layabout, and a quick check of my bank account always sets me straight. Still, fantasies of retiring at sixty bubble to the surface now and then.

*        *        *

Half an hour out of Streator, I decided to make an unplanned stop at Marshall County Airport at Lacon to refuel and check the weather farther south. I carried my "communications bag" of TTY and laptop computer into the pilot's lounge while the line attendant refueled *Gin Fizz*. Afterward I wandered over to the attendant's shack to pay for the gas and then boarded the airplane and rolled out. At the edge of the runway, I had just completed my engine runup when I saw a figure on a little four-wheeled motorcycle of the kind called an "all-terrain vehicle" bouncing madly over the greensward, waving his arms wildly. It was the airport manager. "Your bag!" he mouthed, drawing a little rectangle in the air and pointing to the pilot's lounge. "Your bag!"

"Aw, *shit!*" I shouted into the roar of the engine. This was the third mistake I had made today, the stupidest yet. Nodding to the manager, I swung the plane around to taxi back. He bounced back to the pilot's lounge in the ATV and stood on the ramp, bag in hand, as I rolled up. The propeller still whirling, I opened the door, and he passed the bag to me. In the universal gesture for "I screwed up," I pointed my finger at my temple, grimaced, and fired a mock bullet. The manager grinned and waved me on. Good fortune was riding with me. That bag held not only my only means of communicating with the outside world, but also my logbook, my FAA medical certificate—without which my license is useless—and my airline ticket home from Austin.

As if to emphasize my luck, the weather continued to improve as I approached my next stop, Peoria. In 1911 Rodgers landed there shortly after noon on the grounds of the National Implement and Vehicle Fair to the usual alarums and excursions from a large and enthusiastic crowd. Cliff Turpin, another prominent birdman of the time, had also arrived at the fair, and in midafternoon the two fliers took off, Turpin escorting Rodgers out of town. Today, Peoria Regional Airport doubtless would have been Rodgers's airfield of choice, but it is a big tower-controlled field, and I saw no reason to go through the rigmarole of a light-gun landing, not when a suitable uncontrolled alternative lay close by. This was Mount Hawley Auxiliary Airport, just north of the city, right under the 2,000-foot floor of Peoria Regional's upside-down wedding cake. Mount Hawley, I saw as I taxied to the little terminal, is a modern suburban airfield, its concrete runway and taxiways only a few years old and capable of handling small jets. I shut down next to the terminal, and as I closed the pilot's door, a tall, grizzled old fellow ambled out from the terminal and muttered something.

"I'm sorry, I'm deaf but I read lips," I said, pointing to my ear. "What was that you said?"

He turned his leathery face to me, pointed to *Gin Fizz,* and bellowed, in such a slow and exaggerated fashion that the deep furrows on his cheeks smoothed out with the effort, "I HAD ONE OF THOSE, TOO, ONCE." With that, he peered inside *Gin Fizz*'s pilot's door. After a moment, he turned to me, smiled new crinkles into his wrinkles, and gave me the thumbs-up sign. Then he ambled back into the terminal.

The lounge looked scrubbed and well kept, its magazines arranged in neat cases instead of strewn about, the warbird posters carefully preserved behind glass. A yuppie pilot, I thought, could safely stash a girlfriend or boyfriend here after a round of tennis while he or she went up for a few touch-and-goes.

I saw the old-timer slouched in a chair before a big television set and thought I might be able to coax a few words out of him about his old Cessna 150. But as I approached, I could feel the growl of the television's speaker, turned way up. I realized that the old fellow probably was quite hard-of-hearing himself. Maybe he felt uncomfortable about conversing with everybody, let alone someone who was deaf. An attempted conversation would probably have been awkward and unproductive. He nodded curtly, as if to acknowledge and dismiss my presence in the same instant, and turned back to the television. "Guess if you've seen one 150 you've seen them all," I said to myself, and headed for the vending machines.

Meanwhile, on the television a young woman of startlingly ample décolletage hove into view. Leeza Gibbons was breathlessly interviewing a plastic surgeon and the latest patient to receive his new breast implants, whose success was on display just this side of a Class B misdemeanor. As I passed by the screen with Diet Coke and peanuts in hand, the patient said brightly, "I did it for myself!" and thrust out her chest with pride.

The old fellow looked up and winked at me. Tapping his temple, he said with a contorted expression, "SHE NEEDS A BRAIN IMPLANT, TOO."

\*     \*     \*

I was still laughing over the old-timer's remark as *Gin Fizz* approached Logan County Airport at Lincoln, forty-five miles southeast of Mount Hawley. It was the airport nearest Middletown, thirteen miles west, where Rodgers had landed in 1911 when *Vin Fiz*'s oil tank sprang a leak en route from Peoria to Springfield. While the mechanics worked away, Cal shilled for Mabel's air-mail business, selling postcards and stamps. A day earlier, the U.S. postmaster general had commissioned Mabel as an "aerial postmistress," and so the Rodgerses declared the Peoria-to-Springfield flight their "first official air mail flight." But as Eileen Lebow pointed out, no records of such a sanction exist in Washington, so the service was "strictly private, although it pointed the way to future mail service development."

Even today Middletown, a soybean metropolis of 400 people, isn't big enough to rate its own airstrip. But like so many small towns in the hinterlands, it remembers Cal Rodgers, for his visit in 1911 was probably the biggest event in its history. When Jim Lloyd landed there during his 1986 trip, the city fathers had carved out an impromptu airstrip in a cornfield close to Rodgers's landing site to allow *Vin Fiz II* to set down as the entire village cheered. In the early 1990s, the town's tree commission raised $500 to mount an egg-shaped 2,800-pound chunk of granite on the Rodgers site. On this monument is carved a likeness of Rodgers's airplane and the legend VIN FIZ SKYWAY, 09 OCT 1911.

I couldn't ask the good townspeople to carve out an airstrip in a cornfield for me—the FAA wouldn't have allowed a landing there anyway—but at Logan County Airport, I encountered another bit of found Americana even more charming than that at Streator. It was a scruffy, underfunded little historical treasure-house.

As I flew over Logan, looking for the wind sock by the runway—a handsome 4,000-foot-long expanse of concrete—I spotted two vintage jets, a T-33 trainer from the 1950s and a Vietnam-era Phantom interceptor, squatting near a complex of buildings and hangars. A Phantom in a cornfield way out in the middle of nowhere? I thought as I taxied up to the terminal building, a typical barnlike general-aviation pile in need of a coat of paint. A lonely Cessna 172 and a tattered World War II–era Beechcraft D-18 twin-engine transport, its twin rudders painted in the red-and-yellow stripes of its era, occupied the apron. I dismounted and approached the Beechcraft. Clearly, it had not flown for decades; bird's nests occupied its cowlings and spider's webs crazed its windows.

I turned my attention to the Phantom and T-33, noticing as I did so the long, low building across from them with a sign bravely proclaiming it as the headquarters of the Heritage in Flight Museum. The sun-bleached sand-and-olive air force camouflage paint of the Phantom must have dated from the 1960s, and the sad gray crust on the T-33 failed to hide decades of abuse at the hands of air force fledglings. These were not the meticulously (and expensively) restored examples of their breed one can find at well-groomed big-city air museums; they had been left to molder under the unforgiving prairie sun. I peered into the tailpipe of the T-33; the engine had been removed, leaving the plane an empty shell, its control surfaces welded rigid.

On the door of the low wooden headquarters building, a sign proclaimed the museum closed until the weekend except by appointment. Then serendipity arrived in the form of a comfortable country woman with a spacious smile. After I explained my presence, she extended her hand and said warmly, "I'm Pat Miller. My husband is an aircraft technician in the hangar over there, and I'm a museum volunteer. I answer the phones from nine to five every day. Would you like me to open up the museum for you?"

Would I? She unlocked the building, explaining as she did so its history: It dated from 1943 and originally had housed German prisoners of war at Camp Ellis on the Illinois River in Fulton County. After the camp fell into disrepair, its buildings were scattered about the countryside, and this one had wound up at Logan County Airport, where it served as the airport office for twenty years until the present pile was built.

Inside, the place looks as though every local veteran of World Wars I and II, Korea, and Vietnam had donated his military memorabilia—war booty included. Uniforms, medals, helmets, posters, ration books, medical records, snapshots, aircraft-recognition charts, vintage radio equipment, gas masks, and parachutes lay cheek by jowl with swords, daggers, bombs, Nazi and Japanese flags, and machine-gun belts, as well as aircraft models of every conceivable kind. Old newspapers proclaimed great victories. All the exhibits were arranged in a careful chronology of wars, with those from 1941 to 1945 most in evidence, such as a cracked shearling leather bomber jacket that had clothed a U.S. Army Air Forces crewman at Attu, Kiska, and Adak in the Aleutians.

A lump rose in my throat as I read a faded letter from a soldier from somewhere in Southeast Asia to his mother back home in Lincoln. Certain details had been blanked out by the army censor, but not the short poem with which the soldier finished the letter. It was gaunt, rough-hewn poetry, not worth the quoting, but its simple existence bespoke a profound truth of war: The writer had seen something that had so affected him that he was able to tell his mother about it only in verse. I wondered if he had made it back.

"I'll show you some more stuff," Pat said, beckoning, and we stepped outside to a hangar that must have been of the same vintage as the POW building. Just inside the door lay a Navion that had been painted in the colors of an early U.S. Air Force trainer, with spectacular nose art of a pneumatic blonde beauty. "It's in flying shape," said Pat, "and so is this little Champ back here."

The sixty-five-horsepower Aeronca Champ she showed me had been partially disassembled for its annual inspection. Even smaller and lighter than my Cessna, the high-winged steel-tube-and-fabric airplane had been an Army L-16, in which role it had been used for spotting targets and carrying out wounded soldiers on litters and even as the lightest of bombers. Other L-16s like it had served in Korea.

There was also a little Bell helicopter ("our newest acquisition," Pat said), an original four-by-four truck, a cluster of navy practice bombs, a big radial engine from a B-25, a tow cart, an ejection seat, and too much other military surplus to mention. Pat swept back a curtain from a little alcove in which sat an ancient Link trainer from the 1940s.

Outside she showed me a large rotating lamp on a forty-foot platform, one of the original beacons that, spaced several miles apart across the United States, had once guided aircraft across the continent. A large red air force fire engine lay parked in front of it, and up the airfield sat several more rusting old military vehicles, including a De Soto command car from World War II.

All these things are cared for by only forty active volunteers, half of whom, Pat said, are retirees. Money, naturally, is scarce; it dribbles in from dues, contributions, and a yearly fly-in breakfast. Why do they do it? I asked. "They just want to keep history alive," she replied simply, as if there was no other conceivable reason.

There was nothing hollow about this museum. Shopworn and commonplace as some of its displays may have been, they bespoke many hours of love and caring by ordinary people who wanted, in whatever way they could, to preserve for their descendants a bit of the history they had experienced. This is why little grassroots museums are always so special: They are true people's archives whose exhibits are assembled and cared for by folks who, with their grandfathers and fathers, actually used the implements on display, or at the least saw them in action. "Trust us: this is how it was," they seem to say, "not how other people think it must have been." There is no greater authenticity than that.

As *Gin Fizz* lifted off the runway, I rocked her wings in salute.

An hour after she left Middletown, *Vin Fiz* arrived on the state fair grounds at Springfield. Her pilot, eyewitnesses said, was "almost exhausted" from the strain of the day and "stiff from cold" despite having stuffed many layers of newspapers under his coat for insulation. Early autumn in Illinois can be biting cold. There was also a chill in St. Louis. The next day, October 10, the Hearst Prize deadline was to run out, and so St. Louis had withdrawn its offer of a $1,000 prize for a landing and dinner there. Angered, Cal removed St. Louis from his route in favor of Kansas City, and that night he decided to alter his plans for a more direct flight to that town.

Again I chose to skip the big tower-controlled airport at Springfield and landed instead at Jacksonville, twenty-six miles southwest of the Illinois capital. And when I landed, it was to the biggest welcoming crowd that yet had greeted me—about a dozen people. I was touched when a boyhood friend I had not seen for a decade walked up to shake my hand. Larry Meyer, a YMCA executive in Evanston during my youth who was soon to retire from his post at the Jacksonville Y, had been one of my mentors, and seeing him was icing on what was shaping up as a delightful pastry of a day that, in the morning, had threatened to collapse.

First, the airport manager presented me with a proclamation of welcome from Jacksonville's mayor. I was further touched by the large chocolate cake with "Happy Birthday from IJX" (the airport's FAA identification code) etched in vanilla. I had turned fifty-five the day before, when I was supposed to have arrived but had to stand down for bad weather. The big hello had been orchestrated by Clyde Smith, a fellow Cessna 150 owner, a graphic arts teacher at the Illinois School for the Deaf in Jacksonville and president of the International Deaf Pilots Association (IDPA). A carnival barker at heart, he never misses a chance to wave the banner of our organization.

In its own distinctive way, the IDPA, which at this writing has about 140 Americans and Europeans on its roster, is a testament to the imperfect but genuine fraternity of aviation. It is made up of three kinds of audiologically deaf pilots whose differences both define and divide them.

The first and largest group consists of those who use American Sign Language and are steeped in that linguistic culture. Most of this group were born deaf—many of them offspring of deaf people—but an increasing number are emigrants from the other two groups, the oral deaf and the lately deafened. Many, if not most, of the culturally Deaf—they use the capital letter with pride—do not use voiced speech among themselves, although some can, and do, when they are dealing with the hearing world. They do not regard themselves as hearing impaired and resent the use of that term to describe them. Theirs, they believe, is not a handicap but a language-based way of life that centers on ASL. The only impediment they perceive is the long-standing prejudice of the hearing society, which, they believe, has long tried to impose impossible standards of spoken language on them, denying them their heritage. As a result, some of them are extremely militant, viewing their cause as revolutionary, and are as intolerant of differing viewpoints as are the old-time educators who slapped their young hands when they attempted to use sign language.

Because I am a member of the second group, the oral deaf— those who struggle to speak, lip-read, and use whatever residual hearing they have (I have none)—many of the Deaf militants regard people like me as traitors to the cause, renegades who deny their deafness and seek to "pass" as hearing people. But the oral deaf tend to differ from the deaf-born in important ways. Most lost their hearing in early childhood after they had learned language and speech, as I had. (There are staunch oralists, however, who are deaf-born.) We find the larger hearing world more suitable for us and our capabilities than that of the Deaf culture, which, for all its recent public successes (such as the Deaf movement's 1988 takeover of Gallaudet University, the world's only liberal arts college for the deaf), still remains on the margins of American society.

We believe that learning to speak and to function within the larger hearing world are worth whatever struggle it takes.

The third group is made up of pilots who lost their hearing in adulthood or are hard of hearing, rather than truly deaf. Most of them belong to the larger hearing culture simply by virtue of having grown up within it or having found it relatively easy to make their way through it.

Historically, these groups of the not-hearing have had little to do with one another. The culturally Deaf have preferred their own company, the oral deaf employ Emersonian self-reliance, and the lately deafened have had little in common with the others. Yet exceptions abound—some members of each group are fluent in both speech and sign language and find it easy to mix among the other two groups. Whatever point of view they espouse, it has likely been colored by the increasingly bitter debate over how young deaf children should be reared. The choices are to use sign language alone or as a first language with written English as a second, or to use speech, lipreading, and residual hearing, as well as to undergo cochlear implants, ear surgery that has had varying results in restoring a kind of hearing to some patients—or through a mixture of methods. From time to time, someone will suggest that the groups unite for mutual advancement, but so quarrelsome are the divisions that most such alliances never last.

This is emphatically not the case with the IDPA. So strong are its members' commitments to flying and to giving other deaf and hard-of-hearing people a leg up into aviation that commonality bridges the chasms. I saw that mutual respect at the group's annual fly-in one summer, at Manteo on the Outer Banks of North Carolina hard by Kitty Hawk and the Wright Memorial. A few Deaf pilots and their spouses may have felt diffident about my ignorance of sign language, but they did not show it. Rather, they made every effort to interact with me and with others and even hired a hearing interpreter who knew sign language so we could bridge the communications gap at our meetings and social events. For an hour, one Deaf pilot and I conversed companionably with a laptop computer, taking turns at the keyboard as the other watched the screen. For almost the first time in my life, I felt comfortable with members of the Deaf culture—and I daresay they felt the same with me.

They are teachers, lawyers, and computer engineers, as well as aviation mechanics, auto mechanics, and entrepreneurs. I have found each person fascinating for a different reason, but none more so than the group's most prominent European representative, a handsome and voluble (he converses in fluent Franglais with both sign language and speech) deaf-born French aviation technician in his late thirties with the aristocratic name of Henri Corderoy du Tiers. None has struggled for the right to fly more than Henri has. Though he has held an American private pilot's license since 1990, his homeland refuses to issue him one. France has been much less hospitable to the deaf than the United States; it did not allow them to drive automobiles until 1959 and boats until 1973.

For more than a decade, Henri has been battling the medical board of the FAA's French equivalent, which has refused to issue him the exemption from the rules that would let him obtain his French pilot's license. Early in 1991, the board, faced with Henri's acquisition of an American license, gave him a student pilot's certificate good for solo flights in airspace that do not require the use of a radio. A short time later, Henri passed the rigorous three-hour flight test for the license. That September the board allowed him half a license: He could fly solo, but he could not carry passengers. Supported by professionals at all levels of French aviation, including those the medical board designated to test his ability, Henri appealed. Petulantly, the medical board not only rejected the appeal but also yanked back most of the half license it had given him: Now he could fly only as a copilot. The hidebound doctors on the board feared that other deaf people might want to learn to fly and therefore swarm over French airports like grasshoppers in a wheatfield. That's hardly likely. With all the freedom the much larger United States grants to pilots, only about seventy or eighty aviators hold valid certificates with a restriction reading "not valid for flights requiring the use of radio," and some of these aviators are not deaf but speech impaired. Henri appealed again, to the French Ministry of Transport, and even five years later was still awaiting its decision. He does much of his serious flying in the United States and, indeed, has taken passengers through the Hudson River Exclusion, about which, he has observed with French élan, "I offered myself the incomparable spectacle of the skyscrapers and the Statue of Liberty. *C'est fantastique!*"

My guess is that Cal Rodgers would have had a hard time fitting

Bob Locher, the pilot who reawakened in the author an old boyhood dream of flight, in the cockpit of his Cessna 172.
*(Photo by Judy Locher)*

Tom Horton, the author's instructor, with one of the Westosha Flying Club's Cessna 152 trainers.
*(Photo by the author)*

Calbraith Perry Rodgers, who in 1911 became the first to fly across the United States. Note the ever-present stogie.
*(Photo courtesy National Air and Space Museum, Smithsonian Institution)*

A promotion poster for the Vin Fiz grape drink showing Cal Rodgers's coast-to-coast flight with inset pictures of events and statistics.
*(Photo courtesy National Air and Space Museum, Smithsonian Institution)*

Westosha Airport near Wilmot, Wisconsin, on a sunny spring day. The road below the airport runs from east to west; this view is down Runway 3.

*(Photo by the author)*

The blinking "Locherometer" that served as a rudimentary ear for the author, allowing him to broadcast his intentions over the radio without "stepping on" another pilot's transmission.                    *(Photo by the author)*

The newly purchased *Gin Fizz,* a 1959 vintage Cessna 150 two-seater with registration number N5859E, on its tiedown at Westosha.

*(Photo by the author)*

The author in *Gin Fizz*'s "office."

*(Photo by Jean Hauser)*

Ted Robinson, the former Tuskegee Airman who was the FAA's first black general aviation safety inspector, in the pilot's seat of his Mooney shortly before he and the author took a flight above the Washington, D.C., area.
*(Photo by the author)*

Eileen Lebow, the biographer of Cal Rodgers.
*(Photo by the author)*

Jim Lloyd in the pilot's seat of *Vin Fiz II* before his seventy-fifth anniversary re-enactment of Cal Rodgers's flight.     *(Photo by Susan J. Ogurian, AOCAD)*

Cal Rodgers puts on a show for cheering spectators as *Vin Fiz* begins its epic transcontinental flight at the old racetrack at Sheepshead Bay, Brooklyn, on September 17, 1911.
     *(Photo courtesy National Air and Space Museum, Smithsonian Institution)*

Manhattan puts on a show as *Gin Fizz* cruises at 1,100 feet up the Hudson River barely twenty minutes after takeoff from Old Bridge, New Jersey. *(Photo by the author)*

Max Francisco, probably the Northeast's only one-eyed flight instructor, in the doorway of his headquarters at White Birch Airport, Hancock, New York. *(Photo by the author)*

The wreckage of the Super Cub after the crash that killed sportsman Lee Wulff and cost Max Francisco his left eye. *(Photo courtesy of Max Francisco)*

The battered *Vin Fiz* after a close encounter with a barbed-wire fence on takeoff near Salamanca, New York. Cal Rodgers, however, was unhurt.
*(Photo courtesy National Air and Space Museum, Smithsonian Institution)*

The author and sailplane instructor Shane Lese search for thermals in a glider above Elmira, New York. *(Photo by the author)*

Mechanic Bob Reid buttons up *Gin Fizz* at Marion, Ohio, after a morning of routine maintenance—changing the oil and filter and cleaning the spark plugs.                                                    *(Photo by the author)*

Josephine Richardson, a white-haired dynamo and jack-of-all-airport-trades, mows her runway at Hi-Way Airport near Decatur, Indiana.

*(Photo by the author)*

"It makes a glorious noise." Jim Shuttleworth's P-51 refueling at Huntington, Indiana. BELOW: Shuttleworth in the cockpit of his warbird, one of just two surviving Mustangs flown by an ace in combat during World War II. *(Photos by the author)*

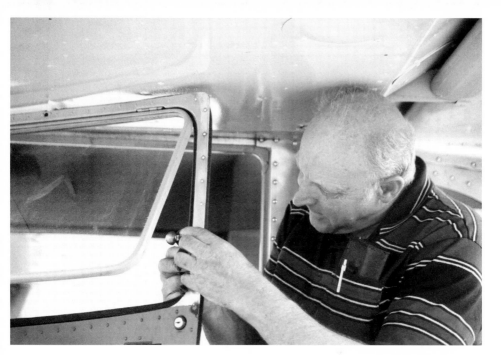

Larry Bub repairs *Gin Fizz*'s pilot door at Valparaiso, Indiana, shortly after the door frame had failed at its thinnest point and flapped alarmingly in the slipstream high above the ground. *(Photo by the author)*

LEFT: Gene and Cheryl Rae Littlefield of Plainfield, Illinois, do their wing-walking act in their much-modified 1942 vintage Boeing Stearman biplane. *(Photo courtesy of Gene and Cheryl Rae Littlefield)*

Virgil (Rocky) Rothrock and his very own Santa Fe caboose near the gas pumps of Streator Airport, Streator, Illinois. *(Photo by the author)*

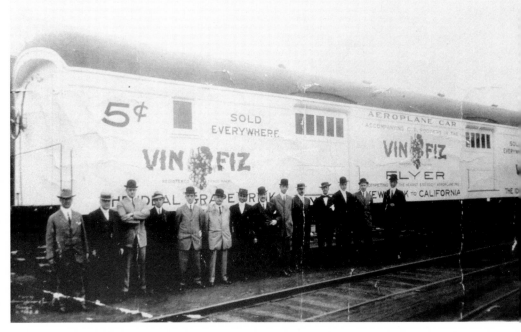

The "hangar car" of the special train that followed Cal Rodgers and the Vin Fiz all the way across the United States in 1911.

*(Photo courtesy National Air and Space Museum, Smithsonian Institution)*

The author and a boyhood mentor, YMCA executive Larry Meyer, upon *Gin Fizz*'s arrival at Jacksonville, Illinois.

*(Photo by Jason Coontz,* The State Journal Register*)*

Once a pilot, always a pilot. Bob Searfoss, who flew B-17s over occupied Europe during World War II, in the model-festooned master bedroom of his house in Mexico, Missouri. *(Photo by the author)*

Supersalesman Sebastien Heintz, president of the Zenith Aircraft Company, in the cockpit of a Super Zodiac kit plane in the firm's factory at Mexico, Missouri. *(Photo by the author)*

An ungainly An-2 biplane, aptly named "Kolkhoznik" or "collective farmer," still in its Soviet Aeroflot markings at the skydiving school in McAlester, Oklahoma.                                                                      *(Photo by the author)*

What, jump out of a perfectly good airplane? The author tries on a parachute at the North Texas Skydiving Center in Gainesville, Texas.
*(Photo by Ernie Long)*

Aerobatic pilot Barbara McLeod puts a Cessna 152 Aerobat into a roll in the skies over Austin, Texas. Just two and a half years earlier she had been grounded by a "lifelong and terrible" fear of flying.     *(Photo by the author)*

Legless pilot Jim Newman steps carefully around his pristinely restored Champ at Georgetown, Texas.     *(Photo by the author)*

This could be an elegant way to travel. *Bud No. 1,* the Budweiser Blimp, swings gently at her mooring mast, a cherry picker–like truck, at Deming, New Mexico. *(Photo by the author)*

A ghost of the Great War. Her pilot creakily extricates himself from the cockpit of a seven-eighths-scale replica of the British S.E. 5a pursuit plane at Lordsburg, New Mexico. *(Photo by the author)*

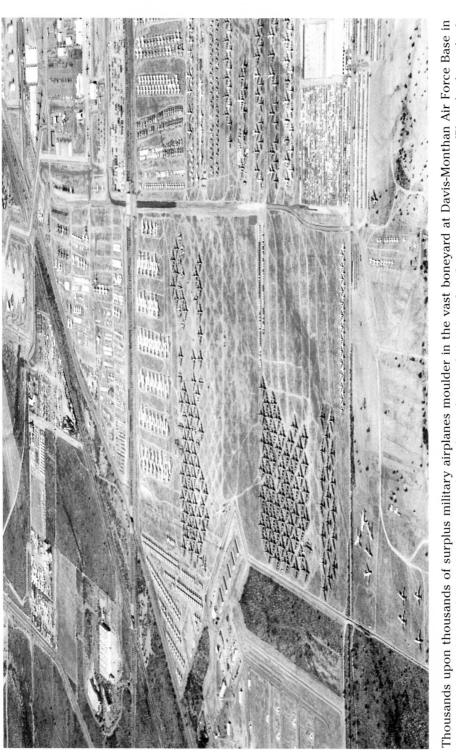

Thousands upon thousands of surplus military airplanes moulder in the vast boneyard at Davis-Monthan Air Force Base in Tucson, Arizona. Many of them, however, can be made combat-ready in just a few days. *(Photo by the author)*

"IFR" ordinarily means "Instrument Flight Rules," but on this trip it stands for "I Follow Roads." *Gin Fizz* drones westward high above Interstate 10 in eastern Arizona.                                                                  *(Photo by the author)*

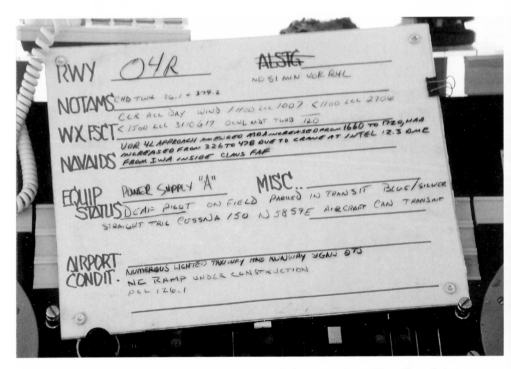

A bulletin board in the control tower of the airport at Chandler, Arizona, announces the fleeting presence of *Gin Fizz* and her pilot.

The Rev. O. Ray Williams's Cessna 172 closes with *Gin Fizz* twenty miles east of Yuma, Arizona, where the airplanes landed as a "flight of two" amid a swarm of Tomcats and Harriers, Herculeses and helicopters on the busy combined marine air station and civil airport. *(Photo by the author)*

Williams, a flying Methodist missionary who looks like a modern Arizona cowboy. *(Photo by the author)*

It is done. Cal Rodgers wets *Vin Fiz*'s skids in the Pacific surf at Long Beach, California.

*(Photo courtesy National Air and Space Museum, Smithsonian Institution)*

*Gin Fizz* arrives in Upland, California, in the eastern Los Angeles Basin, the grail of her coast-to-coast trip.  *(Photo by Bob Locher)*

in with this group of deaf pilots, at least in the beginning. His mother's apparent reluctance to discuss her son's deafness in her correspondence or with reporters indicates that she refused to acknowledge his hearing loss. Perhaps influenced by his mother's attitude, Rodgers may have shunned other deaf and hard-of-hearing people. It is also likely that Cal knew how society regarded what it called the "deaf and dumb" and did not want people to look down upon him. (For many years, I believed the same thing.) On the other hand, he eventually might have been drawn toward the IDPA simply by the powerful attraction of twin currents of solidarity—one of a mutual interest in aviation and the other of indomitable people like himself who, sharing the commonality of being unable to hear, devise novel ways of coping with it.

And cope the IDPA has. In 1995 the FAA proposed new medical rules for private pilots, to deal with an influx of Japanese student pilots on the West Coast. Many Japanese come to this country to learn to fly—instruction is much less expensive in the United States because aviation taxes are far lower here—but their less-than-adequate grasp of English often drives air traffic controllers crazy, especially in the heavily trafficked airspace around Los Angeles and San Francisco. Therefore, the FAA decided to require that all pilots "be able to read, write, speak, and understand the English language." That was sensible enough, but in rewriting the rules, the FAA inadvertently removed the provision for special operating limitations ("Not valid for flights requiring the use of radio") that allowed the deaf, hard of hearing, and speech impaired to become pilots.

Mark Stern, a fellow oral deaf pilot on the West Coast who took the trouble to read the fine print of the FAA's proposal, spotted the new language and told me about it, and I passed the word on to Clyde Smith, a culturally Deaf pilot. Clyde immediately called two IDPA members in Washington—one hearing (several hearing pilots who are interested in deafness belong to the group) and one lately deafened, who, reinforced by the Aircraft Owners and Pilots Association as well as several national organizations for the deaf, met with the FAA and prevailed on the agency to alter the draconian regulations. The provision was restored, and deaf and hard-of-hearing people in America still have the right to fly. Best of all, the FAA also extended the provision to apply to other new regulations. When new technology allows deaf pilots to communicate over the radio with Air Traffic Control, we will be able to earn instrument ratings and fly in bad weather. If that victory doesn't demonstrate the power of solidarity, I don't know what does.

One of the folks who met my plane at Jacksonville was a fiftyish student pilot who, like me, had taken up flying after fulfilling obligations of family and finances. By happenstance, he was making a short solo cross-country flight that evening, and as I passed him on the way back to my airplane, he was sitting in the left seat of a Piper Tomahawk trainer consulting his sectional chart. I waved cheerily, and he responded. Before I climbed into my airplane, I noticed that the wind sock was completely limp. The wind tee—an airplane-shaped indicator that shows which runway is active— was, however, pointing straight down Runway 31, the designated no-wind runway at Jacksonville. As at most airports, the no-wind runway logically points away from the city, in this case, toward the empty fields to the northwest, simply to reduce further the small risk of accident. An airplane suffering engine failure on takeoff would find a place to land without endangering lives or property.

After strapping myself into *Gin Fizz* and checking my own flight plan, I started the engine and taxied to the holding line on the taxiway near the threshold of Runway 31. As I finished the engine runup, I noticed that the Piper was nowhere to be seen and assumed that the student pilot had already taken off. I keyed the mike and announced in the blind, "Jacksonville traffic, Cessna five-eight-five-niner-Echo departing Runway Three-One, Jacksonville"—and opened the throttle. The plane rapidly gathered speed.

It so happens that there is a hump in the center of Runway 13-31 where the cross runway, 4-22, bisects it. The hump is so pronounced that an airplane at the other end of Runway 31 cannot be seen. You guessed it—as soon as *Gin Fizz* had lifted ten feet off Runway 31, the Piper emerged at the other end of the runway, starting its takeoff roll on Runway 13 right toward me.

It was immediately apparent, however, that *Gin Fizz* would clear the Piper by seventy-five feet or more while it was still rolling, long before its wheels left the concrete, so I held my course. And just before my airplane flashed over the Piper, the other pilot's eyes widened in horror and his jaw dropped as he spotted *Gin Fizz,* hit his brakes—hard—and skidded to a fishtailing stop.

I had done all the right things. I had checked the active no-wind runway and broadcast my intentions. But I had made two false assumptions: first, that the other pilot would follow normal no-wind practice, and second, that he would hear and understand my broadcast. Pilots make mistakes, especially when they are students. And there is no guarantee that another pilot will always have his radio on, if his plane has one, at an uncontrolled airport. The law does not require him to have it on. And if he does, there is no guarantee that he will have understood the broadcast.

The mistake I made was not to have kept a better eye on that Piper and all other airplanes on the ground, to be sure they were following normal practice and departing on the designated no-wind runway. I could simply have asked the student what runway he planned to use. I could also have made sure there were no aircraft rolling down the taxiway to the other end of the runway while I was taxiing out for takeoff.

Jacksonville is hardly unique. As I was to discover later in the trip to Los Angeles, the main paved runway of many an airport has a hump in the middle where another runway crosses it. Often the first runway was built long before the second one, and to save money, later builders did not grade the ground for a new cross runway to be perfectly level with the first. Thus the hump.

I shuddered. For the second time that day, I thought, I had been lucky. The same angel that had shepherded Cal Rodgers through that Indiana thunderstorm in 1911 was looking out for me, too.

# 11

hat, really, was the extent of my good fortune? Was I over-dramatizing the perils of the day? As *Gin Fizz* droned along the Santa Fe tracks through the farm fields west of Jacksonville, I could hear faint cries of "You coulda been killed!" "I told you so!" and the like from the many naysayers among my relatives, friends, and colleagues. As the remarks reverberated in my head, I began to contemplate what they revealed about the people who spoke them. So many people, I realized, allowed hardly any daring and adventuresomeness into their own lives, so imprisoned were they by their quotidian routines and so fearful of testing themselves. Like prissy bankers and actuaries, some had warned me that the money I spent flying should instead go into my retirement fund and that my life insurance was unlikely to pay off if I accidentally killed myself while flying. (They were wrong about the life insurance, but as part of the bargain with Debby, I bought double the amount of my ordinary term life policy in pilot's flight insurance, making me worth far more dead than I will ever be alive). Middle age, I wanted to tell them, may give one the wisdom to accept his limitations, his lot in life—but that acceptance has two sides: It can entrap him forever, or it can free the person to explore new worlds.

Exactly how dangerous is flying in a small plane? In 1995, the latest year for which figures are available, the FAA reported a fatality rate of 1.5 deaths per 100,000 hours flown in small airplanes. If a private pilot flies 100 hours a year, a generous number, he faces less than a one hundredth of 1 percent chance of being killed in an accident. In measuring comparative risk, it's difficult to compare these numbers with those for automobiles, which are calculated in miles traveled instead of hours aloft.

A good rule of thumb, however, is that statistically, a pilot has better than a 99.990 percent chance of surviving a small plane ride, and a driver has better than a 99.999 percent chance of surviving an automobile ride. In other words, the risks are tiny and ten times tiny. Furthermore, the chance of a pilot being killed is directly related to the risks he takes. The two biggest killers are flying into bad weather and running out of fuel, traps that are both easy to avoid. On the road, another driver's stupid mistake can kill you; if you die in a general-aviation crash, it's usually your own fault.

My experiences during night flights with Tom Horton convinced me never to fly alone after dark, not without a flight instructor in the right seat. I watch my fuel burn carefully. Instead of keeping the required fuel reserve of thirty minutes, I keep an hour's reserve. I watch the weather diligently, although I admit that that morning I had increased the risk by taking off from Westosha into weather that was below the personal minimums I had set for myself. Even so, the risk was within legal limits. Theoretically, the risk a pilot exposes himself to is largely under his personal control. Practically, he has to be willing to increase the risk on occasion, or he would never get into an airplane in the first place. Those who try to lead lives of zero risk never go out of the house. Arthur Rudolph, the scientist who developed the Saturn rocket that launched the first Apollo mission to the moon, had the perfect metaphor for the situation: "You want a valve that doesn't leak and you try everything possible to develop one, but the real world provides you with a leaky valve. You have to determine how much leaking you can tolerate." In other words, risk exists, but we can manage it. We are not passive in the face of chance.

The episode with the communications bag at Lacon certainly wasn't dangerous, but I *was* lucky that the airport manager had spotted the bag before I took off. Otherwise, I would have had to fly back to retrieve it from wherever I discovered it missing, probably the last stop of the day in Missouri. A major inconvenience, nothing more. And the near miss on the runway at Jacksonville was not as dangerous as it had at first seemed. Even if the other pilot had started his takeoff roll at the same time I had, we were both flying slow training airplanes, and it is likely that we'd have seen each other in plenty of time to follow the rules and make an evasive turn to the right. Nonetheless, I learned a valuable lesson from the incident, and I hope the other pilot did as well.

The event of the day I truly regretted was the one at De Kalb. Had I not let my guard down after following that Aeronca, I probably would have seen the oncoming 182 in plenty of time to lengthen my downwind leg and follow him in, thereby avoiding the unpleasant contretemps that ensued. We were in no danger, for the other pilot had been alert. But I did not dismiss the incident. Again, the lesson I learned made me a safer pilot. "See and avoid," I often say to myself, in one of the FAA's favorite mantras. "See and avoid." At these times I can feel Tom Horton's glare drilling into my back.

Not long after the incident at De Kalb, news broke of a tragedy at nearby Quincy, whose airport is also an uncontrolled field. There a King Air corporate twin carrying two flight instructors began its takeoff roll at the same time a United Express Beechcraft 1900 commuter aircraft with twelve aboard landed on the cross runway. The two airplanes collided at the intersection of the runways, killing everyone. The exact reasons for the tragedy are dim—it seems that radio communications between the pilots failed—but it is clear that the United Express plane had the right of way because it was landing, and that the pilot of the King Air failed to see and avoid the oncoming aircraft. Visibility had been excellent. He simply did not follow the established rules. The lesson was driven deep into my consciousness and, I daresay, that of every other conscientious pilot.

The Quincy accident caused several people who are not pilots to ask if I did not think that all airfields that host passenger traffic—even just two flights a day—should have control towers. I sighed. They could, I replied, but where's the money going to come for a new control tower and its personnel in a climate of cutbacks in governmental spending? The truth is that we already have rules to control landings and takeoffs at uncontrolled airports. Think of highway intersections with stop signs and traffic lights. For the most part, they work just fine. But, given the laws of chance and human carelessness, sooner or later somebody is going to get sloppy and fail to stop, precipitating a fatal accident. Should the state therefore remove the signs and replace them with an expensive traffic cop? The bottom line is that we establish rules for cooperation to help us avoid accidents and expect everyone to follow them. If accidents occur only when someone neglects the existing regulations, does applying more and more stringent rules avoid the problem? Not necessarily. There have been a number of fatal runway collisions at towered airports, too.

As a deaf pilot, however, I feel much less likely than a hearing one to become involved in such an accident—simply because my deafness makes me more vigilant than the average hearing pilot, who often tends to rely too much on the radio for protection. Once, in the lounge after a flight, another pilot, who had been waiting behind me on the ramp, complained that I seemed awfully slow to get rolling out on the runway for takeoff after I did my engine run-up. "There was no incoming traffic," he said. "What was the problem?" Slowly and a little reproachfully, I replied: "I just had to *make sure.*" I'd rather be a live turtle than a dead rabbit.

I felt better as *Gin Fizz* climbed away from Jacksonville on a heading to intercept the Santa Fe line at Nebo, a hamlet thirty-two miles southwest, where Cal Rodgers had landed in 1911 to refuel. Nebo even named one of its streets for *Vin Fiz,* and each October the town celebrates the great event in its history— the arrival of Cal Rodgers—with a parade of folks dressed as historical figures from Illinois and Missouri, just a few miles west. When Jim Lloyd landed *Vin Fiz II* on a city street there in 1986, he was met by Abe Lincoln, Tom Sawyer, and Becky Thatcher.

No airport exists near Nebo, but as *Gin Fizz* droned over the hamlets and toward the lowlands of western Illinois toward the Mississippi River and Missouri, I promised myself to return someday for the annual celebration. Meanwhile, still spooked by the events at Jacksonville, I began woolgathering about other consequences of deafness for pilots. If it is true, as that long-ago newspaper account said, that Cal Rodgers was "timid about associating with other aviators" because of his imperfect speech, then he, like me and every other deaf pilot, would have missed much of the great fellowship of hangar flying.

On every warm weekend morning, when the smell of dew still lies fresh on the grass, pilots at small airports gather inside the yawning mouth of a hangar or a shabby pilot's lounge. Their gathering is as American as PTA meetings, firehouse raffles, and cracker-barrel assemblies. Information is exchanged, opinions vented, lies told, relationships maintained, and friendships cemented before the important business of the day—aviation—begins. Within this broad brotherhood lie several layers of hierarchy.

At the center of the group, dominating the conversation, are the Owners. On the periphery are the Renters, who, for the most part, maintain a respectful silence. Owners are not necessarily better or more experienced pilots than Renters, but they tend to take more conscientious care of their airplanes. Owners keep their airplanes lovingly polished, the windows sparkling. They change engine oil religiously. They are meticulous about maintenance. Renters do few of these things; those tasks fall to the FBOs and flying clubs that own the airplanes, and they often will perform only the legally required tasks. Renters often fly at full throttle at low altitude, shortening the engines' lives. They fail to refuel the planes for the next pilots. They park aircraft haphazardly on the tiedowns. They are less punctilious about shutdown checklists. Sometimes they forget to turn off the master electrical switch, ensuring that the battery will be dead within an hour. Owners look down upon Renters as careless slobs, and Renters resent Owners as anal-retentive snobs. Owners lend each other tools; Renters nod a curt hello. Owners stay around for years; Renters come and go. Within each group, Owners tend to be ranked by the size of their airplanes and Renters, by the number of hours in their logbooks. These rankings are not always exact, however. Many Boeing 747 drivers, bored with autopilots steering their enormous buses at high altitude, own tiny Champs and Ercoupes just for the sensation of flying low and slow.

Layered over this pecking order is one based on experience. The pilots who win the most respect from the others naturally are the former military fliers, especially fighter pilots who flew in combat, for their war stories are the most eagerly greeted. Just below them are the airline captains, holders of Air Transport Pilot ratings. (Former fighter pilots who are airline captains rank the highest.) Then come the commercial pilots, including the certified flight instructors. Below them is the largest group, the private pilots, led by those who hold instrument ratings. At the bottom are the peons, the student pilots, and dividing this group are those who have soloed and those who have not.

The shared conversation often is important to aviators. The

weather, often merely an ice-breaking topic for nonpilots, is frequently discussed with the urgent gravity that physicians give to mysterious lumps in the groin. Both experienced and low-time pilots who are about to fly to a new airport will look for someone who has been there and knows its idiosyncrasies. Stories of a zealous FAA inspector doing surprise "ramp checks" at a nearby airport often spur pilots, Owners and Renters alike, to check to see that the paperwork carried aboard their airplanes is complete and up to date. News of a nearby fatal crash will send chills down everyone's spine. A successful first solo or flight test will bring a round of cheers and backslapping. Learning about the singularities of particular aircraft brands will engross Renters who are thinking of becoming Owners.

There is also a great deal of political discussion. Pilots tend to be conservative, generally for two reasons. First, they have more money, on the average, than most Americans and naturally want to keep as much of it as they can. Second, they tend to mistrust governmental regulations, particularly the bureaucratic minutiae of the FAA that is so often a burr under their saddles. Some seem to obtain their political education from Rush Limbaugh, but others are remarkably well informed about battles on Capitol Hill that threaten to affect their net worth, and it is a feckless liberal who joins argument with them without having done his homework. (Anyway, liberals are usually so outnumbered in pilot's lounges that they keep quiet.)

Within this group are a smattering of types, but the largest representation is heavily masculine and sometimes chauvinist. The older the pilot, the hairier chested he tends to be. For instance, veterans of World War II, Korea, and Vietnam are often appalled that the U.S. military would put women in the cockpits of combat aircraft; younger male Gulf War pilots, however, tend to tolerate and even welcome the idea. Not, however, navy carrier-based fighter pilots. It is not surprising, though, that the old boys show far more manners and even gallantry to female pilots and student pilots than do the younger ones; when the first woman of the day walks into a male-dominated pilot's lounge, the old-timers suddenly clean up their language and even doff their caps. For the same reason, an archconservative pilot with a bitterly jaundiced view of affirmative action and welfare entitlements but a genuine admiration for individual accomplishment will often be the first to give an itinerant black flier a warm welcome to his airfield. His younger, more "liberal" colleagues, I have noticed more times than I care to count, will frequently pay lip service to the yearnings of minorities—African Americans and people with disabilities among them—but wouldn't take one home to dinner. It is for this reason, I think, that despite my own leanings toward the Left, my deepest friendships tend to be with those on the Right. And it may help explain why I have sensed greater acceptance from pilots, as conservative a bunch as exists, than from journalists, as liberal a group as you'll find anywhere.

And the often infectious sense of humor among the old-boy right-wing pilots may lead even the dewiest young leftist to forgive their benighted attitudes. Pilots' humor is singular and usually involves self-mocking stories of brushes with disaster, as well as encounters with bureaucracy. The jokes pilots tell couldn't be altered to fit any other pursuit. The FAA is the butt of many of them, especially the safety inspectors who spring surprise check rides on commercial pilots to test their proficiency in simulated emergencies. A much-hated inspector's trick is to snake back one or more throttles unexpectedly, just as the airplane climbs away from the airport, and crow "Engine failure! Now what?" This led to a hoary old Santa Claus tale that is retold every holiday season, and no matter how many times the pilots have heard it, the laughter will be heartfelt. Here is how I heard it:

One day Santa Claus was preflighting his sleigh when a car drove up and a man in a suit carrying a briefcase got out. "Hello," said the man. "I'm a safety inspector from the FAA, and I'll be riding with you today."

Santa was pissed off. The last thing he needed on the most important flight of the year was an FAA guy in the jump seat testing his skill in emergencies. He protested. "I've been carrying toys to good little boys and girls all over the world for 2,000 years without an accident," he said, "and *now* you spring a surprise check ride?"

"Get in," said the inspector. "Let's go."

As Santa resignedly took up the reins and clucked to Dasher and Dancer, the man from the FAA opened his briefcase and took out a shotgun.

"What's with the shotgun?" Santa asked in alarm.

Said the FAA man: "You're going to lose two on takeoff!"

*      *      *

Except among themselves and on a one-to-one basis with hearing pilots, deaf aviators generally are unable to participate in hangar flying. Group conversations are just too difficult for even expert lip-readers to follow; by the time they figure out the topic of the moment, the conversation often has passed on to something else. There is an adequate substitute for in-the-flesh hangar flying, however, and it's the most commodious hangar of all: the Internet. Every morning and every evening, when I'm not flying, I fire up my computer and, with screen and keyboard, participate as easily and as fully as any hearing pilot, missing nothing of the ebb and flow of online conversations.

First, I'll check the Internet newsgroups—glorified electronic bulletin boards with such specialized titles as "rec.aviation," "rec.aviation.hang-gliding," "rec.aviation.marketplace," "rec.aviation.owning," "rec.aviation.piloting," "rec.aviation.products," "rec.aviation.student," "rec.aviation.ultralight"—and even "alt.aviation.disasters." (Nobody ever seems to post anything on "rec.aviation.lovemaking.") In these forums questions are asked and answered and spleen is vented— "Q. My nosewheel strut is deflated. How much will it cost to fix?" "A. Maybe nothing." "Q. What will Clinton's plan to privatize the FAA mean for small-plane owners?" "A. It'll hit you in the wallet." As with actual hangar flying, a great deal of opinion passes for fact, and one must learn to discriminate between wisdom and twaddle.

Then I'll drop in on the AVweb site on the World Wide Web. AVweb is not a bulletin board but an electronic magazine, with expert color illustrations supplementing news stories, consumer articles, and product reviews. It's operated in the same spirit (and briefly shared an editor with) the highly respected *Aviation Consumer* magazine, one of the few aviation publications that doesn't seem to kowtow to advertisers with puff articles and kid-gloves product evaluations. AVweb is updated each Sunday night with new articles, and old ones are retained in the site's database. It's a class act.

Finally, I'll call up what is at this writing the biggest, liveliest, and oldest forum of all: the Aviation Special Interest Group—AVSIG for short—on CompuServe. With some 80,000 members from all over the world at its peak, this enormous forum—think of it as a hangar bigger than O'Hare Airport—has been a godsend for a low-time pilot seeking to overcome his ignorance. On it I have posted queries and received sensible, cogent answers on such practical matters as overcoming the fear of flying, where to rent oxygen bottles for high-altitude flights, used headsets, computer flight log programs, air-camping sites, federal aviation rules, automobile fuel, instrument repairs, converting aural stall-warning horns to electric warning lights, light-gun landings, fatal accidents, the best places to stop on a transcontinental trip, and how to prevent bird droppings from marring airplanes on outside tiedowns (respondents suggested plastic owls, rubber snakes, and "an inflatable fellow with an inflatable shotgun parked in a lawn chair by your airplane").

I recently posted a message asking whether anyone knew the history of the term *fixed-base operation,* one of the least self-descriptive aviation terms I've encountered. An old-timer came to the rescue. After World War I, he said, barnstorming pilots hopped from field to field giving rides and flight lessons. These characters were colorful but transient. As time went on, other pilots—who were business people at heart—settled down and committed themselves to providing flight and ground services to all customers from a fixed base of operations. "Many old-timers would argue that the first fixed-base operators, or FBOs, were not as committed as they were desperate," said the old-timer. "The profit had gone out of barnstorming, and they became 'fixed' when they ran out of money."

There is naturally a great deal of camaraderie, and certain questions invariably will bring standup comedians out of the closet. For instance, one of the special problems a deaf pilot faces without being able to use the radio is not only determining his location, but also finding the direction and speed of the wind and the active runway at a strange airport. He can't call the pilot's lounge on the radio and ask for "winds and active." Wind socks are tiny and hard to see from the air and sometimes have been blown away in a storm. The old pilot's standby, smoke from local chimneys, has all but disappeared in this age of environmentalism. Checking the direction of wind-blown waves on a pond helps—if there's a pond nearby, but lots of luck if you're flying over a desert. And so I naturally have searched out unusual ways to determine the direction and velocity of the wind, as well as offbeat aids to navigation, and this is why I posted the following message on AVSIG:

The following item appears in the March 1995 issue of *Government Technology* under the heading "Bovine Navigation."

"Back in the 1920s, pilots delivered the mail by following roads, rivers, and landmarks. They had no GPS or other electronic direction finders. But there was one navigational aid—cows. If a pilot saw cows scattering on the ground beneath his plane, he knew he was off course. Why? Cows on the flyway, accustomed to planes, continued to graze. Those not used to planes would run away, thus giving pilots an udder way of navigating."

Well, I don't know. A few months ago, a pilot who lives in the Upper Peninsula of Michigan told me, in all seriousness, that one of the ways he judged wind direction before landing was to look at herds of cows. They face into the wind, he said.

Several times I've tried to test that statement, and every time the cows were facing every which way. Maybe there just wasn't much wind.

But why would a cow face *into* the wind? Horses are just as stupid, and they have the sense to face \*away\* from the wind.

I don't understand it.

This was the first response I received:

Most grazing animals will face away from the wind. If a predator approaches from upwind, they have a shot at smelling it; if the predator approaches from downwind, they have a shot at seeing it.

Quite a sensible answer, and so was the following:

Henry, many years ago when I was in grammar school one of my teachers said cows face *away* from the wind because their hair grows such that facing into the wind raises the hair, and that's uncomfortable. She also said the opposite was true with horses. I often meant to find out for myself. But every time I was near a horse or cow, I'd forget the research.

A former air force pilot offered this confirmation:

In the early '70s I flew C-130s on low-level routes in Kansas. We would bore holes in the sky at 500 feet AGL [above ground level], then pop up and drop jeeps on "Jayhawk Drop Zone" across the road from our base near Topeka.

Cows that were used to the noise of three or more airplanes passing just overhead would just keep on grazing, tail to the wind (unless there was no wind). If the cows were scattering from our noise, we knew the navigator had us off course.

Navaids? That's stretching it a bit. You might be able to define an airway, but using cows for intersections would be challenging.

Another respondent added an interesting dimension:

I've heard it as cows face *away from* the wind, and if they are facing everywhichaway, there isn't enough wind to worry about. I've also heard that if you fly a fabric covered plane, you should not land in a field with cows in it, because they will eat the fabric.

Two other replies carried the discussion a bit further:

They also love doped cotton fabric and will eat it off the plane. I have no idea if they are interested in more modern paints and fabrics. They like to rub up against things and may push the plane around or crush parts.

Same rumor among skydivers. If you have a malfunction and release your main parachute, you don't want to let it lie in a cow pasture for days before you find it. If the cows get to it first, they will eat your parachute. I have never actually seen this happen. I can, however, speak from first-hand experience about a helmet I lost once over a cow pasture. Someone found it about a year later and returned it to me. The foam and fabric lining was gone, and teeth marks were scraped into the edges of the helmet where the cows had chewed on it to get to the foam.

Then the nickel-and-dime Henny Youngmans popped up ("I think the whole thing is a fabric-ation") and punsters of a juvenile bent, of course, felt moved to check in with their unoriginal and unhelpful observations ("I know how to milk a cow. You just pull one thing or the udder" and "Lemme ruminate about this for a while"), of which there must have been a dozen. A pilot from Texas with a well-developed sense of drollery submitted the following (actually only a tiny part of the whole message):

Here is a good way to judge your altitude (AGL) using cows as a visual reference:

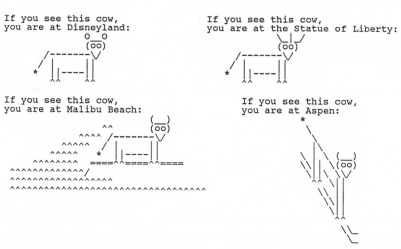

Cow at 50 feet          Cow at 1,000 feet          Cow at 10,000 feet

If you see this cow, you are at Disneyland:

If you see this cow, you are at the Statue of Liberty:

If you see this cow, you are at Malibu Beach:

If you see this cow, you are at Aspen:

The illustrations went on like that for more than two pages, which prompted this rejoinder from a North Carolinian:

"We need to find you a life, son. I think you been 'deep in the heart of' for too long."

At this point I posted the following *cri de coeur:* "My God, what have I started with my innocent cow query?"

To which the same North Carolinian replied: "No such thing as an innocent cow, son. They are all guilty of something."

AVSIG, however, has played host to a number of dramatic exchanges as well as good-old-boy knee-slappers. The most astonishing one I watched unfold concerned a "quiet, unassuming" veteran Minnesota pilot who was the subject of an admiring article in *AOPA Pilot.* The profile began, "Mel Fielder can fool you. . . . He doesn't look much like an FAA official. But then, he doesn't really look like a pilot who used to fly for Air America in Southeast Asia, either. Or, for that matter, a man whose first 20 skydiving jumps were into the mountains between East and West Germany with a German shepherd strapped to his chest so that he could help refugees escape across the border. Or, while we're at it, perhaps the only pilot in history to have made his one and only aircraft carrier landing in a Fairchild C-123 cargo plane."

The article went on to say, among other things, that the C-123 had been loaded with North Vietnamese prisoners the military wanted to interrogate. Saigon was weathered in, Fielder said, and, low on fuel, he "was directed to land on an aircraft carrier off the coast. 'I put it down on the numbers, with the engines in reverse and the brakes locked,' he remembers."

After reading the article, John Deakin, a 747 captain for Japan Air Lines flying the Los Angeles–São Paulo route and himself a veteran of Air America, the famous CIA airline, sent an open message on AVSIG to Tony Broderick, a high FAA official. "Man, he certainly fooled the author and the magazine, and is apparently fooling a lot of people, probably including the FAA," Deakin wrote. Of the sky dives with dogs strapped to Fielder's chest, Deakin said, "It sounds like a four-drink story to me." Then came the heavy lumber. Deakin had flown C-123s for Air America at that time and had never heard of Mel Fielder, nor had he heard of anyone landing such a large and cumbersome twin-engine cargo airplane on an aircraft carrier. Nor, Deakin said, had a large number of Air America veterans—including the line's chief pilot—and a retired admiral who had served in the South China Sea during the period.

"The small group left" of genuine Air America pilots, Deakin finished, "is intensely proud of what AAM did. We revere greatly the many who lost their lives, and honor the real heroes who survived. We are deeply angry at this nonsense."

For the next two days, a flurry of heated messages on the topic of Mel Fielder choked AVSIG. The Minnesotan had his defenders. Judging from other details in the AOPA Pilot article, he seemed a genuinely nice guy, a gentle, steady, and soft-spoken man who went out of his way to help others, and his friends emphasized that. According to one of them, Fielder said that it was a World War II–era British carrier he had landed on, and that is why the U.S. Navy had no knowledge of the incident. This brought the reply that the British had no carriers from that period, and the only likely one that Fielder could have landed on was so small the C-123 would have taken out her superstructure. Other friends speculated that Fielder was in a witness-protection program and could not reveal his real name. ("Then would it be prudent to get your picture in a national magazine?" was one retort.)

And then the terrible news came: Mel Fielder had killed himself. A printout of many of the AVSIG messages, it was said, had been found in his car. Fielder's friends fiercely attacked Deakin in their online posts, charging that his "irresponsible" messages had precipitated Fielder's suicide. Deakin refused to accept the blame, saying his only motive was to find the truth about Mel Fielder, and the majority of the AVSIG members who participated in the controversy agreed. One suggested that Fielder had been suffering from bipolar depression, also known as manic-depressive illness, a speculation that won wide acceptance. Another participant, a well-known and highly respected pilot, wrote with surprising courage and openness, "As a long-time combatant with uncontrollable mood swings, all I can say is: I've been there and done (or tried to do) just that. . . . Mel Fielder took his life for much deeper reasons [than Deakin's exposure]. What John posted on AVSIG was only a trigger, the necessary justification for action by someone who was already wired to self-destruct."

When the story finally simmered down, the editors of *AOPA Pilot* said a published explanation of the Fielder story would take time because Freedom of Information Act requests were involved. At this writing, they have not yet published such a story. In the meantime, all sides agreed that they had learned something useful about their own humanity and that of others and that the entire contretemps was worth it if it helped one person recognize and conquer depression. "Mel's death was not in vain," said one, "because here we are talking about this." Two hundred friends attended his funeral.

Soon the marshes of the Mark Twain National Wildlife Refuge passed below, and then *Gin Fizz* crossed the Mississippi River just north of Louisiana, Missouri. Vast acres of deep green flood plain, part of the glacial Till Plains over which I had been flying since I left the Chicago metropolitan area, stretched from horizon to horizon. *Gin Fizz* droned on along the Santa Fe tracks, and an hour after leaving Jacksonville, I saw the smokestacks and radio towers of Mexico, Missouri, dead ahead, silhouetted in the lowering sun. Rodgers had not landed there. He had been forced down at Thompson, four miles farther west, by a balky spark plug. While the repairs were being made, a delegation from Mexico arrived. Its members offered Rodgers a "substantial purse" to fly around their city, and Cal agreed. Though Mexico was not an official *Vin Fiz* stop, I decided to make it one of mine because of the late hour—and because there were some people there whom I wanted to see.

# 12

year before, in my other life, I had received a letter from a graduate journalism student at the University of Missouri at Columbia. She was writing a thesis on newspaper book-review policies and had sent me a questionnaire. I had been planning the *Gin Fizz* route and noticed that the return address was from Mexico, a town along that route. In my reply I mentioned that I'd be passing through on my way west and asked if she happened to know any good aviation-related stories around Mexico. She said she had, and so Grazia Rechichi Svokos—a small and effervescent Italian-born, Brooklyn-bred former laborer in the New York publishing vineyard—was waiting, three small children in tow, when I shut down at the Mexico FBO.

After we made our hellos, an old-timer walked over and said, "Come with me. Got something to show you." While Grazia fetched her minivan, I followed him to his hangar, a big one, and walked inside. And there loomed a rare airplane, an F8F Bearcat. My eyes widened and my small-boy memory kicked in. The Bearcat was the ultimate piston-engined U.S. Navy shipboard fighter, the smallest airframe Grumman could build around the biggest radial engine available in 1945. It had rolled off the assembly lines too late to see combat service in World War II, but had fought under the French flag in Indochina in the 1950s. Much-altered examples still fly at the annual air races in Reno, Nevada. In 1989 one of them, *Rare Bear,* flown by Lyle Shelton, set the official world's speed record for piston-engined airplanes at 528 miles per hour.

The Bearcat in the hangar was a sorry sight. Her gleaming top half, painted in authentic dark-blue U.S. Navy colors, looked as if it had just emerged from the restorer's hangar—which she had. Her bottom, however, was a sea of rippled, torn, and mud-splattered sheet metal. Her enormous four-blade propeller had been twisted and bent into a pretzel. "Guy in Michigan spent one-point-three million dollars restoring her," said the old-timer, who had introduced himself gravely as Joe Jacobi, "and on her first cross-country flight, to Columbia for an air show, she had an engine failure just east of here. Only thirteen hours on the engine! He put her down perfectly, gear up, in a wheat field. He was lucky. She's repairable. He's coming next week with a flatbed truck, and he'll remove the wings and take her home to rebuild her."

Joe is himself a warbird restorer, albeit on a much smaller scale than either Jim Shuttleworth or the fellow who had rebuilt the Bearcat. In the back of his hangar, he showed me the fuselage of a Taylorcraft L-2 observation plane, which looks like a Piper Cub gone to war. "Been working on it for three years," he said, "and I'll be done in two more. I've just finished recovering the wings." A retired electrician, he no longer flies, having had open-heart surgery three years before.

"Do you miss flying?" I asked.

"I'm satisfied just to be alive."

We shook hands as Grazia collected me in her minivan, first driving into town to drop off the children, then taking me to the other side of Mexico to see "someone you just have to meet." Soon I emerged in the driveway of a substantial home to behold a gleaming seven-foot-long B-17 bomber atop a custom-built automobile trailer, its sides dropped down to display the radio-controlled airplane. On the model's nose was painted the legend "Organized Confusion." On the other side of the trailer stood a tall, broadly smiling white-haired man named Bob Searfoss.

"Ten-foot, four-inch wingspan—the wings detach—three-and-a-half horsepower in four engines, forty pounds," he said, rattling off the figures in practiced fashion. "The radio receiver has eight channels that drive thirteen servos. See, all its control surfaces work." For the next ten minutes, he showed me how the plane worked. It was by far the most elaborate radio-controlled scale model I had ever seen, and I have seen many.

We sat on the shaded veranda by Bob's garage, iced teas in hand, and talked. Dr. Robert Searfoss is a common Midwestern species, a courtly country gentleman with a booming laugh and an easy manner who can make an urban visitor feel at home in an instant. He is a seventy-four-year-old optometrist, a veteran of World War II, and the model was a silvery replica of the full-sized B-17G he had flown from England over Europe. "Have any more airplanes?" I asked.

"Have any more?" he said, eyebrows rising. "Come."

I followed him into his house and then into his bedroom, a huge chamber that seemed to take up one end of the place. It looked like the bedroom of a small boy who had successfully resisted growing up. Scores of model airplanes hung from the ceiling. Not your little plastic shake-the-box-and-it's-built kit models, but big balsa-wood monsters with five- and six-foot wingspans, all built from scratch. A few seemed to be of Searfoss's own freelance design, but most were World War II aircraft—a P-38 here, a P-47 there, a P-51 over here. Some were battered and tattered. Others looked pristine. On a table in a corner sat a half-completed twin-engine aircraft. "An AT-9," Bob said. "It was built as a transition trainer between the AT-6 and the P-38. The P-38 was too hot an airplane for the average pilot to jump into right out of the single-engine trainers, and when the U.S. Army Air Force decided too many pilots were being killed in P-38s, it developed the AT-9. I was an instructor in one. It was made to be unstable. If you could fly this, you could fly anything. I flew down inside the Grand Canyon with it, like so many of us did. The airplane would not climb with one engine, and if you lost an engine in the canyon, you were in the soup. Ah, we were all crazy kids."

In 1943 young Bob Searfoss was a clinician at the University of Chicago optometry school when he signed up for the army air forces. "I didn't tell the army I was an optometrist because I didn't want to be examining soldiers' eyes when I could be flying," he said. After his commissioning as a second lieutenant, he was assigned to Randolph Field in Texas, where he became an instructor. Three days after he won his wings, he married his sweetheart, Mary. "I carved my name in the top of the desk like all the other guys that had sat there. And about fifteen years ago, Mary and I went back down there and saw the desk, still in the same spot as it was in 1944."

Late that year the U.S. Army Air Forces decided it had enough fighter pilots but needed more B-17 and B-24 pilots—the "wastage" of bomber pilots over Europe in 1944 was enormous—and so Searfoss volunteered for the B-17, in which he flew twenty-four missions over Europe between November 1944 and V-E Day in May 1945. "I was the Old Man," Bob said. He was all of twenty-two years old when *Organized Confusion* joined the 365th Squadron of the 305th Bombardment Group at Chelveston, England, on the plains of Northamptonshire. Few of the missions were "milk runs," and Bob nearly lost his life in one.

When his aircraft was closing in on Berlin at 22,000 feet, another B-17 above accidentally dropped its stick of incendiary bombs on *Organized Confusion,* shearing the nose off the bomber. "See, I have a photograph here," he said, pulling out a black-and-white glossy of several military men and a woman gazing up at a yawning hole where the nose of a B-17 should have been.

It was hard to believe that Searfoss, his hands frozen by the 30-degrees-below-zero, 150-miles-per-hour hurricane howling through the exposed flight deck, could have brought home that snub-nosed B-17. It so happened, Bob said, that three people in the photograph—the air marshal of England, the duchess of Kent, and General James Doolittle—the Jimmy Doolittle whose B-25s had raided Tokyo in 1942—were visiting the airfield that day. Since Bob's plane was the only one to suffer battle damage in the mission, they all walked over to have a look at it, and their expressions of shock and disbelief are evident in the photograph.

"And, of course, Doolittle had been one of my heroes," Bob said. "I didn't get to meet him because the meat wagon had already taken me away. I had high-altitude burn. I had flown that plane home 400 miles that way. It was *cold* in there." Oddly, he was not decorated for bringing home his wrecked airplane and its crew, although among the "bunch of medals" he amassed for his combat service is the Air Medal with three oak leaf clusters.

Searfoss's last mission was almost as dangerous. It was the last raid of the European war, and just before the bomber stream reached its target over Germany, the announcement crackled over the radio that the Nazis had capitulated. "Every plane in the air—about 3,000 of them—broke formation and headed for Paris to circle the Eiffel Tower," Bob said. As seemingly the whole of the U.S. Army Air Forces converged in an enormous and uncontrolled traffic jam of celebration, he added, "I flew my crew down the Champs-Elysées." Suddenly, the prospect of a cornfield meet between two little airplanes over an Illinois airport seemed small potatoes, indeed.

After the war Bob and Mary moved to Mexico, where he set up his optometry practice, becoming a lecturer and giving speeches all over the United States. He designed equipment, still in use, to treat visual difficulties in children.

"Did you keep flying after the war?" I asked.

"No," he said. "I walked away from that B-17 and said, 'That's enough.' "

Once a pilot, always a pilot, though, and Bob stayed in aviation through his radio-controlled models, building, flying, and crashing them by the score. "Somebody asked how many I had crashed," he said. "And I set down one afternoon and put myself back through the years, and I'm sure I've missed some, but I think I've crashed over 120 airplanes."

"Doesn't that *hurt?*" I asked. "I mean, when you put all that time into building just one airplane. . . . "

"Noooooo," Bob scoffed. "If you don't crash one once in a while you're not progressing. That's part of the hobby. Of course, I'd hate like thunder to tear up that bomber out there. I've been offered $7,000 for it. I'm going to show it in Kansas City at the reunion of the Second Air Division, about 2,000 people who were in Africa and Italy. They asked me to bring it."

Searfoss had flown the model of *Organized Confusion* a total of three hours and ten minutes, "about twelve minutes at a time. Boy, it's tiring. These models are infinitely harder to fly than a real airplane. A real one's no problem because you're going in the same direction as the airplane. When you fly a model away from you, you're all right, but when you turn it around and bring it back, the controls are reversed."

Once a pilot, always a pilot. "I've been on airliners, but I don't like it at all," Bob confided. "The flaps don't go down at the right time and the wheels don't come up at the right time, the headings are never kept just right, and I'm in the back where I don't know what's goin' on. If I could sit up there in the pilot's compartment, that'd be fine, but sittin' in the back, no way, so I don't fly on airliners very much."

Once a pilot, always a pilot. In a few minutes, I had coaxed out of Bob the information that "about two years ago, I decided to find out if I could still fly. I still had my license. All I had to do was get a physical and go get checked out by an instructor. It was time to have my physical anyway, so I went out and had a flight physical, and passed it fine."

At the airport Searfoss asked the instructor not to do or say anything. "'Let me do the preflight,' I told him. 'Let me do everything. Just get me out of trouble if I get into it.'"

They took off in a Cessna 152. "I took off straight right on out like you're supposed to. We got up to about 300 feet, and I made the procedure turn out of the field and went up and did some power-off and power-on stalls. I did a 180-degree turn and rolled right out on the proper heading. I did a 360-degree steep turn and came back and hit my own prop wash. You know that's a sign of a perfect turn, no loss of altitude.

"My problem was finding the field again. The orientation was so different after all that time. As soon as I had found one of the factories, I knew where I was and headed for the airport. I made a beautiful landing, with just a squawk-squawk-squawk of the tires on the runway—you hardly even knew what was going on. I said, 'Well, this is a fluke, this just couldn't happen,' so I turned around and took off again. Went up and around and came back and put it down again with just a squawk-squawk. I was only a little rusty. And that's the extent of my flying since World War II." He beamed with pride.

Abruptly Bob changed the subject. "I want to tell you about my mother," he said. "She and Dad saw Cal Rodgers and *Vin Fiz,* and even autographed her wings."

After circling Mexico on October 10, 1911, Rodgers flew on to Marshall, Missouri, eighty miles west along the old Chicago & Alton tracks, crossing the Missouri River at Glasgow. He had hoped to reach Kansas City that day, but his fuel was low, and by the time *Vin Fiz* was topped up, it was too late in the day to take off again. All the same, he had set a new long-distance flying record of 1,398 miles since leaving Sheepshead Bay, breaking the old one by 133 miles.

The next morning Cal lifted off at 8:31 A.M. When *Vin Fiz* passed over Higginsville, twenty-five miles west of Marshall, the C&A stationmaster at Higginsville called his counterpart at Odessa, thirteen miles farther west. There lived a young man and a young woman who eventually would marry and become Bob Searfoss's father and mother. The Odessa stationmaster was a friend of the young man, who had just opened a jewelry store there, and called him to let him know Cal was on the way. The elder Robert Searfoss dashed over to Myra Lucy Whitsett's house in his car—"Dad had the first Model T Ford in Odessa," Bob said—and picked up the young woman he had been courting. "They went down to the C&A siding and climbed on top of a boxcar, to get closer and see better. After *Vin Fiz* went over, they got into the Model T to follow Cal to Kansas City. It was a forty-mile drive, and even though the roads were bad, it was a beautiful day and everything was dry."

Rodgers, however, had to put down at Blue Springs, ten miles short of his destination, to refuel and repair a balky magneto. "Dad easily caught up with *Vin Fiz,* and Mother and Dad signed her wings, as was the custom. *Vin Fiz* couldn't take off from that field because of the fences, so everybody had to lift the plane up over a fence to the next field. And Dad got to help lift the plane, being a young man. Then, having seen the *Vin Fiz,* Mother and Dad drove back to Odessa instead of going on to Kansas City." Two years later, they were married.

The elder Searfoss died at ninety-eight and Myra died at ninety-seven, just two months apart. Late into their old age, "they talked about all the things that had happened in their lifetime," Bob said. "Mother had seen the first cross-country auto race across America right in front of her front door. They had seen the first flight across America. They had watched as Neil Armstrong walked on the moon, for crying out loud."

That evening Bob, Grazia, and I dined at the Barbary Coast Seafood Grill and Ballroom in downtown Mexico. This restaurant calls itself "the Damnedest Place You've Ever Seen," and so it was. Its decor can charitably be described as a controlled explosion in a junkyard. A World War II Jeep hanging from the wall above the entrance to the place provides a marquee, and inside the main room hangs the upside-down fuselage from a wrecked Cessna 150. I could cover page after page describing the exotic junk with which the place is decorated, like an insane Old Curiosity Shop, but I'll mention just a few of the items that decorate the several rooms and ballroom of the two-story establishment: lampshades made of a turtle shell; a World War I helmet; a giant oyster shell; a two-story waterfall; toilet seats; a giraffe's head; a polar bear rug; big game trophies; mounted fish, including an enormous alligator gar; a fully stocked library; hot-air balloon baskets; and chandeliers from a defunct New Orleans eatery. A phone booth is the entrance to one back room. The owner, Don Harmon, says he drove 140,000 miles in a truck prospecting for junk to complete the decor.

The cuisine, both workaday Midwestern and exotic game, hardly tastes as if it comes from a landfill. I had alligator tail, which has a calamari-like texture, but I piled on the chutney to mask the sweetish taste. Bob, Grazia, and I shared a "swamp flower"—a huge onion sliced into petals, like a daisy, then deep fried. It turned out that Grazia, who is in her thirties, is my kind of person; she reminds me of Debby at the same age. When our boys were young, Debby quit teaching and stayed home to care for them, but didn't let the grass grow under her feet—she earned a master's degree in library science over four years, and when the boys were sufficiently grown, returned to the fray. Similarly, Grazia had been a foreign literary scout for the Italian publisher Mondadori, smoking out Italian translation rights for American books, when she met and married George Svokos, a chemical engineer for a pharmaceutical company. She also dropped out of the rat race to rear her children, and was now preparing to return to work in more ambitious fashion, with a master's degree in journalism from the University of Missouri. She had earned it over four years and endless forty-five-minute commutes between Mexico and Columbia ("I did get one speeding ticket that cost me more than $150," she said, "but I won't tell you how fast I drove"). She is now a freelancer for a local business publication.

After dinner, I fell exhausted into the bed in Grazia's spare room and slept soundly.

The next morning George drove me to the airport. There I dropped by the Zenith Aircraft Company, which occupies a large building at one side of the field. It is one of general aviation's most successful manufacturers of kits for homebuilt airplanes, and three of its offerings sat on the ramp in front of the factory. All were two-seaters. One was called a CH 701. This airplane looks like a mantis on steroids—an ungainly high-winger with slab sides, clearly a short-takeoff-and-landing aircraft made for flying into the Canadian and Alaskan bush. Another was a CH 601 Zodiac, a pretty little red low-wing speedster with a plastic bubble canopy over the cockpit and sporty "pants" shrouding its wheels. Both are what the FAA classifies as "experimental" airplanes; they are for private use only, not commercial hauling of passengers, instruction, and the like. "Certified" aircraft, which must meet more stringent standards, may be used for commercial purposes. My Cessna 150 is a certified aircraft, and so was the third aircraft on the factory ramp, a CH 2000. The CH 2000 is a bigger two-seater that looks like a serious training airplane, and it is—it is Zenith's hopeful entry into the certified factory-built aircraft market to replace the aging Cessna 150s and 152s and Piper Cherokees that make up most of the American instructional fleet.

The all-metal planes were designed by Chris Heintz (hence the "CH" in their names), a famous name in the kit industry. Chris's son Sebastien, the company's president, met me at the door and ushered me into his office. I asked him a question that had crossed my mind whenever I saw a homebuilt airplane. "I flew here last night in a Cessna 150," I said. "It may be thirty-six years old, but it's an airworthy certified airplane. Tell me, why should I build a kit when, for the same money, I can have a certified airplane?"

Heintz, a short, dark, and handsome man in his thirties, smiled. He is a master salesman, and in a trice he had me under his spell. "The question should properly be, 'Why are we buying thirty-six-year-old airplanes?'" he said smoothly. "The answer is that that's the only choice we've had. There are no new affordable factory-built aircraft—most cost over $100,000—so people have been looking at kit aircraft as an alternative. For the same money a twenty- or thirty-year-old used airplane costs, say $20,000 or $30,000, you can buy and build your own kit. And when it's done, you have a brand-new airplane."

There are other advantages, too, he said. "With the factory-builts, there hasn't been much progress in technology over the last thirty or forty years. In the kit aircraft, we use newer technology in engines, in aluminum alloys, and composite materials. And one of the biggest advantages of building a kit aircraft is that the FAA allows you to do all the maintenance on it yourself, instead of hiring an expensive airframe-and-power plant mechanic for that. When you build a kit plane, the FAA issues a repairman's certificate, which gives you the right, as the builder of that particular airplane, to maintain it and sign off all the inspections." This can save a lot of money. Typically, an A&P mechanic costs thirty-five dollars an hour and a required annual inspection starts at $500 and usually tops $1,000, depending on the worn-out parts that need to be replaced. The maintenance costs are much higher on older airplanes than on newer ones because aging components need to be replaced regularly.

Heintz was just warming up; clearly he enjoys selling a prospect, and I was obviously a live one. "Because you have a new airplane and the technology is newer," he said, "you get more efficiency. Kit airplanes go faster and burn less fuel. And they're just more fun—they're typically lighter than factory-built airplanes, have much more responsive controls, and just feel sportier. Flying a certified aircraft is like driving a station wagon, but flying a kit plane is like driving a sports car.

"Now, I don't think kit aircraft meet all the needs for aviation, but for the market segment of affordable recreational flying, kit aircraft are filling a need. Which is why we're seeing more and more pilots looking at kit airplanes as a way of owning an aircraft."

I decided to challenge Heintz on a common complaint I've heard from owners of certified aircraft—that the Rotax brand engines commonly seen in kit planes, Zenith's included, are unreliable compared with the Continentals and Lycomings that power certified aircraft.

"You have to look at it in perspective," Heintz replied. "About ten or twelve years ago, when people started using Rotaxes, they were basically taking those engines out of snowmobiles and putting them in airplanes. Those particular engines were never meant to be used in airplanes, and that's how they developed a bad reputation. But now Rotax—which is owned by a big Montreal company called Bombardier—manufactures genuine aircraft engines, and their quality is much superior to that of those old snowmobile engines. We've been using Rotaxes for eight years, and we've been pleased with the results. They're economical to operate, they're very reliable, and the parts are affordable and readily available."

So what's it all going to cost?

"The basic Zodiac kit is $12,620," Heintz said. "That gets the customer everything but engine and instruments."

At this writing, a primary set of instruments—airspeed indicator, altimeter, turn-and-bank indicator, compass, tachometer, oil temperature and pressure gauges, coolant temperature gauge, fuel-pressure gauge, hour meter, ignition, and key—costs $1,050. An eighty-horsepower four-cycle Rotax 912 engine with propeller and all the accessories costs $10,600. That all adds up to $24,720—a brand-new two-seater airplane for about the price of a well-equipped family car. Crating costs $500 and shipping is extra, but the buyer can pick up the kit at the factory instead.

The big catch, of course, is the 400 hours of labor required to put the kit together. But Zenith, like some other manufacturers, offers "prejigged" fuselage kits for the Zodiac series—all parts are lined up and predrilled, ready for final riveting. This saves a good deal of time, yet keeps the builder honest—to meet the FAA requirements, the purchaser must build at least 51 percent of the airplane. True, some wealthy pilots have evaded that requirement, buying kits and hiring A&P mechanics to build them, but the FAA has been cracking down on abuse of that rule.

"Who builds kit planes?" I asked. "People with a high degree of mechanical skill?"

"You'd be surprised," Heintz said. "Only ten years ago, the market for kit airplanes was primarily mechanically oriented people. The kits were difficult to build, with a lot less prefabrication. Today we're putting a lot more prefabricated parts in kits, and your basic handyman can build them. You need no specific skills. We know that not all pilots are mechanics, and they want to be flying as soon as possible."

Kit builders used to be retirees, with both time and money on their hands, and only a small percentage of kit airplanes were ever completed because assembling one took five or ten years of weekends, with lots of distractions. Today, however, younger people are building airplanes, Heintz said, because the kits are quicker and easier to build, typically taking just a year or two to construct. "When the work goes by quickly, there's a lot of built-in motivation," Heintz said. "In a few weeks you've got a wing done. You see something happening, and so a lot of momentum is built up, and before you know it, you're nearly finished. Suddenly you're anxious to get flying."

The FAA used to visit the builder two or three times during the construction to make sure the critical parts were built correctly, but because of budget cutbacks, it now does just one final inspection. "But what we try to do here at the factory is exercise quality control on critical parts," Heintz said. "The customer might make one or two little errors, but it won't be a structural mistake." The wing spars, which hold virtually all the weight of the airplane, are built by the factory, "so if the customer misdrills a hole here, forgets to put in a few rivets there, that airplane won't fall apart."

More than 800 Zenith aircraft are flying around the world today, Heintz said proudly, "and they've never had a structural failure. Some customers have made silly mistakes, some engines have failed or run out of fuel, but we've never had an airplane come apart because of weak structure. Some of our airplanes are now twenty years old, so that speaks well for the design."

Heintz hitched his chair closer. "And it also speaks well for the builders, because they're building something for themselves. They're not getting paid by the hour, and they're not going to cut corners. They're going to make sure they do it right because they're gonna be in that airplane. Their wives or their kids are gonna be flying with them, and so they're gonna do a careful job."

Still, I thought, $25,000 is a lot of money, and the average working stiff isn't going to have that kind of loose cash around. The pilot, however, can follow the buy-as-you-build route: He can purchase the components separately—the fuselage first, then the wings, and so on, which costs a little more—so the expense is spread over a longer period. And, Heintz added, getting a bank loan to build an airplane is easy. "Most bankers will tell you that people will default on their houses or their cars before they default on their airplanes because airplanes are something they really enjoy. For most people, however, buying a kit airplane isn't an impulse purchase. They've been planning and saving for several years. And they've also been making sure they have a big-enough garage so they can build their plane in it."

Heintz took me around the factory floor, showing me neatly stacked parts and watching a workman form sheets of aluminum into wing ribs. I sat inside a demonstrator Zodiac, imagining myself hurtling at 110 miles per hour through the clouds. I felt an impulse. "Hmm," I said. "What's the cheapest part of the build-as-you-go plan?"

"The rudder," Heintz replied. "It costs three hundred dollars."

"I'm thinking about buying a rudder and seeing if I could do it," I said. "But I would have to talk my wife into it—she wasn't too happy when I bought that little Cessna."

Heintz beamed. "I've never had a customer who couldn't build the rudder," he said.

It was a good thing, I thought after I made my good-byes and walked out to *Gin Fizz,* that I was on a tight budget; otherwise, I would have ordered a Zodiac rudder kit on the spot. I have a weakness, you see: I am a dreamer. And Sebastien Heintz is the kind of salesman who knows how to persuade people into acting on their dreams.

On the way across the ramp to *Gin Fizz,* I dreamed. Maybe I *will* retire at sixty. I could work part time three days a week and work three days on a Zodiac kit. If I worked on the airplane ten hours a day, that's thirty hours a week, so it should take only thirteen or fourteen weeks to complete that airplane. That's one summer. Oh, I'd take my time. Let's say six months. I could build the wings and fuselage and tail empennage in the garage and then when they're done, I could truck them to the airport, where I could finish the assembly in a hangar and then mount the engine. After which I'd fly it to Watertown, where I'd have the paint shop dress the airplane in fire-engine red, just like that 1963 Volkswagen Bug I owned so long ago. Then I would have a brand-new airplane, and I could save money doing my own maintenance and annual inspections. . . .

Well. Someday, maybe.

On the ramp at 10 A.M. the temperature was nudging 100 degrees when I checked the computer weather. The forecast was good except for a chance of thunderstorms in midafternoon at Kansas City, my target for the day. But scarcely half an hour later, at 4,500 feet, my bladder began to knock at the door of my consciousness, and I swore to myself. *Goddamnit, why did I have that third cup of coffee?* I had gulped a quick eight ounces in the pilot's lounge, thinking the heat would sweat it out of me before it could filter through my kidneys, but no. Coffee is a diuretic—it makes you excrete more fluid than you take in. This may be an indelicate subject, but not a trivial one for any pilot, especially one over the age of fifty who suffers from diminished capacity. Go into any small airport's pilot's lounge and look around. Those of any age who are swilling coffee will not be taking any long-distance cross-country flights that day. They either came down to the airport for a little hangar flying or, at best, a few touch-and-goes.

Pilots will go to great lengths to deal with the problem. The sensible ones avoid that third cup or even that second one and put up with the slight but nagging headache and generalized cranky feeling that mark the onset of caffeine-withdrawal symptoms. Why not carry a plastic milk quart bottle and just pee into that? Or the small "Little John" necked urinals often sold in pilots' shops? The truth is, in most small airplanes there's just not enough maneuvering room under the yoke to open your pants, and certainly not in a Cessna 150. I've tried it and damned near put the airplane in what pilots delicately call an "unusual attitude." I am not alone; an air force pilot once had to eject from an F-16 over northern Iraq when he lost control of his airplane while relieving himself. (Female pilots tend to reject the notion of airborne relief entirely, though some do use adult diapers.)

Several manufacturers market "piddle packs" that are at best partial solutions to the problem. The typical model is a plastic bag with a loose granular powder that turns into a gel when moisture strikes it, supposedly keeping the contents from splashing back onto the user. It also contains a strong deodorizer that infuses the entire cockpit with a sweet porta-potty odor. These seem to me more trouble than they're worth.

The classic military piddle pack, an external condom catheter that runs down to a bag strapped on the lower leg, sounds like a good idea for men. It requires, I am told, some fussing to get on and off and seems most appropriate for long missions into enemy territory or situations in which exposing oneself to the gaze of shocked passengers isn't practical. It's used not only by fighter pilots but also by macho businessmen who want to stay at the table longer than their rivals. It's not particularly cheap—$10 or $12 per unit—but it can be washed and reused.

Before I started on the transcontinental trip, I discovered an inexpensive and workable system for summer use: a cotton infant's diaper folded tightly into a plastic freezer bag with a zip-locking mouth. When one wears floppy, wide-legged shorts, it is not difficult to maneuver oneself into the bag—at least if one is male—and the diaper quickly soaks up the liquid. It costs nothing to raid the kitchen drawers for a couple of freezer bags and beg a few tattered diapers from the young mother down the street. The evidence can be quickly disposed of at an airport, or if one is exceptionally parsimonious, one can wring out the diaper and throw it and the freezer bag into the washer for recycling.

I carry two of these homemade piddle packs in *Gin Fizz* and even managed to bring off the trick once in smooth air at 6,500 feet. I'd never try it in any kind of turbulence, however. It's much easier just to watch the coffee and land every two hours to purge one's tank while filling the plane's. That way one never runs out of fuel.

Three-quarters of an hour after I took off from Mexico, I landed at Marshall Municipal Airport, to off-load the now insistent morning coffee and recheck the weather, which really wasn't necessary—it was still clear and sunny, though the heat was execrable, even at higher altitudes. The temperature drops two and a half degrees per 1,000 feet of altitude, but it was still in the humid nineties at 4,500 feet. I could have climbed to 6,500 feet, but the headwinds were stronger at that altitude. A Pitts Special aerobatic biplane that had been stunting high in the sky to the south followed *Gin Fizz* down. Inside the terminal the Pitts pilot came by and asked me something. "Sorry," I said in long-practiced fashion, "I'm deaf, but I read lips. What was that you said?"

The pilot grimaced, pointed to his own ear, and said, "I'm deaf, too." Not the same sort of deafness, it was clear, but he intended a heartfelt commiseration all the same. It was likely that he had made the same error people all across the country did in 1911 about Cal Rodgers—assuming that a couple of hours sitting behind an airplane engine had rendered me temporarily deaf but that time and rest would put my ears right. It's also possible that he thought years of experience in a noisy cockpit had permanently damaged my hearing. Just about every small-plane pilot who is older than thirty-five or so, and started flying before modern noise-attenuating radio headsets came along, will have suffered at least some degree of hearing loss. Some of them, I suspect, have become fairly adept lip-readers to help make up for it, as Tom Horton had.

Unfortunately, my interlocutor was a member of that 10 percent of humanity I find impossible to lip-read. His thin lips barely moved in an almost expressionless face. "I'm sorry?" I said, bending closer for a better look. He repeated the statement, loudly; I could feel the vibrations of his voice. I didn't understand it that time, either. "You're hard to lip-read," I said. The pilot was undaunted. Once again he repeated his question—I knew it was one because he raised his eyebrows in query—and once again I shrugged blankly.

The fourth time he bellowed and made rotary motions with his right hand on an imaginary surface. I essayed a guess.

"Polish?" I said. "You're asking me if I polish my plane?" He nodded enthusiastically. This always happens: The harder a hearing person and a deaf person strain to communicate, the more banal the original question. Sometimes the result seems hardly worth the effort. But the pilot was pleased that he'd made the breakthrough, and so was I. Even a small connection is sometimes a victory.

"Once a year," I replied, grimacing. He laughed and nodded sagely; he knew what it was to own a shiny aluminum airplane. Then he turned on his heel, climbed back into his Pitts, and was away. I followed shortly later after casting a longing glance at the coffee machine.

An hour after I left Marshall, I landed at East Kansas City airport in Grain Valley, near the spot where Bob Searfoss's parents had affixed their autographs to *Vin Fiz* all those years before. Grain Valley was the funkiest grassroots airport I'd yet seen on the trip, with gravelly runways, foot-high grass growing through their cracks. Lots of airplanes were visible, however, in a warren of hangars and a score or more on outside tiedowns. The gas pumps were modern, and the pilot's lounge was surprisingly spiffy, with pristinely clean bathrooms and half a dozen student pilots talking with their instructors. Clearly, this was a busy suburban general-aviation airport—so busy that no one had the time to shoot the breeze; its denizens clearly had planes to fly and people to see. Shrugging, I paid the bill for several gallons of automobile fuel and took off.

In 1911 Cal Rodgers landed at Kansas City to a roaring welcome. Packing-house whistles had emptied the schools and businesses, and when *Vin Fiz* arrived over the city, Cal gave a crowd of thousands in Swope Park an impromptu demonstration of aerobatics, "the like of which it had never experienced before," a newspaperman wrote breathlessly. After *Vin Fiz* landed, one reporter described Rodgers as "unmoved by the cheers of a crowd, a nerveless, unemotional man." That nervelessness probably was just Cal's lack of awareness of the great shouts behind him. Just think of that conundrum about a tree falling in the forest; if a deaf man doesn't hear its impact on the ground, the tree doesn't exist— as far as he is concerned. The same reporter did observe, however, that Rodgers "is deaf, and it is with some difficulty that he converses with those about him." Still another reporter wrote that "Rodgers's nerves were worn to a frazzle from the strain of the trip and that he spent as much time as possible resting in bed."

Coping with all the adulation very likely was beginning to grate on Cal's patience. When tired and ragged, people who hear poorly or not at all often subside into reticence; conversation requires effort. Cal probably wasn't ever sure he understood the questions asked him. He may have answered so many misunderstood questions with embarrassing non sequiturs that he simply quit bluffing. It is also likely that he was ashamed of his speech, whose imprecision may have been fuzzed more than usual by fatigue. And because his family probably felt his affliction was unmentionable, he may never have had real training in coping with his deafness. He probably just found it easier to blow off strangers like any other tired, wind-buffeted, irascible human being. I'd bet cash money that Cal was just trying to avoid talking to anybody he didn't know.

I've been there, too. As Cal could when he absolutely had to—and sometimes did—I *can* summon up the effort to talk to and even charm large groups of people, but it is a major undertaking that requires rest, energy, desire, and a few weeks of speech therapy. I have to psych myself up for the stadium, like a linebacker before a big game. If I'm just a bit tired, I can bluff my way through group conversations by guessing what others are saying; often the context of the moment makes it easy. But when the going gets tough—when I am having a difficult time understanding and making myself understood—the temptation is to get going, to cut and run. Because trying to raise my voice above loud hubbubs further distorts my speech, making me even harder to understand, I frequently try to escape noisy evening cocktail parties I can't get out of attending after first making polite hellos and having an hors d'ouevre or two, just for the sake of appearances. My quick exits used to annoy Debby, who often would turn around from the canapé table and discover that her husband had disappeared, but now she's quite understanding about it.

The following day, October 11, Rodgers flew nine miles southwest to Overland Park, a suburb of Kansas City, and gave another aerobatic exhibition of spirals, turns, and glides, including a bank with a fifty-five-degree angle, after which one of the mechanics said, "A man has about three times to do that stunt and then they lay him away in a box. Rodgers is usually the most careful fellow in the world but he's done that twice now, and he'd better stop it." So low was the power of those primitive airplanes, and so inefficient the wings, that a bank of more than forty-five degrees was risky. Much more than that and the wings would simply stop generating lift, often throwing the airplane into a nasty upside-down spin. Possibly as a way of communicating his courage and skill to a world that had a hard time understanding him, Rodgers displayed an impulsive streak of carelessness that was far more serious than the nagging small errors in judgment that can plague even conscientious pilots.

For the next two days, rain blanketed Kansas City, and Rodgers holed up sullenly in his room. When he finally could take off on October 14, he circled Swope Park to give the spectators a good look and then headed down the Missouri, Kansas and Texas Railroad main line to Parsons, Kansas. Along the way, he ran into a stiff headwind that forced him to land at Moran, eighty miles south, to refuel.

I had planned to land for the night at the aptly named Heart Airport near the center of Kansas City on the Missouri side of the river, but as *Gin Fizz* approached, I decided against it. Not only is Heart ringed by bristling radio towers, but it is also unattended. Thus, few pilots were likely to be about, especially in the heat, and I didn't feel like tangling with navigational hazards on a day like this. So I simply rocked *Gin Fizz*'s wings at Heart as we passed close aboard and headed southwest to Iola, Kansas, ninety miles south. There I would land at Allen County Airport, which I'd chosen as the stop closest to Moran, ten miles east.

On the way to Iola, the heat and humidity had stirred a lot of low-lying turbulence, so I climbed above 3,000 feet to smoother air. Though haze blanketed eastern Kansas, visibility still was remarkably good—about fifteen miles—and in an hour I found Allen County Airport. It had an almost brand-new concrete runway, 75 feet wide by 4,100 feet long, big enough for small jets. Clearly, the county was trying to attract more aviation traffic and had spiffed up the place. But there was just a single Cessna 185 outside on a tiedown, its multihued paint so mangy that I suspected it had been assembled from pieces of wrecked airplanes.

Inside the terminal the only person I could find, almost hidden in an office off the surprisingly bare pilot's lounge, was the ancient airport attendant, who seemed as moribund as his business. In a swivel chair he sat attached to an oxygen tank through a nose cannula. As I stood in the door, he waved a weak hello and apologized for not being able to refuel my airplane. "You'll have to do it yourself," he gasped. Between rapid, shallow breaths, he started to explain how to throw switches and twirl wheels on the gas pump. I put up my hand. "Never mind. It's OK. I'll just go on to Chanute to refuel." I had plenty of gas to get to that airport, thirteen miles farther south. He waved a feeble thanks for my not adding to his burdens that day—I doubt that he had the strength even to run my credit card through the printer. I wanted to be neighborly and chat a bit, but he was clearly distressed by having to talk to anyone, let alone a deaf person who was hard to understand. So I bade him good-bye; I was not certain he could last out the day in this heat. As I climbed away in *Gin Fizz,* I shook my head. If I ever wanted to convince someone of the economic distress of American general aviation, I now knew which airport to pick as my first stop.

In a few minutes, after descending back into the maelstrom of low-level heat turbulence and making a sloppy landing, I found Chanute no busier than Iola at 102 degrees in the shade. The airport's hangars, however, sheltered at least a dozen airplanes, not counting those at the modern FBO. After refueling and wiping down the leading edges of *Gin Fizz*'s wings, nose, and tail, which had accumulated thick splotches of squashed bugs over the past two days, I accepted an offer from Doug Klaassen, the affable FBO manager, of a ride to "the best motel in town." This was the Guest House Motor Lodge, whose spartan rooms rented for twenty-nine dollars a night, including tax. Still, it had air-conditioning, Home Box Office, and the Weather Channel, and the all-you-can-eat pizza-and-salad buffet at Hungry Howie's next door was at least edible. I napped all afternoon and went to bed at sundown, intending to take off as early as possible while it was still cool and make Muskogee, Oklahoma, by midmorning before the thermals again had a chance to pound me silly.

For an hour I lay awake, thinking about Colin and Conan, and wishing that one or both had gone along with me on the trip in a bigger airplane. How they would have enjoyed it! Both are adventurous, and both have the same happy curiosity about people, as well as a comfortable ease with strangers. Both had often traveled with me by train and car, and having one along on this trip would have extended my range in speaking with strangers, especially away from airports.

But neither had shown anything more than a polite interest in small planes, just enough to keep up their end of the dinner-table conversation. One summer, when Conan was home after graduating from college, I offered to pay for a dozen flying lessons, hoping that he, too, would become hooked. Politely he turned me down, as both boys had turned away my offers to help them become involved in a variety of my enthusiasms, including railroads, tropical fish, and photography. I will admit I was a little hurt, but in time, I came to realize that their acts were not rejections of my aspirations but affirmations of their own. They are of a younger generation—one for whom aviation was a childhood commonplace, not the adventure it was for me—and their dreams are different. This, I realized, is how things should be, and I fell asleep comforted.

# 13

*I* arose at 5 A.M., downloaded the weather to the laptop, and then breakfasted on day-old doughnuts and coffee at an all-night gas station down the road—I hated to abuse my stomach so early in the day, but the only other choice was to go hungry. As I spread out the sectional chart over a table in the station to examine my course, I remembered that on October 14, 1911, Rodgers's flight over the same leg had been a difficult one.

A tempest swept in from the west as Rodgers took off from Moran, bound for Parsons, Kansas, forty miles south, where some 7,000 spectators awaited. There, almost before Cal could react, the storm's long claws plucked at *Vin Fiz,* worrying the airplane as a hawk does a sparrow, lightning pinioning it against the sky. Evidently remembering his harrowing experience in Indiana, Cal instantly decided to skip Parsons and try instead to outrun the clouds. The wind picked up and was howling at a good thirty miles per hour when Cal crossed into Oklahoma and landed to refuel at Russell Creek near the state line. Ten hurried minutes later, he was aloft again, and within half an hour he had landed in the failing evening light at Vinita, where 10,000 people, twice the town's population, awaited him. That day he had flown 220 miles, and he went to bed satisfied with his performance. It was one of the few days during his trip that something hadn't gone wrong with *Vin Fiz.*

At 6:30 A.M. Doug Klaassen picked me up as arranged, and an hour later I was in the air, heading for Oswego, fifty-one miles southeast—the airport closest to Rodgers's refueling site at Russell Creek—skimming the ground at 1,000 feet with the Cotton Belt tracks on my right. At that hour, following the Iron Road down low was a joy. The early-morning air gave a cool and smooth ride, and now and again I spotted deer peering up from copses, watching *Gin Fizz* soar overhead.

At Oswego I landed to a view of two dilapidated hangars, one doorless and containing a Cessna 150, an Ercoupe, and a Taylorcraft, all sun bleached and breaded with birdshit. Obviously, there had been no flying there in weeks, maybe months. I was the only soul around, but in a few minutes a car rolled up. A lone old-timer emerged, photo album under his arm, and shook my hand with grave ceremony. "Mr. Kisor?" he asked formally. I had gotten in touch with Donald Tiffany before I left Chicago, when I had heard that his grandfather had taken a photograph of *Vin Fiz*.

I suggested we talk in the office, but as we approached it, we saw that webs festooned the windows and years of mud, dust, and animal droppings crusted the walls. The place was so godawful that no self-respecting hobo would think of using it for shelter from the rain. So we drove to a homespun café in town and chatted there. Donald Tiffany was a school custodian in nearby Columbus, and as we sat down among other Oswegians, they nodded hello to the two faces, one familiar and one strange.

"Does the flight of *Vin Fiz* mean anything to people here?" I asked. "Does anybody talk about it today?"

"No, sir," he said, shaking his head slowly. "But my grandfather saved this card for my father, who was seven when Mr. Rodgers made his flight over Parsons."

Donald Tiffany spoke with a gentle, polite Victorian formality. At first, his manner seemed amusing, then admirable. Americans generally are not known for their reserve—we are renowned, especially in Europe, for our open willingness to air the most embarrassing personal and family secrets in casual conversation with a perfect stranger. Mr. Tiffany—it was impossible to think of him as Don—was not the kind of man to betray the smallest such confidence, and I felt sure that he had thought deeply about sharing even this information.

The card, carefully preserved in the Tiffany family photo album, was one of the thousands of paper flyers Rodgers had scattered from his airplane. Mr. Tiffany pointed to it with grave pride. It was a tiny thing, smaller than a file card, printed on one side with the legend "Vin Fiz: The Ideal Grape Drink, Refreshing-Invigorating, 5¢ Sold Everywhere 5¢," and on the other side, "Greetings from the Sky: Rodgers in the Vin-Fiz Flyer, *from* New York *to* Los Angeles—*for* the Hearst $50,000 ocean to ocean flight." The card, insignificant as it seemed, may have been his family's only surviving tie with a renowned event in American history—an event whose renown, of course, has all but disappeared. Yet the tiny flyer carried cachet for both Mr. Tiffany and me, and for a brief moment it linked us together.

"Must go to church, sir," Mr. Tiffany said after a few minutes, and we returned in his car to the airport. "Good luck, Mr. Kisor," he added with that unwavering solemnity, and was off. I regretted his departure, for spending that brief time in his kindly grace had been relaxing. In my travels across the rural Midwest, I have often been greeted with the same courteous formality by people whose self-assurance is as solid as their station is modest. To them, conversing with a deaf person seems to be natural and comfortable, if perhaps a little more time consuming than with others. I can't help contrasting these good, gentle people with those I know who judge others patronizingly, measuring human worth not by character and dignity but education, wealth, and power, masking their own shaky self-confidence with snobbery and artificial gravitas.

When nobody else showed up before 9 A.M., I took off downwind—the first time I'd done that deliberately, although of course as a student pilot, I'd misread the wind sock once or twice or maybe a dozen times. Tall telephone poles carrying high wires marched across the road just north of the windward end of the runway, at 2,500 feet long a bit on the short side for a takeoff over an obstruction on a morning that was growing hot. I was pretty sure I could have cleared the wires, but why experiment? The breeze was gentle—not more than six miles per hour, just enough to swing the wind sock gently on its staff—so I chose a takeoff with the wind over the broad, almost treeless fields south of the airport. Soon *Gin Fizz* reached 1,000 feet again heading for Vinita, thirty-six miles south along the tracks, and I decided to climb higher, to 2,000 feet above the ground, to see farther ahead.

As I approached Vinita, I looked down into the sharply defined edge of a deck of seemingly solid clouds 1,000 feet below, about the same distance above the ground. Ordinarily, I will not fly over an unbroken cloud deck, as many VFR pilots will, expecting that they will be able to descend through broken or scattered clouds to land at their destination. (In aviation-weather terminology, "broken" clouds blanket 50 percent or more of the sky; "scattered" clouds obscure less than 50 percent.) If VFR pilots are caught above solid clouds when their fuel runs low, they can call a controller on the radio and ask to be vectored down through the soup on instruments. They're not supposed to get themselves into that fix, but they sometimes do. The FAA usually doesn't discipline them because it doesn't want pilots to be reluctant to radio for help if they need it, and it figures they've already learned a good lesson. In any case, I can't call for help, so I never go "over the top."

But this deck had been forecast to dissipate by midmorning and was just a few miles north of Vinita. I decided to fly over the clouds and see if they were broken enough to allow me to thread my way down to the airport—if I could find it. I was a little nervous; it was the first time I'd ever flown over a broken deck that obscured more than five-eighths of the ground. But I was close to the edge and had plenty of fuel; if the deck turned out to be solid cloud over my target, I could fly back northwest into clear air in a few minutes. So I stretched my self-imposed limits a little more.

Indeed, the clouds over Vinita were beginning to break up, and after circling the town twice, I spotted the airport below, then descended between wisps and landed. Vinita boasts a dozen or more long hangars, all stuffed with aircraft, but the temperature at 11 A.M. had already climbed over 100 degrees. Unless they had to go somewhere, Vinita's pilots clearly were staying home, waiting for the cooler air of evening.

There was, however, a certain attraction I simply had to check out: the self-styled World's Largest McDonald's just a hundred-yard walk from the ramp, an enormous hangarlike building arching over Interstate 44, halfway between Joplin and Tulsa. "It's got a ballroom!" a pilot back home had said. I stepped over for a second breakfast, climbing a stairway to the upper level and looking about. The place was big, all right. Although it had no ballroom, its interior certainly could have hosted a couple of orchestras and a thousand dancers. It was broken up into dining spaces, two large gift shops (one selling "World's Largest McDonald's" T-shirts for an absurd thirteen dollars and postcards for thirty-nine cents, one of which I bought), a children's playroom, and a tourist information office. Even at that hour, the place was crowded with motoring families.

The serving area and kitchen were no larger than those at the average McDonald's, and a plaque revealed that the restaurant had been constructed by the Oklahoma transportation department in 1957, well before Ray Kroc had more than half a dozen burger outlets, and had been leased to a number of concessionaires over the years. Just to be able to say that I had eaten at the World's Largest McDonald's, I challenged my arteries with an Egg McMuffin and just half a small coffee—whatever else may be said about its other products, McDonald's coffee is remarkably tasty.

Unbowed by the heat, I once again took off in a slight downwind on the 2,800-foot runway for Muskogee, forty-five minutes away. I was beginning to accustom myself to *Gin Fizz*'s diminished performance in hot weather and had grown less nervous about her capabilities—just as long as I have lots of runway with no obstacles at the far end. Slowly, *Gin Fizz* climbed to 2,500 feet, then to 3,500 feet, and finally to 4,500 feet, but the Oklahoma heat seemed to ascend with the airplane. Though I turned the air vents in the upper corners of the windscreen so that both blasted directly in my face, the hot stream felt like an assault by high-powered hair dryers. Noon had almost arrived, and I was glad that my last stop for the day lay just a few miles south. Fifteen miles to the east, over the long, sinuous Lake o' the Cherokees stretch of the Neosho River, I spotted two biplanes cavorting in tandem aerobatics and a couple of seaplanes. Their pilots must have been used to the heat. I tied a bandanna around my forehead to soak up the rivulets of perspiration from my pate.

When Cal Rodgers left Vinita, he, too, faced uncomfortable temperatures, taking off in a cold, gusty October wind that cut through the newspaper insulation under his jacket and bounced *Vin Fiz* around like a feather. The ride to Muskogee took just one hour and fifteen minutes, but that must have been a draining flight, for the press reported that Rodgers was silent and sullen upon his arrival. I'm sure it wasn't just because of his hearing loss; after a frigid and bumpy hour in the air in a primitive airplane like *Vin Fiz*, anyone would have been exhausted and thoroughly out of sorts. But when I arrived over Muskogee on that brutal summer afternoon, I was still fresh and eager, heat or no heat. I'd been looking forward to landing at Hatbox Field, as historic a working airport as you'll find anywhere in the United States. After fighting my way down through the reverse avalanche of thermals to the runway, shimmering in the 102-degree heat, I shut down by the FBO. All I could see in the way of activity was an itinerant 172 picking up a passenger. The place looked tidy, except for some long uncut grass between the runways.

Inside the FBO, I was greeted by a comfortable couple named Joe Cunningham and Mary Kelly, editor and publisher, respectively, of the monthly newspaper the *Oklahoma Aviator*. We had gotten in touch when I was planning my flight, and I was determined not to display any of Cal Rodgers's taciturnity.

"Not very busy today?" I said, just to break the ice.

"No," said Mary, gazing out the window sadly. "I used to be the airport manager a few years ago, and it was busier then. Each year it's just got a little less busy. But the place is so historic."

We gazed at the old photographs of the airplanes and pilots on the walls of the musty, high-ceilinged pilot's lounge, including one of *Vin Fiz* and a poster promoting Jim Lloyd's 1986 reenactment. A plaque proclaimed that Charles A. Lindbergh stopped at Hatbox on October 1, 1927, during his triumphant transcontinental air tour after the epochal New York-to-Paris flight. I asked about a large photograph of two big single-engine biplanes.

"Hatbox hosted the Douglas World Cruisers on their round-the-world trip in '24," Joe said. "The place was the Oklahoma stop for the army airplanes, first to circumnavigate the globe." This flight, like Rodgers's accomplishment, is remembered today only by aviation enthusiasts. In 1923 Billy Mitchell, an irascible army colonel and aviation visionary, commissioned four large single-engine airplanes from a small California manufacturer named Donald Douglas. The open-cockpit biplanes, which carried fittings for floats or wheels, boasted a cruising speed of ninety miles per hour and a ceiling of 8,000 feet above sea level—less on both counts than *Gin Fizz*. Mitchell sent advance teams to find suitable landing fields and to store crates of gasoline, tools, parts, and spare engines at these fields, for the Liberty engines the planes used were good for only fifty hours of flight. Each plane would require nine complete engine changes over the trip.

On April 6, 1924, four World Cruisers named *Seattle, Chicago, Boston,* and *New Orleans* left Seattle, heading up the coast of

British Columbia for Alaska. Their mishap-plagued odyssey was just like Rodgers's in *Vin Fiz*, albeit on a global scale. Almost immediately, the pilot of *Seattle* was blinded by snow and flew into the ground, totaling the airplane. *Chicago*'s engine blew up over the Gulf of Tonkin, and the plane landed on its floats. A fleet of sampans towed *Chicago* to a dock, where a U.S. Navy destroyer delivered a new engine. *Boston* was forced down into the North Atlantic. On September 18, 1924, the remaining planes—*Chicago* and *New Orleans*—called at Hatbox to the cheers of a crowd of 25,000 after following the route Rodgers had blazed across the United States. The mission ended at Seattle ten days later, after the planes had flown 26,345 miles in six months.

"Wiley Post landed here, too," said Joe. "So did Amelia Earhart. Lindbergh's instructor ran this airport at one time. And here you come doing your little deal. I think it's great. I'm excited about what you're up to. Mary and I have done some similar things."

I was fascinated by Hatbox's history, and I asked the Cunninghams about those "similar things."

"I'm just a private pilot," Joe said. "I've never done anything spectacular, just accumulated a little flying time through the years since serving as a crewman on a B-17 in World War II." That was one of the most modest statements I have ever heard from a pilot.

On their honeymoon in 1988—Mary is considerably younger than Joe—the Cunninghams flew to Alaska to commemorate the fatal 1935 trip of Wiley Post and comedian Will Rogers, who died when their airplane crashed near Point Barrow. Post, one-eyed since an oil-field accident in 1924, was a pioneer high-altitude pilot who in 1931, just seven years after the World Cruisers' odyssey, had circumnavigated the world aboard *Winnie Mae,* a Lockheed Vega. He and his navigator flew over Newfoundland, England, Germany, Russia, Siberia, Alaska, and Canada before he landed in New York City. Sixty years later, the Cunninghams made a similar round-the-world flight. "It took them eight days and fifteen hours," Joe said, "but it took us three weeks. That's progress."

In 1987 the Cunninghams flew a Cessna 172 ("Mary did all the flying," Joe said proudly) to Ireland to commemorate Amelia Earhart's fifteen-hour transatlantic trip of 1932. Flying a Vega similar to Post's, Earhart took off from Newfoundland and endured a violent thunderstorm; wing icing; and, at one point, a vertical drop of nearly 3,000 feet. A rough-running engine forced her to land in

Ireland, rather than Paris, but she still had set three records: the fastest crossing of the Atlantic, the first transatlantic flight piloted by a woman, and the first solo crossing by a woman. Her Vega hangs in the National Air and Space Museum near *Winnie Mae,* just down the hall from *Vin Fiz.*

"We're kind of into the history angle of flying," Joe said, in the second greatest understatement of the day. "That's why we're caught up in what you're up to. What you're doing and what we've done can only help promote aviation."

Among the things that this man who is "only a private pilot" does in the service of aviation is help his wife—a certified flight instructor—run a summer camp for teenagers at Tenkiller Airpark, a turf strip in Cookson, twenty-five miles east on Tenkiller Lake and tucked into the Boston Mountains. Twice every summer the Cunninghams host a handful of youths aged fourteen to seventeen. "We work them from daybreak to dark, giving them five hours of flight instruction and four hours of ground school," Mary said. "We have them wash airplanes—you'd be surprised how much you can learn about an airplane by washing it—and when the week's over their tongues are dragging. We have a full quota of students every time."

Of course the Cunninghams had some good advice for a fellow reenactment enthusiast. On their Alaskan trip, they said, they took along a survival kit much like mine, though theirs contained a shotgun for protection against grizzlies and a large box of trail mix. On the second day out, Joe discovered he could reach the box from the pilot's seat, and the emergency supply diminished with every mile north. I'll admit that my stock of granola bars also tended to shrink the farther west I flew.

Now they recommend a twenty-five-pound bag of dry dog food as emergency rations for the wilderness pilot. "Not only will it stay edible in a variety of weather conditions," Joe said, but also "it has all the necessary nutrition and food qualities to keep you alive. Yet you wouldn't want to snack on it along the way."

By that time, the midafternoon heat had grown so oppressive that I decided to stay overnight at Muskogee, rather than press on to Texas, so the Cunninghams dropped me off at the Ramada Inn, whose restaurant had closed for the day. Starving, I looked in both directions for a supermarket but could see none. I was almost ready for a fistful of kibble, but instead staggered across the griddle of the highway to a Denny's and had a ham sandwich.

*         *         *

The next morning I took off at 9:30 A.M. after posing for pictures with Joe and Bill Richardson, the airport manager. Even at mid-morning, the temperature had soared into the nineties, but I found calm air at 2,500 feet and cruised at 3,000 feet, once climbing to 4,500 to see if I could get above the haze. Nonetheless, the air remained silky through most of the morning, and the haze stayed minimal—I could see twelve miles or more. Crossing the 100,000-acre Eufaula Reservoir, formed by the impoundment of the northern and southern branches of the Canadian River, I gazed down at roads that seemed to disappear abruptly into the lake, betraying its man-made origin. Oklahoma is Swiss-cheesed by more than 200 reservoirs formed by dams, twice as many lakes as those nature created. For the first time since I left the Allegheny Mountains at the western edge of Pennsylvania, the land below seemed to take on a personality. The flat Till Plains farm landscapes of the upper Midwest had been pleasant enough to gaze upon, but often boring to fly across.

At Muskogee, I recalled, Cal Rodgers had taken off just before noon, hoping to reach Fort Worth, Texas, but the gremlins had come home from their brief vacation. Before long, Cal noticed that *Vin Fiz*'s engine was laboring, the radiator water steaming. In the fashion of the reciprocating engines of its time, it had worn out after only a few hours of use. Cal made a precautionary landing on a farm field five miles north of McAlester and discovered that water had leaked into the engine. Draining the water, he took off again and flew on to McAlester, where he landed to wait for the mechanics on the special train. They found a cracked cylinder that needed to be replaced, and flying was over for that day. The memory spurred me to make a quick scan of the gauges on my instrument panel. The tanks read full, the oil pressure was in the green, and the ammeter showed a slight charge. Everything was fine, and I pressed on southward.

Shortly after 10 A.M., *Gin Fizz* hove into view of the high sandstone ridges that marked the beginning of the great Ouachita Mountains range straddling eastern Oklahoma and western Arkansas, and fifteen minutes later I landed at McAlester. Just behind me, an Ercoupe marked N113WM rolled in to refuel. Ercoupes are extraordinarily cute little low-wing tricycle-geared two-seater airplanes with bulbous cockpit canopies and a distinctive twinruddered tail. Even smaller than Cessna 150s, they were first de-signed and built before World War II and came off the assembly lines of a variety of manufacturers until 1970. Conceived as an easy-to-fly airplane for the ham-handed Sunday pilot, the original Ercoupe has no rudder pedals. Its control yoke moves the rudders and ailerons simultaneously for turning, and the angle of climb and descent are controlled in the usual fashion by pushing and pulling the yoke. The wheels swivel from side to side, enabling the plane to be landed at an angle in a crosswind. Many legless pilots fly Er-coupes because these planes lack rudder pedals, and other avia-tors simply love the Ercoupes for their distinctive looks and economy—with only sixty-five to eighty-five horsepower engines, they are one of the cheapest airplanes to fly.

Three Whiskey Mike, a beautifully polished, bare-aluminum air-plane whose rudders were emblazoned with the name *Waltzing Matilda,* so outshone my Five-Niner-Echo that I felt envious. Partly for that reason, I approached its pilot, a slim, handsome gray-haired woman in her midfifties, in the lounge.

"I own that 150 over there," I began, "and I have the devil's own time keeping her polished. How do you keep that plane so shiny?" I asked.

"Well, I haven't polished it for two months," she said deprecat-ingly, which made me quail because if that's so, *Gin Fizz* looks as if it hasn't been shined for two years. For the next couple of minutes, we sounded like housewives in a supermarket discussing the rela-tive merits of laundry soaps. "I use Rolite," she said—that metal polish, a standard in the airline industry, is a favorite of mine also, but it still requires lots of hand rubbing—"and Treem. It comes in a little black can, and it has pink felt in it. You have to get it from an automobile chrome shop, and it works real well. I also use Glass Wax. It just polishes the airplane as you wipe it down, and you don't have to polish it every couple of months. Works real good. Comes in a pink can, and you usually can get it from Ace Hardware. You have to ask for it." Carefully, I wrote down the names of all the products.

Her name is Carol Morris, she lives "on a little strip in Fort Worth," and this Ercoupe is actually an "Aircoupe" made by a Kansas firm called Alon, which briefly manufactured the airplane, turning out 214 examples. *Waltzing Matilda* is her third airplane, she added, and she has been flying since 1982, when as a forty-two-year-old widow, "I met a gentleman, and he introduced me to aviation."

Carol has owned a Cessna 140 and a large, powerful Cessna 185. "We also own a Bonanza and a J-3 Cub," she added. "I've just been up to Montana in the Ercoupe. I took it across to Belvidere, Illinois, then Oshkosh, Wisconsin, where I got weathered in, and now I'm on my way back home. And now I've got to go," she said, plunking down her coffee cup, shaking my hand, and striding briskly out to her airplane.

As *Waltzing Matilda* lifted in a silvery arc into the sky over McAlester, I wished I had more of an opportunity to talk to Carol. She was the first female pilot I had encountered since leaving New Jersey. Women certainly are not unheard of in aviation, but of the 600,000-plus licensed pilots of all ratings in the United States, only 6 percent are female. That is hard to believe in a feminist age, but it's true. So few women are seen in the left seats of airplanes that their presence is instantly noticeable.

Why should the subject fascinate me so? It is simply that a member of one minority (in my case, the deaf) is always interested in the experiences of another; perhaps I might learn something new and useful about the struggle for acceptance by the majority. Besides, the female pilots I have encountered all seem to be remarkably self-assured and even commanding. Are they confident because they became pilots, or did they become pilots because they were confident? As someone whose gumption is sometimes shaken by events, I wanted to know.

Historically, society has had a hard time accepting female aviators as anything more than fleeting curiosities. In 1929, on the second day of the Women's Air Derby (patronizingly dubbed the "Powder Puff Derby" by Will Rogers), Marvel Crosson died in the crash of her airplane, precipitating the headline "Women Have Conclusively Proven They Cannot Fly." Nine years later, Lindbergh, whose wife Anne Morrow was a leading aviatrix of the 1930s, was dismayed to find women flying for the Red Air Force when he toured the Soviet Union. "I do not see how it can work very well," he told his diary. "After all, there is a God-made difference between men and women that even the Soviet Union can't eradicate." The storied Soviet women fighter and bomber pilots who helped crush the Nazi war machine proved him wrong, but half a century later, many American men still doubted that women had the "killer instinct" to excel in combat.

It's not hard to pinpoint why women are still so rare in aviation after two decades of influential modern feminism. Today earning a
simple private pilot's license, let alone a commercial or air-transport
rating, takes thousands of dollars. The average working woman's
income is three-quarters that of her male counterpart, which limits
her spending on nonessentials. Parents and schools still tend to
guide boys and girls into traditional roles. Among working couples,
husbands still expect to be the principal breadwinners, their wives
serving subsidiary functions. Male pilots tend to be ultraconserva-
tive about social change. They tend to be skeptical about women's
ability to perform male-dominated skills, so women have to work
harder to prove themselves professionally.

I have encountered fascinating stories about such hard-to-kill
cultural imperatives on CompuServe's Women in Aviation Online
forum. Annie Mattos, a pilot for a Colorado commuter airline,
posted this message one day: "I was at an airport the other day in
my uniform. I was waiting for a flight next to a family and this little
girl kept staring at me and pointing. Her mother hushed her up and
told her that if she was good maybe someday she could be a stew-
ardess, too. Maybe this is why there aren't more lady pilots—because they don't grow up hearing they can be whatever they want
to be, like I did."

Angela Elgee, an FAA inspector who often does safety-check
rides on airliners, responded: "Annie, I've had similar experiences
and I don't even wear a uniform! I have come off the flight deck to
go to the lav and have had passengers hand me all kinds of articles,
including empty brandy glasses and dirty diapers."

Nancy Novaes, another airline captain, offered: "I can stand
there with four stripes on my shoulders and still have fuelers and
gate agents address my first officer, looking past me as if I weren't
even there."

Annie Mattos has had experience with the Invisible Woman syndrome, too. "When I was building my hours," she said, "I flew a vintage Ercoupe. My husband—who is not a pilot—and I flew together
a lot. At most FBOs we would have three-way conversations in
which somebody would ask my husband a question about the airplane, fuel or tiedown, and I would answer it. We'd continue like
this until we got whatever we needed accomplished. My husband
and I would die laughing about it afterwards."

This struck a powerful chord with me. Frequently, strangers talk right past me to Debby as if I am not there, even though I may be asking the questions. They just don't believe a deaf person can have anything intelligent to say. It can be maddening.

"Sometimes I have to repeat important information several times to make sure I am being listened to," Annie said. "I think men have a tendency not to listen too closely to what women are saying. It sometimes takes an attention-getting phrase like 'Did you hear me? OK, then, what was that altimeter setting?' Some guys tell me that this is because of a woman's higher pitch, but I think men are just really good at tuning women out. Maybe it's all that 'take out the trash' stuff they heard from their wives and mothers."

One of the most interesting female pilots I have met is Patrice Washington, the first black woman to become a captain for a major airline, flying DC-8 freighters for United Parcel Service. She is one of only 500 of her sex flying the left seat for major carriers. Her colleague Bill Kight, the 757 pilot who had written about me for *AOPA Pilot,* told me about her. Later Patrice and I met in a northwest suburb of Chicago, where she lives with her husband Ray Washington. Ray is a former B-52 pilot who is now one of American Airlines' few black captains.

She said she is never sure whether the prejudice she encounters is addressed to the color of her skin—or its shape. On the job, she says, she feels accepted most of the time. "We have something in common. We know about airplanes. We speak the same language. We can share our experiences. But am I really more accepted as a female because I'm a pilot? I don't know about that. Some men feel that by my being in the cockpit, I've taken a job away from another male, a white male. I've had some negative experiences also with black male pilots. It couldn't have been because I was black. It had to have been because they were having difficulty relating to a female and a professional." And she may be accepted at work, "but when it's over, the other crew members go their way and I go mine. I never get invited home. The others do. Whether it's because I'm female or I'm black, I don't know."

As do so many female pilots, Patrice feels that she has had to prove that her flying skills are superior to most men's, not only to get a job, but also "every day because someone is questioning your ability."

She was born and raised in the Bahamas and immediately after graduation from Embry-Riddle Aeronautical University in Daytona

Beach, Florida, found a job with a Bahamian charter outfit, Trans Island Airways, flying twin-engine Piper Aztecs and Navajos. It was in a Navajo on a flight from Nassau to Governors Harbor on Eleuthera that she was "blooded" by an engine failure.

"I remember that propeller turning," she said. "It stopped. And my heart stopped. I was almost two-thirds of the way to Eleuthera, about eighteen miles out." In an airplane as small as a Navajo, the single pilot is not separated from the passengers by a bulkhead. "I decided it was important to remain calm and not show I was nervous because then the passengers would be, too," she said. "They were watching. They could hear me breathe." The airplane landed without incident, and a passenger told Patrice he felt reassured when he saw how cool she was.

Patrice then signed on with the regional airline Bahamasair, flying bigger airplanes—HS-748 twin-engine turboprops and Boeing 737 jets—to Florida and New York. When UPS advertised job openings, she sent an application, and in 1988 went to work for the freight carrier as a flight engineer. Two years later, she "upgraded" to first officer, and just a few months before we met, sewed on her fourth stripe as a captain.

When I heard about Patrice, I said, I had done a bit of a double-take. "To me, like to most Americans, United Parcel Service means big brown trucks," I said. "I know UPS flies airplanes—I've seen them at O'Hare—but I never realized it was a major airline as well."

Patrice laughed. "One of the comments I often hear after 'That's neat, you fly an airplane,' is 'Well, are you ever going to get a *real* airline job?' They think since I'm flying for UPS, I haven't reached the top yet, that I'm still going up the steps, American or Delta or United being the top. The pay is no different. The only difference between me and my husband is that I fly cargo and he flies passengers."

She and Ray don't see much of each other nowadays. "Last year we had a good year," she said. "Because I was flying as a copilot, I was able to bid my trips so I could go home almost every day he was home. But because I've just been upgraded to captain, I've gone to the bottom of the captain's seniority list, and so my ability to bid for trips I want is nil. I think I saw Ray five days last month."

Being low on seniority means spending a lot of time as a reserve pilot. At the moment we talked, she was "on call" at UPS's headquarters in Louisville, Kentucky, sixteen days out of each twenty-eight-day month, in eight-day stretches. She checks into a Louisville hotel and waits to be called. "And if they don't call me," she laughed, "I just wait some more."

All this having been said about professional women pilots, it's undeniable that women who fly on the grassroots level today enjoy a great deal of acceptance from their male peers. Partly because female private pilots aren't competing financially with them, the male pilots are "very supportive," said one who more or less spoke for them all. Therese Brandell, with whom I enjoyed a long E-mail correspondence, is in her late thirties and flies out of Pontiac, Michigan. "I do get surprised looks from some of the male students, but that's typical," she said.

Therese grew up in Lansing, the only girl among four brothers "and the only one of us interested in flying. It's in my blood. My dad was a pilot. I went for my first ride at age ten and just loved it, and flying was always in the back of my mind." In the early 1980s, she was introduced to hang-gliding by a cousin in hilly California, but since that sport isn't popular in flat Michigan, "I found ultralights and started flying them in early 1983. I bought my own, custom-made wings and all." She loved the ultralight social culture, much of which consists of sitting around the airport talking, waiting for the breeze to die down—these featherweight airplanes cannot handle a lot of wind. "I flew with a group of three women, and it was great fun to go out and shock people. They'd say, 'I couldn't believe it when you landed and I saw that you were girls!'"

Her instructor became her boyfriend. "While my interest was already there, he really cultivated it. He had a private license and was an airframe-and-power-plant mechanic, so his job and his life were aviation. I was constantly at the airport with him. He used to talk about the romance and adventure of it. He wanted to take off and go barnstorming around the country. He was daring. He lived for the moment."

Therese's boyfriend was an aerobatic pilot and died in a crash at an air show, flying inverted. "He was too low and descending and tried to pull out of the dive, but there wasn't enough altitude. It was shortly after his thirtieth birthday. I remember him saying then that he was surprised he lived that long."

After that, she said, the fun temporarily disappeared from flying. "I remember Wayne asking me one time what I would do if he was gone. Would I still fly? I don't think I really answered him. The topic came up only because he was going to be gone for a weekend and I wasn't planning on flying then. I thought about that conversation a lot after he died. I realized that I really did want to continue flying, but not in ultralights. So although it took me eight years to get back into flying, I finally did, and I know he's always there with me."

I could understand Wayne, I told Therese. When my children were young and Debby had put aside her teaching career to care for them, I, of course, had to shoulder the major financial responsibility for the family, so I was a cautious breadwinner, never taking any kind of chance. Now that my children are grown and my wife is back in her profession, I can afford to take a few risks—not that flying a little Cessna 150 low and slow is a particularly dangerous pursuit. A little risk, I said, adds spice to life. As Wayne did, I am breaking down self-imposed limits, and that gives me a new sense of accomplishment at an age when physical and mental powers are otherwise beginning to flag. "There is something about living for the moment that gives life a new clarity," I told Therese. "Wayne knew that."

So comfortable have many grassroots pilots of both sexes become with one another that they can enjoy an ironic humor about gender differences. I was once at a Texas airport whose bathrooms were marked Pilots and Stewardesses, and as I started to enter the men's room, the woman behind the counter called out to me, "Watch out—the women pilots *never* go into the Stewardesses'." And why should they? A sense of humor always is a powerful weapon against adversity.

Also on the field at McAlester sat a curious-looking airplane I immediately recognized, a huge, sun-bleached biplane called an Antonov An-2, still with Soviet Aeroflot markings. The An-2, the biggest biplane still flying, looks extraordinarily ungainly, like a fat heron with dragonfly eyes. Inside the FBO, I pointed to it and asked the woman behind the counter, "What's it used for?"

"Skydiving," she replied. "We have a skydiving school here. It's for sale. Are you interested?"

"How much?" I asked.

"Fifty-nine thousand dollars, but make us an offer," she answered. I was surprised. That was a lot of airplane for the money.

"I'm tempted to offer you my Cessna 150 in trade, but I'm not qualified to fly an airplane like that," I said.

She laughed. "Well, why don't you go down and take a look before you make up your mind?"

"How many skydivers can it carry?" I asked.

"As many as are willing to get into it," came the snickering reply from the line attendant. Probably twelve jumpers, I estimated. (Twenty-nine Cubans escaped to Florida in an An-2 in 1991, but they presumably weren't wearing bulky chutes.)

"Why are you selling it?" I asked.

"It burns one gallon of gas a minute," said the woman behind the counter.

"Oh," I said, quickly doing the arithmetic in my head. At $2 per gallon, that's $120 an hour, more than ten times *Gin Fizz*'s fuel cost. "I'm going to go down and look at it. But I'm not kicking its tires, mind you."

"Just the same, we'll listen to any reasonable offer," she pressed, only half kidding. "We'll even throw in the original Aeroflot crew uniforms. They came with the plane."

She was being a little disingenuous. Months later I learned that the An-2 has never been used as a skydiving plane in the United States, at least legally. Since the collapse of the Soviet Union, Aeroflot has raised cash by selling some of its older Antonovs to private parties in the United States. But the type has not gone through the rigorous and expensive FAA certification process to allow it to be used commercially, so it is limited to "experimental exhibition" flying—that is, flying in air shows. It can carry no passengers, just its crew. In America, it is nothing more than an expensive museum piece.

But what a museum piece! The An-2 has been to Soviet domestic air transport what a DC-3 has been to American aviation. More than 20,000 An-2s have been built in the Soviet Union and its satellites and used as short-haul airliners across Russia, Siberia, and Eastern Europe, as well as crop dusters, forestry and fishery survey ships, and air ambulances. The An-2 was originally called the *Kolkhoznik,* "collective farmer," a name that suits it perfectly. It first flew in 1947 and is still in production in Poland.

It is extraordinarily slow—its cruise speed is not much faster than *Gin Fizz*'s—but it has a keen ability to take off and land on a postage stamp of an airfield—a roughly cleared one at that. Usually, if the only engine of an airplane should fail during a dark night without lights on the ground or in bad weather when the ground cannot be seen, the pilot and passengers are in deep trouble. Not in the An-2. Its pilot drops full flaps and pulls the control yoke all the way back. An ordinary airplane would stall and perhaps spin, but the An-2 simply mushes forward at twenty-six miles per hour, descending gently like a parachute. Yes, the landing is a hard one, but everybody usually survives.

Half an hour later, I was ascending the rickety stairway of light turbulence through the clouds, setting course along the railroad for Eaker Field at Durant, seventy-two miles southwest, my last stop in Oklahoma. I flew over the easternmost ridge of the Ouachita range, climbing to 6,500 feet before emerging above the annoying heat turbulence, and felt a little cooler at the higher altitude. At that height, the railroad tracks below looked tiny, yet I could still follow them. I exulted in the solitude.

But flying alone does have disadvantages. The old cliché about two pairs of eyes being better than one is even truer in the air than on the road. No matter how carefully a pilot scans the sky and the instruments—neophyte pilots are taught to concentrate their gaze on one pie-slice of the sky at a time and to sweep the instrument panel regularly to make sure the needles on the gauges point where they should—it is impossible to see everything. Other airplanes are hard to discern, especially against the ground and toward the sun. They're just too small to see until you are almost upon them.

More than once I have peered down at my sectional chart for just a moment—is that peculiarly shaped lake with a dam at one end the same one I'm looking at on the map?—then glanced up to spot an airplane passing uncomfortably close aboard and wondered if the other pilot saw me.

Around airports, it's easy to miss another plane entering the landing pattern, especially if the plane is above and behind my field of vision. Occasionally, there is a fatal accident when a fast low-wing airplane, whose pilot can't see below and forward, descends atop a slow high-wing airplane, whose pilot can't see above and behind. A second pair of eyes cuts down the risk.

Another disadvantage is that when there's nobody to talk to in the right seat, it's hard for many pilots to stay alert, especially if they're flying airplanes with automatic pilots; more than once, such a pilot has dozed off and awakened to find himself hundreds

of miles past his intended point of landing, short of fuel. Hearing pilots with nondirectional radio-beacon equipment can keep awake
by tuning their receivers to local radio stations for talk shows,
sports news, or soft rock. Deaf pilots have to guard against drowsy
woolgathering.

It's a little easier to stay alert in a skittish Cessna 150, which
needs to be tended every mile of the way. A brief glance at a hawk
cruising on a thermal below, and you've gained 200 feet and departed five degrees from your course. I am an inveterate lollygag-
ger, too—always wondering, for example, *Is that train below an
Amtraker?* I nudge *Gin Fizz* toward it for a better look, losing 2,000
feet of altitude in my eagerness to identify the locomotive. My
course through the airlanes sometimes resembles a dog trotting
veeringly down the block, following its nose higgledy-piggledy.

In a solo aerial odyssey, there are few other dogs to sniff. The
joy of riding a train, for instance, lies largely in the people one
meets. With them, one can share opinions and insights on the
world that passes by outside the window. One can enjoy the
serendipity of new friendships over cocktails in the lounge car or
at dinner in the dining car. Not so at 2,000 feet in a little Cessna,
and not so at zero feet in a fast-food restaurant on a motel strip.
Only on weekends at busy grassroots fields, I had discovered, is
there fellowship for the cross-country pilot. Time and again, I have
landed at an outlying rural airport between Monday and Friday to
find myself the only pilot out and about. The few pilots I run into at
these times always seem to be concerned with their preflight tasks
and anxious to get away. Who can blame them?

And still, there are advantages to boring lonely holes through
the air at altitude, rather than on the highway. There's nobody to
roar up behind you and flash his brights into your rearview mirror,
then shout "Asshole!" as he passes you. If you're self-centered
enough to enjoy your own company, you can converse with yourself over endless miles without the guy in the next vehicle looking
over and thinking you're a couple of sandwiches short of a picnic.

Without a second person aboard, the plane takes off more
quickly and climbs faster. There's no unexpected "Gotta go. Would
you stop at the next airport?" You can wallow in selfishness;
there's no asking if a 6 A.M. takeoff time is OK with your passenger,
no negotiation over Long John Silver's versus McDonald's, no
power grabs for the television remote control in the motel room.

And more than most solo pilots, I have had to make no adjustments. A deaf pilot flying solo does not need to learn how to accommodate himself to isolation; he has experienced it all his life, come to terms with it, and even turned it to his advantage. Isolation is not the same thing as loneliness. Aloneness has many faces. The serenity of solitude is one of them.

# 14

*A*fter landing at Durant, I taxied to the FBO, shut down, and walked inside to a yawning but air-conditioned emptiness. The place was fairly modern and clean but bare and, as I was coming to expect, utterly uninhabited on a summer Monday noon. As I was washing down my lunch of peanut butter crackers with Diet Coke, a mechanic walked in from the hangar and asked if he could help me. When I said no, he nodded, turned, and walked back to the hangar.

The emptiness of Eaker Field was deceptive, however. Underneath an open-air hangar outside sat nine pristine Cessna 152s, all done up in the same new blue-and-white livery and with consecutive N-numbers. A tenth blue-and-white 152 landed on the long runway as I did the run-up at the end of the field, preparing to leave. Doubtless the place is busier later in the week—and in the fall, winter, and spring; the Southeastern Oklahoma State University aviation school occupies a large terminal-like building across from the FBO, with a couple of large Cessna 414 twins in the hangar. This certainly was not a down-at-the-heels airport.

For Cal Rodgers, the mechanical imps had again settled in for the day. *Vin Fiz*'s engine had overheated, so Rodgers landed in a cotton field just east of Durant after a seventy-five-minute flight from McAlester, to let the motor cool down. Twenty-five minutes later, he was back in the air, and within ten minutes had crossed the storied Red River, entering Texas. At Denison, just fifteen miles southwest of Durant, where arrangements had been made for refueling, thousands of people were waiting to watch *Vin Fiz* land. They were disappointed because Cal, who had been told at Durant that the country around Denison was "rough, rugged and timbered with wire running in every direction," decided to pass up the city and instead headed along the Missouri-Kansas-Texas tracks to Pottsboro, five miles west, where he put down to refuel. The Denison oil company, annoyed that Rodgers had not landed there, refused to deliver fuel to Pottsboro, and Rodgers had to hustle up other supplies. After departing, Cal took *Vin Fiz* ten miles farther west, over Whitesboro, where he missed the white markers near the depot indicating which track to follow, instead taking a branch line toward Wichita Falls, rather than the main track to Gainesville. He flew on, passing close by Gainesville, sixteen miles west, and continued another twenty-five miles to Bonita, where men atop boxcars flagged him down. Cal landed, realized his mistake, and returned to Gainesville, where his chase train—and still more thousands of rowdy spectators—waited.

The crowd besieged *Vin Fiz* and Rodgers, the people surging around the airplane trying to write their names on the fabric. They did not understand that doing so might poke tiny but dangerous holes in the muslin. The mechanics had not yet arrived to guard the plane, and since he had had his fill of these situations, Rodgers was "edgy and in no mood to be interviewed," Eileen Lebow wrote. "One reporter tried and wrote that Mr. Rodgers had lost his patience 'as well as his way.' . . . He later said the crowds were so unruly that he would not have landed for two thousand dollars had he known how they were going to behave." An hour and a half later, fed and at last calmed, Rodgers took off, heading south along the Santa Fe tracks to Fort Worth.

When I left Oklahoma, the airborne perils—not other airplanes, but other flying objects—became Texas sized. As I climbed through 3,000 feet, heading for a 4,500-foot cruising altitude, I saw, about two miles in the distance and a little higher than me, a pair of almost imperceptible black specks turning lazy circles in a thermal—large birds, I thought. When I was a student pilot in southern Wisconsin, I learned that Canada geese and other migratory birds usually—but not always—could be trusted to hold their course, altitude, and speed and therefore could be easily evaded.

But these birds weren't geese. They were buzzards, enormous turkey vultures with six-foot wingspans. And turkey vultures don't often fly from Point A to Point B like geese. They fly in tight circles, hovering on a thermal for long periods before swooping over to another. As the distance between airplane and birds closed to a mile, the birds still dead ahead, I put *Gin Fizz* into a gentle right turn to go around them. At the same time, the birds altered their glide path onto a course that would intercept mine. As *Gin Fizz* closed the distance at more than 100 miles per hour, I decided to jink to the left and press the control column forward to dive—and the damned birds altered *their* course toward mine again, like a pair of feathered heat-seeking air-to-air missiles. At the last moment, I pulled the control column back and the birds flashed by, not more than ten feet away—one below the plane and one above.

My heart trip-hammered. A strike from a bird of any size is dangerous, but those buzzards were large enough to punch right through the windshield, bang the propeller into a pretzel, or pound a deep groove into a wing. We three were very lucky, indeed. For the rest of the way to Los Angeles, I scanned the sky as never before and frequently made a point of asking what kinds of birds I was likely to encounter and how best to avoid them. (The invariable answer: "Buzzards. Just stay clear of 'em.") That's one thing the student pilot's syllabus doesn't discuss, especially in Wisconsin.

The airfield nearest Pottsboro is Grayson County Airport, between Denison and Sherman. It is the largest airport I've ever landed on—its runway is 9,000 feet long by 150 feet wide, so huge that I felt swallowed up as I touched down. Since most of my landings habitually tend to be "short-field" landings, in which the pilot aims to put his wheels on the runway just past the threshold, I touched down on the numbers and had to taxi 2,000 feet to the first turnoff and then another 3,000 feet to the FBO. I could have taken off again and flown there. As befits such a place, the FBO was huge and modern—and utterly empty. The manager had gone to lunch, and absolutely nobody was about. It was lonelier even than Eaker Field.

I wanted to ask about the dozens of 727s and DC-9s parked all over the field, some of them in various stages of disassembly, some of them looking almost new. Was it a boneyard? Later I discovered that, like many airports in the dry Southwest, it is a repository for surplus airliners, the older ones serving as sources of parts to keep others flying, the newer planes often refurbished and sold to start-up domestic low-cost airlines and foreign carriers.

Instead of taxiing down to the beginning of the runway to take off, I started the roll at midfield—but that was just fine, for there was a good 4,500 feet of runway to use up, and *Gin Fizz* was at least 300 feet above the ground when she crossed the threshold.

The turbulence was beginning to grow ferocious twenty minutes later when *Gin Fizz* touched down at Gainesville just before 2 P.M. I took the weather as a sign that I had done enough flying for that day. "Anyplace to hangar my plane for the night?" I asked the line attendant. "Lemme ask the parachute school if they've got room," he answered. He pointed to a hangar across the ramp. NORTH TEXAS SKYDIVING CENTER, said a small sign above its office.

After the attendant refilled my tanks, I paid the bill inside the tiny and windowless but air-conditioned skydiving office to a skinny, wispy-bearded, tough-looking man in his thirties. Sitting around the place watching a soap opera on a television with a lop-sided rabbit-ear antenna were a dozen men, women, and young children, some in menacing tattoos, T-shirts, and denims with all the subtle taste of Hell's Angels.

Meekly I asked, "Is it possible to put my plane away in the hangar? I'm worried about the heat damaging my instruments." I was also concerned about nighttime vandals, some of whom, it seemed, could be in the room with us.

"Oh, sure," said the skinny man with un-biker-like friendliness. "C'mon around, we'll put her away now. I'm Ernie Long, and I manage the skydiving operation," he said, thrusting out his hand as he led me inside the hangar, where two large, well-worn Cessna 182s, high-wing four-seaters that are a much larger and twice as powerful version of *Gin Fizz,* nestled against the far wall. All but their pilot's seats had been removed, their interiors—walls and floor—were covered with quilted foam padding, and their right doors had been converted to hinge upwards; clearly, they were skydiving planes.

Many, if not most, small-plane pilots will grouse at the yank of a ripcord that they see "no earthly reason to want to jump out of a perfectly good airplane." Their disapproval is partly generational; while pilots tend to be older and fettered by responsibilities, sky-divers tend to be young, carefree, and unattached, like the ski bums our fathers hated. A middle-aged pilot once told me rather crankily that he had heard that some young female skydivers finance their pastime by selling their bodies.

Ernie has been skydiving for thirteen years, he said after we had rolled down the hangar door on *Gin Fizz*. "I just wandered into it. I'm an electrical engineer, and I was working on a project for American Airlines at Dallas/Fort Worth. A relative who was a skydiver invited me to go make a jump just to see what it was like, and I've been skydiving ever since."

"Were you frightened on that first jump?" I asked.

"Yes, to a degree. I didn't really take it seriously. I thought it was a carnival ride, that they could just take someone off the street, give them three hours of training, and throw them out of an airplane. I didn't realize the gravity of the sport." He eyed me to see if I got the joke.

In the old days of parachuting, the military would first teach a jumper to "fly" a chute under a canopy tethered to a tower. On his first jump, a static line tied to the plane pulled the chute out of its pack as he leaped from the door. Today, Ernie said, most skydiving schools instruct under a system called "accelerated free fall."

"After a six- or eight-hour ground school, two instructors go out with you. We all exit the aircraft at the same time, each of the instructors holding one of your leg straps. As we fall, we help hold you stable while you learn to 'feel' the air. We act as training wheels. In seven jumps you'll be a skydiver."

The school handles about 100 student jumps a week, Ernie said, and there are about fifty active experienced skydivers who jump in the afternoons and on weekends, paying twelve dollars a ride. "It's like a bus pass, only instead of going across town we're going straight up."

I'd always thought jumpers leaped out over farmland, but Ernie set me straight. Jump planes always stay right over the airport. "Safety's a big concern with us. If we ever have a problem with one of our aircraft, we can just glide back to the runway. We fly a box around the airport and drop the jumpers from the windward side.

"Now, on the way down, an experienced jumper must open the main parachute by 2,000 feet above ground level, but on the way up, he starts having oxygen concerns at 12,500 feet, just like a pilot. So, from 12,500 to 2,000 feet, he has seventy to seventy-five seconds of fun time." Twelve dollars for seventy seconds of bliss? That didn't sound like a bargain to me.

"Does the pilot use the radio to let other airplanes know he's dropping jumpers?" I asked.

"Oh, yes. When we first take off, we notify everyone and give them a time frame. Between 2,500 feet to about 8,500 feet, we talk to the air-traffic center in Fort Worth, and then we give a two-minute warning, a one-minute warning, and then 'Jumpers away!' Finally, we notify air traffic when all the jumpers are back on the ground."

I sighed. "I'll tell you, Ernie. I'm fifty-five years old and learned to fly just a couple of years ago. Honestly, I cannot imagine what's so great about jumping. How would you sell the sport to a reluctant pilot?"

Ernie thought a moment. "Well, I'm sure you love to fly. I can tell by the way you take care of your airplane how much you like to fly. You know flying is not only steering your plane around 360 degrees, but up and down also. In free fall, you steer yourself, too. You can go in any direction. You just think about what you want to do or where you want to go, and your body will take you there. It's the only thing you'll ever do that's totally three dimensional. It's such *freedom.*"

Ernie was on a roll. "And I've spent the last thirteen years learning to get better and better. That's another thing about this sport—it's so open-ended, with freestyle jumping, jumping in big formations, even skysurfing. You could do this forever and never do everything or be as good as you really want to be."

"And there's competition, too, isn't there?"

"Oh yes," Ernie said. "On the state, national, and world levels. Here at Gainesville we have small competitions from time to time, just for fun, to give you a chance to show what you've learned."

Ernie is able to make only a "really pretty meager" living teaching skydiving, but he loves it. "Look," he said, "I'm taking a break for a year or two from my profession, and I've known the owner for a long time, and I just took the opportunity to take some time off and just skydive full time."

Aha, I said to myself. A skydiving bum. "Married? Family?"

"No."

"That helps."

"In skydiving, you could catch AIDS."

AIDS? Maybe that crotchety middle-aged pilot was right, I started to think. Ernie caught the expression on my face. "That's 'aeronautically induced divorce syndrome,'" he said, laughing.

"I can understand that," I said wryly, adding tentatively, "What if I wanted to make just one jump, just to see what it's like, and then never do it again?"

"For people like you," Ernie said, "we have a system called 'tandem jumping.' You have about a forty-five-minute ground school, and when you jump, you're tethered to the instructor by a harness that's attached to the shoulders and hips. You get to experience free fall. Skydiving is not for everyone, but everyone should make a skydive."

"I'll think about it," I said, thinking about it and realizing that I risked an instant case of AIDS if Debby ever heard about it.

"I've got an idea," Ernie said. "Tomorrow another skydiver and I are getting some practice. Want to go up with us and watch?" Forest McBride, the owner of the school—a black-bearded middle-aged man with a midriff as ample as mine, who looked as if he'd be comfortable on a Harley-Davidson in a Wehrmacht helmet with Viking horns—would fly the plane, and I'd sit beside him and watch. I accepted with alacrity.

Then it was time to head for the Holiday Inn, nine miles away. I wandered over to the line attendant's office and asked if he'd call me a cab. "Naw," he said, "I'll drive you." He refused my offer of five dollars for his trouble, even "just for gas." I wasn't surprised. His was just one more example of the airport neighborliness I was beginning to grow used to.

The next morning a fellow guest overheard me at the front desk asking for a ride to the airport in the motel's courtesy car. He tapped my shoulder. "I'm a pilot, too," he said. "I'll give you a lift. I'm heading in that direction anyway." In the car, he said he was a computer-hardware salesman, and by the look of his brand-new Chrysler, he was a prosperous one. In response, I told him about my trip, and he became so interested that twice he lost his concentration and missed the turnoff to the airport on the interstate— once northbound and once southbound.

"Wish I could go along," he said, as he dropped me at the sky-diving center.

"As they say in the sneakers commercial," I replied, "just do it."

At 9 A.M. the two skydivers arrived. After I cleared *Gin Fizz* out of the hangar and helped roll out the airplane we'd fly that morning, Ernie used the open floor space to repack his chute, a red-and-yellow nylon high-tech sports model. "Most students use 240-square-foot chutes," he explained conversationally as he gathered the nylon into neat pleats, "but this is a 153-square-foot model. It lets you glide faster."

The chute, he explained, is not the circular white silk parachute familiar in World War II movies, but a rectangular wing. Much like a crude glider, it allows the user to soar after a fashion, controlling his direction as well as rate of descent.

"I'm not that meticulous a person," he said, as he folded and tucked, "but this is a brand-new parachute, and I want to take care of it." A typical parachute rig begins with a tiny pilot chute that yanks the main canopy out of its bag and ends with a smaller reserve chute. The whole, Ernie said, costs $3,000.

"Forest will take us up to 4,500 feet today," he added, and "we'll free-fall for 2,500 feet before pulling our rip cords at 2,000 feet." With that, Ernie finished folding the chute, then repeatedly lay on it with his entire torso, pressing the air out of the folds, smothering the nylon into submission.

"Is making a few mistakes in folding the chute critical?" I asked.

"Oh, you can make lots of mistakes," he said, "but not certain ones."

Before Ernie finished speaking, he had the nylon folded into a tiny bag the size of a woman's purse. It was hard to believe that so much material could be stuffed into such a small space. Ernie then gathered the score or more of 15-foot-long risers into foot-long lengths, snubbing each of them into a series of rubber loops along the open edge of the bag. Packing the chute had taken twenty minutes. "I'm slow," he said. That's because you're *really* meticulous, I thought.

"Here, try it on to see how it feels," he said. I slipped my arms into the shoulder harness and fastened the chest strap while he pulled the two leg loops under my crotch and shackled them tight. "How much does this thing weigh?" I asked, taking a few crablike steps across the hangar.

"Eighteen pounds."

The weight felt like that of a hiker's day pack stuffed with a generous lunch for six people. But the leg straps cut into my crotch; I was wearing light shorts. I wouldn't want to hike more than a few yards in this rig.

In the meantime, Ernie was donning a skintight black nylon

jumpsuit, as was his companion. "We don't have to wear these today," he said. "They're just for looks, really." The jumpsuits lessen
air resistance and help equalize the rate of fall among several
jumpers. They also sport padded grips along the outside of the
legs and upper arms for other skydivers to grab in a group jump.
Each jumper wears a wrist altimeter, which looks like a large plastic stopwatch with a red pie section at the 2,000-foot mark. Before
going up, the skydivers zero the needles.

As McBride walked out to his airplane, the two jumpers donned
their packs. Then Ernie turned to me with another parachute and
said, "Here, you wear this."

I pulled back slightly. "Why?" I asked. "I'm not planning to
jump!"

He laughed. "It's for safety," he said. There's no seat in the plane
for you."

"There isn't?" Then I remembered that all but the pilot's seat
had been removed.

"Here, you sit on the floor," Ernie said. Clumsily, encumbered by
the parachute, I climbed into the big Cessna and sat facing backward, my chute against the forward bulkhead of the airplane below
the instrument panel. Ernie reached down and fastened a web belt
firmly about my upper thighs, clamping me to the floor. "You won't
fall out," he said, not very reassuringly.

Then the skydivers scrambled aboard, crouching in the rear of
the cabin, and McBride started his engine. In just a couple of minutes, we had taken off, the plane clawing for altitude. I couldn't see
anything outside—I was sitting below window level. One thousand
feet, then 2,000, then 3,000, and 4,000, and as the 4,500-foot mark
approached, McBride throttled back and radioed that he was
about to drop jumpers over Gainesville Airport. Ernie reached
over, pushed the door up, and on McBride's "Go!" stepped out in
the eighty-miles-per-hour slipstream onto a step above the landing
gear, gripping the wing strut. I pointed my camera as the second
skydiver stepped out—and suddenly they dropped away just as I
pressed the shutter release. I had no idea whether I did so in time.
(I did, but when the pictures came back from the drugstore, that
one showed only two disembodied torsos against the sky.)

Quickly McBride reached over, shut the door, and put the plane
into a long descending circle, careful to stay well clear of the
jumpers. I levered myself high enough to peer briefly out the win-

dow and caught a quick glimpse of the two skydivers, who had completed their free fall and were gliding down under their chutes. The view was much too brief to photograph, so I had to be content with the ride down.

On the final approach, McBride had to tunnel down and behind me to yank up the flap handle, almost bringing me up with it, so tight were the confines. On the ground I opened the door and saw the two skydivers marching across the apron, their chutes gathered in front of them, grinning. Only then was I able to take the second picture of the day.

"Well, what about it?" Ernie asked. "You gonna do it some day?"

"Aaaah," I said. "I think flying an airplane is exciting enough for me."

As I struggled out of the chute, Ernie presented me with a North Texas Skydiving Center T-shirt. "We want you to have this," he said.

I thanked him, and a few minutes later I was off, glad to have witnessed the details of an interesting sport, but having absolutely no desire ever to participate in it. My marriage is safe.

It was 10 A.M. and growing hotter as I banked *Gin Fizz* northwestward through a thick cloudless haze—visibility was about five miles—toward Bonita, twenty-two miles west, where Rodgers had flown after misjudging the direction to Fort Worth. The nearest airfield is at Nocona, seven miles farther west. It was no more than a 3,200-foot-long concrete strip with no airplanes visible on the ramp, indeed no buildings of any kind nearby. I circled and saw no one. I throttled back and did a touch-and-go and then headed south toward Fort Worth.

On his way to Fort Worth in 1986, Jim Lloyd had a singular encounter in *Vin Fiz II*. "On the way there my engine gave me problems. It would stop and start, stop and start. I was able to hold altitude, but I didn't think I could make it to Fort Worth/Dallas airport." The nearest field was a private one with two hard-surfaced runways, one almost 5,000 feet long. Private airstrips are not for public use, but FAA regulations allow aircraft to land on them in emergencies. "When I landed, this place was absolutely empty. There was a hangar here and a big mansion there—a huge, huge house, brand new—and another big building, one that looked like a small industry of some kind. I figured I'd landed at an industrial air park."

Almost before the propeller stopped, "a uniformed guard came out and said, 'Why did you land here? You're not allowed!' I said, 'I know. I had engine trouble.' I told him what I was doing, and he said, 'Oh, OK. You know, if it wasn't an emergency, I would have to have you take the wings off your airplane and truck it out of here because we're not supposed to allow this. We really don't want anybody landing here.'

"It turns out that the place belonged to—have you seen this preacher on television?" And Lloyd named a charismatic evangelical whose face is familiar to devotees of the Christian Broadcasting Network. Kenneth Copeland is known for a singular theology that emphasizes material prosperity, especially his own: "It would have been impossible for Jesus to have been poor," he has declared. "Give generously to my ministry, and you'll get abundantly multiplied returns," is how a mainstream Protestant minister friend of mine characterizes Copeland's message. Unlike the careers of some other televangelists, however, Copeland's has not been tainted with scandal. Getting rich may be doubtful as a moral virtue, but there's nothing illegal about it.

Copeland "had this beautiful, beautiful house worth several million dollars, and he had two Learjets plus another airplane in that hangar," Jim said. "We were there for a while fixing the engine, and I got to know the guard a little. He was not one of the members of the church, just a hired hand. He was willing to talk. He said, 'Look, I don't know what Jesus needs with two Learjets, but He's got them here.' In that industrial building, the preacher makes religious videotapes and sells them. In Texas, religion is a big moneymaking business. I mean, this guy was *rich*. It was disgusting."

Cal Rodgers's flight on October 17, 1911, over the sixty miles from Gainesville to Fort Worth, was unmemorable for a change, but as usual, his landing precipitated a harrowing encounter with crowds. More than 20,000 people had gathered in the early afternoon to watch *Vin Fiz* land, though the delay owing to Rodgers's side journey to Bonita caused most to grow impatient and go home. Still, between 8,000 and 10,000 packed the landing site when Rodgers finally arrived. The chase train was still an hour away, so Rodgers had to busy himself shooing eager hands away from his delicate machine, but the crowds at Fort Worth were more tractable than most. There was some other good news. At the state fair in Dallas, an aviator named J. A. D. McCurdy had been scheduled to put on an exhibition, but had severely damaged his machine the day before. Earlier Rodgers had offered to fly at Dallas, but the fair planners thought his fee was too high. Now they had no choice; they hired Rodgers to put *Vin Fiz* through her paces for two days. On October 18 he suited up in leather breeches and newspaper insulation and mounted his machine for the thirty-two-mile flight to Dallas. Again a crowd waited, but when *Vin Fiz* touched down at the fairgrounds, armies of guards kept grasping hands away from the airplane.

As usual, Rodgers proved that Coolidge was not the only "Silent Cal" of the century. "The famous birdman is rather a hard person to approach in a conversational way," one account said, "and he had little or nothing to say about his trip from Fort Worth. He merely expressed pleasure at being in Dallas and said that he enjoyed the trip over from Fort Worth." Meanwhile, the Armour subsidy had been reduced to four dollars per mile. Although it was to have been five dollars per mile to the Mississippi, then four, Armour had kept paying the extra dollar. But from then on, the country was sparsely populated. "Listen, Rodgers," an Armour executive pointed out, "even jackrabbits three feet tall don't buy Vin Fiz."

The next day, October 19, Rodgers's backers breathlessly announced that Cal planned to cover the 288 miles between Dallas and San Antonio in one day. "Rodgers made no comment," Eileen Lebow wrote. "Instead, possibly to make up for his lack of small talk on arrival, he told of an experience that happened the previous day. He was flying at about two thousand feet on his way to Dallas when an eagle spied the *Vin Fiz* from far below. Curious about the strange contraption that had invaded his air space, the bird came winging up for a closer look. Rodgers said he was not well versed in the ways of eagles, but this one seemed genuinely puzzled by his flying machine. Floating closer to the *Vin Fiz*, it was almost directly in front of it when, suddenly, frightened perhaps by the propeller, it swooped down and out of sight. The relieved aviator continued his flight, reminded again of the role of chance in air travel, a point he hoped was not lost on his listeners." It wouldn't have been lost on *me*.

Shortly after 2 P.M., two hours behind schedule, *Vin Fiz* took off for Waco, down the Missouri-Kansas-Texas tracks.

Under the huge controlled airspace of Dallas/Fort Worth Airport lie about seventy landing fields, many of them nothing more than grass strips. About half are hard-surfaced airports, and eight of them are towered fields. For a no-radio pilot, flying under an unfamiliar upside-down wedding-cake circle of controlled airspace sixty miles in diameter requires great care, and blundering uninitiated through one so crowded with airports might, I thought, be foolhardy. I therefore decided on Parker County Airport, near Weatherford, ten miles west of Fort Worth and on the edge of the wedding cake, as my stop for that city. Since it was about noon, I decided to land, gas up, ask for a hangar, and stay over for the rest of the day. As I landed, I saw a score of small planes shaded under open hangars, and I hoped some interesting folks might be around.

Only two men lounged in the airport office, and neither seemed interested in me or my story. One observed that he understood my speech when I radioed my entry into the landing pattern, but the other said he could make neither head nor tail of it. I asked if he was perhaps a little deaf himself. "Nope. Just can't understand you," he said, understanding me just fine.

I was bemused. Why weren't my radio broadcasts reaching the people to whom they were addressed? Although I had felt—and still feel—incrementally more secure being able to announce my presence when arriving over an airport, the truth is that the enhancement of my safety is minuscule. Around uncontrolled airports, radio communications are frequently less efficient for hearing pilots than they can be. Often a dozen or more airports are on the "common traffic advisory frequency" of 122.8 on the dial, and pilots have to listen carefully as others broadcast their intentions, sometimes forgetting to say which field they're entering. The safest course is to keep a weather eye out for traffic, and I had been doing that religiously across the country since I let down my guard at De Kalb. But I was growing obsessed with making radio announcements, and the reason, I was beginning to realize, was that I *wanted* to link up with the world this way, even in a one-sided fashion. We deaf people often feel estranged from the hearing world because of our inability to communicate easily with it. To us, every picayune method of communication that helps connect us with others is a straw to be grasped. My difficulties making myself understood on the radio were making me feel alienated, although in practical terms, that was irrational. I couldn't help it, though. In the matter of the radio, I'm like an anal-retentive neurotic who fusses over a minor smudge on the windshield of the car and has to stop and wipe it off before driving on, even though the glass may otherwise be perfectly clean.

Shortly both men arose with polite excuses and left in a pickup truck, doubtless for lunch. Suddenly the airport seemed bereft of hospitality. I decided to try my luck elsewhere. Cleburne, twenty-eight miles southeast, looked like a substantial place, and it was also five miles outside the Dallas/Fort Worth airspace ring, well clear of any other airport.

The half-hour flight to Cleburne was uncomfortably rough, and I was glad to plunk *Gin Fizz*'s wheels on its ample 5,000-foot runway, especially since the crosswind was both high and gusty. Mine was the lone operating plane, although the huge FBO hangar sheltered more than a dozen aircraft, some of them big twins, and several other hangars on the field probably held as many as sixty or eighty planes. This was a serious airport, and the terminal building looked new and modern.

Inside, the manager seemed forbiddingly busy, although the line attendant said he'd gas up and shelter *Gin Fizz* inside the FBO's hangar for the night. The woman behind the counter gaped in apparent disbelief and dismay when I spoke to her, as if she could neither understand a word I said nor figure out a way to deal with it. I was surprised. As a youth and a young adult, I'd often met extreme reactions such as hers—this kind of thing sometimes happens in parts of the world that have never before encountered a deaf person—but in America of the '90s, far more knowledgeable and accommodating about disabilities than it used to be, such responses are rare. Had Rodgers met people like her in 1911? Probably, but in the upper-middle-class stratum where he most often moved, acknowledging infirmities, let alone remarking upon them, would have been considered ill mannered. As late as 1945, when I was five years old, polite society did not mention President Franklin D. Roosevelt's useless legs, paralyzed from polio. The woman at the Cleburne FBO was a challenge. Could I coax her into the sun of understanding? The phone rang, and she picked it up with obvious relief, turning away. Suddenly it seemed as if a cloud had darkened the sky, so I did not press the conversation. I simply shrugged and adopted the Cal Rodgers method of doing business. Sometimes silence is the only sensible alternative.

Fortunately, a more interesting encounter awaited. I used the TTY to call for the local Days Inn courtesy car, and in ten minutes a smiling, slender, dark-skinned Hindu woman picked me up in a new Buick. She nodded and smiled brilliantly at my small talk during the ride; I have no idea whether she understood me. As I stopped at the front desk of the motel, her husband opened the door from their private quarters, loosing a powerful odor of curry and garlic into the lobby. It was a surprise to find a small patch of the Indian subcontinent in deepest Texas, and I was intrigued, although almost overcome by the aroma.

As I flew farther west, I would discover that Indian motel keepers are no rarity; I was their guest more often than not. In fact, I learned a few months later, from a long and admiring article in the *Wall Street Journal,* that theirs is an immigrant success story of surprising proportions. Over the past quarter of a century, Indians have carved out an increasingly larger share of the American hotel industry, beginning with generic roadside inns in the South and later buying more and more economy franchises, such as Days Inns, Econo Lodges, and Rodeways. By the mid-1990s, Indians owned more than 12,000 motels and hotels, including 46 percent of the economy lodgings in the United States and more than a quarter of the nation's 45,000 hotels and motels. And now they are going upscale, acquiring Radissons, Sheratons, and Hiltons.

Like other groups of hardworking immigrants—most Hindu hotel keepers are from Gujarat State in India, and their surname more often than not is Patel, the *Journal* article said—they have invested astonishing amounts of sweat equity in the American Dream. They have risked their labor and savings in marginal enterprises that most native-born Americans won't touch. And they have endured a great deal of prejudice. In the beginning, bankers refused to issue loans to them, and insurance agents would not cover them. In the early 1980s, say some of these motel keepers, the insurance industry suddenly canceled policies willy-nilly for Indian-owned hostelries on the strength of a wild rumor that Indians were conspiring to buy properties and burn them down for the insurance money. And their native-born competition often resents them. All over the Southwest, especially in Texas, I saw AMERICAN OWNED emblazoned in large letters on signs outside rival motels.

The Indians' niche success, the *Journal* article continued, mirrors that of other immigrant groups in the 1990s. We are all familiar with generations of Chinese laundries and restaurants and, today, toy wholesalers. Cambodians and Vietnamese own restaurants, too, as well as doughnut shops and manicure parlors. Koreans and Palestinians excel in the grocery business. Chaldeans, Iraqi Christians, have done well with convenience and liquor stores. Barbadians dominate the short-haul trucking business in Queens and Brooklyn. But no group, the *Journal* concluded, seems to have come so far and so fast as have the Indians in the lodging industry.

The motel had a coin laundry, and I spent the afternoon separating lights from colors and refreshing my meager kit. When I woke up from a nap, I felt logy and out of sorts and realized that I had not had any real exercise since I started the transcontinental flight. Grassroots aviation may be a wonderful sport, but it is hardly an aerobic one, though the concentration required to fly 400 miles in one afternoon may often be as wearying as a 4-mile run. In my mid-fifties, I am less inclined to exercise for its own sake—gravity pulls me away from the hard-body ideal with every passing year—and tend to be willing to indulge in just enough activity for good cardiac health. From time to time, I must remind myself to get up off my duff to stretch the muscles and jangle the arteries. So I set out that afternoon on a brisk walk down the dusty highway. After a couple of miles, I found a convenience store presided over by a doughy, pimply-faced Anglo-Texan postadolescent, but it carried fresh oranges, apples, and carrots, out of which I made myself a meal far more healthful than that I would have found on the fast-food strip near the motel. When I made my nightly call home that night, I told Debby proudly what I had for dinner. "Good for you!" she said. "Keep it up!" I went to bed feeling disgustingly virtuous.

That night, arising in the dark for a midnight foray to the bathroom, I painfully banged my right thigh on the desk, which wasn't in the same place as the desk back in Gainesville, which wasn't in the same place as the desk back in Muskogee or in Durant. Motel-room geography is an inexact science, although roadside hostelries may seem to most American travelers to be cookie-cutter copies of one another. My bruised thigh smarting, I finally stopped swearing and went back to sleep, longing for my own bed at home, with Debby on one side and Stan the half-Lab on the other.

# 15

*A*t 6 A.M. I arose to the usual east Texas summer fog and set out for a little more exercise before breakfast—not for reasons of fitness but just to kill time while the mist lay on the ground. Hidden around the corner of a strip mall was a small café that, praise God, featured genuine *oatmeal* on the menu, a heaping bowl of which I gratefully scarfed with orange juice and melon. Debby would have been proud of me.

Because of Cal's appearance at the air show, the Rodgers route now took a forty-mile jog east, from Fort Worth to Dallas, before proceeding south again. Back at Cleburne Airport, I launched at 8:45 A.M., bound for Lancaster Airport, forty-two miles to the northeast, just south of Dallas, and immediately landed. The fog had dissipated, but the remaining haze was so turbid that visibility couldn't have been better than four miles. An hour later it had improved to about five miles, and I took off again—but the eastward course meant that I was flying into the sun, which made seeing things more difficult than they needed to be. I flew at 2,500 feet, which enabled me to view enough of the ground below to keep my bearings. I was glad for the loran and GPS—without them I'd never have found my way. Pilotage and dead reckoning work best when one can get high enough in clear air, 4,500 feet or more, to compare landmarks with those on the charts. In thick haze it's impossible to see landmarks unless one is on top of them.

Lancaster Airport, I was glad to discover, was a busy place, with a score of hangars and a dozen planes on tiedowns, including big twin-engine craft. A couple of student pilots shot landings in the pattern, and a mechanic tested repairs on the engines of a big Beechcraft. There seemed to be enough business on the field for two or three FBOs, and the place looked as a general aviation airport must have looked in the early 1980s before the crunch hit. Of course, airports that are close to oil-rich Dallas and Fort Worth are bound to enjoy a plumper economic cushion than are those out in the starving boondocks of Kansas and Oklahoma.

The terminal boss, an old fellow, said he had heard my broadcasts but had not understood them. I was disappointed but glad for his honesty. I decided to keep on trying with the radio. If *some* people can understand my transmissions, I thought, I am that much ahead of not being heard at all. Maybe the radio was old. Or maybe it was just my breathy deaf voice and imprecise articulation. Whatever the truth, I was making myself crazy.

But I was delighted by the Happy Landings Café attached to the terminal building, only the second airport restaurant I had encountered since leaving Westosha. The café was small, bright, and sparkling, unlike the dank, dim lunch counters so common at airports of old, and its windows winked invitingly under chintz ruffles. Three cheerful women worked the place—a middle-aged cook, an attractive thirtyish manager, and a Hispanic waitress of the same age who handled the dozen tables. The special of the day was made-from-scratch beef stew, tossed salad, and cornbread for $4.50, and I found it not only a bargain but also a welcome change from McFood and vending-machine eats. The place was warm and welcoming, and I wanted to hang out and chat with the women, but it was almost noon and the tables began to fill up; not for a couple of hours, it seemed, would they be able to catch their breath. All the same, the small-airport café is a fast disappearing bit of Americana, and I was delighted to find it prospering in this Texas town.

Outside, I wandered about the hangars and introduced myself to a couple of pilots, both of whom were gravely courteous, but neither seemed interested in conversing about a long-distance flight in a commonplace Cessna 150. Neither unfriendly nor dismissive, they just politely waited for me to finish explaining my story so they could get back to their business. Texans are difficult to impress.

Time to move on, I thought. In a few minutes I was off again, this time to McKinney Municipal Airport, forty miles north, which had been recommended by a number of pilots on CompuServe as a good place to visit. The area under the 4,000-foot eastern floor of the Dallas/Fort Worth wedding cake was much less crowded with airports than the area west, but I kept a weather eye out for traffic all the way. McKinney, like Lancaster, is a busy place, although its massive apron, which could hold 100 or more airplanes, hosted only about 20 or 25—as many as I'd seen anywhere else. Like others in the vicinity, it's evidently geared to business aviation, though it still seems to be home to small Pipers and Cessnas of every kind.

Since the fenced airport looked secure—it was early afternoon and thunderstorms were not forecast—I decided to tie down outside for the night. McKinney's hangar space cost twenty-five dollars a night even with refueling. I unloaded my gear and entered the big, new terminal building.

"Can I do anything for you?" asked the woman at the counter, friendlier than most FBO attendants I'd encountered so far in Texas. I explained my deafness. Could she call a motel for me? Ordinarily, I phone motels myself with the TTY—it's important to me to be independent of reliance on hearing people—but I'm delighted to accept offers of help from people whose business it is to provide these services. The woman struck out at the Holiday Inn but connected at the Comfort Inn four miles away and asked a line attendant to give me a ride there. No registered taxi firms operated in the area, he said, as we climbed into the FBO's pickup truck, but a gypsy cab would pick me up in the morning and deliver me to the airport. "They're unlicensed," he added, "but we've had good luck with them." He gave me the owner's card, on which was printed only a name and a phone number. "Call them tonight and make a reservation for the morning."

On the way over, I chatted with the fellow, a tall, skinny, Lindberghish young man in his late teens named Jack. As he drove, he chattered happily. He professed surprise at my flying from New York to Los Angeles in a Cessna 150. "You're *what?*" had become the customary first question asked when I explained my project. "In *that?*" was the second. After I said the longest flight I made any day was 135 miles, he nodded and agreed that a more substantial airplane would be superfluous.

He was a pilot, too, Jack said eagerly, and was studying for his flight instructor's certificate—a classic "ramp rat," Tom Horton as a youngster. Before the slump struck general aviation, airports were often full of ambitious young people who were willing to pump gas and wash airplanes in exchange for a few hours in the air. They first would earn the private pilot license, then an instrument rating. They'd then step up to a commercial ticket and a flight instructor's rating, eventually earn an air-transport pilot certificate, and go to work for an airline. I hoped Jack knew that teaching flying is no way to make a living, especially when fewer and fewer new students join the flow each year, and that winning commercial flying and air-transport work today is almost as hard as breaking into the National Basketball Association. Still, he seemed a bright go-getter and, I thought, had as good a chance to make it in professional aviation as any young person I'd encountered at an airport.

Earlier in my trip, I'd watched as a balding, dissipated-looking line attendant in his late thirties sullenly filled *Gin Fizz*'s tanks in a smog of boredom.

"Not very friendly, is he?" I whispered to the pilot standing next to me.

"That one is a sad case," he said, shaking his head slowly as the attendant walked out of earshot to the FBO with my credit card. "He once was the chief instructor here, but a couple of years ago he lost his medical certificate. High blood pressure. He drinks. I've seen a lot like him."

The attendant, he said, was a member of a common species around airports: a kind of graduate ramp rat, adequately intelligent but feckless and unambitious. They're bright enough to learn to fly but incapable of much else. Because of their interest in aviation, they're accepted as part of the furniture, although not taken very seriously. This one lived at home with his mother, ate bad food, and drank too much, hence the high blood pressure. He had a couple of DUI citations over the years. And now, having lost the means to his meager livelihood as an instructor, he was reduced to pumping gas and cleaning windscreens. Wordlessly, he emerged from the FBO; wordlessly, he handed me my card and receipt; and wordlessly, he returned to the fuel pumps to attend the next customer.

When the pickup arrived at the Comfort Inn, I shook Jack's hand, thanked him, and wished him luck. He'd need it.

\*       \*       \*

The next day began with a good omen. At the appointed hour—right to the minute—I opened the door of my room and found the gypsy cab driver, a young Hispanic woman, waiting outside. She greeted me in a hail of American Sign Language and reached for my bags.

"Thanks," I said, as we walked to her cab, "but I don't know sign." Frowning, she opened the right front door and motioned me inside. Her vehicle was indeed a gypsy cab, for neither meter nor hack license was visible. "Were you assigned to pick me up because I'm deaf and you know sign?" I asked as we drove away.

"Naw, learned it in school," she said in a distant and chilly manner. "I've got lots of deaf friends."

"I never learned it when I was growing up," I said, choosing to let her think it was by chance and not choice that I didn't use sign language. No use arguing these things with strangers, especially hearing people who have fallen in love with American Sign Language and Deaf culture. Many of them remind me of "wannabe Indians," white folks so in love with Native American culture that they wear bolo ties and turquoise jewelry and sometimes claim to have had a Cherokee great-grandmother. Most deaf people are live-and-let-live about modes of communication, but their hearing champions more often are intolerant, refusing to accept diversity among those who do not hear. I am certain the driver thought I was a horrible reactionary oralist who scoffed at ASL and Deaf culture.

"Sign is wonderful," she said vehemently.

"It is," I agreed, refraining from adding, "So is speech and lipreading."

For a few miles we drove in silence.

Suddenly, rapping the steering wheel with an open hand, she exclaimed, "Oh, God, I hope my baby is born deaf!" This sentiment, which often appalls hearing people, did not surprise me. Many who embrace Deafness rejoice at the birth of a new member of the clan, so strong is their pride in the language and culture. I stole a glance at her midriff—if she was pregnant it was still early days—and nodded noncommittally.

"Where are you flying?" she asked, as if to steer the increasingly awkward conversation onto neutral ground.

"Los Angeles," I replied.

She turned and stared at me. "You're *not* flying to Los Angeles from McKinney Municipal!" she exclaimed. "You're going to Dallas/Fort Worth."

"No," I said. "I'm flying my own airplane."

*"Your own airplane?"* she said slowly, her mouth falling open. I was surprised, too, never having encountered such a disbelieving reaction even from the most ignorant hearing person. "But . . . " She may have known a great deal about Deaf culture, but she certainly hadn't heard of the International Deaf Pilots Association. I told her about it.

Her mouth still gaped. "But the radio?"

I explained and was still explaining when we arrived at the airport. She pulled up at the open gate to the tiedown apron and stopped.

"Where's your airplane?" she asked skeptically.

"That little aluminum-and-blue job over there," I said, pointing out *Gin Fizz*.

"I'll drive you over." She pulled out on the ramp and stopped in front of the plane.

I stepped out of the car, unlocked the pilot's door, and stuffed my bags inside. "Take a look," I said.

Astonishment still wreathing her face, she peered inside *Gin Fizz*. "You're going to L.A. in *this* today?" she asked.

I laughed. "Not all in one day. I'm writing a book, you see, and . . . "

"A *book*?" She looked askance at me, as if *now* she'd heard everything.

"Yeah, never mind," I said. "I've got to get going." I paid her and started the preflight check. As she slipped into her car, I said, "I hope your baby grows up to be a pilot." She didn't respond, but drove away. She may love the deaf, I thought as I walked to the FBO to check the weather, but she still has a lot to learn about us.

On my way back to the plane, I spotted her car behind the fence in the parking lot. Intently she was watching me, hands on the steering wheel, and as *Gin Fizz* took off into the hazy sky, she was still watching. That was one Texan I finally managed to impress.

---

The evening after Cal Rodgers landed at Waco, he was treated to an old Texas entertainment: a battle between a bulldog and a badger. Rodgers left early, partly because he never cared for blood sports and partly because he had received news that Eugene Ely, the first flyer to land an airplane on a ship converted to an aircraft carrier, had died in a crash at Macon, Georgia. There is nothing to make a pilot consider his own mortality more deeply than a report of the violent death of a colleague. And Rodgers would have been even more depressed had he learned of the ghoulish behavior by the 10,000 spectators who scrabbled for souvenirs of the accident. The crowd broke through police ranks and, in a few minutes, not only had scoured the field of every bit of wreckage, but also had plucked the collar, tie, gloves, and cap from Ely's corpse.

Sobered by the news, the next morning Cal and his crew performed a much more meticulous preflight examination than usual and discovered that some of *Vin Fiz*'s control cables had been worn alarmingly thin. The crew spent two hours rerigging the cables, and *Vin Fiz* did not lift into the air until late in the morning. The engineer of the locomotive of the special train had trouble making steam, and after circling impatiently, Cal banked his machine toward Austin. He refueled at Granger and then passed over Georgetown and Pflugerville before he arrived over the outskirts of Austin just before 2 P.M. Naturally, thousands were waiting, and Cal stopped for lunch and refueling before proceeding southward toward San Antonio.

My flight through the light haze from McKinney south to Waco took an hour and three-quarters. Just down the road from Waco, after overflying two large controlled airports, *Gin Fizz* landed at McGregor Municipal Airport, to be greeted by a cheering throng of one: Kevin Collins, manager of Brazos Air, the FBO. In his office we chatted briefly. "How do you pronounce it?" I asked. "Wah-co or Way-co?"

He blinked in mild surprise. Surely, after the spectacular and disastrous FBI raid on the Branch Davidian compound in 1993, everybody in the United States knew how that word is pronounced. But I didn't. We deaf people often have to ask how the most commonplace words are pronounced; reading them in print doesn't give us a clue, and lipreading them doesn't always help, either. For decades I thought *com*-pro-mise was pronounced com-*pro*-mise. It's a small thing, but an often vexing one; mispronouncing a word can make one seem like an ignoramus who just rolled off the turnip truck.

"Way-co," Kevin said.

"Not like the airplane?" I asked, just to be sure.

"No, that's Wah-co." The famous Waco biplanes of the 1930s were made by Weaver Aircraft Company in Troy, Ohio.

And he gave me a T-shirt that said BRAZOS AIR, MCGREGOR, TEXAS.

That was the seventh T-shirt or baseball cap that friendly FBOs had bestowed on me during the flight from New York. Too bad, I thought, that socks and undershorts weren't part of the largesse; I wouldn't have to hunt down coin laundries.

Fifty-eight miles farther south, just as the early afternoon bumps started to get troublesome, I landed at Georgetown Municipal Airport. After tying down *Gin Fizz* and wiping the flattened insects off her leading edges, I strode to the FBO. There I encountered an extraordinary woman who had become a pilot at about the same time I did, in the process conquering a crippling phobia and fulfilling a lifelong dream.

Barbara McLeod is a voluble and energetic academic in her early fifties who sounds like a cross between a stunt pilot and a Jungian psychologist. Just the previous day, she had been flying a Cessna 152 Aerobat on a ferry hop back to Austin Mueller Municipal Airport from a field eighteen miles away when the engine spluttered, faltered, and stopped. She was lucky that she had enough altitude to glide to Georgetown and alight on the runway instead of having to put the plane down among houses, at worst, and rough pasture, at best. The cause was water in the fuel, and she blamed herself for not catching it before she took off.

As all conscientious pilots do as part of the preflight routine, she had drained a sample from the tanks before going up. A little water in aviation fuel is common—it collects from condensation or leakage into underground tanks—but it pools at the bottoms of the airplane tanks where it can be drained before flight. Often as much as a pint of water can get into a tankful of avgas, and that's more than enough to drown the carburetor.

Water is heavier than avgas, which is dyed (blue for 100LL, red for 80 octane). Like a multicolored parfait, clear water settles under the dyed avgas in the long transparent tube of a fuel tester. A pilot drains gas until the fluid in his tester shows completely blue or red. Barbara, however, had been wearing blue-blocker sunglasses that day and had failed to spot the clear water in the tube.

Once the engine stopped, however, she kept her cool. "I stayed focused on survival," she said proudly. "I didn't indulge my fear until I was safely on the ground."

Barbara's story is remarkable because two and a half years before, she had been grounded by a "lifelong and terrible" fear of flying. She had not been aboard even an airliner in many years. After the engine-out landing and a flush of the fuel tanks, she took off again for thirty minutes before calling it a day, just so she wouldn't worry that the day's emergency had stirred up old terrors.

Beating the fear of flying is just one of the many professions of this self-described freelance anthropologist. She not only co-teaches a course called "Beyond Fear of Flying" at Austin Mueller, but also holds a doctorate in anthropology, specializes in Mayan languages and ancient Native American hieroglyphic writing, and teaches Yucatec Maya during the summers at the University of North Carolina. She is an itinerant academic, leading archeology tours to Mexico and Central America and participating in research projects hither and yon. For four years she crawled through holes in the ground as a professional speleologist, or "caver," with the Peace Corps in Belize. She writes ballads and performs in a small folk/country band. And now she calls herself an aviation bum.

"It's a tough way to support a flying habit," she said. "I've marginally managed it by leading a very frugal lifestyle and making sacrifices. Flying has enriched my life so much that I don't mind doing without." She does odd jobs for the owner of the Aerobat that she regularly flies. "I feed his dogs; wash the plane; help with the oil changes and maintenance; take his parachutes for repacking; and do ferry flights, such as the one that resulted in the engine failure. I was his flight-school office manager one winter and got flight time in return. That's how I financed most of my primary training." At this writing, she is again the manager, financing her training for the instrument rating.

Barbara fell into her Indiana Jones life early on. In fourth grade in St. Louis, she was the only girl in the model airplane club, dreaming of flying Cubs and Champs and Cessnas. Missouri is riddled with caves, and after she learned the spelunking art at a summer camp, she joined a caving club in St. Louis. "My parents gave me a lot of freedom," she said. "I just spared them the hairiest details."

As much as she enjoyed caving, she sometimes suffered terrible moments of anxiety in remote, tight spots underground. "Once my brain said 'Stop!' in a low crawlway so wide I couldn't see the walls," she recalled. "I was afraid I'd get disoriented, so I offered to be anchor while other cavers went ahead. It was a genuine jolt of fear, but I turned it to practical ends and took control of it. I've never panicked in a cave, but I've had moments of memorable, acute fear, always for good reason—deep, fast water; falling rock; getting lost; hypothermia; or exhaustion. These confrontations with danger always opened a door to my inner resources."

When she was twenty years old, two close caving friends were killed in a whitewater canoeing accident, and Barbara suddenly became phobic about lots of things, even crossing the street. She beat down most of her phobias, but one persisted—the fear of flying. "I had to talk myself into getting on airliners—lightplanes were out of the question. Once on them, I had to constantly wrestle this irrational conviction that any minute we'd be screaming straight down with pieces falling off." Then she took two back-to-back flights in rough weather, and her fear grew worse. By June 1993, she had not been aboard an airplane in thirteen years.

She decided to get professional help and got in touch with a fear-of-flying specialist, a former psychiatrist for American Airlines who practices in Chapel Hill. Barbara had taken the bus to North Carolina for her summer teaching, but before she even met with the psychiatrist, she decided to force herself to fly instead. "I went through a stressful two weeks before the flight, getting little sleep, and almost backed out," she recalled, but a friend pushed her aboard the thirty-five-minute flight from Austin to Dallas/Fort Worth, during which she "literally beat the fear." On the next leg, from Dallas to Raleigh-Durham, she exulted when the plane popped out on top of the clouds at 15,000 feet into a clear dome of pale blue. "The fear was gone, then and there," she said. "The rest was just details."

"And what were they?" I pressed.

"The first was realizing I was in a state of gross inflation of reality," she replied. " 'This plane's chances of crashing go up astronomically if I get on it.' The second was taking the scary step of asking for help. And the third was my buried yearning to fly. I'd completely forgotten about building those models and all the flak I took from the boys. It finally broke loose."

For a few days after that breakthrough flight, she worried that the fear would return, but working with the psychiatrist "anchored things," she said. "He gave me the arsenal of relaxation and visualization techniques that are widely used in treating phobias." Among the techniques she and her partner, a psychiatric nurse, use in their fear-of-flying classes are these:

*Breathing exercises.* "These involve deep, slow breaths and visualizing changes in color, such as reds to blues. This slows heart rate, reduces blood pressure, and deactivates the fight-or-flight response."

*Thought-stopping.* "A shout in the mind with a snap of a fat rubber band on the wrist. This interrupts catastrophic images, which can then be replaced deliberately by positive ones."

*Heroic "rescripting."* This is "thinking about times past when you've been brave and bringing that to the feared situation, taking control. Recognizing that this fear is an accident that happened to you, like a broken leg, and no reason for shame or secrecy."

*Visualization.* "Reading or hearing a story in which a flight is taken happily and successfully, with lots of rich visual stimulation and positive association—great scenery, great seatmates, great flight and cabin crew, great friends and relatives waiting at the gate, a great learning experience."

*Education about aviation.* "Learning about the reliability of the flight crew, the mechanics, the machines. About redundant systems. Learning the statistics, that the odds against an accident are overwhelmingly in your favor. You meet pilots and air traffic controllers and realize they're human but highly trained and trustworthy. You take a tour of the tower and Air Traffic Control."

*Desensitization.* "We take people gradually into the feared situation. First, we take them to the airport; then on board a stationary airliner; and, finally, on a graduation flight."

It is quite rare, she said, for the "cured" to go on to become pilots. Still, that old dream and the adventurer in her helped her not only to learn to fly but also to become an aerobatic pilot, a gymnast of the sky who flings herself through dizzying precision maneuvers thousands of feet above the earth. This was born in a "Eureka!" moment during her primary training—her first spin. "It scared the devil out of me, and I liked it. And I didn't understand that strange mix of emotions. Here's something that's so scary, and at the same time I just couldn't wait to do it again."

She did it again—and again. Barbara's instructor, a former air force pilot, gave her her head, introducing her to aerobatic flight even before she learned to land. "I was doing loops and rolls even before I soloed," she said. It's fairly unusual for a student pilot to need thirty-five hours of flight training before the first solo, but Barbara had great problems with landings. "I would forget everything I learned," she said. Her instructor persisted, "and if I had a frustrating lesson with landings, he'd always reward me by letting me do a couple of loops and a roll." And so an aerobatic pilot was born.

The weekend before our meeting, she said, she had taken advanced aerobatic training in a Champion Super Decathlon and a Pitts S2B, the latter a tiny, hot aerobatic biplane. "I spent a lot of time inverted, as much as they'd let me, and loved it. I learned to do tail slides, saw my first inverted spins, did a ten-turn spin, worked on hammerheads, and got taken through a demo sequence of all the radical maneuvers I could think of: English bunts, lomcevaks, torque rolls, outside snaps. Those beautiful maneuvers just set the hook deeper in my soul."

Barbara and her instructor once set their sights on the National Aeronautic Association record for most turns in a spin. "We needed sixty-eight turns to beat the record and wanted to do it in an Aerobat, but the NAA turned down our petition to challenge the existing record, set in a Pitts in 1989, because of a conservative turn their board has taken recently. They want to avoid sanctioning 'stunts' and anything that gives the appearance of being dangerous. I understand their reasoning, but I think that neglects some of the spirit and chutzpah of aviation." The longest spin she has ever done is fifty-two turns, shared with the owner of the Aerobat she flies. "Now everyone is either egging me on or joking about how crazy I am."

She smiled. "Shall we go up?" she asked. "I've got the Aerobat reserved for a couple of hours."

I hesitated. "Well . . . " I said, and confided in her about my childhood meningitis and its effects on my senses of balance and self-preservation. "I don't even like to do spins. They scare the hell out of me."

She replied like the reassuring professional terror therapist she is. "We could start off with a few gentle maneuvers like wingovers and then see what they feel like," she said. "Any time you feel uncomfortable, we could just go back to the airport. OK?"

"OK," I said, only slightly mollified. And when she dragged out the two parachutes, I felt even less so.

"We won't need them," she said, "but the FAA requires them for aerobatic flight, just in case."

"Just in case," I replied with a casual nod, suppressing a gulp. That would be twice in two days I'd worn a chute. A third time, and I might just have to use it.

We walked out to the Aerobat, the one that had choked on the water in its windpipe. I was familiar with these airplanes, an Aerobat having been one of the three Cessna 152s in which I had trained at Westosha. They are slightly heavier than conventional 152s, certain stress points in the airframe having been beefed up. Their ordinary seat and shoulder belts have been replaced by heavy leather aerobatic harnesses that clamp the pilot and passenger firmly to the seats. The seat backs reverse, to make room for parachutes. The doors are affixed to the fuselage with breakaway releases, so in an emergency, the pilot and passenger can bail out.

"How many hours do you have?" I asked, just to make conversation as we strolled across the ramp.

"Two hundred ninety," she replied. Again I stifled a gulp. I had far more hours in the cockpit than she.

Barbara, however, turned out to be a far better stick-and-rudder pilot than I am, one who is much more comfortable with the capabilities and limitations of her airplane than I ever will be. She is a natural, if there is such a thing; I am merely trained. Expertly, she lifted the Aerobat, carrying its maximum load, off the runway in a brisk crosswind and set course for the southwest, over the Bergstrom Air Force Base, several miles southeast of Austin. "I want to stay within radar range of Austin Mueller so that approach control can keep us on the screen and warn other airplanes away from us," she said, dialing a squawk code into the transponder. That reassured me; clearly safety was on her mind.

By and by we reached 7,000 feet. "Ready?" she asked. I nodded and gripped my camera tightly in my lap. "Ready."

Smoothly, Barbara firewalled the throttle and dropped the nose, to pick up speed. Then she pulled back the yoke, and the Aerobat sailed up nearly to the vertical, before nosing over to the right as if pivoting on one wing. My eyes widened, but I did not panic. I could see the horizon at all times. "Shall we do another wingover?"

At my nod she repeated the maneuver, this time to the left. I smiled.

"We'll do a loop now, OK?"

"Sure."

Again a shallow dive at full throttle, and then, pulling the yoke briskly back, Barbara put the Aerobat into a long, smooth loop, the centrifugal force keeping us firmly in our seats at the top, and then pulled out smoothly, climbing back to the altitude at which she had started the dive. "Cool!" I shouted with a grin. This was not half bad. Again we did a loop, and again. I looked over at Barbara at the top of the last one. She was grinning broadly, seemingly lost in a parallel universe of boundless joy. So this is what aerobatic flight does for a pilot.

"An Immelman?" This is half a loop, at the top of which the pilot rolls the plane straight and level, flying in the other direction.

"Yeah."

Now I was all smiles.

"Reverse half Cuban eight?"

I still am not quite sure what that was, but it had to do with a roll inside a loop. At the top of the maneuver, the airplane hung for a moment, and my camera—resting ungripped in my lap—obeyed gravity and struck the cabin ceiling of the Aerobat. We were both startled, and I reached up to pull it down, but Barbara completed the maneuver briskly.

"A roll?"

"Go right ahead."

That one scared me at last. In wingovers and loops I could keep a level horizon in my mind's eye without difficulty, but a roll took one through a different plane. A spinning horizon triggers my discomfort—and with it, my *fear*. But I was beginning to rebel against it, angry that it made me so lily-livered in front of a fellow pilot.

"We're going to do a snap roll now," Barbara said.

And before I could reply, she snapped the yoke hard left and stomped on the rudder pedal. In the blink of an eye, the Aerobat corkscrewed through the air, the G-forces threatening to separate my head from my neck and lifting me a good inch out of my seat. Afterward I tremblingly looked down at the accelerometer, or G-meter, an instrument that measures gravitational pull. We had pulled four and a half Gs, or four and a half times the force of the earth's gravity. That was enough for me. This was a violent maneuver, and I am a peaceable fellow.

"A two-turn spin?"

I shook my head and pointed back to the airport. "That's enough," I wrote shakily on the kneeboard, a small clipboard I had attached to my leg so I could write notes to Barbara over the din of the engine.

"Why not?"

"Chickenshit," I muttered, shaking my head. I simply was suffering from temporary sensory overload. A few hours later, I regretted my diffidence, but felt that the next time I went up with an "akro" pilot, I would not feel such fear. Having been taken through the high-G routines and topsy-turvy horizons of aerobatic flight just once, I no longer felt terrified of the unknown. I knew what to expect. It was like having ridden a world-class roller-coaster at a theme park; the first hop may have been an exercise in sheer terror, but the second would be a snap.

After a deep and satisfied sleep that night, comforted by having sent some more of my demons packing, I arose to return to Georgetown Municipal Airport. I called a taxi, and when I climbed in, I told the heavyset Mexican American driver that I was deaf but read lips, as I customarily do to forestall misunderstandings. He looked at me intently and then nodded.

Scarcely had we pulled out of the motel lot when the driver leaned over the seat, pointed to his ear, and said, "You're deaf?" I nodded.

A mile later he turned around and jabbed a finger at the ceiling. "Me and Jesus can make you hear again," he said lugubriously. I shook my head.

"Me and Jesus, we can do it," he insisted, widening his eyes and pointing to the sky for emphasis.

"No," I replied, "I'm fine."

Several times more on the five-mile trip to the airport, he looked back and said with great conviction and a skyward gesture, "Me and Jesus, we can make you hear again." He did not spell out the monetary consideration that he and the Lord no doubt required to perform the miracle, and I was not about to give him the chance to do so. I may be a naïf who blindly gives people the benefit of the doubt, but I am not stupid. This was a hustler.

"No," I shook my head. "I am happy as I am." The truth is that I wouldn't mind hearing again—I know what I'm missing in a world of silence—but I'll put my trust in medical science before I throw myself on the dubious mercy of a taxi-driving healer. After his umpteenth "Me and Jesus," I was about to point to the earth and invoke "Me and Old Scratch," but we fortuitously arrived at the airport. In my haste to escape the cab, I overtipped the driver. That, I realized as he drove away, had very likely been his intention all along. I had indeed been hustled.

I chuckled and cursed ruefully at myself as I did the preflight and rearranged the furniture inside *Gin Fizz* for the last hop of this leg, seventeen miles south to Austin Executive Airpark. Absorbed in thoughts about the cabbie, I failed to duck automatically before striding under the wing toward the front of the airplane. Only a couple of times during my life has my diminutive height of five feet, six and three-quarters inches troubled me. The first time was when I rode twenty stories up in a Houston hotel elevator with what must have been the entire Oilers defensive line. I felt as Jack must have far from the beanstalk and deep in ogre country. The second was the first discovery (of many) that my vertical growth had ended one inch above the sharp corrugated aluminum trailing edge of a Cessna 150's wing. From time to time, even when I wear a baseball cap, the top of my forehead sports a flaming red, sometimes bleeding diamond-shaped indentation, and at Georgetown I collected a new one, with much cursing and moaning.

I bade good-bye to the friendly denizens of the FBO after inquiring why a student pilot was taking off on Runway 36, straight north, instead of using the calm-wind Runway 18—in the opposite direction—as posted in the airport guides. A three-miles-per-hour zephyr wafted down from the north, the airport's automated weather station said, and it was barely twitching the wind sock—but the airport had nonetheless declared 36 the active runway. Up in Wisconsin, airports don't change from the calm-wind runway till the breeze tops six miles per hour, enough to swing the wind sock. The Georgetowners may have thought me fussy, but one close encounter of the oncoming-airplane kind was enough for me, and I intended to go with whatever flow the authorities had decreed.

Austin Executive, just north of the Texas capital, is a busy uncontrolled airport any day of the week, and I had almost come to prefer that kind of airport, rather than fields in the boonies with little traffic. That's no paradox. As I gained experience, I found it simply much easier to slot myself into the flow of traffic in the landing pattern and follow other airplanes to the runway instead of noodling about above the airport, trying to decide which way the wind was blowing and which runway I would land upon. Looking for wind socks, chimney smoke, and wave patterns on ponds distracts a pilot's attention from traffic. There's always an unseen airplane in the vicinity when you think you're all alone.

After a ten-minute flight down from Georgetown, I overflew

Austin Executive, holding my altitude at 1,900 feet to stay underneath the controlled airspace of Austin Mueller, the big airport, and saw a line of airplanes entering downwind for Runway 18. I tucked *Gin Fizz* in behind a 172 and followed her in, touching down just as she turned off at midfield. The line attendant at Awesome Aviation shook my hand as I alighted from the airplane—the first official welcome I had had for many days.

In the hangar I made arrangements for Awesome to hangar *Gin Fizz* away from the broiling sun and pounding thunderstorms for the next couple of weeks while I returned to Chicago via a commercial airliner to resume my family and day-job responsibilities. A few minutes later, my brother-in-law Steve Bangs, a retired air force lieutenant colonel who had flown RF-4C Phantoms on reconnaissance missions over Southeast Asia during the Vietnam War, arrived to collect me. Steve took one look at *Gin Fizz* and chuckled, shaking his head. To this veteran of high-altitude, high-performance combat jets, the little Cessna 150 must have looked like a child's toy. But this "toy" had safely brought me two-thirds of the way across the country.

# PART IV

# LANDING

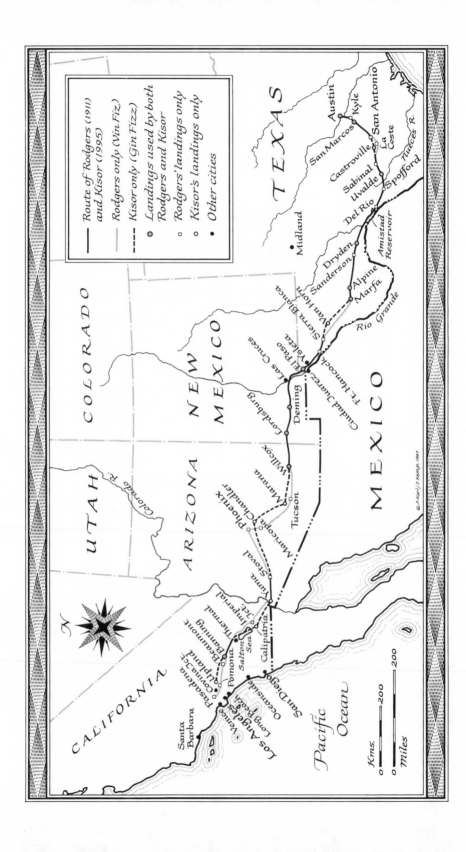

# 16

During the first two legs of my odyssey, I had not only repressed my anomie about the *Sun-Times* but also had thought little about Debby and the boys—and was grateful for that. I had been able to focus on the trip without worrying about events at home. Both Debby and I feel fortunate that our sons have grown up to be solid and reliable young citizens without suffering the usual crises from youthful peccadilloes that bring heartache to so many parents. And the luck of the draw had also given Debby and me a stable, happy marriage, one stressed by few untoward events. Home for us has always been a rock, a haven against adversity. Not having to think about domestic crises enabled me to devote all my concentration to flying across the country. This was no small thing. Flight physicians often counsel pilots to stand down if they are dealing with personal problems; deep anxiety can result in impaired judgment.

My furlough this time was to have been two weeks, until the first week in September. Scarcely half of it remained when bad news upset our applecart. Our HMO reported that a suspicious spot had appeared on Debby's latest mammogram. She would have to have another one, and then the physicians would have to consult in the matter. The procedure—this being a HMO—would require two or three weeks.

From the first, there was no question that I would have to postpone the last leg of my trip—and not because I needed to be anxiety-free in the cockpit. If ever there was a time Debby needed my presence, it was now. Together we would draw our wagons into a circle and wait for events to sort themselves out. I was glad Debby had insisted on my breaking up the trip into three legs; if she had received this news when I was gone, I would have had to drop everything and return home—*if* she had told me. She is a stoic person where I am not and would, I think, have borne the burden alone for my sake.

For more than a fortnight, we quietly stewed, reflecting on the awful possibilities of that spot on the mammogram, even more so when the follow-up X ray revealed the same anomaly. I called Awesome Aviation in Austin to extend *Gin Fizz*'s stay in the hangar. We told friends that I had delayed the trip because I had a slight summer cold. Finally the meeting with the physicians arrived—and the radiologist pronounced the spot insignificant; the mammogram had been initially misread by an inexperienced eye. Consultation with a surgeon confirmed the radiologist's opinion.

In a few minutes of rapidly deflating anxiety, our household returned to normal. But shortly thereafter, I gritted my teeth with annoyance when I discovered that American Airlines refused to honor the return portion of my deep-discount ticket from Austin to O'Hare for another four weeks, *if* seats were available. If I needed to depart in the next couple of days, however, it would be happy to sell me a standard one-way coach ticket to Austin for more than twice what I had paid for the round-trip fare. "Those are the rules," the agent said. "Sorry." I found a cheap one-way fare on TWA and took that airline instead.

Had I not been told that Jim Newman's legs had been amputated below the knees, I never would have guessed. Jim met me outside the TWA baggage area at Austin Mueller in early October, and together we walked to his pickup truck in the parking lot. Even if I had noticed his slight limp, I would have dismissed it as perhaps a result of arthritis from advancing age. Only when we negotiated curbs, stairways, and rough ground did I notice that he placed his feet carefully, looking down to be sure they would not catch on a crack or slip out from under. "The ankles are metal," he said, "and spring-loaded." They give with and articulate each stride almost normally.

The seventy-year-old aviator and I had been introduced by a

mutual acquaintance, a fellow pilot who was an English professor I knew from my work as a book review editor. Jim, a retired contractor, is a thrifty fellow. As we pulled out of the parking lot on our way to Georgetown, where he keeps his airplane, he said, "I've just bought several loaves of day-old bread, and I want to stop at my house in Pflugerville and drop them off into my freezer."

As we drove there, Jim told me how he lost his limbs. His right leg was amputated in December 1965, after a case of phlebitis turned into Buerger's disease, a complete collapse of the arteries in the leg. The same disease claimed his other leg almost ten years later.

Legless pilots are no more unusual than deaf ones, and they have their own organization, the International Wheelchair Aviators. Some two hundred pilots belong to the group. The majority cope with spinal cord injuries or the aftereffects of polio, though some are amputees. Some have muscular dystrophy, some are battling multiple sclerosis, and still others cope with spina bifida. All of them have been licensed by the FAA after the same sort of medical flight test I had.

Most wheelchair pilots fly airplanes whose rudders are manipulated with hand controls, rather than foot-operated pedals. Some of these controls are installed permanently into an airplane, but others are portable and can be carried from aircraft to aircraft. Jim does not use hand controls; he relies on his prosthetic legs to operate the rudder pedals. "If the amputations are below the knee, you still have very sensitive feelings in your stumps and knees. If I am sitting at a dining table and someone just gently brushes a foot, I know it. Though I have feeling, I don't know where my legs are positioned unless I look to see where they are. In my truck or plane, I look to see where they are, and from then on it's automatic, like using a typewriter. Hell, Henry, I'm not too sure I know how I do it."

Jim is a veteran pilot of 2,500 hours, having learned "under the good auspices of the old United States Army Air Forces." Like his contemporary, the black pilot Ted Robinson, he trained in Stearmans and then flew Cessna UC-78 Bobcat twin-engine trainers and B-25s before he was mustered out in November 1945, months too late to have seen combat. "The war was over before anything real exciting happened to me, with the exception of obtaining some absolutely wonderful flying education. And we had loads of fun. Since then, I haven't done much as a pilot except fly," he added.

"No exciting accidents or experiences except a few stupid flights into inclement weather in aircraft unequipped for it. Oh, I did have a tailwheel blow out on my old Cessna 195 while taking off. The takeoff was great, but the landing was exciting."

Losing his legs, Jim said, has not affected his flying. "I have no particular trouble handling an airplane, provided that there is sufficient room above the rudder pedals to put my feet. If I'm flying an airplane other than my own, I prefer to sit in it awhile and taxi around until I feel comfortable with it and learn how far I have to relocate my feet to use the brakes. I do check to make sure my feet are not on the brakes when I first start taxiing an airplane, and I look down on the final approach to make sure I'm off the brakes. I have never goofed up." After a beat he added, "So far," invoking another variation on the old aviation standby: There are two kinds of pilots—those who have goofed up and those who are going to.

When we arrived at Jim's house, the first things I noticed were the aircraft parts on the back porch—an engine mount and a horizontal stabilizer that had been reskinned with new aluminum, the riveting job as neat as any I've ever seen. "Hail damage," he said. He took me to an outbuilding next door, his shop. "I bought this basket-case Ercoupe because I was going crazy after putting my wife in the nursing home." Jodi Newman had to be institutionalized after a three-year bout with Alzheimer's disease. Rebuilding that Ercoupe, I could see, was Jim's way of coping with the anguish caused by his wife's slow and inexorable decline.

In a few minutes, we were back on the road and soon arrived at his hangar at Georgetown Municipal. Jim keeps his plane there, rather than at Austin Executive, just a mile and a half south of his home, because "there are no hangars I can afford at Executive, and I will not leave my bird outside."

The 1958 Champ he had rebuilt from the ground up is only a little smaller than my Cessna. It looks like a Piper Cub with a slight potbelly. Like the Cub, it is a fabric-covered high-wing airplane with a tailwheel and a narrow fuselage containing two seats, one in back of the other in tandem fashion. All white with brown-and-red stripes, it's in pristine condition, with wheel pants giving it a jaunty air, like Fred Astaire in spats.

"Want to go for a ride?" Jim asked. If I had been a dog, I would have gone into paroxysms of wagging. My eager grin was enough for him, and he pushed the airplane out onto the apron. "I'll have to get in first," he said, "so I can get my legs in." The Champ is equipped with a front seat that slides on rails, instead of the usual fixed seat, to make climbing in easier for him. "I had to get an FAA supplemental type certificate for this. It allows modifications of airplanes."

Like all Champs, Jim's airplane has heel brakes—in fact, his pilot's certificate limits him to airplanes equipped with heel brakes. He cannot press down the fronts of his prosthetic feet to operate toe brakes like those on *Gin Fizz*. As I crawled into the back seat and pulled the door to, I was intrigued to see that there was far more elbow room in the narrow fuselage than in the wider side-by-side cockpit of *Gin Fizz*. It was a comfortable fit.

Jim turned around and motioned for me to put on the radio headset, hanging on the rear throttle. "Why?" I asked.

"Save your hearing," Jim said. "It's *loud* in here."

"I haven't got any hearing to be saved," I replied. Jim threw back his head, laughing at his own absent-mindedness. Most people would have been painfully embarrassed, fearful that their thoughtlessness might have offended me. Only someone who copes with a disability every day of his life would treat the event with the nonchalant humor it deserves. Jim makes light of his handicap—"I can wade in high water without getting my feet wet," he says—and so I felt comfortable with this man. I put on the headset anyway, just to have a place to hang it, and was immediately struck by how heavy and awkward it was, even though it was of a brand famous for its lightweight construction. There are, I thought, a few compensations for being deaf, and one of them is not having to wear a headset.

In a few minutes Jim pressed home the throttle, and the ninety-horsepower Champ lifted off in just a couple of hundred feet despite its full load. At 1,500 feet above the ground, Jim turned around and said, "You take over now." The Champ is equipped with dual controls, but the instruments are on the front panel. Jim obligingly leaned to one side so I could see the turn-and-bank indicator. It was the first time I had ever flown an airplane with a stick, not a yoke, and I yawed badly into my first turn, the ball on the turn-and-bank indicator flopping to the inside instead of being perfectly centered. "Got to lead the turn with rudder!" Jim said, noticing my embarrassment. My subsequent turns were better, but still ragged. A Champ, like any other airplane, needs to be gotten used to. Its roll, for another instance, is stiff, compared to that of a Cessna 150, but it was still light on the controls. I could easily get used to an airplane like this, I thought—if I could rig up a mirror to talk to the passenger behind me. Side-by-side seating makes communications a lot easier.

After a while we returned to Georgetown, and I was intrigued to see how carefully Jim picked his touchdown spot on the long runway so he could roll out onto the taxiway by steering only with the rudder, not the brakes. "The only time I use the brakes," he said, "is to turn the plane around in front of the hangar. It's my army training. I can't remember the last time I had to use brakes on a landing rollout or in an emergency." A light tread on the brakes saves wear and tear on expensive tires and brake pads and is the mark of the veteran and competent pilot. To this day, I often must slow down and turn with my brakes—one masters brakeless steering only with long experience.

In the car on the way back south to Austin Executive, where *Gin Fizz* awaited, I asked Jim how other pilots treat him. "I have not, to my knowledge, received any negative or unusual feelings from other pilots," he replied. "They all accept me, showing no special interest one way or the other. I'm just one of the gang. They are considerate and aware that I can't walk more than a quarter of a mile or stand for long without sitting a spell. This is because of the poor circulation in my legs. I'm sure I still suffer from phlebitis. My legs begin to cramp, and sitting for a few minutes restores circulation. It's also because of the way the artificial legs are fitted in order not to drop off when I walk. All my weight is resting on my kneecaps, and my weight compresses my stumps into the sockets of the legs. It's like wearing shoes that are too small. Sometimes I carry a small folding chair, not a canvas one. The chair has steel legs and a molded seat. It's light and can be used as a walking stick or cane. I hate wheelchairs and refuse to use one until the absolute last day I can stand up." He said this last calmly, without bitterness.

Jim's remark about being "just one of the gang" reinforced my notions about a pilots' brotherhood. But maybe, I thought, Jim was also welcomed because he is not only an exemplar of quiet self-reliance, but also accepts his situation stoically. Unlike some disabled people, he does not try to force a guilt trip on the healthy, blaming them for his lot. He simply endures.

\*       \*       \*

At Austin Executive I collected *Gin Fizz* from her baby-sitters and prepared her for takeoff. It had been a month since my layover in Chicago had begun, but the summer heat had abated and the convective turbulence no longer would be so annoying. I could now fly all day without being tossed around like a feather. As the line attendant rolled *Gin Fizz* from the open hangar out into the sun, I saw that she had a coating of Texas dust and that the Velcro strips holding a kitchen timer I use to measure fuel burn had slipped down, leaving a sticky glue trail. This was a sure sign that the airplane had been wheeled out into the hot sun for part of every day. Long periods in the hot sun can damage delicate instruments as well as fade paint. Still, *Gin Fizz* was otherwise in fine condition, and after refueling, I shook Jim's hand and was away into the haze for San Marcos, thirty-six miles southwest. Rather than head directly to San Marcos, I flew twelve miles due west to avoid the Austin Mueller controlled airspace, then turned south after clearing pretty Lake Travis. At 2,000 feet above ground, the haze was slight and the bumps gentle, and in a few minutes I flew over Kyle, where eighty-four years earlier, Cal Rodgers had been forced down for a day and a half.

After taking off from Austin, Rodgers circled the state capitol three times at 800 feet to give the citizens a thrill. He then ascended to 3,000 feet, taking advantage of a brisk tailwind, and headed for San Antonio. But after ten miles, the gremlins struck again. Cal felt a sudden snap and a jolt. The engine had thrown a valve and began bouncing wildly in its mounts. Cal shut down and "volplaned"—the 1911 term for "glided"—to a rough landing in a cotton field just north of Kyle. The damage to *Vin Fiz* was minimal, but the aviator was shaken and dazed. He needed rest—he had lost fifteen pounds since leaving New York—and that night a wet Texas norther screamed through. All the next day *Vin Fiz* remained wind bound in the slashing rain.

Late in the morning of October 22, *Vin Fiz* labored into the air, her skids and wheels caked with heavy loam softened into muck by the storm, and a few minutes later reached San Marcos. The ride down had been cold, and while *Vin Fiz* took aboard fuel, Cal added an extra layer of clothing. His takeoff from San Marcos was routine but slightly hairy—Cal chose to take off downwind across a small meadow—and the flight to San Antonio, forty-two miles southwest, turned out to be smooth and pleasant. The usual crowds bent on plunder greeted him, but this time a detachment of infantry and cavalry waited at the polo grounds of Fort Sam Houston with orders to "cut the toes off those who get too close." A thirteen-year-old boy was the first to reach the aviator. "How do you do, Mr. Rodgers," he said. Cal, according to newspaper accounts, ignored the boy, leaving him hurt and disappointed. Probably Cal never heard the youngster, who mistook his silence for a rebuff. After the official greetings and speechifying, Cal flew *Vin Fiz* to suburban Harlandale to collect a small purse, and there his plane was stored under guard for the night.

The next day, sobered by reports that the rugged terrain west of San Antonio was carved by canyons and carpeted with scrub mesquite with few clear spots for landing, Cal's crew—slowly getting smarter—rerigged *Vin Fiz* from nose to tail, restringing flying wires and scrubbing or replacing fabric, and overhauled her engine. Shortly after noon on October 24, *Vin Fiz* lifted off, once again heading due west after the long southerly course from Kansas City, following the Sunset Route of the Southern Pacific Railroad.

As *Gin Fiz* approached San Marcos Municipal, I thought it a huge airport for such a small city, with four long and wide runways and massive expanses of concrete ramps. Like so many Texas airports, it is a former training field handed over to civilian use after World War II, and I could visualize rows upon rows of parked B-17s, B-24s, and B-29s on the hardstands. At first, the place seemed lonely, but a fair amount of aviation activity was going on, concentrated in one corner of the huge expanse.

"Anything happening here?" I asked the young woman at the terminal desk. "Oh, just the usual. A little training, a little business flying, a lot of fun," she said. "Next month they're gonna make a movie here, though, and Meg Ryan and Denzel Washington are starring in it." Her eyes brightened at the thought.

The film, she said, was *Courage Under Fire,* a Desert Storm epic produced by Fox, and Ryan was going to play a hard-nosed army helicopter pilot. I was surprised—judging from the Meg Ryan movies I have seen, the sweet, loopy actress seemed better suited for romantic comedy than combat. Part of the airport, around an old World War II–era hangar, had been cleared of airplanes in preparation for the shooting. The *Rashomon*-like plot, I learned later, had to do with Ryan being considered for a posthumous Medal of Honor after being shot down and keeping the enemy at bay with rifle fire until her men could be rescued. Washington plays a colonel who investigates the incident. Each of Ryan's surviving crew presents the colonel with a wildly different picture of the pilot, painting her variously as a coward and a brave leader. It was a juicy if risky role, and Ryan would later win respectable reviews for her performance. Perhaps she had listened to the army recruiting commercial that ends with "Be all that you can be."

As I walked back out to *Gin Fizz,* I mused about how in the span of a single generation the military had changed from a constant presence to an almost invisible one in American life. When I was a college student in the 1950s and 1960s, the draft was on. Had I not been deaf, I am sure I would have yearned for a naval career, following in the footsteps of my father, just as Cal Rodgers had hoped to emulate his forebears. But our mutual deafness had squelched any hopes in that direction for both Cal and me. Twenty years after that, Colin had hoped that naval ROTC would pay for his college education, but the rapid shrinking of the military in the wake of the collapse of the Soviet Union and the end of the Cold War meant intense competition for the fewer and fewer ROTC slots in American colleges and universities. Briefly, Conan, who followed Colin four years afterward, worried, as did his college compatriots, about a resumption of the draft during the Persian Gulf War, but that was short-lived. But those were universal experiences they shared with all the young men (and women) of their generation. Mine weren't. During the Vietnam era, I could only look on from the sidelines as my friends and acquaintances fell into the deadly morass of the draft, finagled their ways into safe National Guard berths, or, when all else failed, fled to Canada for their lives. At the time, I smugly thanked my deafness for keeping me aloof and alive during dangerous events—a selfish emotion for which I now feel vaguely ashamed, for it means that I never paid my dues during the sixties. Like so many of my contemporaries, in the beginning of the decade I favored American intervention in Southeast Asia, then, as the war was transformed into an endless meat grinder, I turned against it. As a journalist who still believed that his profession ought to be as objective as possible, I could hold opinions and deliver them in print—but could not demonstrate them in public events, for that would be making the news, not reporting it.

As time passes, not having been able to participate except as an ineffectual onlooker in the central public event of my young manhood has made me feel increasingly detached from the entire decade, as if I had never experienced it. I have no real answer to "What did you do in the sixties, Granddad?" except "Nothing."

The enduring lesson I learned from that episode in history is that nobody has much control over his own life, except in the most superficial ways. As a young man, I liked to think that I was master of my fate; but like everyone else, I was really being guided by the dice of chance. All the same, I have discovered, we can from time to time nudge our lives onto interesting new courses. That much is possible.

Still, the military had enough of a presence to affect my progress westward. Flying from San Marcos to Castroville required some thought before takeoff to avoid tangling with both the controlled airspace of the San Antonio International Airport and the military alert area of Randolph Air Force Base. I could either go around or go over, and I chose the latter. After takeoff, I put *Gin Fizz* into a steep climb, and in a few minutes she leveled off at 6,500 feet, well above the 4,000-foot ceiling of the Randolph alert area and the 4,800-foot limit of the San Antonio airspace. There was no compelling reason to ask for a light-gun landing at the busy international airport, so I had chosen Castroville, twenty-five miles west, as my San Antonio stop.

Castroville is a deceptively dusty and well-worn municipal airport, but it was busy when I landed, with a couple of students and instructors flying Cessna 152s in the circuit. "We have about twenty-five student pilots," said Joan McCasland, who, with her husband Lou—one of the flight instructors—runs the FBO for the city of Castroville. She is a pleasant, trim, attractive woman who may be forty or fifty—it is hard to say with many of both sexes who live in this part of the country—and displays a mien of friendly but no-nonsense competence. "There's a deaf pilot here, Carlos Freytes," she said. I knew the name from the International Deaf Pilots Association, although I had not met him.

I was still concerned enough about the radio to ask Joan if she had heard my transmissions from the air. "We heard you," she said, "but it was all garbled. Speak very slowly when you're on the radio." I thanked her for her candor, commenting that many people told me what I wanted to hear, not what they had actually heard.

"I always tell the truth," she said firmly. "I'm a former school-teacher." In heartland America, that profession is known for candor and uprightness. Indeed, she reminded me of a junior high school teacher I had, who, on the first day of school, invariably looked her pupils in the eye and said, "I expect the best from you, and if you give me the best you can, we will get along." This teacher, like so many during my childhood and youth, had high expectations of me; she did not pigeonhole me in a special education slot, as just about all deaf children are today.

Among Castroville's amenities were two small dogs, the most interesting I had seen so far during the trip. Mitch and Sadie were miniature pinschers, ten-pounders by the look of them. The smaller dog, Sadie, wore a radio receiver of some sort around her neck, an eight-inch "rubber ducky" antenna sticking out.

"What's that?" I asked Joan.

"It's a GPS," she said, "so I always know where she is." Then she laughed. "It's a shock collar," she said, showing me a tiny transmitter with sending button. "When I press this button, it causes the collar to zap her. She chases cars. Behavior modification, you know."

"What would she do with a car if she caught one?" I asked rhetorically. As if to display her disdain for the question, Sadie stood up, padded stiff-leggedly to the screen door, shouldered it aside, and disappeared into the pilot's lounge. I could have sworn she curled her lip. A year later, I learned that Sadie was with pup, her first litter, and has sworn off chasing cars. Mitch, of course, was the daddy.

No airport is complete without at least one dog, the odder the better. Among pilots, airport dogs are a common topic of conversation, and some are legendary. I once heard of an Oklahoma border collie that was so smart, the teller of the tale swore, he learned some of the duties of a line attendant just by watching. Airplanes would land and taxi up to the gas pumps as the dog barked furiously, sidling right and left and backing up as the pilots followed its lead, and then the dog would sit down smartly, a signal to the pilot that his airplane was positioned correctly and he could shut down his engine. Then, the yarnspinner said, the dog would run around past the tail of the airplane and guide the next one to a stop. That way he could herd half a dozen airplanes into a perfectly straight line.

One of the 152s landed, and a middle-aged student pilot of Mexican descent got out and asked about *Gin Fizz*, and we chatted briefly. He sounded just like any other student pilot I had met, displaying a transparent eagerness and a barely suppressed wish not to seem ignorant. Only two years before, I had been just like him. The 340 hours I had amassed in the air since then, however, had subtly changed my outlook. I was starting to take on the world-weary mien of an old pro, even to the point of being slightly patronizing, although as helpful as I could be, with student pilots. With a professorial air, I carefully explained the differences between the Lycoming engine in his 152 and the Continental motor in my 150 as the student listened intently.

That night, in my comfortable but isolated motel on the other side of Castroville, I sat at the bar nursing a Lone Star beer. It was only my first night on the road after leaving home, but I was already missing Debby and our ordinary domestic conversations. Cal Rodgers never had to cope with solitary evenings on the road; there was always a warm berth with his wife in his railroad car or a big overstuffed bed in the best room in the best hotel of every town after a welcoming banquet. Today, however, flying solo across the country is largely an exercise in navigating the margins of civilization. Conversation is rare, and when it occurs, it tends to be about airplanes.

Back at Castroville Municipal the next day, morning fog greeted me. While waiting for it to lift, I asked Joan about flying to Del Rio, two stops west on the Rodgers Route, on the Mexican border. That city's airport lies right on the other side of Laughlin Air Force Base, around which is a thirty-five-mile-wide alert area warning transiting civilian pilots to be wary of military traffic—of which there is a great deal, Laughlin being an intensive student jet training center. Joan gave me a booklet about Laughlin published by the air force. Reading it made me nervous, and I decided to call Laughlin approach control and ask how best to steer clear of the high-performance jets. The phone rang and rang. Nobody answered. I decided to follow the Southern Pacific tracks to Uvalde and then to Spofford, ninety miles west of Castroville, at which point I would head northwest in a wide sweeping circle around the air force base until I reached the eastern shore of the huge Amistad International Reservoir on the Rio Grande. There I would turn southeast to land at Del Rio International Airport, despite its name an uncontrolled field on the western outskirts of town. That route seemed safer than climbing to 6,500 feet to overfly the Laughlin controlled airspace ceiling. It's best to stay low, I thought; the students in their jets most likely will be high.

And I figured it best to file an official flight plan, the first of the trip. West of San Antonio, distances between towns are great, and the Southern Pacific line diverges from U.S. 90 at several places. If I suffered a forced landing, I figured, it was possible that no one would see *Gin Fizz* go down, and help might be many miles away. For the first time during my odyssey, I filled both my water bottles and made sure my shrinking stock of granola bars could keep me alive.

On the laptop I called the computer weather service and filed a standard flight plan online, keyboarding the data into the blanks: Type, VFR; aircraft identification, N5859E; aircraft type, C-150/U for Cessna 150 equipped with Mode C altitude-reporting transponder; true airspeed, 86 KNOTS; departure point, CASTROVILLE MUNICI-PAL; proposed departure time, 1400 ZULU (9 A.M. central daylight time); cruising altitude, 4,500 FEET; route of flight, DIRECT CAS-TROVILLE-UVALDE; destination, UVALDE; estimated time en route, 30 MINUTES; remarks, PILOT IS DEAF, CANNOT RECEIVE ON RA-DIO, FILING ASSUMED DEPARTURE; fuel on board, 4 HOURS; alternate airports, NONE; pilot's name, address, and telephone number, mine; color of aircraft, SILVER and BLUE; destination contact, GAR-NER AIRPORT, UVALDE.

Hearing pilots activate their flight plans shortly after takeoff, radioing the nearest Flight Service station and giving their aircraft identification so the briefer can call up their plans and open them. Before takeoff, I used TTY and the Texas Relay Service to telephone Flight Service, telling the briefer I was deaf and could not receive on the radio and asking that he activate the plan at my proposed takeoff time, 9 A.M. He assented. "By the way," he said, "we're looking for pireps, so please let us know what you encounter en route." A pirep is short for pilot report, a summary of whatever weather conditions the pilot experiences, radioed to Flight Service at the instant he experiences them. "Sure thing," I replied, chuckling to myself at the briefer's absent-mindedness.

The Castroville-Uvalde route, however lonely it seemed on the sectional chart and whatever Cal Rodgers was told in 1911, did not follow unbroken wilderness in 1995. From takeoff *Gin Fizz* flew over lots of farms along the Hondo and Frio rivers, lots of human habitation, lots of clear and open space for emergency landings near the route. The Southern Pacific tracks followed the northern edge of the fertile lowlands of the West Gulf Coastal Plain of Texas, the hills of the dry Edwards Plateau of the high Great Plains bordering the route to the north. After landing at Uvalde, I took my TTY into the terminal to try the tower at Laughlin Air Force Base again, and again I couldn't raise anybody. Hmm. I dialed the FBO at Del Rio International. "It's Sunday," came the response. "Laughlin is inactive today."

"It is? So I can go under the 2,500-foot floor of Laughlin's airspace and get to Del Rio International?" I asked.

"Yes sir," said the fellow at the airport. Today I am not sure that any of the Laughlin controlled airspace was active at all, and I might have been able to fly directly over the airport to Del Rio. But at that time, in my uncertainty, I decided to stick with my original plan: to fly around Laughlin instead of over it. It's better, I thought, to do things the conservative way, even if it takes longer.

Moments later, *Gin Fizz* was off again, and when I suddenly jinked the airplane to the left to avoid a flock of birds that had risen from the runway, I shouted, *"Oh, damn!"* Not at the birds, but at myself. I wrested *Gin Fizz* around into the pattern and landed again. As I strode past the puzzled line attendant into the terminal, I growled, "Forgot to close my flight plan." He chuckled. He must hear that half a dozen times a day.

Lulled by the obvious signs of civilization along the Castroville—Uvalde route, I decided not to file a flight plan from Uvalde to Del Rio. This was, I soon learned, not a good idea. This time, the farther west I flew onto the Edwards Plateau, the scrubbier and lonelier the terrain became. Only a few dwellings along the Nueces River bespoke the presence of people. "Engine, do your stuff," I whispered. Seventeen miles west of Uvalde, the Southern Pacific line veered toward the southwest while U.S. 90 turned northeast. I stayed with the highway, bypassing the military alert area around Spofford, and at a point twenty miles east of Del Rio, I turned *Gin Fizz* slightly northwest to fly a large sweeping arc seven to eight miles away from the center of Laughlin Air Force Base, staying at 2,400 feet, 100 feet under the floor of the outer shelf of the controlled airspace. Even only a few miles from Laughlin, the land seemed vast and lonely. Out there, if I suffered distress and had to put the plane down, it could have been hours, even days, before I was found. If the airplane's emergency locator transmitter did not go off in a crash, the expanse of bush looked so forbidding that I thought the buzzards would find me long before rescuers could. Henceforth, I decided, I would religiously file flight plans—and weigh down *Gin Fizz* with another gallon of drinking water.

At Del Rio International, I had to exercise care not to fly over the Rio Grande into Mexico while approaching the runway for landing. *Gin Fizz* does not have foot-high numbers on its fuselage, required by the FAA on aircraft crossing the border. As a thirty-six-year-old airplane restored to as-built appearance, she has three-inch-high numbers on her vertical stabilizer and eighteen-inch-high numbers on her upper right and lower left wings, but those don't count. The big numbers must be on the fuselage of every aircraft crossing the border in either direction.

On the ground, the line attendant agreed, for a ten-spot, to stash the plane in the FBO hangar for the night—which made me feel better because of all the dark stories I had heard about this military border town. I looked up motels in the phone book and found a Best Western on F Street, the motel strip near the airport. The co-owner of the motel picked me up in his van, and since he was also a pilot, we had a pleasant chat about flying cross country in these parts.

"Don't go across the border," my sister-in-law Prissy, Steve Bangs's spouse, had told me back in Austin. "It's too ugly and dangerous and awful." Telling a journalist not to go somewhere for those reasons is like waving a Milk-Bone in front of a starving dog. Almost three decades before, as a college student, I had tasted the dubious pleasures of wide-open Tijuana, and I wanted to see if Ciudad Acuña was similarly a hotbed of sin and iniquity—just a glimpse of a dancing señorita would do, and maybe a draft or two of *cerveza*.

From the motel I could see a bridge about three miles south, doubtless the one across the Rio Grande. Eagerly, I set off down F Street, past the fast-food joints, pawnshops, and psychic readers. No sidewalks assisted the footsore traveler; west Texas is not designed for pedestrians. But when I fetched up at the bridge, dog-tired and drenched with sweat, I discovered that it was not the international span over the Rio Grande. Ciudad Acuña lay three miles farther, a roadside sign said. The hell with it, I said to myself. I'm too old for this. On the way back, staggering on the graveled verge like a parched prospector across alkali sands, I turned in several times at filling stations and fast-food joints to slake my thirst with draughts of Diet Coke. The reckless adventuresomeness of my youth was now just a ghost.

At Harlandale near San Antonio, *Vin Fiz* took off at 12:35 P.M., Rodgers taking his airplane to 3,500 feet. He was as nervous about the terrain to the west as I was ignorant of it, but on October 24, 1911, he had greater reason for concern: This part of Texas was less than sparsely settled, and he hoped to keep his chase train in sight all the way to El Paso. Half an hour later, *Vin Fiz's* weary engine again began to splutter, but Cal nursed it along for a while. Just before Lacoste, the motor coughed again, so he put the plane down in a cotton field. He adjusted the magneto while his crew hired boys to pull cotton plants to clear a takeoff space for *Vin Fiz*, and at 2:24 P.M., Rodgers was in the air again. He landed at and took off from Sabinal and Uvalde and was soon off for Del Rio, flying as far as he dared before dusk turned to dark. At suppertime he landed on a road just west of Spofford, several miles short of Del Rio, puncturing a tire on a cactus spine but otherwise coming to a stop without incident.

Rodgers was growing wearier and wearier, his silences longer, his words sharper edged. Eileen Lebow wrote that Cal's determination urged him on, but I think it was sheer stubbornness that fueled Rodgers's mighty effort to communicate his innate capabilities to the larger hearing world. Meanwhile, in Pasadena, excitement began to build. Cal was coming closer and closer, and it looked to the world as if he might make it after all. His cousin John Rodgers announced that he had chosen Tournament Park as the best site for Cal's landing, and a prominent hotelier there grandly offered the aviator 1,000 gold pieces if Rodgers landed in Pasadena.

On the morning of October 25, Cal started his engine, but on takeoff the right propeller struck a small mound of earth. The plane swerved and crashed, both propellers splintered, the skids collapsed, and the left lower wing crumpled. Cal emerged unhurt, announcing offhandedly, "These wrecks are part of the game and to be expected." But the truth is that just as he had done in the Northeast, Rodgers could have avoided them if he had been more meticulous. Had he surveyed his takeoff site a little more carefully, that wreck might not have occurred.

While the mechanics worked to repair *Vin Fiz*, a chastened Rodgers went ahead by train to scout out the rugged country west of Del Rio. Meanwhile, a scoffer in Spofford started the story that as a result of the accident, the hangar car was now carrying a coffin in case Rodgers was killed. The next afternoon, shortly after one o'clock, he took to the air again, the brisk wind propelling him thirty-seven miles in thirty-one minutes to Del Rio, where he landed to collect still another purse. This time the crowd stayed well behaved.

*Vin Fiz* took off at 2:50 P.M. for Sanderson, 110 air miles west. On this part of the Texas–Mexico border, the Rio Grande doubles back on itself in sweeping loops a dozen times, and Cal flew straight over the loops, from Texas into Mexico and back into Texas and then into Mexico again three times. At Dryden he landed to replenish oil and then proceeded to Sanderson, where he landed for the night. The next day, October 27, the wind blew hard, and Cal stayed fidgeting on the ground.

On October 28 he tried too soon again, and the still-capricious wind blew *Vin Fiz* into a fence on takeoff, breaking a skid and tearing the lower left wing fabric. Just before noon, the patched and repatched airplane took off again, and this time Cal kept control of it. The country had grown rough and hilly, with mountains on both sides of the flight path, and almost immediately *Vin Fiz* flew into a thick mist. Cal could barely see the ground and fretted over running out of gas or losing his way. Soon, however, he flew out of the murk and finally reached Alpine, seventy-five air miles west of Sanderson. The town's citizenry turned out en masse. The entire country was perking up its ears, watching as each new edition of the day's newspapers reported the aviator's progress. BIRDMAN NEARS WEST COAST, the headlines blared. WILL RODGERS MAKE IT? Little by little, the whole United States was coming down with aviation fever.

At 2:30 P.M. Cal took off and navigated Paisano Pass to Marfa, twenty-one miles west of Alpine, landing in a field just as the sheriff arrived to rope off the plane, keeping away the eager residents. Again some tinkering needed to be done, and Cal lost two valuable hours of daylight before taking off again. Ninety-five miles later, he had to put down for the night at Sierra Blanca, considerably short of El Paso, his day's goal.

\*         \*         \*

"Stay north of the Rio Grande," the Flight Service briefer said when I activated my flight plan from Del Rio to Dryden. On takeoff down the southeast runway, I had to bank sharply into a steep right turn at an altitude of 100 feet, just past the end of the runway, instead of continuing to pattern altitude of 800 feet before making the turn, as conscientious pilots normally do, so approaching aircraft can see them more readily. Otherwise I would have blundered over the Rio Grande into Mexico and perhaps brought an U.S. Customs jet down on my head. I had had visions of spending hours applying temporary twelve-inch numbers made with plastic tape to both sides of *Gin Fizz*'s fuselage, but an exchange of messages on CompuServe with an FAA official had assured me that as long as I didn't cross the border, I'd be legal. It was close, however.

After flying over Amistad Reservoir, the huge man-made lake northwest of Del Rio that is a fifty-mile-long septic tank choked with silt, I followed the Southern Pacific, rather than the river. I was tempted to fly straight over the looping Rio Grande from the United States into Mexico and back again, as Rodgers had done, but I couldn't take the risk. It is likely that somebody had me on radar. From the blip on the screen, the operator couldn't tell that *Gin Fizz* was just a little old Cessna 150 and not the drug-running plane of choice, a big Cessna 206 six-seater with its interior gutted to enable it to carry a ton of dope.

Since Del Rio, the land elevation had climbed gradually, from 900 feet to more than 2,000, as the low front porch of the Rocky Mountains approached. Except for a few low-level hops and a couple of climbs to 6,500 feet to overfly military areas, I had been flying at 4,500 feet above sea level since the middle of Oklahoma. That altitude had kept *Gin Fizz* at 2,000 to 3,500 feet above the ground, low enough to enjoy the sights below but high enough to see where I was going. As long as the air wasn't turbulent, 4,500 feet had been a nice, comfortable cruising altitude for a small airplane across the middle of the United States. Flying at that height had brought a kind of equilibrium to my trip, and it also seemed symbolic of the new balance my life was reaching, thanks to the heartening effect of the events of my coast-to-coast adventure on my self-esteem. *I can do this,* I thought to myself. And now it was time to go higher, to cross the Rockies.

An hour later I landed at Terrell County Airport at Dryden, elevation 2,322 feet, on the most desolate airstrip I'd yet put down on during the entire trip. Its two 4,500-foot runways had deteriorated badly, huge tufts of grass growing through long cracks in the asphalt, rolls of tumbleweed strewn willy-nilly between them. Some of the tumbleweed was so large that I had to slalom the plane around it. Not a single other airplane or hangar, except for an empty T-hangar—a roof without walls—could be seen.

As I walked to the low terminal building, a large mixed-breed hound bounded up with a mixture of booming barks and timid licks, and a short time later his owner, for whom "airport manager" must have been simply one item on a long list of jobs, rolled up in his pickup. The dog leaned so affectionately against my leg he nearly caused me to topple over. I did not ask his name; saying it might have impelled him to adopt me.

The manager, a wiry, weathered Texan named C. D. Curry, opened up the pilot's lounge—spiffier and more comfortable than the rest of the airport, with a small kitchen that had a microwave and refrigerator and two neat bathrooms—and offered to brew a pot of coffee. "No," I said, envisioning a long pull ahead to Alpine without a bathroom, "but thanks anyway." Even for a lonely airport manager, Curry was exceptionally affable. Only three planes land there every week, he said, and seemingly every one of them is enshrined in a photograph under the glass counter, including a good-sized executive jet that had brought in a party of hunters—presumably they had used the old camouflage-painted Suburban in the lounge's lot, bench seat and back bolted to its roof, to hunt mule deer in the scrub. Curry then stepped outside with a camera to capture *Gin Fizz* under glass.

I plugged in my laptop, closed out my flight plan, and filed a new one. Then I called Texas Relay to bounce my call to Flight Service to activate the plan. This call took a while because the operator—a man—was confused by the number I gave him. He insisted steadfastly that 1–800-WX-BRIEF, the standard number that will link a pilot to the closest Flight Service station, was a garble of numbers and letters. I finally persuaded him to punch WX-BRIEF into his computer instead of translating the letters into numbers, and got through to Flight Service. The experience did not surprise me. In my years of using the state relay services across the United States, I've found that female operators are quicker than their male counterparts to get a handle on unfamiliar language. I have even used relay services to obtain complex weather briefings over the phone. Female operators rarely are buffaloed by the heavy jargon, such as

"En route, broken to overcast cirroform clouds . . . surface winds zero two zero at one one, peak gusts two eight, with standing lenticular altocumulus southeast through west." They simply repeat what they hear, asking the briefer to spell an unfamiliar word or spelling it themselves phonetically. Men, I think, are conditioned to try to understand what they're passing along, and that slows down the proceedings. I can't blame them; I'm that way, too.

At 10 A.M. I lifted off from Dryden and headed west. Half an hour later, the flat scrubland of the Great Plains had changed to the rolling foothills of the Stockton Plateau, an outpost of the Rocky Mountains, and they gained altitude the farther west I flew. The clouds were lowering below the mountaintops—or, rather, hadn't yet risen above them with the heat of the day. Never having flown through the Rockies, I decided not to chance getting caught in clouds. When the base of the broken cloud cover dropped below 1,500 feet above the climbing valley floor, I would put *Gin Fizz* into a 180-degree turn back to Dryden. Soon it happened, and on the flight back, I calculated that if I landed and tried again for Alpine that day, I'd be burning my fuel reserve—and it is not a good idea to be in the mountains without plenty of gas. I thought I'd ask Curry to run me into town and get a couple of five-gallon cans of autogas to top off the tanks. I prayed that the autogas sold at the service stations there wasn't laced with alcohol.

Curry hardly seemed surprised when I told him I had run into low clouds in the mountains. He turned and pointed to a fifty-five-gallon drum under the open hangar roof. It contained 100LL avgas, he said, and was just for emergencies such as mine, and, of course, he'd top me off so I could make another assault on the mountains with full tanks. Cheerfully, he filled a five-gallon plastic can with a rocker pump and used a funnel to fill my tanks, splashing a good couple of quarts on the ground. I didn't care, nor did I blanch at the $25 charge for ten gallons of avgas; I was just glad for the full tanks.

At noon I mounted my counterattack on the mountains, and at that hour the clouds had lifted to where they were supposed to be two hours earlier, a good 3,000 feet from the valley floor, leaving plenty of room for me to fly under them and between the peaks. I made it to Alpine in an hour. The ride through the cliffs and dales of west Texas on a clear day was glorious, and I exulted in the landscape. At low flight levels, the crags and pinnacles of the Rockies are far more interesting than the Great Plains and eastern flatlands—and naturally more dangerous. Winds over the mountains dip and swirl and can catch a lightplane in a bottomless vortex. That day, however, the winds blew gently and from the east, and *Gin Fizz* maintained a ground speed of 112 miles per hour, a good 12 miles per hour faster than her airspeed.

Soon I arrived at Alpine, tucked on a valley floor between the Davis and Del Norte mountain ranges, just before the four-times-a-week stagecoach—a commuter jet—from Dallas landed with a dozen passengers. When the jet left, Alpine was not such a busy airport anymore, but the FBO attendant seemed more interested in fixing his truck than talking with me, so I remounted and flew to Marfa, down the road around a 5,500-foot peak. Again the ride was glorious.

Alpine and Marfa airports, however, both lie above 4,500 feet, and I noticed that *Gin Fizz*'s engine power had shrunk noticeably in the thinner air. I had to lean the air and fuel mixture before takeoff to gain full power, instead of leaving the mixture control at full rich for best engine cooling. Takeoff runs took much longer, even with ten degrees of flaps extended to help *Gin Fizz* get unstuck from the runway, and climbing was slow. I was now cruising at 7,500 feet above sea level, only 2,500 feet above the ground, and the terrain kept gaining altitude the farther west I flew.

Marfa looked like a ghost town's airport, but the white-haired FBO manager who filled my tanks with the help of his wife was friendly and interested in what I was doing, though he had little to say about himself in that shy way one sees in so many Westerners. He did say he heard me on the radio but could not understand me. By now, however, I was growing philosophical about the situation and shrugged. Compared to the woes Cal Rodgers had had to suffer, I was way ahead on points.

It was such a good flying day that I decided not to stop for the night in Marfa, as I'd planned, but press on to Van Horn, sixty-five miles northwest, to cut down the next day's distance to El Paso. There is no airport near Sierra Blanca, where Rodgers had spent the night in 1911, so I used Van Horn as my Sierra Blanca stop. The afternoon was beautiful, the engine humming happily, and I was not at all tired. I filed and opened a flight plan for Van Horn.

Not far out of Marfa, I flew past a tethered blimplike balloon that was marked on the charts with a circular restriction zone four miles in diameter. I could see the balloon "flying" through the clouds at 8,500 feet, now obscured, now standing out in clear relief against the cumulus. What sort of balloon it was I wasn't sure, but I surmised that being so close to the border, it contained some sort of detection equipment to spot drug-smuggling aircraft. I felt unseen eyes upon me as *Gin Fizz* droned past. I was glad I had filed that flight plan. Whoever they were, they knew who I was and where I was going and that I was not a potential bad guy to be intercepted and searched.

The fool's luck that had followed me all the way from New York landed with me at Van Horn. Even at 4 P.M., Culberson County Airport, I discovered as I walked to the terminal, was closed, locked, and deserted. Only a pay phone hung in the lounge for the itinerant pilot—and how was I going to use that with a TTY to phone Flight Service to close my flight plan? After all, I could not hear the clinks, beeps, and instructions to insert more coins. The town was three miles away, a good hour's walk. I had visions of the FAA sending the Civil Air Patrol out on a search for a missing pilot who was hardly lost. (Later, I was told by a Civil Air Patrol veteran that when nobody at an airport responds to a call, Flight Service simply phones the local sheriff's department, which sends a cruiser to the airport to look for the missing airplane.)

A few minutes after I landed, however, a tall Texan—a former Dallas Cowboy by the look of him—arrived at the airport in a brand-new Ford Explorer. The fellow was a pilot himself, and when I explained my predicament, he dropped a quarter and closed out my flight plan for me. He had arrived to meet his wife, coming in aboard an executive jet, and kindly offered to drive me to a motel on the other side of town, which he assured me would have plenty of room for pilots without reservations. By and by, his wife arrived—in a Learjet. As her copilot stored the plane in a hangar, the two Texans drove me to town, chuckling and marveling at the audacity of a low-time Midwestern pilot thinking he could fly a Cessna 150 all the way across the country. "You be careful, heah?" they both said as they dropped me at the Best Western.

My first concern was being able to get back to the airport the next morning, for it lay a good five miles east of the motel. To my question, the female clerk said, "We don't have a taxi service in town, but maybe the Reverend Taylor will drive you." For a small donation to his church, perhaps? I asked. It seemed reasonable. She smiled.

Later I went for a walk and was bemused at the utter emptiness of Van Horn. It was like a ghost town, the loneliest stop so far on the whole trip, and I wondered if some natural disaster had emptied the place. At the deserted Tex-Mex restaurant next door, the waitress said with a sigh, "The whole town's gone to Alpine for the high school football game." In this part of Texas, schoolboy football is considered world-class entertainment; coaches and players are regarded with respect and awe. Doubtless Alpine was the jumpingest place in west Texas that night.

The loneliness of the long-distance pilot was beginning to get under my skin. At midnight I awoke restlessly and after tossing and turning for an hour, arose, dressed, and walked a mile on the highway west of town into the clear, cold black night. The stars glistened like sapphires, and moonlight limned the jagged horizon. The air in the remote West, untouched by pollution and the lights of distant cities, was astonishingly clear; I had forgotten that heavenly bodies could be so bright and sparkling. I wished I had brought along an astronomy primer to identify the constellations that were laid out across the sky like a giant panorama. Breathtakingly beautiful in its dark austerity, the night reminded me of a Georgia O'Keeffe painting. Although I am not ordinarily a spiritual person, here in the desolate wilderness of west Texas I felt not isolated but blessed, as if something unseen was touching my soul.

# 17

he next morning I eagerly looked forward to meeting the Reverend Taylor. Doubtless he was some sort of Southwestern character, befriender of the traveler, who in exchange for listening to a Bible verse and a small donation to his storefront church (no doubt housed in a sun-bleached, crumbling adobe building), operated an impromptu taxi service in an ancient sandblasted Ford pickup. He was probably an old-timer who had seen it all and had lots of good stories to tell.

By and by a brand-new Plymouth minivan arrived in the parkway, and a handsome young man and a pretty young woman alighted. Both were in their late twenties and were dressed in crisp, casual clothes that could have come from L. L. Bean. Not the reverend, I thought, and turned to look in the other direction. Then came a tap on my shoulder. It was the minivan's driver.

"I'm Vic Taylor," he said.

"The reverend?" I said, feeling a twinge of surprised disappointment that must have shown in my face, for he peered at me with concern.

"Yes. Ready to go to the airport?" he asked.

"Sure," I said, and we piled in. As the reverend—"Call me Vic"— drove out to the airport, Tay, the young woman, told me that Vic was the local Baptist minister, that she was one of his flock, and that they were on the way to do some church business.

"Vic doesn't do this sort of thing all the time, does he? He's not a minister to the lone traveler?" I asked.

"Oh, no," she said. "He's the pastor of a big church."

"Then how come he's driving me to the airport?"

"Why is that important?" she replied, puzzled.

"Well," I said, "I thought that maybe—oh, never mind. But maybe you'll accept a small donation to the church for your trouble?" She looked at the ten-dollar bill and then at me.

"I don't think so," she said, and Vic shook his head, too.

"Oh, well," I said, trying to cover my embarrassment at having been so self-deluded, "I do appreciate your taking the trouble. How did he come to do this today?"

The desk clerk, Tay said, is a friend of Vic's wife. The clerk knows that Vic drives past the motel each morning to the church near the airport and had called Vic's wife the previous night and asked if he'd mind picking up this pilot who had no way to get to his airplane. "Oh sure," Vic had said, and there he was.

We chatted a bit about my trip west, and as we arrived at the airport, I said I'd be refueling, then calling to file a flight plan and going on my way. "Don't you know that the airport is unattended?" Vic asked.

"It is?" I said. The *Flight Guide* to airports I carry in the plane hadn't reported that fact. "I thought it had just closed early last night." No, he replied. An auto garage mechanic is on call to refuel airplanes, but otherwise nobody's around. How was I going to get out of town? Vic fished a cellular phone from under the seat of the van and began punching numbers.

"I'll get the guy out here to fill you up," he said. It took a while to find the attendant that early in the morning—it was just past 8 A.M.—but Vic finally located him. "I got him out of bed, and he'll be here in half an hour. Now I've got business to attend to. Good luck on your trip," he said, shaking my hand firmly and climbing back into the van with Tay. They drove off. Half an hour later, Jeff, the attendant, arrived, topped off my tank, and sold me a quart of oil. He waited in the lounge while I used the office phone to file a flight plan and call Flight Service to activate it. He didn't leave until I started *Gin Fizz* and taxied away.

At Sierra Blanca the morning of October 29, 1911, Rodgers arose with the sun and was in the air by 9 A.M., on his way to El Paso, where he had a date to see a bullfight that night across the river in Ciudad Juarez. Ill luck dogged him once again. Scarcely fifteen miles west of Sierra Blanca, he discovered water leaking from the water pump and nursed *Vin Fiz* along for another ten miles, searching frantically for a landing spot in the hostile terrain. At Fort Hancock Rodgers spotted a plowed field and glided down toward it. When the plane had descended to barely five feet above the ground, the pump connection to the engine sheared off and the engine froze. Without power *Vin Fiz* plunged like a wounded grouse into mesquite brush just short of the field, smashing the skids and bringing the auxiliary gas tank down on Cal's head. Poor Cal rubbed his aching pate, helped his mechanics rebuild the skids, and was away again early in the afternoon. A bit more than a hour later, *Vin Fiz* hove into view just east of El Paso. Seeing that crowds choked his planned landing site at the racetrack, Cal chose to land instead on waste ground near Evergreen Cemetery. That night at the bullfight, Cal turned away at the moment of truth, saying, "I can't watch it. It would make me sick."

The following day the mechanics discovered that *Vin Fiz*'s engine had crept half an inch to the rear, upsetting the plane's carefully calculated center of gravity. They decided on a complete overhaul. The plane had flown 3,204 miles and was getting tattier and tattier. Meanwhile Robert Fowler, who had departed Los Angeles in a second west-to-east attempt, had followed a southern route and reached Maricopa, Arizona, just as Rodgers arrived at El Paso. On October 30, while Rodgers's mechanics worked on *Vin Fiz*, Fowler crashed into a barbed-wire fence in Tucson, damaging his plane's undercarriage. Plans were laid for the two battered aviators to meet there.

Late in the morning of October 31, *Vin Fiz* left El Paso, bound for Deming in the Territory of New Mexico (it would not achieve statehood until the following January 6). The dry desert air made for good flying, and Rodgers landed at Deming shortly after noon. There, the pilot and airplane took on nourishment, and Rodgers reached the mining town of Lordsburg in midafternoon. A control wire, corroded by the elements despite a protective coating of petroleum jelly, broke during the landing, but Cal glided *Vin Fiz* to a safe stop. Mabel slathered the same jelly on Cal's face to protect him from wind and ice. "Even so, his face was pockmarked as if he had been hit by buckshot," Lebow wrote. "After one particularly scarring day, Cal joked, 'Why doesn't somebody provide a barrel to slide over me with two eye-holes to see through? Why, I could even make my cigars last longer.' " The enclosed cockpit had not yet appeared on airplanes.

At 4:12 P.M. *Vin Fiz* lifted off for the Territory of Arizona, and at 5:30 he landed for the night in the cow town of Willcox, where local ranchers had arrived in horses and buggies to see the first man to fly across the country. They looked on as Cal worked on his airplane, commenting that the newfangled flying machine looked far too fragile to be dependable. As Lebow noted, "For their money, a good horse was still a better way of getting around."

As I left Van Horn the weather cooperated with me, despite having dumped a thunderstorm on the town just before dawn. The clouds drifted off to the southwest while the wind, still blowing from the east, pushed me to El Paso through clear skies, mountains on each side hugging the route as I followed Interstate 10 through the valley. To the south, the Rio Grande drew closer and closer, the tracks and the interstate following the river toward El Paso.

Here the river is anemic, thanks to a warren of irrigation dams and impoundments upstream, and grossly polluted from the runoff of pesticides and fertilizers, as well as human waste. It is a waking nightmare that grows worse the closer one gets to the El Paso–Ciudad Juarez urban sprawl, where more than 600,000 people live on the American side of the river and more than 800,000 reside on the Mexican side. A yellow pall of filthy air hangs over both cities, and each year Juarez drains 60 million gallons of raw sewage into canals, which leak huge amounts into the river. Each year, depending on who's doing the estimating, anywhere from 1 million to 10 million illegal immigrants squirt over the poorly guarded bridges and crossings of the 1,254-mile-long riverine border into the United States. To the illegals, the river is an escape valve, but to the legal residents of the land, it is a breach in the dam that inevitably must transform the southern United States into a Third World frontier that will slowly creep northward like an encroaching tide, bringing with it overpopulation, poverty, and crime. El Paso has become a town of window bars, long steel rods crisscrossing the windows and doorways of those who can afford them.

I banked *Gin Fizz* over the interstate, closer to the Southern Pacific tracks, and peered ahead as I saw a mile-long freight train stopped below. Descending to 500 feet above ground, I saw three men clustered before a boxcar. Were they train crew checking out a hotbox—or were they perhaps modern train robbers?

Almost daily during the 1990s, enterprising Mexican gangs in armored pickup trucks have crossed the Texas and New Mexico border where the railroad passes close by and have fallen upon Southern Pacific trains like *bandidos* out of a Wild West movie. To force the trains to stop, they roll boulders and railroad ties on the tracks, even spray-painting signal lights red to make the crews think they're seeing orders to stop. Sometimes the robbers leap aboard a slowly moving train, breaking into sealed boxcars and throwing the loot to waiting confederates. They haul away VCRs, wide-screen televisions, microwaves, computers, athletic shoes, and other easily fenced goods, escaping over the border with the swag. A few days later the goods turn up in the black markets at Ciudad Juarez and other Mexican border towns. Some gangs are so sophisticated that they send scouts aboard westbound trains to leap aboard eastbound freights at sidings and start searching through the cars. By the time the eastbound trains reach the spot where the gangs' confederates have set up the ambush, the scouts already know what's on board and have the loot all ready to toss out. The Southern Pacific has hired private guards to protect the trains, as well as the sidings where trains stop to let other trains pass, but the guards are spread thin over many hundreds of miles of main line.

Even stretches of highway are not immune to bandits. One of the worst sections is the Paisano Drive corridor just east of El Paso, where the four-lane highway skirts the Rio Grande only a few feet away. There the bandits cross the border, throw up roadblocks, and toss rocks at passing cars. When a motorist stops to check for damage, the highwaymen charge the car, seizing cash, jewelry, and sometimes even the vehicle itself. At that spot the river is only a foot deep. Large boulders carefully placed in a neat path across the trickle of a river allow bandits to make their escape dry-shod.

Seeing no pickup trucks near the freight, I concluded that the figures gaping up at *Gin Fizz* from the train were its crew and banked northeast toward West Texas Airport near Ysleta, eight miles east of El Paso. The airport looked promising as *Gin Fizz* completed her rollout. It was clearly a popular grassroots field, with a long wooden verandah attached to the old mobile home that was the airport office. Under the verandah a long line of picnic tables attested to the likelihood of activity, and most important, an autogas pump stood out among the jet fuel and 100LL pumps. Where there is autogas, there are likely to be lots of older Cessnas and Pipers and antique airplanes. *Gin Fizz* took a healthy drink, the first time since Kansas that it wasn't burning 100LL. But it was Monday morning and all the weekend fliers were laboring at their day jobs.

I opened a new flight plan, this time for Deming, and took off, heading north just 1,000 feet above the ground to stay under the bottom shelf of El Paso's controlled airspace, skirting both the big airport and Biggs Army Air Field just west. I turned west with plenty of room to spare, threaded a wide pass between two mountain ranges, and picked up Interstate 10. The Southern Pacific main line had branched off from the road thirty-five miles to the southwest and was invisible. I decided to hug the interstate, rather than the railroad, through this part of the Southwest, since the Southern Pacific main line often veered twenty or thirty miles away from the highway. It was better to have a well-traveled interstate nearby in case of a forced landing, I thought, than alight somewhere in godforsaken country near the tracks, hoping a train would come through that day. I headed for the Las Cruces airport, just west of the New Mexico city of the same name, and used that for a waypoint, turning west, for Deming forty-five miles away. The Rio Grande flows south to El Paso in the middle of the valley from Las Cruces, and from 3,000 feet above ground, the irrigated greenery on either side of the river stretches richly two or three miles from the river. Past that greenery, there is only empty desert. As *Gin Fizz* droned on, leaving Texas farther and farther behind, I felt lonelier and lonelier.

I am Eastern born and Midwestern bred, utterly unused to the wide open spaces of the West, where one could hike for days without encountering another human being—or even seeing another living thing. In Wisconsin and Illinois, there is something comforting for the traveler in knowing someone will be awake at the farm over the next hill, that under the welcoming copse of trees at the next crossroads there will be a filling station or tavern to pull into for a tankful of gas or a bite to eat. Even a few lonely cows lying on a hill, slowly chewing their cuds, as they have for hundreds of thousands of years, bespeak a benign presence. But up high in the desert Southwest, at 2,500 or 3,000 feet above the ground, I could see nothing. Roads disappeared toward the horizon or into mountain ranges. Not even a shack broke the endless solitude, and I was glad for the distant companionship of another human being, however unseen he might be, when *Gin Fizz* passed over a car or an eighteen-wheeler thousands of feet below.

An hour later I landed at Deming. It was one in the afternoon, and the thermals and gusts down below caused a good deal of bumpiness. I could not find the wind socks and took a guess which runway to use—the wrong one. Just before I crossed the threshold in a sharp slip, I saw the wind socks, which stretched straight out at a ninety-degree angle from the runway I had chosen. The crosswind was just too great—it was seventeen miles per hour, I later learned—for *Gin Fizz* to handle; even with the rudder all the way to the stop and the left wing almost brushing the asphalt, I could not keep the nose straight down the runway. I poured on the coal and climbed away into the landing pattern for the cross runway, which pointed much closer to the wind. My landing was terrible. I came in fast against the gusts and touched down with too much speed, bouncing back into the air and touching down twice more in gooney-bird fashion before the wheels gripped the runway. I hoped nobody was watching.

The FBO on the south side of the field, the one listed in *Flight Guide,* was moribund. Workmen were busily digging the fuel tanks out of the ground, and the pumps lay on their sides. I had hoped to refuel with the advertised autogas, but the harassed middle-aged woman in the FBO said the place was going out of business—her father, the owner, had passed away, and her mother didn't want to run it anymore. She was kind enough, however, to let me plug in the laptop to call Flight Service to close out the flight plan and pointed out the big new FBO on the other side of the field. I started *Gin Fizz*'s engine, rolled her onto a new taxiway and hardstand that didn't show in the *Flight Guide* map of the field, and shut down. An attendant came out and helped me tie down, then called a motel for me—the Grand Hotel. The FBO had been open just two months and showed its rawness. But it was doing brisk business on a Monday morning. A big Cessna 441 executive twin landed shortly after me, followed by a Mooney single-engine speedster with a husband and wife who rode with me in the courtesy van to the Grand Hotel—

decidedly ungrand although clean and adequate—and lunched there. They were flying to Las Vegas from their home in Midland, Texas, for a week of gambling. Both were pilots, both were young, and both were neighborly in the fashion of traveling aviators. They offered to help me check into the hotel—their first thought clearly was my deafness—but I declined with thanks.

That afternoon I discovered that I had finished the Ed McBain mysteries and had run out of reading matter. I should have taken along a dozen books, but hadn't wanted the added weight. It was time to replenish the library. I decided to take the three-mile hike into Deming under the hot sun along the motel-and-auto-parts-store strip, and find a newsstand or bookstore.

Scarcely had I walked a mile along the verge of the highway when a police cruiser pulled up beside me. "Help you, sir?" said the sheriff's deputy in the driver's seat. He appeared courteous but wary, the way cops do when they approach an unidentified sub-ject; he clearly wasn't assuming that a lone man on foot in the dusty heat was necessarily a stranded motorist. Sunglasses hid his eyes, making it more difficult for me to understand him—eyes carry a lot of expression, helping the process of lipreading. But I wasn't about to ask an officer of the law to remove his sunglasses in the blinding daylight just so I could understand him better.

I told him I was deaf but read lips. "I'm at the Grand Hotel," I added, "and I'm going into town to find some books to read. Can you direct me to a bookstore?"

"Where's your car?" he asked suspiciously.

"I came by airplane," I said. "It's at the airport."

He relaxed. "Hop in and I'll drive you," he said. I smiled inwardly. A veteran pilot had once confided to me that in the sticks, the local gendarmerie can often be used as an impromptu taxi service, espe-cially after dark. "We're not a cab company!" a cop will argue crossly when asked for a ride from the airport to town, but since your safety is his business and he doesn't want you surprised on the highway like a deer in the high beams of an eighteen-wheeler, he'll more often than not give you a ride. Something like that must have been in the deputy's mind—or maybe he just had a soft spot for pilots.

As we rolled into town, he asked conversationally, "What kind of plane are you flying?"

"A Cessna 150," I said.

"A 150," he said slowly, his features softening into a smile. "My oldest son used to own one. I went up with him quite a bit before he sold it and went into the service. Nice little airplane." For a while we discussed the merits of the littlest Cessna, then fell silent for several blocks.

"Ever think of flying yourself?" I asked at a stoplight.

"Well, sure," he said after a pause. "It's too expensive, though. And I've still got kids at home." The glint in his eye was brief but unmistakable. It said he was a dreamer, too.

As we rolled up to the store, a used-book emporium, he picked up the radio mike, listened, and spoke into it. "Got to go," he said wistfully. "Good luck." I emerged from the cruiser. Without looking back, he drove away, all business again.

On the paperback shelves inside, I found a well-thumbed Ruth Rendell I hadn't yet read, plus an almost new John Mortimer *Rumpole* opus. While they turned out to be good entertainment, they weren't the best bargains of the day. Those were the rides with the reverend and the deputy.

The sun had just risen, and well before the courtesy van delivered me back to Deming Aviation, I could see the huge red-and-white air-ship rising from the ramp above the hangars, swinging gently in the soft breeze. It was *Bud No. 1,* the Budweiser blimp—the first one I had ever seen close up. She was tethered to a big red-and-white cherry picker–like truck whose extended cupola served as a moor-ing mast. As the line attendant refueled *Gin Fizz,* I ambled over to the airship and took a few snapshots. Three other trucks, including a van, accompanied the cherry picker, and all were gaily decorated in the blimp's Budweiser colors. A young man sat inside the rear "office" of the van. He smiled sleepily as I waved.

"How fast does she go?" I asked.

"About fifty to fifty-five miles an hour," the young fellow an-swered amiably, "less if there's any wind the wrong way."

"Where've you been and where're you going?"

"Where are we now—Deming, New Mexico? He laughed. "It's hard to remember when you're in a different town every day. I think yesterday we were in Midland, Texas. We're going to Los An-geles."

"Me, too, in that 150 over there."

"Where you gonna land?"

"Cable Airport."

He brightened and stood up. "Hey, I'm from Upland, that's where Cable is. Nice airport, too. Hey, you want to look inside the gondola? Climb right in." I did, and was surprised at how comfortable and roomy it was, with airliner-style seats for half a dozen passengers. This, I thought, could be an elegant way to travel, slowly and in stately fashion, with a suitable box lunch and maybe a little champagne. The dirigible companies of the first third of the twentieth century surely had the right idea. This would be *voyaging,* taking your time crossing the country, seeing not only where you're going but also where you've been and exchanging impressions with your fellow passengers—much like laid-back train travel, surely the most relaxed and civilized form of journeying mankind has yet devised. Of course, dirigible flight is hardly economical, especially for a time-conscious age in which people have forgotten how to travel.

Or is it? Even though airships are expensive to operate—hangars, mooring masts, vehicles, and helium supplies make up a costly infrastructure—the storied Zeppelin company is returning to the business. Zeppelin quit making and operating dirigibles after the *Hindenburg* disaster in 1937, choosing instead to manufacture aluminum cookware and other metal goods. At its famous headquarters in Friedrichshafen, Germany, in July 1996, Zeppelin unveiled the framework of a new prototype airship, hoping to launch the finished product the following year. The new Zeppelin, about the size of the Goodyear blimps like *Bud No. 1,* is a hybrid. Like a blimp, the airship's nonrigid shape is to be maintained by internal helium pressure, but its internal frame, like a dirigible, is rigid, made of an aluminum-and-carbon-fiber composite. Another innovation is twin engines that can swivel, providing thrust up, down, or straight ahead, enabling the pilot to maneuver the airship without the huge, labor-intensive ground crew needed for airships of old.

Zeppelin says it wants to fill "a niche between helicopters and airships" with a highly maneuverable craft that can hover in place for hours at a time at high and low altitudes for atmospheric research, surveillance (like the balloon I passed in Texas)—and sightseeing. The current $7.5 million model is designed to carry twelve passengers, and forty-two- and eighty-four-passenger versions are already on Zeppelin's drawing boards.

I looked about a bit more and then walked over to *Gin Fizz,* where the line attendant was rolling the fuel hose back into his truck. "That thing's going to L.A., too," I said, pointing to the blimp.

"Better get going now," the attendant chuckled, "or he's gonna beat you." I wasn't the least bit insulted.

During the forty-five-minute flight to Lordsburg, New Mexico, *Gin Fizz* crossed the Continental Divide, the invisible line snaking across the flat basin-and-range desert floor from between the Mogollon Mountains and the Mimbres Range, twenty miles to the north. If I should crash, I thought blackly, my blood would run into the Pacific instead of the Atlantic.

But the vistas from 2,500 feet above the ground were achingly beautiful, and it was with regret that I glided down to land at Lordsburg, tucked into the foothills of the Pyramid Mountains of the great Peloncillo range of New Mexico. As I shut down, I saw a neatly kept small airport, with six single-engine planes of varying sizes on tiedowns, plus the friendliest airport dog I have ever encountered—even more affectionate than the hound at Dryden. As I opened the pilot's door of *Gin Fizz,* the dog stood on her hind legs and put her paws in my lap, slathering me with joyous licks and gladsome cries. When I told her she was a good girl, she wiggled ecstatically. She was a big mixed-breed, colored like a shepherd but with short hair and an odd triangular-shaped head, her eyes seemingly too close together.

"What is she?" I asked Anna Lee Heemsbergen, the smiling manager of the FBO. Heidi, she said, was the result of an unsupervised encounter between a German shepherd and a shar-pei. Instantly, I saw the wrinkly Chinese breed in Heidi's distinctive head. "Got to take a picture of her," I said, and walked back to *Gin Fizz* to get my camera, followed by the dog, gamboling all the way. But when I pointed my Pentax at her, she turned aside and then put her tail between her legs and slunk away, camera-shy. I shot off a few snaps as she trotted away and hid in the narrow space between a refueling truck and the wall of the FBO, insulted, her privacy violated. I should have asked her first, perhaps proffering a granola bar. The camera-toting traveler must ever be sensitive to the feelings of the natives. Clearly, I had committed a cross-species faux pas. Maybe the dog felt that I was stealing part of her soul by capturing it on film. Or maybe she just didn't like having large black cylindrical objects pointed at her.

I changed the subject. "Did you hear me on the radio?" I asked Anna Lee.

"Sure," she said.

"Did you *understand* me?"

"I guess so. I don't know. I was doing something and wasn't really paying attention." I looked her in the eye. She was being truthful, I decided, not evasive. The radio crackles all day long; in these wide open spaces, transmissions can carry more than 100 miles, and most FBO operators pay little attention to them, unless they hear the word *fuel* or *emergency.* I sighed. I just couldn't let it go, this fretting about the radio.

Just then the British landed—in the shape of a flight of three gaily painted single-seater biplane fighters, the kind the Red Baron fought over the skies of France during the Great War. They were Royal Flying Corps planes, judging from the red-and-blue roundels on their fuselages. After snapping several photos, I put down the camera and followed the airplanes to the gas pumps. Though they looked a little smaller than I would have expected, they still seemed genuine, down to the black Lewis machine guns mounted above their top wings, and so did their pilots, three white-haired men who looked almost old enough to have flown over the Somme in 1917. The pilots were done up in regulation silk scarves, leather helmets, and goggles, and as soon as they awkwardly shoehorned their bulks out of their cockpits and staggered about, loosening up their arthritic legs, they made a dash for the men's room.

When the tallest of the three returned, I engaged him in conversation. The planes, he said, were seven-eighths-size replicas of the S.E. 5a, perhaps the most famous British pursuit plane of World War I. They had been built from plans, everything sized down in perfect scale, except for their engines, whose cylinders poked out from the cowlings. The engines were modern four-cylinder Lycomings of the same model used in the Cessna 152s in which I had trained. The pilots were bound for their homes in Tucson from Midland, Texas, where they had participated in an air show at the museum of the Confederate Air Force, a large private organization that keeps old warbirds alive and flying all over the United States. (So that, I thought, is where the Budweiser blimp had been.) These homebuilt airplanes, I saw, were warbirds on the cheap, and their genuine brothers had flown over the Western Front scarcely six years after Cal Rodgers had landed at Lordsburg. One does not, I gathered, need to be rich to own and fly a warbird—well, a pretend warbird; a real surviving S.E. 5a would likely be too valuable to risk in the air.

"Where are you going?" I asked.

"Tucson," he said. "Avra Valley Airport."

"Hey, that's where I'm going, too."

"In *that?*" he asked, nodding toward *Gin Fizz.*

"Yup."

He shook his head. I chuckled inwardly. His airplane was no bigger than mine and not much faster, either. I could have said the same thing. "See you there," he said.

A few minutes later I took off for my next stop—Willcox, Arizona. *Gin Fizz* crossed into Arizona just twenty miles west of Lordsburg near the Kathrine Playa dry lake, a low spot in the desert basin where water has no place to drain, so just evaporates. The Peloncillo Range receded northwestward, and the desert floor broadened into the San Simon Valley, relieved only by a few low ranges of rock. The air was superdry, hence infinitely clear, and I could see for hundreds of miles in all directions. Far below I could see *Gin Fizz*'s shadow, sharply etched on the sand, pacing me at 100 miles per hour. Shadows are remarkably distinct in the Southwest, where the dry air holds little water vapor to diffuse their edges. Soon *Gin Fizz* approached the gap between the Pinaleno Mountains, topped by 10,720-foot Mount Graham to the north and the 8,300-foot Dos Cabezas range to the south. Interstate 10 and the Southern Pacific main line swing southwest through the gap, a few miles past which lie Willcox and the Cochise County airport.

Cochise County airport seemed bigger and busier than the one at Lordsburg. A dozen singles plus two big twins sat on the ramp; they were executive transports. I saw no executives nor anyone else save a lone woman inside the FBO, so after topping off *Gin Fizz*'s tanks at the self-service pump, I left. This time I trimmed *Gin Fizz* for a long cruising climb to 8,500 feet above sea level, the highest I had yet had her on this trip, so I could fly over the 6,600-foot ceiling of the controlled airspace belonging to the Tucson International Airport and Davis-Monthan Air Force Base, fifty miles west. *Gin Fizz* droned past the Winchester Mountains to the north and then 7,550-foot Mount Glen and the Dragoon Mountains to the south, with Dragoon Pass below at an elevation of 4,351 feet. Benson, Arizona, passed by, and the railroad and interstate slowly turned northwest toward Tucson. On the right, 8,482-foot Rincon Peak, pinnacle of the Saguaro National Monument, stood sentinel against the sky.

I was feeling pleased with my navigation skills. I had not used either the loran or the GPS since I left El Paso, trusting instead on pilotage and dead reckoning—navigation with nothing more than a compass, a watch, and a chart. At long last, I was beginning to look down at the earth in the manner of a bird. It takes time for the human brain to get used to seeing things from a mile up instead of looking at everything straight on, as I had done all my life. Following a lonely interstate highway and a solitary railroad track across the desert had not been a difficult exercise, but determining *Gin Fizz*'s actual position along the asphalt and iron roads demanded a sharp eye to compare features on the sectional chart with those outside the cockpit. Almost unconsciously, I had been timing and marking off checkpoints—mountain ranges and peaks, towns, rivers, dry lakes—as the landscape unfolded and at all times knew exactly my location on the chart and when I would reach the next checkpoint.

This wasn't a simple exercise in old-time navigation just to show that I could do it. Modern electronic navigation systems like VORs, the loran, and the GPS can and do fail from time to time, and when they do, a pilot must rely on skills and instincts first honed by ancient navigators. I was developing "a sense of where you are," the graceful term the writer John McPhee applied to the innate ability of the basketball player (and later U.S. senator) Bill Bradley to pinpoint in his brain the position of his body in relation to the ball, the basket, and the nine other players on the court. After hundreds of hours of apprenticeship, I was at last becoming a pilot.

As the urban sprawl of Tucson approached, two U.S. Air Force A-10 Warthog ground-attack jets flashed over *Gin Fizz*, heading in the same direction but only about 400 feet higher. I braced myself. A minute later *Gin Fizz* struck their wake turbulence with a mighty bump and swerve. Having expected the jolt, I recovered after a moment of wrestling with the yoke. Like ships, airplanes churn up wakes, but the rolling, roiling trail of bubbling air behind an airplane is invisible. Wake turbulence from large airplanes can be dangerous, especially down low near a runway where there is little room to recover. For this reason, pilots of small airplanes avoid landing close behind big jets. Single-seat Warthogs aren't all that large, but *Gin Fizz* is very small, and wakes are relative. For a moment I wondered if the pilots in the A-10s even knew I was there, for *Gin Fizz* presents a small profile from the rear, and by the time it was big enough to be seen it might have been below their line of sight. Or perhaps they had seen me, and one had said to the other, "Let's give the civilian in that Cessna a little surprise." We were not in controlled airspace, but above it. Nothing illegal happened, but the encounter still shook me.

Directly over Tucson, *Gin Fizz* flew over Davis-Monthan Air Force Base and its vast boneyard of thousands upon thousands of surplus military aircraft. Some of these aircraft have been mothballed for the long haul, their cockpit windows coated with a plastic spray to hide the interiors from the hot desert sun, their delicate instruments removed and stored in cool warehouses. Most of these airplanes can be reactivated in case of war, some made mission-ready within seventy-two hours of call-up. They are F-4 Phantoms, A-6 Intruders, C-130 Herculeses, P-3 Orions, and even F-14 Tomcats. From aloft they were lined up in perfect rows with military precision; had I been on the ground I would have seen that the four-blade propellers of the turboprop Herculeses and Orions were positioned in perfect symmetry from top to bottom and left to right.

Other airplanes—in particular Vietnam-era B-52s and Boeing 707 tankers—lay in pieces awaiting the smelters, their wings unceremoniously chopped off, their fuselages torched through in the middle as if guillotined, part of an arms-reduction treaty with the former Soviet Union. They stretched over acres and acres of land, their aluminum skins bleaching in the sun. To a pilot, the sight of a dead airplane, its limbs hacked off, is as unnerving as a slaughterhouse is to a small boy, and I felt chastened. Though most of the airplanes will be cut up and their aluminum sent to be recycled, many of their parts will survive, sold to foreign air forces and airlines. Some entire airplanes go through a rebuilding process and are sold off. Davis-Monthan, however, is not just a graveyard; it is also an active airfield. U.S. Air Force and National Guard squadrons train there, and doubtless those two rude Warthogs were based there as well.

In a few minutes I saw the two cross runways of my destination for the day: Avra Valley Airport at Marana, ten miles northwest of

Tucson. I was still at 8,500 feet, having just left behind the edge of the 6,600-foot ceiling of Tucson International/Davis-Monthan airspace. Since Tucson/Davis-Monthan's ceiling was higher than 6,500 feet, I had been forced to the next higher legal cruising altitude, 8,500 feet. Thus, I had to lose almost 6,500 feet of altitude to land at Avra Valley, whose elevation is 2,031 feet, so I put *Gin Fizz* into a wide, descending spiral turn toward the valley floor, being sure to stay safely clear of 4,687-foot Wasson Peak, just seven miles south of the airport. The task took ten minutes; I kept *Gin Fizz* in a shallow, power-off descent at slow speed to prevent damaging "shock cooling" of her engine by air rushing in through the cowling. My ears popped repeatedly and I swallowed heavily. This was a new and interesting maneuver for me. Ordinarily, I am able to start a gradual descent to an airport from many miles away, like the airliners, and arrive overhead at the proper height.

After the long spiral down, I rolled out from the descent at the precise point at which I had aimed—about 1,000 feet above the ground, approaching the active runway at a forty-five-degree angle, just as the book required. I had not needed to watch the altimeter; I judged my height simply by eye. I made the turns onto base and final, glancing at the airspeed indicator to make sure *Gin Fizz* had sufficient forward speed for safety. My touchdown came with just a small thump. The whole thing had been almost instinctive, and I grinned with pride.

On the rollout, *Gin Fizz* swept past a clump of old four-engine propeller-driven transport planes baking in the sun, mostly DC-4s of 1940s vintage. These planes were, I later learned, old "firebombers," their cargo spaces filled by huge tanks to carry water for dumping on forest blazes. One of the planes was a rarity, a high-winged, twin-engine Fairchild C-123 Provider, once the favorite steed of the Central Intelligence Agency's Air America in Southeast Asia. It had been purchased from the air force's boneyard at Davis-Monthan in the mid-1980s by a warbird collector who intended to fly it to California for restoration, but it developed engine trouble soon after takeoff from Davis-Monthan and diverted to Avra Valley, where it has remained ever since.

Otherwise, I saw that Avra Valley is the kind of airport that many others around the country must have been during the heyday of grassroots aviation in the 1970s and 1980s. It is a large general-aviation airport, with scores of single- and twin-engine planes on

tiedowns under the sun and many rows of long hangars holding aircraft belonging to wealthy pilots. At one end, next to the FBO, is the
airport restaurant, the most picturesque I'd yet encountered, with
saguaro cacti and aloe decorating the short path to the ramp where
I parked *Gin Fizz*. As I sat in the large picture window admiring
N5859E framed by the saguaro, all sorts of planes, from battered
Cubs to expensive Barons, landed for lunch. As the waitress approached, I suddenly remembered that the jury in the murder trial
of O. J. Simpson was to have announced its verdict that day. "I've
been in the air all morning," I said as the waitress approached.
"What was the O. J. verdict?"

"Not guilty," she said with disgust as she plunked down the
menu.

Suddenly, I experienced a deep sense of disorientation. While
flying across the country, I had been reading the local papers and
watching the national television news, dutifully keeping up as well
as anyone else with the events of the day. Yet I had become
detached from them, perhaps affected by my need to forget my
day job, literally living on another plane of existence. Over the
months I had not spent much time thinking about the Simpson
trial, feeling, as did many of my more thoughtful colleagues in the
media, that the nation was wasting far too much time and attention on it. And yet, the details of the trial, particularly the DNA testimony and the revelations of police racism, had entered my
consciousness despite my hypocritically high-minded efforts to
dismiss them as trivial. Like most white Americans, I believed that
the preponderance of evidence was against Simpson and that a
guilty verdict or, at worst, a hung jury would be the result. When I
returned home from this trip, I thought, I would have to push aviation out of my mind if I was to understand what had been going on
in the country while I was away. "A sense of where you are" is a
relative thing, too.

After lunch I taxied *Gin Fizz* from the slot by the restaurant out
to the transient aircraft tiedown and put her away for the day.
Then I took a walk around the airport. On it, there is a museum devoted to transport airplanes, among which is a recently restored
four-engine Lockheed Constellation in the 1950s-era colors of the
Military Air Transport Service over bare polished aluminum. With
her triple rudders and sinuously curved fuselage, the Connie (as
she is called) is to me the most beautiful propeller-driven airplane

ever built. But she was also complex and expensive to keep flying; therefore, few Constellations remain in service while many of her simpler, more robust competitors—the DC-4s, DC-6s, and DC-7s—still labor for freight haulers and firebomber services around the world.

A middle-aged man who had been working on the Connie's landing gear saw me admiring her. Putting down his wrench and wiping his greasy hands with a rag, he walked over. "John Travolta used to own her," he said.

"John Travolta, the actor?" I asked. This wasn't surprising—Travolta is a well-known aviator and aircraft owner, even something of a hero among pilots for landing his Gulfstream IIB executive jet safely after a complete electrical failure in bad weather one night over Washington.

"Yes," came the answer. "He bought her in the early 1980s and was going to restore her, but never got around to it, and in 1987 Vern Raburn bought her and did the restoration. She's been flying since 1991. Goes around to air shows." Now I recalled that I had seen the plane before—at Oshkosh, the big air show visited by hundreds of thousands of aviation enthusiasts each summer in Wisconsin.

The man then told me about the plane's accident the previous summer. One morning, while the aircraft was being taxied across the ramp, a hydraulic line ruptured just behind the instrument panel, spraying fluid around the cockpit and temporarily blinding the crew. Without hydraulic pressure, the Constellation's brakes and steering failed, and she wallowed on down the taxiway. To stop her, the pilots put the propellers into reverse pitch and increased engine power. The reversing mechanism failed to engage, and the airplane accelerated forward toward the perimeter fence. The pilots shut down the engines, but the Constellation kept rolling, plunging through the fence, going across a road and drainage ditch, and finally plowing up part of a cotton field. Nobody was hurt, and the worst damage to the Connie was bent propeller blades. The forty-year-old propellers of the kind the Constellation uses are hard to find, however, and it was many months before replacements were located and the airplane was back in the air.

I returned to the FBO, the Tucson Aeroservice Center, and asked the motherly Hispanic woman at the counter if she knew of any nearby motels that had washers and dryers. My meager kit was again running low on clean clothes.

"I'll find you one," she said instantly and began making phone calls. On the third try she hit pay dirt at a Motel 6, ten miles away, and made me a reservation. Then she called to a line attendant: "Pick up this gentleman's bags and drive him to the motel, please." The friendly young attendant drove me to *Gin Fizz* for my luggage and then headed out to the Motel 6 on the northern outskirts of Tucson. This was, I thought, nice service for a twenty-dollar fill-up. An added fillip to the afternoon was a long glimpse of the S.E. 5as I had seen that morning at Lordsburg. They were parked outside their hangars, their white-haired owners sitting in lawn chairs chatting, no doubt reliving the day's journey from Texas. I rolled down the window of the airport car, waved, and shouted "Yo!" Grins split their ruddy faces as they waved back.

And the Motel 6 turned out to be one of the few I had encountered on my trip that not only had television sets with closed-caption decoders, but also TTYs. I didn't ask for a TTY—the affable woman behind the counter simply asked, when I checked in, whether I wanted one, and I said, "Sure."

This was a pleasant surprise. In the years since the passage of the 1990 Americans with Disabilities Act, which mandates that hotels and motels must provide not only closed-captioned televisions for their deaf and hard of hearing guests but also TTYs, flashing smoke alarms, and doorbell signals, I have stayed in few lodgings that provide these things. In my experience, most hotel keepers simply blow off their legal obligations, reasoning that so few deaf people will stay in their establishments that it is cheaper to stall until they are finally threatened with a lawsuit. Most deaf travelers, like me, haven't the time or inclination to press the issue, and many are too timid anyway. From time to time, especially when provoked by a desk clerk's snippy response to my query about the availability of this equipment, I make a stink, but it's always a useless exercise in frustration. A Montana hotel manager once informed me that he had spent $20,000 several months before complying with the wheelchair-accessible provisions of the ADA, and so far no disabled guest had made use of the new facilities. For that reason, he wasn't going to spend a nickel more on things like TTYs and flashing smoke alarms that nobody was going to use because "disgruntled liberals like you" were unlikely ever to stay at his hotel more than once a decade. So, on the road I always carry my own TTY and hope that the television sets are all newer models that are required by law to have closed-captioning circuitry built in. Sure enough, the televisions at that Motel 6 did, and I turned in, happily gruntled.

# 18

*A*fter first feeding and watering my steed and then myself like a good Arizona cowboy, I phoned the control tower at Chandler Airport in Chandler, a few miles south of Phoenix, and requested clearance for a light-signal landing. Briskly and cheerfully, the tower boss gave me the instructions. The flight took just an hour, and I arrived directly over Chandler at 3,000 feet above the ground, 500 feet above the ceiling of the controlled airspace, and found the runways, tower, and wind socks handily. Taking a deep breath—I hoped to see the light signals easily—I announced my presence to the tower, then approached the airport. Two miles away, a surprisingly bright green light winked welcomingly from the tower. It was unmistakable. As I turned onto the downwind leg, two more bright green blinks affirmed the clearance. And the steady green proclaiming "cleared to land" came on and stayed on throughout the base leg. I had never thought a light-signal landing could be so easy.

As I walked to the terminal past the gas pumps, I noticed a tank emblazoned "80 Octane." "That's the first 80-octane gas I've seen since leaving the Mississippi River," I said.

"And maybe the last," said the line attendant. "Ryan (a big controlled general-aviation airport close to Tucson) stopped pumping it just a couple of months ago."

Chandler, perhaps, was a better place to sell 80-octane gas. On the ramp and in hangars were scattered at least 100 lightplanes, the majority of which seemed to have been built before the late 1970s, when 100LL became the libation of choice for newer airplanes. Unfortunately, I had burned only five gallons of gas since leaving Tucson, so refreshing my tanks with 80-octane gas merely diluted the 100LL in them by 20 percent.

At the FBO I was greeted by two pilots with whom I had corresponded months before on CompuServe. Doug Ritter is a black-bearded fellow in his mid-thirties, and Steve White is a tall, Andy Gump–mustached man about forty-five years old. They drove me to a little airport café on the other side of the field for a burger and a schmooze.

Doug is a freelance writer, a species familiar to me, one committed to lifelong penury. "Fortunately," he said, "my wife makes a good salary." His is a well-known byline in the aviation press; he sells his articles to *Aviation Safety, Aviation Consumer, Flight Training,* and *AOPA Pilot* magazines, but none pays much. However, he had contracted to do his first book, on survival equipment, and had hopes for the future. Even so, I advised him not to give up his day job.

Steve makes a decent living as a professional photographer and is part owner of a Cessna 182. With the Cessna, he flies missions for the Civil Air Patrol (CAP), a half-century-old volunteer auxiliary of the air force that was born during World War II as a civilian early-warning system against infiltrators and saboteurs on the East Coast and the southern border.

The CAP's finest hour came in early 1942, before American industry was able to churn out enough military aircraft for coastal defense. With impunity, German submarines were devastating Allied shipping off the East Coast and in the Gulf of Mexico, often within sight of the American coastline. The fledgling CAP, formed December 1, 1941, came to the rescue. From bases in New Jersey, Delaware, and Florida, CAP pilots—providing their own airplanes and equipment—flew as far as 200 miles offshore (40 miles if the planes were powered by a single engine), looking for U-boats and for survivors of sinkings. They wore military uniforms and U.S. insignia so they would be treated as prisoners of war if captured and not executed as guerrillas. The pilots coordinated efforts to rescue shipwrecked sailors and, though unarmed, made mock bombing runs on surfaced U-boats to drive them underwater. Some airplanes later carried small bombs and depth charges. Of the fifty-seven attacks that CAP pilots pressed home, ten or twelve resulted in hits, and at least one U-boat was sunk. By 1943 "those country-club pilots," as many in the army air forces called the volunteers, had become an official military auxiliary. During that year, the army and navy, now sufficiently equipped, took over coastal patrol duties.

The CAP continued on, towing targets and making courier, liaison, and cargo flights between war plants, patrolling the Mexican border, and flying search-and-rescue missions. In all, the auxiliary flew half a million hours and suffered fifty-nine fatalities during the war. After V-J Day, 1945, the CAP soldiered on; two years later, President Harry Truman signed a bill giving the CAP a national charter similar to that of the American Red Cross, and it was permanently designated an official air force auxiliary. Today the CAP still focuses on search-and-rescue operations—if I had failed to close out a flight plan and the FAA could not find me, the CAP would have sent planes out looking for me. It performs 85 percent of the aerial search-and-rescue tasks in the United States while doing public-service flying, carrying law-enforcement officers into the hinterlands. Few outside the aviation community know of its disaster-relief missions, which included being in charge of all emergency airspace operations during the big Midwest floods of 1993.

More controversial is the CAP's newest task, flying counterdrug missions for the Drug Enforcement Administration. Many pilots believe that the "war on drugs" is a misguided and counterproductive boondoggle, but others, perhaps more pragmatic, consider flying along the Mexican border looking for suspicious activity a legitimate form of assistance to the government. Still others point out that flying low and slow in rough terrain looking for out-of-the-ordinary sights enhances the skills used in search-and-rescue missions.

Steve White has flown his Cessna 182 twenty times along the border, looking for suspicious activity. "If we see something weird," he said, "we radio customs about it, and they decide what, if anything, they want to do." Weird things include seeing a couple of trucks parked back to back or a group of vehicles gathered where nothing agricultural seems to be going on. Such flights don't often hit pay dirt, at least for Steve. What he finds more interesting are "radar evaluation flights," in which CAP planes fly mock intruder flights over the border to test the alertness of radar defense installations. "We'll fly into Mexico and then return without a flight plan in the 'usual places,'" he said of these missions. "Various supervisors know we're coming. Sometimes we're intercepted by F-16s, sometimes the Customs Citations."

"Anything interesting happen yet?" I asked.

"Not really, but I've been flying in the program for only a year. Seeing a Citation at your six o'clock and twenty feet at 120 knots is pretty dramatic, but that's about it for me."

On the way back from the café, I stopped at my plane and found a message on the windscreen from Bob Earl, the tower chief, complimenting me on a "well-executed light-gun landing." "Let's go visit the tower," Steve said, and we took Doug's car around to it.

The tower was a temporary structure, an old military portable installation, in the middle of the field on the edge of the main runway. Climbing up and entering the air-conditioned control room, I saw a large bulletin board affixed to the radio panel. Under "Misc." was the notation *"Deaf pilot* on field parked in transit. Blue/silver straight tail Cessna 150 N5859E. Aircraft can transmit."

"Thanks for bringing me in with the light gun," I told the duty controller, Bob Hifler. "I've never seen one so bright."

Hifler pulled it from a corner. It was a heavy, barrel-shaped model that seemed to date back to World War II days. Its beam is far brighter than that emitted by the modern lightweight model most towers use today. Sometimes old technology works better than new.

"Do you give light-gun clearances much?" I asked Earl as he loomed in the doorway.

"All the time," Earl said. "This has been a towered airport only three months, and a lot of pilots don't know that, and just barrel their way in without clearance or without using radio. We use the gun to keep them away or let them know they've got to call for clearance."

"Don't they read the notams?" I asked. The Notices to Airmen at the end of that morning's weather briefing had clearly spelled out that Chandler was now a towered airport.

"Not often enough," Earl replied.

I just couldn't help asking the chief if he had heard my radio transmission and how it was. "So-so," he said, waggling his hand, and I took that to mean "We heard you but we don't know what you said." Damn.

*       *       *

On the other side of the globe on November 1, 1911, Italian pilots mounted history's first air raid. They dropped bombs on Turkish troops at Tanguira oasis in Tripolitania, Libya, in one of the young century's incessant colonial wars. Nobody realized it at the time, but humanity was stumbling blindly toward World War I and the birth of weapons of mass destruction.

Cal Rodgers knew nothing of the Italian attack. He was less concerned with ominous events in North Africa than with *Vin Fiz*'s battered propeller chains, and not until they were replaced was he finally able to take off from Willcox, Arizona. The wind at Dragoon Pass was blowing at thirty-five miles per hour against *Vin Fiz*, cutting her forward progress down to about twenty miles per hour, but once the airplane had threaded the pass, the wind became a quartering one, improving her ground speed. At Tucson Robert Fowler's airplane was still under repair, and when *Vin Fiz* landed, Fowler rushed to the field to meet his competitor.

According to contemporary accounts, the small talk was brief. "I hope you get there," Rodgers said.

"Thank you, and I hope the same for you. You've had lots of hard luck," Fowler replied.

"We've both had that," Rodgers agreed.

"These few words," wrote Eileen Lebow, preserved Rodgers's popular image as "the daring aviator as a man of few words, but fearless deeds." Both men were also probably anxious to get on with their flights. Fowler left Tucson the next day, but would not reach the Atlantic coast at Jacksonville, Florida, until February 8, 1912. Two hours, two sandwiches, and two glasses of cream later, Cal took off for Phoenix but landed in the moonlight at Maricopa, eighty-five miles down the tracks and twenty-five miles short of Phoenix. The next day, though the propeller chains again needed repair, Cal was still able to take off in midmorning and landed at the Circus Grounds in Phoenix to the usual frenzied crowd. The crowd flooded through a fence around the field, bent on one goal: wresting pieces off the plane to take home as souvenirs. The police, however, arrived in time.

The end was in sight. According to the accounts, Rodgers spoke with a promoter in Pasadena by phone. It is not clear whether he actually listened to the phone himself, which would have been difficult with his badly diminished hearing, or with a go-between serving as interpreter. Cal expected to reach Pasadena within three days, collect a $1,500 purse for landing on the roof of the Maryland Hotel, and wind up the trip at Tournament Park. Collecting a fat purse for his stop in Phoenix, he scrambled aboard *Vin Fiz* and was away for Yuma, 170 miles to the west, hard by the Arizona–California state line.

Reaching the Southern Pacific line just west of Maricopa, he put *Vin Fiz* onto a westerly course with a stiff following breeze, making a ground speed of eighty miles per hour and outdistancing his chase train. With fifty-six miles still to go before he would reach Yuma, Rodgers decided to land at Stoval Siding, a tiny station, to refuel. "For the first and only time on the trip," Lebow wrote, "no one appeared after Rodgers landed, 'not a living soul.'" And not a quart of gasoline was available. For two hours and ten minutes, Rodgers cooled his heels, impatiently waiting for the train, repeatedly trying to telegraph the crew to bring gasoline. When the train finally arrived, Rodgers discovered that not only was the hangar car out of fuel, so was the buffet car. The party would have to wait for another train to bring fuel for both the airplane and the stove, and when it finally arrived, the party had decided to make the best of it, camping for the night in the desert while the chef used a section hand's shack as an impromptu kitchen.

Back at Maricopa that morning, the crew aboard the train had had what was probably one of the last genuine Wild West adventures of those waning days of the frontier. "In the middle of that trying afternoon," Lebow wrote, "the porter suddenly cried, 'Them's Indians at the windows.' Sure enough, the side of the car with its dozen or more windows was a collage of painted faces, as the Indians outside peered through the windows. Mabel was terrified, certain that the Indians were about to scalp the group in retaliation for Cal's landing his 'big bird' among them.

"Mabel sat frozen as the chief entered the car and approached her, showing teeth that looked 'for the world like the fangs of a serpent.' Then he spoke.

"'Me come to thank "White Bird."'"

"Mabel was astonished. 'You speak English?'

"'Yes, ma'am. I go to college.' To her great relief, the chief explained that most Indians used English, except for their names, which were traditional. He had come to wish the aviator well on his journey. Learning that Rodgers had left earlier, the chief brought out a beautiful Indian necklace as a gift for Mr. Rodgers's squaw.

Placing it around her neck, he said, 'I christen you, squaw lady of Mr. Rodgers, the human birdman, with the name of "White Wings."' Mabel was speechless as the chief kissed her hand with a parting blessing. 'I leave you White Father's peace,' whereupon he turned and left. The entire group disappeared as silently as it had come."

Early the next morning, *Vin Fiz* was away again. Impatient to reach Pasadena, Rodgers decided to skip his planned breakfast stop at Yuma and keep going while his airplane was running well and at a good speed. At 8:30 A.M. he crossed the Colorado River and reached California, then turned northwestward along the Southern Pacific line toward the Los Angeles Basin. But the end of his trip was not in the cards, not that day at least. As if in a last effort to thwart him, the "hoodoo" that had accompanied him all across the Southwest struck again, with exceptional viciousness. At 4,000 feet just past tiny Imperial Junction, the No. 1 cylinder of *Vin Fiz*'s engine blew out, damaging the right wing and shooting splinters of metal into Cal's right arm. Now powerless, *Vin Fiz* twice lunged downward before Cal regained control and put her into a wide six-mile glide back to Imperial Junction, where he landed gracefully despite his bloody arm.

When the chase train arrived, Cal, ignoring his injuries, already had the wrecked engine disassembled. While the mechanics rebuilt it, a doctor painstakingly plucked steel splinters out of Cal's arm for two hours. The incident was highly revealing. Today pilots are trained and trained again to handle emergencies instinctively, and the incident was testimony to Rodgers's coolness under fire. He had learned a great deal since he had left Sheepshead Bay. By any standard, that of his day or our own, he at last had become an imperturbable veteran pilot.

Perhaps I have been a little hard on the poor fellow, I thought, as I began to approach the end of my journey. He, and the other pioneer aviators of his day, had to invent the arts of piloting as they went along; they had to learn from experience. If a little common sense had leavened their impetuousness, more of them might have survived to die in bed. But it was that headstrong passion for flying that led to both their discoveries and their deaths. In those days, one could not separate the two.

As Rodgers's party retired for the night aboard the train at the junction, all Pasadena squirmed in excitement, getting ready to let its hair down the following day when Rodgers finally arrived. No planning detail was too fine to be ignored. Automobiles that were parked in front of the grandstand at Tournament Park must lower their tops, the promoters decreed, so spectators in the stands could have a fine view of the landing.

Back in Phoenix, I was getting ready for my own arrival on the West Coast. At Chandler Airport, I first dialed up the weather service and downloaded the forecast for that day and the next. Then I called Bob Locher—the pilot who had introduced me to flying two years before—in Geyserville, California, north of the San Francisco Bay area. He had moved there from Illinois the previous summer. The weather was to be splendid that day and the next, I told Bob; then I asked if he would he like to be my welcoming committee at Cable Airport in Upland, California, just east of Pasadena. Of course, he said, and we made a date for noon the next day. Bob would fly his 172 down in the morning, arriving a bit before my ETA.

Meanwhile, there is no airfield at Stoval Siding, so I would land at Yuma, whose airport is a combined commercial and general aviation field and Marine Corps air station. Months before, I telephoned Yuma Tower to see whether it would give me clearance for a light-signal landing, and the gunnery sergeant in charge of the controllers said, "No problem whatsoever. We'll be looking for you." During the interim, however, the controllers had thought a little more about the implications of my arrival, prompted by the Reverend O. Ray Williams, a local flying minister with whom I had been corresponding by fax and CompuServe ever since he read the article in *AOPA Pilot*.

When I phoned the tower with TTY and relay that morning, the marine tower chief, Gunnery Sergeant Paul Bell, instructed me that Williams would intercept me in his Cessna 172 at 4,500 feet twenty miles east of Bard VOR, a navigational radio station north of Yuma, on the 095-degree radial, an electronic beam extending out from the ground antenna. Williams and I would then fly side by side to Yuma, where the controllers would give him radio clearance for us to land as a flight of two, just like a brace of jet fighters. This, Ray and the sergeant had said, would keep my presence in the controlled airspace at a minimum and make for the most efficient possible landing.

Yuma Tower also asked me to call Albuquerque Flight Service and request a transponder squawk code so that I could be followed all the way to Yuma on radar and Williams could be guided to my location for the interception. In the beginning, I was not enthusiastic about the arrangement—I had been doing light-gun landings all by my lonesome and didn't think I needed patronizing help from anybody—but in the end, I was happy for it.

At Gila Bend I picked up the Southern Pacific main line and Interstate 8. The 160-mile Chandler-to-Yuma flight along the broad Gila River valley was the longest of the whole trip from New York. It took nearly one hour and forty-five minutes, most of it in smooth early-morning air. *Gin Fizz* thrummed steadily across the Sonoran Desert past mountain ranges lined up like regiments in formation: Gila Bend, Sauceda, Castle Dome, and Mohawk. When Williams, flying east, reached a spot about thirty miles east of Yuma, he radioed Yuma Approach and asked for my location. I was, the radar operator said, right on course and right on time. Shortly thereafter, I looked up and to the south and saw an airplane silhouetted against the sky three miles away. It was traveling on a course almost parallel to mine and closing slowly. A minute later I recognized the outline of a Cessna 172. When she was about 500 yards away, I rocked my wings and was answered by the same salute. The Skyhawk pulled in just above and slightly ahead. I picked up my camera and took snap after snap until the film ran out just as the other airplane rose slowly under my left wing 100 feet away, presenting the perfect shot—which I missed. Nonetheless, a thrill coursed through me, and I'd swear that *Gin Fizz* answered with a delicious shudder. Flying formation with a wing tucked under another airplane's was a genuine thrill, and for a moment I was once again a dreamy small boy in a Hellcat, flying combat air patrol with my wingman.

By then, we were approaching the last mountain range before Yuma, getting close to the controlled airspace, and Ray opened his throttle to pull ahead. As I had been instructed, I tucked *Gin Fizz* into line behind him and tried to keep up. Ray, whose 172 was a good twenty-five miles per hour faster than my 150, slowly opened the distance between us—he wanted half a mile to separate the two airplanes when he touched down. As we flew past Telegraph Pass and lost altitude, thermal bumps started tossing *Gin Fizz* like jackstraws on a card table. Coping with them, keeping the fast-receding Skyhawk in view against the ground clutter, and making sure my descent was neither too steep nor too fast made me extremely busy in the cockpit. Then I finally understood why neither the tower nor Ray wanted me to do a lone light-gun landing.

Yuma is an immense warren of eight runways and three different landing-pattern altitudes. At any time of day, Cessnas and Pipers mix it up with airliners, as well as Harriers, Herculeses, and Tomcats. That day two navy F-14 squadrons were visiting Yuma, and if I had been given the usual clearance for a solo light-gun landing, the jets would have had to be vectored away from the airspace for ten or fifteen minutes, effectively shutting it down for radio-controlled traffic while I tootled across the landscape at eighty miles an hour, scoping out the wind sock from 1,000 feet directly above the light-plane pattern altitude, and then entered the pattern for a landing. That would have wasted a good deal of taxpayers' money. But Yuma Tower did not want to turn me away. The intercept and escort solved everyone's problems.

As *Gin Fizz* turned onto final approach for Runway 35, a Marine Harrier hovered near the control tower. A flight of four helicopters approached from the west at 700 feet, two navy F-14s sailed northeast at 1,700 feet, and an Embraer turboprop commuter transport departed on Runway 8. As I touched down, a big Hercules transport loomed lordly and bored on the runway to the right, holding for takeoff while the upstart little civilian finished its rollout.

On the ramp Ray—a whipcord-lean man of fifty-one, who looked more like a weather-beaten rancher in faded jeans and Western shirt than a Methodist clergyman—ducked under *Gin Fizz*'s wing and grasped my hand in welcome. He had invited me to spend the night at his house, but before taking me there, he made me pay the piper. We drove by Cibola High School, where I stood on stage and spoke to the special education students, telling them about Cal Rodgers and the fulfillment of dreams. I was not sure I had reached them—I am not a good public speaker unless I prepare for hours with a speech therapist, and this time I hadn't—but later Ray said, "It's very important to me that they understand that God made them with the same ability to carry on and succeed in spite of perceived hardships. Your courage, confidence, and commitment eloquently attest that one does not have to consider himself a victim of circumstance."

I don't know about "courage"—flying a small airplane is not an exercise in valor, and I am anything but stout of heart—but I agreed wholeheartedly with Ray that deafness does not necessarily mean one must be a victim of circumstance. Not being able to hear can be viewed as merely an inconvenience and only occasionally a major one.

Afterward we stopped by the Yuma Landing Restaurant, built on the site where Rodgers's rival Robert Fowler had landed on his way east. At the time, it was shuttered before reopening, but the owner, John Peach, unlocked it so we could see the aviation memorabilia inside. That evening we went to a meeting of the local chapter of the Experimental Aircraft Association, where I told the two dozen homebuilders about Cal Rodgers and deaf pilots.

I loved being the center of attention after a long and often lonely trip. After long stretches of solitude, interspersed with a few encounters with interesting people, I needed the comfort of an enveloping community, and I found it in Yuma. Of the many good people I had met on my coast-to-coast adventure, few were in the league of Ray Williams, whom I came to know a little during that day I spent in his gentle, amiable company and that of his wife, Carol. We enjoyed a meal together, during which the three of us linked hands while Ray said a blessing. My warm response to the touch of their palms surprised me, for intimate sharing of faith ordinarily makes me edgy.

Part of the reason for my diffidence was that my childhood in a flinty branch of Protestantism had ingrained in me the idea that prayer is an intensely private act, a confidential exchange between sinner and savior. More important, like Cal Rodgers, I had been unable as a youngster to soak up the easy Sunday fellowship of church. Cal and I could not hear sermons, psalms, hymns, or prayers. In my case, services at the local Congregational church were austere and puritan, with a pastor who dispensed an icy brand of damnation. Even if the message had been warmly encouraging, he stood too far away in his pulpit for easy lipreading. As others sang and prayed, I woolgathered, counting the colors in the stained-glass windows and wishing mightily that I was elsewhere.

Sunday school was similarly chilly. In fact, I doubt that any of my fellows in those classes, hearing or deaf, felt any sense of ingathering—if we had any commonality, it was that of prisoners of war with one thought in mind: escape. I suspect that religious indifference, if not outright skepticism, is a common spiritual state among the deaf and hard of hearing of my generation.

Linking hands at Ray's table may just have awakened the sudden self-awareness of a fiftyish fellow facing his mortality, but it also showed a mirror to a man who, in the past few years, had slowly become disconnected not only from his community but from his workplace as his closest friends left and scattered around the country. I was beginning to realize that it was up to me to grasp hands offered in great sincerity. Many of these hands had been held out by members of the aviation community, and that was what had led to my feeling that flying is a special kind of brotherhood. And at Ray's table, our simple linking of palms felt like an acknowledgment of my desire for connection with my fellow human beings—itself a prayer of sorts—and, indeed, affirmed my growing sense that the world was gathering me back in.

Besides, such was my respect for Ray that his invocation seemed the most natural thing in the world. Ray is a pilot, a member of the brotherhood; for me, that fact confers more authority than a whole synod of bishops. Naturally, I wanted to know all about how a Methodist clergyman became an aviator, and Ray told his story simply and directly. He is the son of a Texas restaurateur who settled in Yuma after World War II and, like me, took an early ride in a two-seater that spurred him to build "every airplane model I could get my hands on. I don't remember ever telling anybody I was going to be a pilot, but there was never any question in my mind."

Nor was there any doubt in Ray's mind when he received the call. He and Carol were in church one Sunday night "when I heard a voice. It said authoritatively, 'Choose you this day whom you will serve, but as for me and my house, we'll serve the Lord.' I had no idea at the time that it was from Joshua 24:15." In the same place, a couple of Sunday nights later, "it looked to me like the whole world was standing before me and that God was saying to me, 'There they are: Reach them, help them, teach them.'"

Ray was ordained in 1966 and immediately left with Carol and the first of their three children for Mexico, where they remained for eleven years, working in an orphanage and starting and building churches, homes for the elderly, and a Bible college. They later did missionary work in Guatemala, Nigeria, Central Africa, and Europe.

When Ray was still in his "young and adventuresome" twenties, he met a missionary who had been a pilot for many years. "His adventures were very exciting, and so were his stories," Ray said. "He had walked away from five airplane crashes in Mexico. With his encouragement, I became a student pilot. Immediately after I got my private license, I preached at his funeral. He died while crop dusting. He did a hammerhead stall, and then—it was a foolish thing for him to do."

Ray is now pastor of the Great Commission Christian Center in Yuma and administrator of a missionary organization called I Care, Inc., that has started churches in Mexico, Central America, Africa, and Eastern Europe. In that mission, Ray has used various airplanes, including a big Cessna Turbo 206 that he sold "because we were building a Bible college in Mexico and had nowhere else to turn for money." Two years later, he received the 172 he has now as a gift, and he's had it nine years.

Like most pilots, Ray has a "My Most Unforgettable Moment in the Air" story, and he tells it with humor and relish. "Carol and I were flying over southern California in a rented plane one day. A young gentleman who was working for me sat in the backseat with his wife. It was their first time in an airplane. We were circling at 1,800 feet above the ground over a farm we were considering purchasing. Sudden silence. The fuel tanks had plenty of fuel, but the fuel pump couldn't find it.

"I spotted a highway close by without power lines running alongside it and went for it. This little blue Ford Pinto had the green-style California license plates and was going far too slow. I almost altered the shape of the rear license plate, but, in fact, probably made the most perfect landing of my life. The next vehicle by was a Chevy pickup, driven by a local farmer who happened to be a pilot. He took us to his house to phone the FAA, the California Highway Patrol, the aircraft owner, and a mechanic. As we walked in the door, his mother immediately said, 'I know you. You preached in our church. Thank you for coming to see us.'

"Both the CHP and the FAA said, 'No harm, no foul.' We rented a car for my wife to drive back to Arizona. The mechanic repaired the fuel pump. He blocked one end of the road, and the highway patrolman blocked off the other, a half mile down the road, and I took off. That was the last time I ever rented an airplane."

"Trust in the Lord," I mused, "but fly your own machine."

For Ray the airplane has been a practical necessity, not a luxury. Thirty years ago, Mexico had poor highways, but every ranch had an airstrip. "It would take us four hours by air what had taken twenty hours on the ground," Ray said. "For instance, there's a place called La Villita in Durango, about forty-five minutes by air from Culiacan in the adjoining state of Sinaloa, on Mexico's Pacific coast about 700 miles northwest of Mexico City. La Villita is at the bottom of a box canyon along the San Pedro River. To get there, you either fly, or take a mule for three and a half days."

And at La Villita you just have to rely on God as your copilot. Ray continued, "You approach over the top of a very short dirt strip, head straight for the wall of the box canyon, and suddenly make an 180-degree turn just short of the wall, apply full flaps, remove all power, drop like a rock, and just before your wheels hit the river, give the engine full power to arrest the sink. When the wheels are on the ground, brake hard. On takeoff, put the tail over the river, hold brakes, run up to full throttle, lean for max power, release brakes, and start the uphill takeoff roll. Almost to the end of the 'runway' you ignore the stall warning, put on twenty degrees of flaps, leap over the rocks and house, dive for the river, and follow it until your shuddering airplane starts to climb.

"The first time I went in there, we chartered an air taxi in Culiacan. I went to the dispatcher and complained that our assigned pilot was swigging whiskey. The dispatcher said very matter-of-factly, 'I can't get a sober pilot to fly into La Villita.' The next time I was at the airport in Culiacan, they told me that the pilot had been killed in a crash up in those mountains."

Ray's planes helped him and his organization gain influence with Mexican officials: "Military officers, mayors, senators, the chief of customs always need to go somewhere, and do not always have a way to get there. With the planes we were able to accumulate points and gain influence. Now, when we need a building permit or register a new church, we can always find some government official to help us."

"Is the Mexican version of the FAA difficult to deal with?" I asked.

"Not at all, unless they suspect you are hiding something or violating a law," Ray answered. "Usually they're very helpful. Most speak good English, but I talk with them in Spanish—Spanish was my major in college. The Mexican aeronautical officials are not difficult to deal with at all. They're good people, easy to work with. Sometimes, when I've landed at an airport, they'll say they need someone to fly a rescue flight. They'll put someone in my airplane, and we'll go out on a search mission."

I asked Ray whether he had encountered any hostility as a Protestant in a Catholic country. "In the early years we did," he said, but after Vatican II in the 1960s, the attitude of Catholics all over the world toward Protestants and Evangelicals changed, "and the antagonism and persecution began to cease. In 1960 Mexico was ninety-five percent Catholic, and now it's probably twenty-five percent Protestant. I have a number of friends who are Catholic priests who are content for us to be there, and most Evangelicals do not sense a warfare with Catholicism. We realize that we should be brothers, and we have a common enemy. That enemy is darkness and ignorance and evil."

Ray's flying also gives him respect in some circles that he might not otherwise have, while piquing curiosity. "In Mexico, unlike the United States, only the very wealthy own airplanes," he said. "In the States, the average working person can have an airplane. In Mexico the very wealthy are treated with more respect than they deserve. When you are introduced as a gentleman who owns his own airplane, Mexicans immediately presume you are part of the ruling class and therefore show you an automatic respect. They, however, also presume pilots to be intelligent, and so you are also respected because of that presumed intelligence.

"Only rarely does airplane ownership create a barrier. Only occasionally does someone say, 'Why would you spend your money on an airplane when there are all of these hungry people that need to be fed?' Of course that is a misunderstanding. I say to them, 'Were it not for the airplane, I could not be here to help the hungry people.' The airplane has facilitated my coming, seeing and helping. It is not a curse. It is a blessing."

And that is how I view *Gin Fizz,* too. It has not been merely an expensive toy for an aging boy, but a genuine instrument of liberation for the spirit.

# 19

A sorry-looking *Vin Fiz* slumped before Cal Rodgers in Imperial Junction at dawn on November 4, 1911. Her engine had once again been overhauled, but the parts hemorrhaged oil and glistened with wear. Dirty oil soaked her raggedly patched muslin covering. Twine and glue bound together her tail section. The once-shiny flying wires had corroded to a greenish hue. Secondhand bearings held together the propeller chains. Everyone prayed that the wounded Cal and his tattered machine would be able to hold out during the homestretch of what they hoped would be the last day of his adventure.

Rodgers, now smart enough to be wary of risky takeoff sites, mistrusted his surroundings, choked with sagebrush and mesquite. A couple of miles away, he found an open stretch of sand, and the crew laboriously carried *Vin Fiz* to it after a bout of brush-chopping to clear a path. Cal aborted his first and second takeoffs when the engine misfired. One spark-plug adjustment later, *Vin Fiz* finally was away at 10:40 A.M. for Pasadena.

With less fanfare and less anxiety, I activated the last flight plan of my journey at Yuma shortly before 8 A.M. The plan spanned Yuma to Banning, California, 150 miles away near the eastern edge of the Los Angeles Basin, and I padded the expected time aloft by half an hour because I wanted to do a touch-and-go landing at Calipatria, the airport closest to Imperial Junction, where Rodgers had his run-in with a blown cylinder. Besides, Calipatria, just south of the Salton Sea, is the second lowest airport in the United States, at 180 feet below sea level—only Death Valley's, at minus 211 feet, is lower—and I wanted to make a note of that in my logbook.

Otherwise I felt little excitement that this was the last day of my journey; in fact, I felt regret that it would soon be over and that I would have to start back to Wisconsin. The trip had not been wearying—far from it. In fact, my spirits had soared all the way on the wings of the friendly and generous people I had met along the way. My little airplane had done all that I had asked of her, with nary a complaint except for the cracked door over Indiana. Like Cal, I was becoming a bona fide pilot, as confident and competent in the air as I was on the ground. My only real bellyache had been with the lousy food and lonely evenings of strip-mall America.

Again *Gin Fizz* was a flight of two in company with Ray and his 172. We were doing a tandem takeoff as much for Ray, with the help of a passenger, to capture some in-flight photos of N5859E as it was a safety measure, getting me out of the bristly Yuma airspace as quickly as possible. We had to hold on the taxiway for a couple of F-14s to depart on the cross runway, and the thunderous noise of their engines rocked *Gin Fizz* on her wheels. When the fighters roared off the asphalt, the tower cleared Ray to take off, and when he was about 100 yards into his roll, I opened *Gin Fizz*'s throttle.

As soon as *Gin Fizz*'s wheels lifted off the runway, my blood ran cold. The airplane climbed anemically, and her engine vibrations thrummed slightly rougher than normal. Was the "hoodoo" that had dogged Cal Rodgers that morning in 1911 at last leaping through time to present me with the pilot's worst nightmare—an engine failure on takeoff? Quickly I glanced at the tachometer, then the oil pressure gauge, the ammeter, and the fuel gauges. All read normally except the tachometer, whose wavering needle revealed that the engine was developing only 2,400 revolutions per minute instead of her customary 2,600 on takeoff. Something was not right, but I couldn't put my finger on it.

I looked out the window. The trees at the far end of the runway approached rapidly. Too late to abort the takeoff. Should I climb as best I could, then circle and land? Stupidly, I hadn't made a note of the tower frequency, and I was too busy trying to keep the airplane climbing at a safe speed to read the numbers on the chart. I could have turned the radio to 121.5, the distress channel, declared an emergency, and returned to the airport, hoping the pilots of all that heavy military hardware could hear and understand me and stay out of my way.

But my heart stopped pounding when I realized that the engine was running steadily, not spitting and coughing. Maybe the spark plugs had become slightly fouled from a steady diet of leaded fuel and would burn themselves clean after a few minutes of full-throttle running. I decided to keep going, and if the problem did not disappear by Calipatria, I would land there and hunt up a mechanic.

Meanwhile, Ray had pulled steadily ahead until he was out of sight. As I tucked *Gin Fizz* onto our agreed course just to the west of the Southern Pacific tracks, I saw him ahead, slowing down so I could catch up at the eighty miles per hour that was all I could squeeze out of *Gin Fizz*. Now that I was at the planned cruising altitude, I pulled back on the throttle slightly and then rammed it forward to the stop, trying to clear the engine. No good. Applying carburetor heat for a brief time—maybe ice had formed in the carburetor throat, although that was highly unlikely in the dry Arizona air—did nothing to clear the engine. The tachometer wouldn't show more than 2,450 RPM at full throttle, 300 below normal.

Then I spotted the culprit: the ignition key was misaligned on the RIGHT magneto instead of one click farther right to BOTH magnetos. The ordinary four-cylinder lightplane engine has eight spark plugs, two to a cylinder instead of one, as in an automobile motor. Not only does the extra spark plug provide a safety measure, but it increases the combustion in the cylinder, helping it develop more power as well as run more smoothly. The engine has two magnetos, each providing the spark to one plug in all four cylinders. The ignition key can be set to OFF, the LEFT magneto, the RIGHT magneto, or BOTH magnetos. The pilot starts his engine with the key on BOTH, and during the run-up to test the engine before takeoff, the pilot first turns the key one click left from BOTH to RIGHT, turning off one magneto and its set of plugs so the other magneto and set of plugs can be tested. The pilot returns the switch to BOTH. Then the pilot turns the key two clicks left to LEFT to check the other magneto and its plugs, finally returning the key two clicks right to BOTH. I had missed the second click after checking LEFT.

I laughed in relief, cursed ruefully, and turned the switch to BOTH. *Gin Fizz* surged forward, her engine winding up to a smooth full-power 2,750 RPM. I throttled back to an economical 2,500 RPM cruising speed and leaned the mixture, and *Gin Fizz* settled down to her normal happy roar. I was greatly relieved—and very embarrassed, since taking off on one set of magnetos is a typical stupid student-pilot trick. It is not harmful to the engine, but I was glad I had made the error close to sea level, where the loss of power was relatively small. Among student and low-time aviators, this variation on the pilot's cliché is legion: "There are two kinds of pilots: those who have taken off on one set of magnetos, and those who are going to."

Meantime, *Gin Fizz* had caught up to Ray's plane, and for a few minutes we cruised along chummily, wing to wing, Ray's passenger snapping photograph after photograph as I returned fire with my own camera. By then, our "flight of two" had reached a spot ten miles northwest of Yuma, well clear of its controlled airspace. At the appointed hour Ray rocked his wings in farewell, I did the same, and he peeled away to return to base.

I had to stay carefully to the west of the Southern Pacific main line because for forty-five miles it followed the edge of a restricted military area to the east—a gunnery range—in the Chocolate Mountains, which mark the western boundary of the Sonoran Desert. For another twenty miles, another restricted area to the west of my course kept me on the straight and narrow. Soon Calipatria hove into view, right in the center of the green irrigated squares of the Imperial Valley south of the Salton Sea, a vast lake in the middle of the California desert. I banked to the left, dropped down to pattern height, and when *Gin Fizz*'s tires touched the asphalt at Calipatria Airport, opened the throttle and climbed away at full revolutions.

During his 1986 reenactment of the *Vin Fiz* flight, Jim Lloyd had an embarrassing adventure at Calipatria. At the time, Jim said, the runway was unusable because a ditch had been cut right across it, so the crop-dusting airplanes used the adjoining taxiway for landing and takeoff. "The taxiway was lined on one side by a string of crop dusters of all varieties, and the other side was populated by some rather sobering wrecks. In the hangar, which smelled of banana oil as if someone had spilled a bottle of nail polish, were hundreds of fifty-five-gallon drums with all manner of strikingly colored fluids, red, green, and orange, leaking onto the floor. It was a scene the EPA and the OSHA both would have savored with bureaucratic glee."

As Lloyd pushed *Vin Fiz II* into the lineup of airplanes to take off from the taxiway, he said to his crew, "We'd better get out of here, or any unborn children we may have will arrive with three heads and even numbers of digits on either hand."

He looked up too late to spot the two locals standing nearby, both of whom had heard Jim's remark. They muttered darkly. "I thought, 'Oh, my God, what a faux pas!' I weaseled out of it somehow. I don't remember what I said exactly, but it had something to do with how glad I was that somebody was willing to risk their necks in crop dusters so that we could all eat good food. Later my crew told me I got out of that pretty well."

Jim's remark came to mind as *Gin Fizz* sailed over the Salton Sea, just five miles northwest of Calipatria. A curious place with a curious history, it is an ancient seabed that was originally the northern extension of the Gulf of California. Millions of years ago, silt from the Colorado River formed a natural dam, blocking the gulf and creating a landlocked sea. Over time, the sea evaporated, leaving a dry alkaline sink. In 1905, six years before Rodgers's flight, an engineer named Charles Rockwood and a land developer named Anthony Heber carved a small channel from the Colorado River to a canal they had dug just south of the Mexican border. They wanted to divert water from Mexico to the farmlands of the Imperial Valley. Unfortunately, their channel was so poorly built that when the spring flood of the Colorado coursed downriver that year, it smashed through a headgate in the channel and flowed into the old seabed. By the time the Southern Pacific was able to construct dikes to contain the flow, the water had formed the Salton Sea, thirty-five miles long and fifteen miles wide, California's largest inland body of water. There is no outlet except evaporation, and the sea has become progressively saltier—and dirtier.

The travel-guide prose of the *Smithsonian Guides to Natural America: The Far West* describes the 380-square-mile salt lake, 200 feet below sea level, as a wildlife haven supporting four hundred species of birds, including several endangered varieties, as well as saltwater sport fishing. The reality, however, is that the two river systems created by the blunder that filled the sink, the Alamo River and the New River—the latter often cited as the nation's most polluted—deliver to the Salton Sea the lethal runoff from those barrels Jim Lloyd saw at Calipatria, as well as pesticides from elsewhere in the Imperial Valley and, as a noisome garnish, millions of gallons of frothy untreated sewage from Mexico. The sea has become a toxic toilet that cannot be flushed. Its banks smell of sulphur and feces. Its birds lay cracked eggs and deformed embryos. Its seafood has been declared off-limits for children and pregnant women, and healthy adults are warned to eat only eight ounces of Salton Sea fish in any six-week period. Tourism has dropped off precipitously, and adventurous souls who still swim in the sea make sure to shower immediately after emerging. As *Gin Fizz* droned past its northern shore, I looked down at the pale green water and thanked my stars that I was passing by at nearly a mile up.

Near Thermal, seven miles inland from the Salton Sea's north shore, I put *Gin Fizz* into a descent to just under 3,500 feet to avoid the Palm Springs Terminal Radar Service Area, an oddly shaped 800-square-mile piece of controlled airspace rising 10,000 feet from the desert floor. Strictly, I did not need to do so, for radio communications are not required within a TRSA. But traffic is likely to be heavier inside one, and it simply seemed prudent to give it a wide berth. Spotting the cross runways of the airport at Thermal reminded me of Jim Lloyd's story of his run-in with the FAA there.

A safety inspector had come out to Thermal, Jim said, to do ramp checks at a balloon race, making sure the entries met all the legal requirements for airworthiness. "He wanted to bust balloons. And the race didn't happen because it was too windy, so he had to find somebody else to give a hard time, and that was me. He wanted to see all my papers. I was missing one—the aircraft registration. I had lost it somewhere. I told him I was trying to get a 'ferry permit' from FAA headquarters at Oklahoma City, but had had no cooperation. I needed to finish this flight, I told him, since President Reagan was supposed to call me when I arrived in Long Beach. He was typically unimpressed and wrote me up."

Later, when Jim landed at Long Beach, the FAA cited him again for not having the document. "The female inspector who busted me was embarrassed about it," he said. "She didn't want to do it. She waited until the welcoming crowd had evaporated, and she came out meekly and said, 'I have to do this, you know. I didn't want to do it with all the people around because frankly, I'm ashamed to cite you.' But this guy at Thermal had turned me in, and she had to do it. After it was all over, I got a nasty letter from the FAA. I wrote a long and apologetic reply, telling them what happened, why I didn't have the registration, and I also told them about the political pressure and the patriotic nature of the flight. Safety was never compromised, I said. It was only that I didn't have a single piece of paper. And the FAA replied, 'Yeah, it's no problem. We're not going to do anything. We have to put this in your file, but we won't take any action. They knew it was ridiculous. It was a slap on the wrist."

As it turned out, Reagan never called Lloyd. "He couldn't wait for me since I was about three hours late. The plane was slowly falling apart." The propeller had to be replaced in Pomona, and the landing gear was disintegrating. "He sent a telegram instead, and I never saw it because the Armour PR people kept it."

After passing Thermal, I hugged the western edge of the Little San Bernardino Mountains along the Joshua Tree National Monument, to avoid having to descend below 2,000 feet to evade another piece of the radar service area. Remaining at 3,400 feet, I slowly turned east toward the Los Angeles basin and pointed *Gin Fizz* toward the San Gorgonio Pass, also known as Banning Pass for the city in its midsection.

Banning Pass, which runs between the 10,000-foot peaks of San Jacinto and San Gorgonio two miles apart, is an enormous wind tunnel, a natural venturi shaped by mountain ranges that pinch a westerly wind from the Pacific Ocean at the waist, causing it to gather speed—and turbulence. The pass is an infamous graveyard for lightplane pilots who are cheeky enough to challenge it on a gusty day. So strong are the winds that California harvests them for electricity. On the eastern edge of the pass lies a vast "wind farm," thousands of acres of propellers mounted atop tall columns, spinning in the breeze like a forest of pinwheels. In the middle of the farm is a power station that collects current from the generators mounted below the propellers and sends it all over southern California.

The morning Cal Rodgers flew through Banning Pass, the wind was blowing, he said later, in "five or six directions," turning *Vin Fiz* into a handful to keep level and steady. Worse, the engine was once again protesting the steady abuse it had received for thousands of miles. The magneto worked loose, a connecting rod broke, and the radiator leaked. With one hand grasping the jumping connecting rod steady and one knee holding a control lever, Cal nursed *Vin Fiz* toward Banning. Just as the magneto finally broke away from its mountings, Cal put his machine into a glide and landed safely in a plowed field.

The special train lagged an hour behind *Vin Fiz*, however, so the mechanics did not arrive to attack her problems until after lunch. Once its magneto was refastened and the leaking radiator was repaired, the engine seemed ready. But Cal found another loose connecting rod, and after he ordered the crankcase opened, the mechanics discovered that a bearing was missing. Heavy repairs were needed. By then it was 4:30 P.M. Clearly *Vin Fiz* would not make Pasadena that day, and the expectant thousands at Tournament Park were sent home disappointed to await the flier the next day at noon.

I was a good deal luckier the morning *Gin Fizz* flew through Banning Pass. The breeze blew gently from the east at eight or ten miles per hour, instead of blasting out of the west at thirty-five to forty miles per hour and slowing my forward progress to a crawl. The propellers on the wind farm rotated—the ones on the side of the mountain briskly, the ones in the valley lazily. Flying through this notorious pass that October morning was like strolling in the park. Within minutes *Gin Fizz* landed into the wind on Banning Airport's Runway 8, with an unusually long rollout, because, I discovered, the runway slants sharply downward to the east in a 2.4 percent drop. In fact, there seems to be no level space on the airport; wheels have to be carefully chocked so airplanes don't roll away and break something. While *Gin Fizz,* well chocked, took a drink of 80 octane, I walked into the FBO with my TTY and closed out the flight plan.

"It's rare for the wind to be blowing from east to west, isn't it?" I asked Dan Hunt, the airport manager, as I looked up from the TTY.

"Yeah, it happens only three or four times a year," he said, "usually in the summer when the monsoon comes up from Mexico."

"Do those propellers at the wind farm turn to face the wind?" I asked.

"The ones on top of the hill do. They're mounted on gimbals. The ones in the valley stay stationary—they can generate either forwards or backwards."

"That was my guess, too," I said. Then I bent to the TTY and called Cable Airport in Upland, the grail of my flight. I had chosen Cable not only because it was the uncontrolled airport closest to Pasadena but also because it seemed the most convenient and perhaps least dangerous in the almost impossibly crowded Los Angeles Basin, whose airspace is a crazy quilt. To get to Cable from Banning, I had to avoid the controlled airspace of March Air Force

Base and then Riverside Airport and climb to 5,500 feet to elude the Ontario International Airport airspace. To make matters more complicated, the controlled airspace of Brackett Airport at Pomona lies just five miles west of Cable. Cable's uncontrolled airspace is a mere three-mile-wide semicircle, cut out of the edge of Ontario Airport's 20-mile-wide controlled airspace like a bite taken out of a pie. In short, Cable is surrounded by controlled airports on three sides and the mountains on the fourth. It was going to be a tight fit, and to make matters easier, I decided to phone Cable's flight school and ask for the winds and active runway so I wouldn't have to drag the airport to find the wind sock and maybe bust airspace I wasn't allowed into. The active runway was Runway 24, and the wind was from the south, the attendant said. She seemed confused, asking if I was really a deaf pilot. I learned later that she thought my relay call was from a deaf student pilot at Cable who wasn't due to start his lesson there for another hour.

On Sunday, November 5, 1911, all Pasadena cheered excitedly at the news that *Vin Fiz* was at last in the air. By midafternoon in Tournament Park, thousands of pairs of eyes scanned the sky to the southeast, looking for Rodgers, who had stopped at Beaumont to fix a broken fuel line, then Pomona to catch his breath and refuel. A great shout arose as a speck appeared, then materialized into wings and fuselage. *Vin Fiz* soared over the park and the city, did a spiral and a dip, and glided gracefully to a landing on a white-cloth marker in the center of the park.

"A maelstrom of fighting, screaming, out-of-their-minds-with-joy men, women and children" enveloped Rodgers, according to an onlooker. Policemen burst through the human tide and rescued the aviator, struggling through the crowd to bring him to the grandstand some twenty minutes after *Vin Fiz* had landed. A delegation of wives of the town's pooh-bahs presented Cal with a bouquet, and someone draped an American flag around his shoulders. He rode an open car in triumph around the track.

"He remains outwardly unimpressed, the same cool imperturbable aviator as when people were joking of his efforts to cross the country," the *New York World* announced the next day. It mentioned "the man's utter coolness and indifference to the plaudits of the crowd," and other reporters noted that he stayed "unflustered and wreathed in a cloud of cigar smoke."

Swept off to his hotel, Cal signed the registry, the press reported, as "C. P. Rodgers, New York to Pasadena by air" and held forth like a visiting potentate, bellboys scurrying to do his bidding while newsmen gathered around worshipfully.

"The trip was not a hard one, all things considered," he said in one of the age's most astonishing understatements. "Indeed, I believe that in a short time we will see it done in thirty days and perhaps less." He had covered 4,231 miles in a total flying time of eighty-two hours and six minutes over forty-nine days, at an average speed of 51.59 miles per hour.

At breakfast the next day, Cal and Mabel Rodgers totaled up the statistics of the flight. Not only had it taken 1,230 gallons of gasoline to make the flight, the enterprise had used up six back skids, five front skids, eight propellers, six double sets of wings, three seats, two radiators, six cylinders, two steering rods, two engines, two tails, two tail springs, four propeller chains, four back-tail skids, four fins, one elevating plane, countless struts, and an unknown number of fabric patches and pieces. The only original parts remaining from *Vin Fiz* that had flown all the way from Sheepshead Bay were the vertical rudder and drip pan—and the bottle of Vin Fiz that had been tied to a strut; it had made the trip unbroken.

The flight was officially over, but Cal wanted to wash *Vin Fiz*'s skids in the Pacific and looked about for the coastal town that would offer him the largest purse to do so. Long Beach, Santa Barbara, San Diego, and Venice offered bids, and Long Beach won with a $1,000 offer. The mechanics repatched and repaired *Vin Fiz* from their stock of rapidly diminishing parts while Cal was driven around Pasadena giving countless short speeches, receiving innumerable plaques, and accepting plaudits at dinner parties.

At 3:34 P.M. on Sunday, November 12, *Vin Fiz* took off for Long Beach, twenty-three miles southwest of Pasadena, an easy half-hour flight. Shortly after his climb-out, however, Cal's engine began coughing and then stopped. Cal put *Vin Fiz* down safely in a small valley just east of Covina Junction and discovered a broken feed line from the gas tank. While the repair was made, Cal blamed himself for not checking the machine thoroughly before takeoff. Henceforth he would do it himself and not trust the job to others. "The mechanics had heard that before," Lebow wrote. I think that this was another indication that despite his long education in hard knocks, a tendency to hastiness underlay Cal's outward coolness; the conscientious pilot then, as now, always made a meticulous preflight examination of his airplane before takeoff.

Though *Vin Fiz* was in no condition to continue the flight, Cal, ever bull-headed, insisted on making it. As onlookers lighted bonfires at Long Beach to guide the aviator through the twilight and darkness, Cal took off at 4:57 P.M. What happened fifteen minutes later is unclear—the *Vin Fiz* entourage tried to spin-doctor the event with a "theory" that Cal had suffered from "ethereal asphyxia," which lurks in "air pockets." An eyewitness said, however, that the engine suddenly stopped, Rodgers leaned forward to pull a lever, and *Vin Fiz* plunged nose first 150 feet to the ground near Compton, throwing Cal face first into soft dirt. When rescuers arrived, he was lying face down, a fuel line across his neck and the engine pinning his legs. "Where's my cap?" he asked, and fainted. He was bruised and concussed, his face burned, and an ankle badly sprained. Once again he was extraordinarily fortunate to have gotten away with that stubborn impetuousness.

His ankle healed slowly, and a month passed before he made a second attempt. Finally, as 50,000 spectators waited at Long Beach Pier, Cal lifted off at 3:44 P.M. on Sunday, December 10. He flew south over Signal Hill and out across Devil's Gate at 1,500 feet. At Long Beach two other pilots joined up in welcome: Beryl Williams in a biplane of his own design and Frank Champion in a Blériot monoplane. At 4 P.M. *Vin Fiz* touched gently down on the sand. Hundreds of onlookers helped push the tattered plane the last few yards to the Pacific, where cameras clicked as *Vin Fiz*'s skids touched the surf. It was done.

Eighty-four years later, *Gin Fizz* lifted off from Banning and flew west into the deep smoggy haze that so often envelops the Los Angeles Basin. It was just after noon, and the sun was still high. Veteran California pilots warn newcomers not to attempt an east-to-west arrival much after early afternoon because the glare of the sun slanting through the smog makes it almost impossible to see ahead. "Fair is foul, and foul is fair / Hover through the fog and filthy air," I sang with the three witches of *Macbeth* as *Gin Fizz* cut through the murk. The visibility was just over the legal minimum of three miles, so I relied on the GPS to guide me to Cable Airport.

As it turned out, there was a bit more room than I had expected between the mountains and the northern edge of the Ontario controlled airspace, so *Gin Fizz* was able to descend in uncontrolled airspace from 5,500 feet to the Cable traffic-pattern height of 2,250 feet in a shallow power-off dive. Because of all the surrounding controlled airspace, entering the landing pattern for Cable's Runway 24 is a bit odd. The pilot first flies west, paralleling the east-west runway about four miles north of it, then turns south and crosses the western threshold of the runway at an altitude of 800 feet—enough to avoid departing planes. The pilot then turns east to parallel the runway again on the downwind leg and just past it, turns north on base leg and west on the final approach to the runway. It is a perfectly four-sided, rectangular landing pattern. The landing all went well, despite the gathering, gusty wind, which kept *Gin Fizz* bouncing merrily all the way down the final approach.

Just as *Gin Fizz* crossed the threshold, I spotted, out of the corner of my eye, the unmistakable bearded figure of Bob Locher looming just off the runway numbers, a tiny camera in his fists. He was my crowd of thousands come to hail the conquering hero at the end of a long and arduous journey. I was gliding in a little high and fast, however, and my landing was an embarrassingly inelegant three-bounce crow-hop.

On the rollout and taxi to the ramp, I felt slightly disappointed. It all had seemed so easy. The weather had been nearly perfect since I left Chicago. There had been no challenging hurdles, no skin-of-the-teeth adventures except for the near collision over Illinois and the encounter with the buzzards in Texas. I had not risked my neck. I felt exactly as I did during those first few hours after being awarded my private pilot's license, that I had been presented with an unearned gift.

But I quickly stifled the emotion because Bob clearly had no doubts. At shutdown he strode forward and clasped my hand in his enormous paw, a brilliant grin wreathing his face. "Congratulations!" he said in heartfelt welcome. As my mentor, instigator, henchman, co-conspirator, and partner in crime for the last year and a half, he had invested nearly as much thought and emotion in the flight as I had. That evening, after checking in at the curry-scented lobby of the Comfort Inn nearby, we celebrated in our room with the gifts he had brought: a can of smoked oysters and a bottle of Sonoma County merlot. Later we repaired to a Mexican restaurant down the street for a huge dinner, washed down with a couple of bottles of Dos Equis, all the while reliving the saga of *Gin Fizz* and laying plans to complete my journey to the Pacific. The next day we planned to fly together in N3979Q, the Skyhawk in which he had introduced me to the joy of flight a little more than two years before, to Santa Catalina Island, twenty-five miles southwest of Long Beach. There I would ceremoniously dip my toes, in lieu of *Gin Fizz*'s wheels, into the Pacific surf.

Before we got up to leave, slightly wobbly, I said: "Bob, you never told me how you got into flying. Was it the fulfillment of a childhood dream?"

"As a boy I didn't really dream of being a pilot," he replied. He had built the usual plastic airplane models, but the idea of becoming an aviator never occurred to him. For one thing, his mother had done her best to instill in him a fear of heights and of small planes. As a youth, however, he was "in a small way a daredevil. I was always trying new things that would have terrified my mother, but at the same time was always careful. I was a climber—I'd climb any tree as high as I could with nary a slip. And later I climbed antenna towers most of my ham life, and still do."

There is a kind of affinity between a ham and a pilot because amateur radio shares a distinction with general aviation: Practitioners of either need a federal license. Also, "both amateur radio and flying are full of technical points, and both are potentially dangerous. High-voltage transmitters can kill you. Being a ham who does antenna work on top of towers means putting your faith in the work that was done before: that the tower is strong enough to hold you, that the guy wires are properly attached, and that your climbing belt is secure. You are putting your life into it.

"But maybe my mother's fear of small planes did have some effect. I never feared them until the neighbor across the fence from our house gave her husband a certificate good for a trial flight, one of those twenty-five-dollar half-hour specials to see if you like flying. He was hooked, and that led to lessons and a private pilot's license. He started in on me to give it a try, and finally I agreed." Bob's friend set up an appointment for him with his instructor, who happened to be a tiny, attractive young woman.

"The day of my ride came. I drove up to Waukegan Airport. As the car neared Waukegan, I grew progressively more terrified. I was desperately trying to figure out a way to get out of it. That the instructor—whom I had not yet met—was little and a gal only added to my dilemma. How could I, a macho male, be afraid of something if she was a accomplished pilot? How could I explain that to my equally macho neighbor?"

Unable to come up with a convincing excuse, Bob arrived at the FBO. True to his friend's reports, the instructor, Cindy Kilgore, indeed was "young, cute, and weighed not 100 pounds soaking wet. I suspect she sensed my fear and wasted little time shoehorning me into the Cessna 150. Into the *left* seat! God. She fired up the engine, talked to the tower, taxied to the active, and began the takeoff roll. Moments later we were airborne, and by the time we were fifty feet off the ground, I was absolutely in love. As you know so well, there is nothing like the feeling when the ground falls away from a light-plane—it's so different from the takeoff in a big jet."

Less than five minutes later, Cindy told Bob to take over. "I took the yoke, and in little ginger steps started feeling out what the airplane would do. It was fantastic. Then Cindy showed me a steep turn, using a farmer's silo as the center point. It was fascinating to look almost straight down in a forty-five degree bank through the side window into the barnyard. That scares the pee out of a lot of people." He grinned broadly.

"Yup," I said, remembering a March day with Tom Horton a couple of years before and matching his grin cheek for cheek.

"I think Cindy was calibrating my pucker factor," Bob said. In one of his old flying books, he added, Richard Bach rated his green-horn passengers the same way. "If, in a sharp turn, they kept their heads level with the airplane's attitude instead of trying body English to bring the world back to level, he knew they had potential as pilots and would tell them so after the flight. While I was a painfully slow learner, I think I did have, in my own small way, the right stuff."

Bach, I mused, never would have thought *I* had the right stuff, not during that terrifying second lesson in 1993. But Tom had. If I was not a "natural" pilot, whatever that is, I still could be trained into a competent one. And that was all I needed.

"When we landed," Bob continued, "Cindy thanked *me* for a nice ride and asked if I wanted to do another lesson. I said 'Yes!' On the spot she sold me a logbook and logged the flight. I am still using that logbook and still carrying that entry."

Did the yen to fly, I asked, perhaps involve a bit of a midlife crisis?

Not really, Bob said. At that point in his life, learning to fly was "not inappropriate for my interests, my financial situation, and the fact that I had been unconsciously looking for something that would expand my life, to put a little pizzazz into it." He paused. "Which I guess one could call a midlife crisis."

# Epilogue

A fter the cheers died down, Cal and Mabel Rodgers settled in Pasadena, which had given them such a warm welcome. Cal talked about opening a flying school, but never got past the talking stage. He spun grandiose dreams of flying the Atlantic to collect a $100,000 prize offered by the Aero Club of France. He would need, he said, an airplane capable of 100 miles per hour and an endurance of twenty-four hours. Part of his scheme was to station ships at 100-mile intervals between New York and Southampton, England, as a safety measure. The practical details were vague. Someone else would take care of money matters, as had happened all the way across the United States. Courageous and tenacious he may have been, but Rodgers was neither an organizer nor a businessman.

On January 1, 1912, Cal—as king of Pasadena's Tournament of Roses—flew along the parade route, dropping carnations on the wildly cheering crowd. Later that month, he took a train to New York, where on January 27 he received a medal at the Aero Club dinner, with President William Howard Taft in attendance. His short, shy speech of acceptance was so quiet that only those nearby heard him, and he sat down quickly with relief. Only the French ambassador had anything of consequence to say, and it was this: In future wars, nations would have "to defend themselves skyward." Scarcely two years later, he would be proved right.

On the way back to Pasadena, Cal visited his cousin John

Rodgers in San Diego and flew the navy's Wright "hydroplane," a float-equipped airplane. Out loud Cal contemplated a flight along the length of the Pacific Coast to Alaska, then a Winnipeg-to-Mexico City flight, and finally wondered about flying surveillance for the federal government along the Mexican border. And at Long Beach he sold rides in his airplane, the freshly re-engined Model B he had bought from the Wright brothers the previous summer—not *Vin Fiz*, too worn out ever to fly again.

Wednesday, April 3, 1912, was a sunny, warm spring day. Cal gave one student a lesson, then prepared to take up a young woman for a ride. Just before 3 P.M., Cal took the Model B up for a short spin, flying out over the pier and the Pacific at an altitude of 200 feet. He turned back toward the pier, diving his airplane through a scattering flock of seagulls to pick up speed for a flashy roller-coaster hop over the pier. In the middle of the forty-five-degree dive, Cal was seen to look behind him suddenly and then try to stand. The Model B struck the surface of the sea, then the sand two feet below. It crumpled. Cal died instantly when the engine, torn from its mounts, shattered his spine.

Friends and fellow aviators proffered various explanations for the tragedy. Cal had been drinking, some whispered, but this rumor was absurd because he was a lifelong teetotaler. Others said he had grown careless, which was more than likely. His cousin John Rodgers said Cal had pulled out of his daredevil dive too late, the Model B's skids catching the water. One of Cal's crew said the wind had been gusty that day, and a puff had caught Cal's tail in the dive, delaying the pull-up that might have saved him. Weeks later, Mabel announced that a seagull had been found wedged between the fuselage and rudder, preventing the machine from maneuvering. Nobody knows the truth, but I often wonder if Rodgers's determination to prove to hearing people that a deaf man could make good—in itself an attempt to communicate with them—led him to show off one time too many.

Rodgers was the 127th pilot to die since records had been kept. He was buried on July 6, 1912, near the grave of his father in Allegheny Cemetery in Pittsburgh. On his monument is the motto "I endure, I conquer."

When asked what he thought about Cal's epic flight, Thomas Sopwith, his contemporary and fellow pilot, said: "Not much." But Cal's accomplishment was a real one. He was the first. He proved that flying from coast to coast could be done, although the way he did it—with short hops and an expensive entourage, including a chase train—was hardly practical. He did not advance the arts of aviation. Still, his mark stood until the end of the decade. Not until 1919, after a quantum jump in aviation technology, was Cal's record for a coast-to-coast flight broken. Lieutenant Belvin Maynard of the U.S. Army flew a de Havilland D.H.4 over a more direct route—2,701 miles from Mineola, New York, to San Francisco—in three days, eight hours, forty-one minutes, and thirty seconds.

After 1911, the pace of aviation progress accelerated so rapidly that Cal and his primitive Wright Model EX quickly faded into the dust of memory. During the four wartime years between 1914 and 1918, speeds jumped from 55 miles per hour to 120 miles per hour. Airplanes became bigger, with enclosed cockpits, and larger, more reliable engines. Most important, they became useful—first, of course, as instruments of war, but immediately thereafter as vehicles of commerce.

During our interview in Washington, Eileen Lebow said she thought that if commercial radio had been around in 1911 to lend a timely immediacy to his feat, Cal would have been better remembered. Just sixteen years later, Charles A. Lindbergh landed in Paris while the world listened in live; he was the world's first electronic media hero. In our own time, Neil Armstrong set foot on the moon as the entire globe watched on television, and people remember his name.

Cal, for all his taciturnity, was a colorful fellow. By turns he could be careless, impulsive, defiant, cheerful, and stubborn. Always he was extraordinarily courageous, persistent, and enduring. But these things—as well as having been the first to fly across the country—cut no ice with today's packagers of commercial heroism. "We have a cousin in California who deals in movie and television properties," Eileen said. "She contacted somebody at Disney because they've got the money and they could do a very good job doing a movie of Cal Rodgers flying across the country. The man from Disney wrote back, saying, 'Well, gee, he only did this for money and for a reputation. We're looking for more uplift.'"

As far as riches are concerned, Rodgers left behind an exceedingly modest estate, Eileen wrote: just $12,960 in cash and letters of credit, a $5,000 Wright biplane, a $1,200 Wright wreck, a $1,500 automobile, and a $10 watch. Total, $20,670.

What happened to *Vin Fiz* afterward is not clear. Most sources say the airplane went back to the Wright company and was destroyed after the brothers' shop in Dayton was closed. Others say that Rodgers's widow donated it to the Carnegie Museum in Pittsburgh and that it eventually ended up in the National Air and Space Museum. Whichever story is true, a collection of parts was completely restored and has been known as the real thing ever since. It hardly matters; the airplane that arrived at Long Beach, except for a stick or two, was not the craft that took off from Sheepshead Bay.

The day after my arrival in Upland, Bob and I paid for our excessive celebration—or, rather, Bob did. I have the digestion of a goat, but Bob had just spent an arduous week at his various businesses, and the combination of the ensuing stress and our generous feast gave him terrible gas pains. All morning we tarried around Cable Airport waiting for Bob to recover and finally returned to the motel, but it was not until late afternoon, after a rest and most of a roll of Tums, that his bellyache departed. A good night's sleep would complete the recovery. I was not bothered, for there was another chance to wet my toes in the ocean. The next day, after Bob left for home, I was to fly sixty-four miles southeast to Oceanside, on the coast, to meet a pilot who flew missions for Angel Flight, a charity organization that ferries patients between home and hospital. Then I would start the long trip back to Wisconsin.

Murphy's Law, however, had settled in for the weekend after gently brushing me for so long. That morning thick fog squatted over the Los Angeles Basin like a great gray toad. Not until 10 A.M. did visibility over Upland improve to the legal three miles. After a round of handshakes and solemn promises to meet the following summer at the big fly-in at Oshkosh, Bob climbed into his Skyhawk and soared over the mountains to clear air and a smooth trip back to Healdsburg Airport, down the road from his home in Geyserville. Elsewhere in the Los Angeles Basin, airports were reporting surface visibilities of two and a half to three miles. I hate to fly in anything less than five miles' visibility, so I waited several hours for the mist to clear.

The hell with trying to reach the coast, I told myself. I could be stuck here for days, unable to start back to Chicago. I had only a week left of my vacation, and who knew what weather extremes I'd find between here and there to keep me grounded? I'd just declare

Upland my last westbound stop, and if I could get back through Banning Pass to the clear air of the desert, I thought, I'd have a good start for home the next day. By early afternoon, the fog toward the east had lifted enough for safe flight, and I finally took off and emerged from the Los Angeles Basin.

Two days later, at Gallup, New Mexico, *Gin Fizz* experienced her only mechanical woe of the trip, other than the broken door in Indiana. During the night, the temperature at that lofty airport—more than 6,000 feet high—plummeted to twenty-four degrees, and the cold plus the steady diet of 100LL gasoline finally got to *Gin Fizz*. She started easily enough, but during the runup, the engine quivered and rocked like a dog in intestinal distress, and twice the roughness at full throttle caused me to abort my takeoff. I looked up a mechanic, a young Navajo, who got right to work and cleaned the plugs, which were badly caked with lead deposits. *Gin Fizz*'s troubles after a transcontinental flight seemed picayune, however, compared with *Vin Fiz*'s. Half a century had made a great difference in the durability of airplanes.

When I finally unfolded my weary frame from *Gin Fizz* two days later on the ramp at Westosha, a pilot whom I had last seen the June morning I left for New York to begin my adventure walked out from the lounge to greet me. "Where'd you go?" he asked.

"Los Angeles."

He blinked. "What took you so long?"

That was an anticlimax of a greeting, and I burst out laughing. But a far warmer welcome home awaited me. It was late evening on a Friday, and I reasoned that after a long week of work, Debby would be fresher the following morning for the drive up from Illinois to pick me up. I persuaded Mel Everhart to drop me at a motel just outside Wilmot, and there I called Debby to tell her I had at last returned and would spend the night. Nothing doing, she said. Two hours later, she arrived to collect me, Conan with her. To see the glowing warmth and pride in their faces was worth the entire trip.

Just a few days later, I heard about an inexpensive space inside a three-plane hangar at Burlington, Wisconsin, thirteen miles northwest of Westosha. I investigated and rented it on the spot. *Gin Fizz* now sits safe out of the elements there, although she visits Westosha regularly, to refuel with 80-octane avgas—Burlington sells only 100LL and jet fuel. It was also at Burlington that I finally solved my difficulties with the radio. The real problem, I discovered after much experimentation with the generous help of Eric Weis, the operator of the Burlington FBO, was a worn-out carbon microphone that just could not handle my breathy voice. I bought a secondhand pilot's headset with an adjustable boom mike, and now my transmissions ring out loud and clear all over southern Wisconsin. "We hear you all the time," Tom Horton said the other day at Westosha, after coming in from a ride with his newest student. "And we understand you just fine."

The first time I flew into Westosha wearing the headset, a pilot I'd known since my student days strode out of the lounge and demanded, "What do you want with a headset, Henry? You're deaf!"

I struck a pose. "It *looks* cool," I told him. All the pilots within earshot burst into laughter.

Of course, the reasons for my obsession with the radio went deep. They were part of my longing to fly, itself grounded in a deeper wish to prove my continuing worth as a human being. I wanted to thumb my nose at a world ignorant of and condescending to the deaf, yet at the same time show it that I could interact with it on its own terms and do the things hearing people could do—if not quite in the same way. Talking to the world on the radio was an oblique way of showing that I was not a handicapped and middle-aged fellow to be patronized but a seasoned and skilled old hand to be valued. If flying across the country was Cal Rodgers's way of declaring, "Here I am: I am a man," it was my way of saying, "Here I am: I am *still* a man."

Yet once I had experienced that welcoming, though imperfect, community of aviation, it was hard to maintain that defiant pose. Yes, human beings are often petty, foolish, cruel, and treacherous, but they are also capable of a surprising decency. Who could keep a chip on his shoulder after encountering so many of those good people who crop up like corn all across America—not to mention those pilots who conquered far greater challenges than I had, both within the cockpit and without? Not I.

As a deaf person, I sometimes have difficulty persuading the world that I am what I claim to be: a journalist and a writer. During conversations aboard trains, for instance, I often found it hard to lip-read different accents, which, combined with my own imperfect speech, caused some people to conclude that I was just another pathological lounge-car liar like so many others. Breaking down their disbelief often took hours, and in the end I had to resort to taking along hearing friends and family members as impromptu interpreters. This tactic worked, but made me aware that I was dependent on others.

In the aviation community, however, most people immediately accept me for what I am. If I fly an airplane, they seem to think, I must be a person to take at face value, never mind how hard my speech may be to understand. Because of this acceptance, we will find ways to connect. On this coast-to-coast trip, I didn't need an interpreter at all—and that was one reason I was able to fly solo. I may be dependent on the kindliness of my fellow humans in some ways, but not in others—and especially not in the air. The ingathering I had felt among pilots had given me a new freedom as well as new friends to replace the ones I had lost over the years.

I made still other connections, ones I had never thought about as a worker in the literary arts. I learned, among other things, not only the physics of a reciprocating engine, the geometry of angle of attack, and the chemistry of aviation fuel, but the rigorous technical discipline of aviation. It begins with a meticulous preflight checklist, continues with a wary ritual of scanning sky and instruments by turns, and ends with a careful postflight shutdown routine. The consequences of omitting any step can be fatal, if not merely expensive, and accepting the need for systematic routines aloft, in turn, led to more orderly habits in my daily life.

Today I am better at planning more carefully, both at home and at the office, anticipating events before they happen, rather than living from day to day and reacting to things as they occur. Maybe I no longer enjoy a vigorous youthful creativity as a book review editor, but I have learned to use my long experience more efficiently. (Things are also better at the *Sun-Times,* where a new editor has improved morale.)

Over Arizona I developed a more intuitive sense as well, that "sense of where you are" by discovering how to "read" weather and terrain while flying low and slow. The views from a small airplane are both sweeping and oblique; no map can duplicate them. Watching the early sun cast long shadows, highlighting and coloring the topography, gives the pilot the eye not only of a hawk, but of an artist. He learns to see—and appreciate—the world in new ways. In cinematic terms, life becomes a panorama, rather than a narrow close-up. Becoming a pilot enlarged my world, making it richer in view as well as in experience.

Outwardly, learning to fly and flying a small plane from coast to coast transformed neither my life nor my identity. I am still Henry Kisor, writer, husband, and father, a man who happens to be balding, overweight, and no longer young—hardly an unusual combination, except perhaps for the almost-lifelong deafness. But I did change within. I shed terrors and stretched limits, expanding the bounds of my physical envelope further than I ever had as an energetic young man. Retracing the route of Cal Rodgers was less a feat of self-reinvention than of self-rediscovery—of old dreams and capabilities that had never quite disappeared—and revival of a flagging self-esteem brought on by advancing age. In emulating a forgotten hero, I became one to myself. I may be the only one who thinks of me in heroic terms, but who cares? I flew from coast to coast alone in a small plane. How many men of any age can claim that?

My odyssey is now in the past, and Debby and I no longer talk about it at the dinner table. We converse far more about the lives of our sons, about their plans for the future, and how we may best support them. I do so unreservedly, for at the same time I learned to fly, I also learned to let go, to allow them to pursue their own interests with my full blessing. Letting go has given me a far better appreciation of my own parents' willingness to cut the umbilical when I was a young man who was not at all certain what he wanted to do with his life.

I still have not enticed Debby aboard *Gin Fizz*—but I accept her reluctance to fly, just as she accepts my love of flying. I have come to realize that she showed a great deal of courage, compassion, and understanding in allowing me to learn to fly, as well as to make the transcontinental trip, despite her well-grounded fears—and in supporting me once she knew that I was going to do it, come hell or high water. She knew how important all these things were to me. In return, I try to show as much encouragement and understanding of the things in her life that I cannot experience. As we approach the twilight of our lives, we know that for both of us, together as well as separately, there will be other frontiers to explore, other lives to intersect.

And on those frustrating days when the world seems to be closing in, when nothing seems to be going right, I can still drive north, climb into my little airplane, and rise above it all.

# Acknowledgments

any people helped in the making of this book. Grateful thanks to these airmen and airwomen: Steve Bangs, Paul Bell, Charles Brodie, Therese Brandell, Larry Bub, Teddy Clemons, Kevin Collins, Henri Corderoy du Tiers, Mandy Coronado, Rick Cremer, Joe Cunningham, C. D. Curry, John Deakin, Bob Dubner, Bob Earl, Angela Elgee, Larry Ely, Mel Everhart, Max Francisco, Bob Guy, Jean Hauser, Anna Lee Heemsbergen, Sebastien Heintz, Bob Hifler, Tom Horton, Dan Hunt, Joe Jacobi, Andy James, Mary Kelly, Bill Kight, Doug Klaassen, Sally Lese, Shane Lese, Cheryl Littlefield, Gene Littlefield, Bob Locher, Ernie Long, James R. Lloyd, Forest McBride, Joan McCasland, Barbara McLeod, Annie Mattos, Jim Marsters, Don Medernach, Carol Morris, Jim Newman, Nancy Novaes, Riley O'Brien, Brian Petri, Bob Reid, John Rich, Bill Richardson, Josephine Richardson, Doug Ritter, Ted Robinson, Virgil Rothrock, Judy Scholl, Doug Schoonover, Bob Searfoss, Jim Shuttleworth, Clyde Smith, Mark Stern, Dan Stover, Jimmy Szajkovics, Mike Waynen, Pat Waynen, Patrice Washington, Ray Washington, Eric Weis, Scott Weis, Steve White, Stephan Wilkinson, Ray Williams, Sam Williamson, and Doug Wixson.

Thanks also to these "ground crew": Prissy Bangs, Charles Berlin, Anne Feiler, Debbie Guy, Judith Halper, Lynn Horton, Conan Kisor, Colin Kisor, Judith Kisor, Manown Kisor, Eileen Lebow, Mort Lebow, Judy Locher, Pat Miller, Karen Moody-Karpf, Susan Ogurian, Jolee Robinson, Linda Scott, George Svokos, Grazia Svokos, Vic Taylor,

Donald Tiffany, Bonnie Tucker, Selden West, Carol Williams, and my agent, Eugene H. Winick.

Special thanks to the curators of the National Air and Space Museum of the Smithsonian Institution for their invaluable aid.

As always, thanks to my longtime editor, Paul Golob, for his usual patient wizardry with a sow's ear of a manuscript.

And most of all, fervent love and gratitude to Deborah Kisor, my wife, for her astonishing indulgence and unwavering affection.

# Index

# About the Author

HENRY KISOR is the book review editor and literary columnist of the *Chicago Sun-Times*. A graduate of Trinity College and the Medill School of Journalism at Northwestern University, he began his newspaper career at the Wilmington (Delaware) *Evening Journal* in 1964. He joined the staff of the *Chicago Daily News* a year later and became book review editor in 1973. Since moving to the *Sun-Times* in 1978, Kisor has earned numerous prizes and citations, most notably his selection as a finalist for the Pulitzer Prize for criticism in 1981. He has served as an adjunct instructor at the Medill School of Journalism and is the author of two previous books, *What's That Pig Outdoors?: A Memoir of Deafness* (1990) and *Zephyr: Tracking a Dream Across America* (1994). He lives in Evanston, Illinois, with his wife, the children's book author and critic Deborah Abbott Kisor. They have two sons, Colin and Conan.

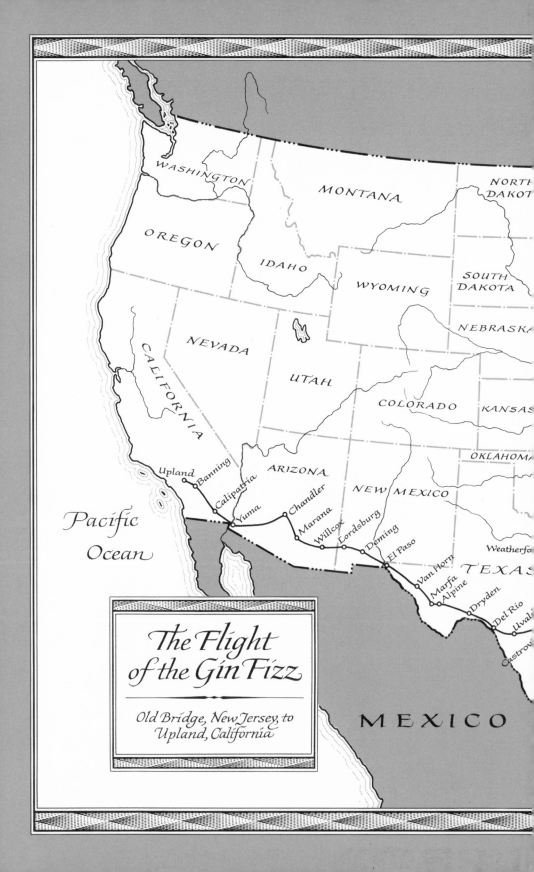

The Flight
of the Gin Fizz

Old Bridge, New Jersey, to
Upland, California